O9-CFU-341

"In the Beginning..."

"In the Beginning..."

A Verse-by-Verse Commentary on the
Book of Genesis, With Detailed Studies
on Creation Vs. Evolution, the Flood, etc.

by
John R. Rice

SWORD of the LORD
PUBLISHERS
P. O. BOX 1099, MURFREESBORO, TN 37133

Printed and bound in the United States of America

Table of Contents

GENESIS 1 (cont'd)

THE EVOLUTION FANTASY 55

GENESIS 1 (cont'd)

THE SIX DAYS OF CREATION 75

GENESIS 1 (cont'd)

CREATION WAS COMPLETE AND PERFECT 84

GENESIS 1 (cont'd)

NO CONFLICTING ACCOUNTS OF CREATION IN GENESIS 93

ABEL THE RIGHTEOUS, GOD'S FIRST HERO

GENESIS 5

THE GENEALOGIES FROM ADAM TO NOAH

GENESIS 6

PRECEDING THE FLOOD

GENESIS 7

THE WORLD WAS DESTROYED IN A FLOOD AND MORE THAN A YEAR OF VOLCANOES, EARTHQUAKES AND TIDAL WAVES

GENESIS 20

GENESIS 21

GENESIS 22

GENESIS 23

GENESIS 24

TABLE OF CONTENTS

INTRODUCTION

Many noble men of God have written comments on the book of Genesis. How sweet in spiritual blessings are the notes of Matthew Henry. They are devotional, enriching and good. And so with the *Notes on the Pentateuch* by C. H. Mackintosh. Many have referred to these again and again with blessing, but they do not deal much with the scientific importance of the flood and they have no answer to the evolutionists, no explanation of the fossils, the coal beds, so-called Ice Age or Ages. They do not deal much with the chronology of the Bible.

Hastings, on *Great Texts of the Bible,* gives good preaching suggestions but no answer to the evolutionist, to the Graff-Wellhausen hypothesis of unbelievers.

Edward J. Young, in his *Introduction to the Old Testament,* is fine, especially on bibliography on these matters, and he is one of the best in wholehearted adherence to the verbal inspiration of the Bible, but he gives only limited comments on Genesis.

Oswald T. Allis, in his book, *The Five Books of Moses*, wonderfully answers the foolish Graff-Wellhausen theory of higher critics. He is not quite adequate on verbal inspiration, thinks Moses probably made use of ancient documents and oral tradition but only as God inspired their choice and use. In that he goes beyond what the Scripture claims. But he does attack the folly of the critics who would make the Pentateuch a patchwork of assembled traditions collected by a fraudulent "redactor" long after Moses. The book is absolutely unanswerable and very valuable on these themes.

Dr. Scofield, in the Reference Bible, has many fine notes on Genesis. However, we think he, without justification, makes room for endless ages before Adam and then has a second creation. Thus he tries to concede all he can to the unbelieving evolutionists and scientists. We think he is wrong on the "gap theory" and so we deal with it here.

Martin Luther and Leupold have done strong, scholarly works on Genesis which we have consulted with pleasure and profit.

But no commentary on Genesis, with which we are familiar, adequately deals with creation, the folly of evolution, the flood, the fossils, the coal beds. Only a few Christian writers seem aware of the extra ages which unbelieving historians have assumed from the records in Egypt. So they will suggest the old town of Byblos in Lebanon goes back seven thousand years! That is only a farfetched guess, of course. Historians rashly make the dynasties suggested by the Egyptian priest Manetho, who wrote many centuries later than the kings whose reigns he listed, and make those dynasties consecutive instead of some being parallel, as they must have been. The exodus and the conquest are misplaced by Miss Kenyon and other scholars. Most historians are unsure about the Pharaoh of the exodus and usually mistaken.

Immanuel Velikovsky, an unsaved Jew but a great scholar, in his remarkable books, *Ages in Chaos, Earth in Upheaval* and *Worlds in Collision,* calls attention to and proves the misplacement of hundreds of added years in Egypt. And Dr. Donovan A. Courville in the two volumes of *The Exodus Problem and Its Ramifications* is very convincing and scholarly in backing up the historical accuracy of the Bible itself in its chronology. These men show that hundreds of years extra have been added without proof and that the Bible is to be trusted chronologically as well as in doctrine. Ussher's chronology is not perfect but not seriously wrong by more than a few years or scores of years, we believe. Commentaries have not dealt adequately, we feel, with these matters in comments on Genesis.

We have felt we must deal with the problem of the unproven claims of the (continually retreating) evolutionists. We must deal with the flood, the civilization before the flood, the world convulsions that destroyed and made over the face of the whole earth, made the layers, the fossils, the coal beds, the radically different climate after the flood.

We feel it is necessary to contradict the silly claims of man's climbing from beastly ancestry up towards civilization, the so-called Stone Age, etc. The unbelieving scientists should be challenged that their methods of judging ages of the past are all unreliable.

We gladly commend the books by Byron C. Nelson, *After His Kind* and *The Deluge Story in Stone*. The book, *The Genesis Flood*, by Henry C. Morris and J. C. Whitcomb, Jr., is very valuable—and *Why We Believe in Creation, Not in Evolution* by the late Fred John Meldau.

We received help and encouragement from *The Bible-Science Newsletter* and from many, many authors we cannot here mention. We are profoundly grateful for all these good men—Bible believers and scholars—who stand up for Christ and the Bible, for the historic Christian faith.

Now what excuse need this author give that we write on Genesis? I am not the scholar that some are. My constant labor in editing the weekly SWORD OF THE LORD and superintending more than ninety workers in our office, in preaching weekly on many radio stations, in preaching usually six or eight times a week in churches or conferences mean that I cannot retire from all other duties and do the research some might do.

Yet the Bible is mine, gladly and fervently believed. We believe and defend the thesis of the Bible that "every word. . .proceedeth out of the mouth of God" (Matt. 4:4), that the Bible is a revelation "not in the words which man's wisdom teacheth, but which the Holy Ghost teacheth" (I Cor. 2:13). Besides I have in the past written comments on every chapter in the Bible, and every principal verse. With holy joy this evangelist and editor writes of the Scriptures with constant pleading for Holy Spirit guidance as I read and write and for all who might be helped by my writing.

Yes, and thousands who have read my writings, thousands who have found the Bible sweet and life-changing through my humble ministry might read my comments on Genesis before those of some other author. So, compelled by the urge from God and the need among the people, we write.

Let all remember that Christ and salvation by faith in His atoning blood are the real themes of all the Bible. May He our Saviour and Lord smile on those who read and may the blessed Holy Spirit move and enlighten and bless all who study His Word here.

John R. Rice

Murfreesboro, Tennessee
1975

"In the Beginning . . ."

GENESIS 1

The Creation of the Earth

VERSE 1:

IN the beginning God created │ the heaven and the earth.

All the Bible, Christ and Christian Faith, Stand or Fall With Genesis

Genesis is included in that clear statement of II Timothy 3:16, "All scripture is given by inspiration of God. . ." or literally is breathed out by God. Jesus believed in Genesis as the very Word of God and quoted or referred to it. And He said, "Think not that I am come to destroy the law, or the prophets: I am not come to destroy, but to fulfil. For verily I say unto you, Till heaven and earth pass, one jot or one tittle shall in no wise pass from the law, till all be fulfilled" (Matt. 5:18).

"The law" here specifically refers to the first five books in the Bible including Genesis, and Jesus quoted from that law, from Deuteronomy 8:3, when He answered Satan, "It is written, Man shall not live by bread alone, but by every word that proceedeth out of the mouth of God" (Matt. 4:4; Luke 4:4).

And the resurrected Jesus spoke to the two sad, doubting

Christians on the road to Emmaus: "O fools, and slow of heart to believe all that the prophets have spoken: Ought not Christ to have suffered these things, and to enter into his glory? And beginning at Moses and all the prophets, he expounded unto them in all the scriptures the things concerning himself" (Luke 24:25-27). Jesus quoted Scriptures "beginning at Moses" about Himself and so "in all the scriptures."

So Genesis is the very inspired Word of God. And the first verse of Genesis is as inspired and authentic and as authoritative as John 3:16 or any other verse in the Bible.

"In the beginning God created the heaven and the earth."

"In the Beginning God"!

God was in the beginning. Where else could God be than there—at the beginning? No earth, no sea, no sun, no stars, no planets, no animals, no matter, no energy before God! God was at the beginning of creation. Here we find God was at the beginning of the Bible.

That there is a God is the basic fact of all this universe. He made all things. He made life. He is all knowledge, all wisdom, all power. He is all goodness, all mercy and all loving-kindness. Everything good in the universe stems from God. All evil is rebellion against God.

Genesis starts at the beginning. So also does the Gospel of John. We read in John 1:1-4:

"In the beginning was the Word, and the Word was with God, and the Word was God. The same was in the beginning with God. All things were made by him; and without him was not any thing made that was made. In him was life; and the life was the light of men."

We are told the same thing in Colossians 1:15-17:

"Who is the image of the invisible God, the firstborn of every creature: For by him were all things created, that are in heaven, and that are in earth, visible and invisible, whether they be thrones, or dominions, or principalities, or

*powers: all things were created by him, and for him: And he
is before all things, and by him all things consist."*

Jesus Christ not only created all things but they were
created for Him and "by him all things consist" or hold
together. When creation was done, the Lord Jesus kept His
hand on the universe and He keeps planets in their orbits.
All the planetary processes are supervised and continue
under Jesus' controlling hand.

We are even told that the animals look to Him and are
fed, just as Jesus said that God notes the sparrow's fall.
Jesus is the Creator.

Hebrews 1:2 tells us that God "hath in these last days
spoken unto us by his Son, whom he hath appointed heir of
all things, by whom also he made the worlds." The next
verse continues the story that Christ is "upholding all
things by the word of his power."

But Genesis 1:2 says, ". . .the Spirit of God moved upon
the face of the waters." In some similar way the Holy Spirit
works with Jesus now. Jesus is the Saviour, but the work of
regeneration is actually done by the Holy Spirit and He it is
who moves into the Christian's body to live and there
represents Christ so much that the Scriptures may say,
"Christ in you, the hope of glory" (Col. 1:27).

If we understand that Jesus Christ is the Creator, we
need not be surprised that He will come back to reign on the
earth again and make it into a new Garden of Eden. We
need not be surprised that in His life on earth Jesus created
bread and fish enough to feed the five thousand besides
women and children, and that He created the wine out of
water in John, chapter 2.

We see that all of the Trinity had part in creation:

1. *"In the beginning God created. . . ."*—Vs. 1.

2. *"And the Spirit of God moved upon the face of the
waters."*—Vs. 2

3. *". . .his Son,. . .by whom he made the
worlds."*—Heb. 1:2, like John 1:3.

So Father, Son and Holy Spirit all had part in creation.

There is no contradiction here, no conflict. Christ, the Word, the *Logos*, the revelation of God, the Son of God, another person of the Godhead, was there at the beginning, too. Christ is the Light of the world shining into the night of this dark world to fallen men, alien from God, even enemies of God.

Who did the creating: God the Father or Christ the Son? Well, Christ was active in creation.

"Who is the image of the invisible God, the first-born of every creature: For by him were all things created, that are in heaven, and that are in earth, visible and invisible, whether they be thrones, or dominions, or principalities, or powers: all things were created by him, and for him: And he is before all things, and by him all things consist."—Col. 1:15-17.

"In the beginning God. . . ." But the Hebrew word for God, *Elohim,* is plural, including all the three: the invisible God, of whom Christ is the image; Christ, active in creation and the "Spirit of God" who "moved upon the face of the waters" (Gen. 1:2).

But there is no jealousy, no competition, no aloneness in the Godhead. They are not separate but one. There are three manifestations of God, three persons, but they are one. We say that Jesus is "the Saviour of the world," but He is not alone in saving sinners. First, "God so loved the world." Then, "Christ died for our sins according to the scriptures." And then it is the Holy Spirit who convicts the sinner, who brings about the miraculous regeneration of salvation in the believer, so that one is "born of the Spirit." Whatever Christ did, the Father and the Spirit did. When the Holy Spirit moves into the body of a convert as a Comforter, Guide and Witness, then through Him, Jesus said of both Himself and the Father, "And we will come unto him, and make our abode with him" (John 14:23). There is a sense in which God is always "we." What one person of the Godhead does, all have part and do.

The importunate friend in Luke 11:5-8, begging the Bread of Life for hungry sinners, says, "Lend me three loaves." He seeks the soul-winning help of the Father, the Son and the Holy Spirit, to give the Bread of Life. All work together. God—*"Elohim"*—created. Christ created. And the Holy Spirit had part, too.

Then to whom should we pray—to the Father or to the Son? Why, to either or to all three. We should pray, "Our Father," or like Bartimaeus and the Canaanite woman, "Thou son of David," or if you like, to the sweet Spirit of God. Would it be wrong to ask help of your divine Teacher, your Guide and your Comforter? Or wrong to ask the Spirit of God to make plain the Scriptures you read? Or to pray that He will convict a sinner? Or that He will breathe upon you in power for soul winning? Jesus said He is really *"another* Comforter," meaning One just like the Lord Jesus Himself, the first great Comforter they knew.

So the Godhead created, but Christ was active in creation along with the Father and the Spirit.

God's Creation Proves to Every Open Heart There Is a God!

Creation is proof of God. Since there is a world, there must be a World-maker. Sensible men need not argue about whether there is a God, for only a fool, a perverted one, could say, "There is no God."

All the universe speaks of a mighty all-powerful, all-wise God.

Psalm 19:1-6 says:

"The heavens declare the glory of God; and the firmament sheweth his handywork. Day unto day uttereth speech, and night unto night sheweth knowledge. There is no speech nor language, where their voice is not heard. Their line is gone out through all the earth, and their words to the end of the world. In them hath he set a tabernacle for the sun, Which is as a bridegroom coming out of his chamber, and rejoiceth as a strong man to run a race. His going forth is from the end of the heaven, and his circuit unto the ends of it: and there is nothing hid from the heat thereof."

Oh, the voice of the sun in the heavens says there is a God! His glory, His handiwork is evident. "There is no speech nor language, where their voice is not heard." The heathen sailors on Jonah's ship knew there was a God, so they begged Jonah to pray. All the idols and spiritual blindness among the most depraved races cannot wholly shut out the clamoring voices of the heavens and all created things that proclaim there is a God.

Dr. Bill Rice went to Africa to work with missionaries for a season. Far into the jungle they went to a tribe of little black Pygmies who had never seen a white man. By shooting monkeys for their food and then intriguing them by showing them a book that talks (the Bible), he assured them he could tell them where their fathers had gone. At last he could tell them of a God who loved them and who sent His Son to die, to forgive and save them so they could go to a happy, blessed hereafter in Heaven.

Then a most surprising thing happened. A tiny man named Tarasi said, "Bwana, I thought it must be something like that. Many times I have climbed the highest tree and have looked far into the sky, trying to see God. I felt sure He must be up there some place. And again and again I have called, God, are You there? Can You hear me? Do You see little old Tarasi? God, I am afraid—come and help Tarasi. But," the old fellow continued, "I never could hear Him answer me a word. I thought God surely must have some way of helping poor old Tarasi. . . .I am glad to hear of Jesus and to know that He died for me. . . .I thought it must be something like that!"

Oh, God has not left Himself without a witness! Men are without excuse who do not seek God and love Him and serve Him.

In Romans 1:18-22 the Lord tells us clearly of this fact: All of creation proves there is a God:

"For the wrath of God is revealed from heaven against all ungodliness and unrighteousness of men, who hold the truth in unrighteousness; Because that which may be known of God is manifest in them; for God hath shewed it

unto them. For the invisible things of him from the creation of the world are clearly seen, being understood by the things that are made, even his eternal power and Godhead; so that they are without excuse: Because that, when they knew God, they glorified him not as God, neither were thankful; but became vain in their imaginations, and their foolish heart was darkened. Professing themselves to be wise, they became fools."

What may be known of God is manifest in creation. We do not believe, as some have, that the Gospel is written in nature, but God as a Creator is revealed by His works. Those races after the flood, here spoken of in Romans, chapter 1, had no excuse. They knew about God but preferred idols. "They were not thankful" (vs. 21). "They did not like to retain God in their knowledge" (vs. 28). So God darkened their sinful hearts and "gave them up to uncleanness" (vs. 24). He "gave them up unto vile affections" (vs. 26). He "gave them over to a reprobate mind" (vs. 28). "Professing themselves to be wise, they became fools" (vs. 22). Ah, so that is how atheists happen! That is the way of the fool who says in his heart, "There is no God."

The Fool Who Says, "No God for Me"

Yes, Romans 1:22 says that the people descended from Noah after the flood, and enlightened people, with great civilization and who knew about God, turned away from God with unthankful, wicked hearts. They did not want to retain God in their knowledge. So "professing themselves to be wise, they became fools."

But Psalm 14:1-3 tells us about this:

"The fool hath said in his heart, There is no God. They are corrupt, they have done abominable works, there is none that doeth good. The Lord looked down from heaven upon the children of men, to see if there were any that did understand, and seek God. They are all gone aside, they are

*all together become filthy: there is none that doeth good,
no, not one."*

That is repeated almost word for word in Psalm 53.

Only a fool can say, "There is no God." The term *fool* in
Scripture does not mean only ignorance or poor judgment
or lack of intelligence; it speaks of one whose judgment is
warped and tainted by an evil mind and by wicked desires.
The rich fool of Luke 12:16-21 had plenty of sense, but his
mind was so obsessed with worldly goods, eating and
drinking, and riches, that he took no thought that he must
die and meet God. So God said to him, "Thou fool, this
night thy soul shall be required of thee." The fool in the
Bible is a perverted person who is blinded by sin and by his
own wicked heart. It has to do not primarily with the mind
but with the soul, the heart, the intentions, the desires. So
is such a man who says there is no God.

But read again that first verse, Psalm 14:1: "The fool
hath said in his heart. . . ." Where did he say it? Not in a
logical and intelligent mind, considering all the facts. No,
in a wicked heart that did not want God. Atheism and all
unbelief is a heart matter. The fool has said, "There is no
God," but the words *there is* are in italics, showing they
were not in the original but were supplied by the
translators to make sense. Actually the fool really said,
"No God! No God for me! I'll not have a God!" He is saying
not so much that God does not exist but that he will have
no God. He wants no God. Unbelief is from a wicked heart,
rejecting the light and the truth as he rejects God.

Let Us Illustrate

Look at this watch in my hand. It is marked Accutron. It
is a lovely gift from my brother, Dr. Bill. Now let us talk
like an evolutionist or any other atheist or agnostic.
Suppose that we say, "No one planned this watch. No one
made it. It just accidentally happened as a result of
concomitant forces, circumstances, accidental movements
or impulses in thousands of years. It just happened.
Nobody planned it."

But you would protest. "There are twelve equally distant marks around the face of it, and they are divided into exactly sixty smaller measures exactly the same size. Surely somebody planned it to show twelve hours of sixty minutes each."

"No (let me reply as a fool would), it just happened. Perhaps it was first a chip of wood or a bit of iron ore, then it was a button, then a compass, then a steam gauge, then a watch. The similarity of size and shape proves evolution like that. It just happened."

But some sensible one would say, "But how could it accidentally happen that the hour hand goes from twelve to one in exactly one hour and so on around the face of that watch? The minute hand goes sixty minutes in one hour. The tiny second hand goes sixty seconds in one minute. Why?" You insist, of course. "Somebody planned it! Somebody made it." You say, "Dr. Rice, you talk like a fool. If there is a watch so intricate, then there must be a watchmaker."

Yes, you are right. One talks like a fool who says there are watches keeping good time, fitted to the wrist, adjusted, powered with tiny batteries that last a year or more, and all keeping good time always, but that there is no watch factory! Only a fool talks that way. That is like the fool who says there is no God!

To say that man, plants, animals, the seas, the air, the earth turning on its axis, the sun around which we orbit, and the infinite riches and wisdom and planning of all nature—to say it just happened without a personal Creator is to speak like a fool. God says one who says it is a fool and I say, Amen.

It is said that Sir Isaac Newton had someone make an intricate machine representing our planetary system; a central sun, an arm revolving about that with a ball representing the earth, a moon then that went around the earth and all the planets proportionately, proportionate in size, and on arms a proper distance to represent their course in the heavens, turning with the relative speeds of the planets. A crank turned the beautiful and accurate planetarium,

A scientific friend came in, we're told, and marveled and exclaimed, "Wonderful! Who made it?"

"Nobody," answered Sir Isaac.

"Oh, don't joke. Tell me who made it."

Again the brief, indifferent answer, "Nobody made it."

Indignantly, that infidel scientist protested. "Such a marvelously planned machine, actually a model of our planetary system showing how all moved in proper order around the sun, could not just have happened. Who made it?"

Dr. Newton replied that the actual earth and sun and planets and moons were a million times more detailed and wonderful than the mechanical model, and the infidel thought no one made it! What a fool anyone would be to say of this universe, "There is no Creator!" It is not sensible. It shows a perversion, a wicked preference against God.

The Lord Jesus said in John 3:18-21:

"He that believeth on him is not condemned; but he that believeth not is condemned already, because he hath not believed in the name of the only begotten Son of God. And this is the condemnation, that light is come into the world, and men loved darkness rather than light, because their deeds were evil. For every one that doeth evil hateth the light, neither cometh to the light, lest his deeds should be reproved. But he that doeth truth cometh to the light, that his deeds may be made manifest, that they are wrought in God."

Only those who hate the light because their deeds are evil run from Christ and say, "No God." That same unbelief is why sinners reject Christ and go on their wicked way to Hell.

Yes, "In the beginning God created the heaven and the earth."

God Who Created All Things Sustains
Life and You Must Answer to Him

Is this matter of creation, then, simply a theological matter, and does it really concern you and me? Well, the God who made the world sustains it and controls it. Again note Colossians 1:16, 17:

"For by him were all things created, that are in heaven, and that are in earth, visible and invisible, whether they be thrones, or dominions, or principalities, or powers: all things were created by him, and for him: And he is before all things, and by him all things consist."

". . .all things were created by him, and for him: And he is before all things, and by him all things consist." Christ not only made all things, but "by him all things consist," or hold together! The Christ who made this giant solar system, the original of the little copy (the man-made planetarium), turns the crank that makes the universe go! Christ keeps the earth in its orbit, sets the bounds for the seas, sends the rain or withholds it, gives the wild beasts their food, notes the fall of every sparrow, and paints the beauty of every wild flower.

He sets up kings or dethrones them. "The earth is the Lord's, and the fulness thereof; the world, and they that dwell therein" (Ps. 24:1).

The God who creates you keeps your heart beating. He starts the juices that digests your food. He supervises the kidneys that eliminate the poisons from the blood. He creates the antibodies in your blood to immunize you against certain diseases, or He does not, as He chooses.

So a man is not only a fool in heart to say there is no God but he is a fool who would ignore, with arrogant and unthankful heart, the God who loves and provides for him, who nurtures and seeks him. It is ". . .in him we live, and move, and have our being" (Acts 17:28).

When King Belshazzar sinned, Daniel told him, "And the God in whose hand thy breath is, and whose are all thy ways, hast thou not glorified." So a king or a pauper who ignores God is a fool in God's sight.

Remember, Unbelief Is a Heart Sin

The Scriptures repeat the truth that unbelief is a sin, a wickedness. To the two disciples on the road to Emmaus Jesus said:

"Then he said unto them, O fools, and slow of heart to believe all that the prophets have spoken: Ought not Christ to have suffered these things, and to enter into his glory? And beginning at Moses and all the prophets, he expounded unto them in all the scriptures the things concerning himself."—Luke 24:25-27.

So a Christian who knows Christ as Saviour may be guilty of unbelief about some Bible truths and so Jesus said, they may be "fools, and slow of heart to believe." Make sure your heart leaps gladly to believe "all that the prophets have spoken," all the Bible, lest Christ should call you a fool!

Remember that unbelief is "the sin which doth so easily beset us" in Hebrews 12:1,2 and we should make sure to deliberately, again and again, "lay aside" that wicked tendency of our carnal nature to unbelief.

And in this universe, where Jesus is to be the only atoning Saviour, He is to come back to reign, and He who created man must do the new creation, making one a new creature in Christ.

He who created the world can create a clean heart in you and in me.

GENESIS 1 (cont'd)

In the Beginning, God and Miracle

It was "in the beginning." That reminds us of the first statement in the Gospel of John: "In the beginning was the Word, and the Word was with God, and the Word was God. The same was in the beginning with God" (John 1:1, 2).

Before there was an earth, before there was a sun or moon or stars, we suppose before there was force or matter, there was God, God the Father, God the Holy Spirit, and God the Son. The Son was there in the beginning with God.

We suppose that the angels, heavenly beings, were there with God. Later, the archangel Lucifer would sin and become Satan and some angels would fall with him; but we suppose it was after this time, for in Isaiah 14:12-17 the prophesied fall of the Antichrist someway typifies the fall of Satan, and there Lucifer had ambitions mentioning the heavens and the clouds and things. So Satan's fall was after this time "in the beginning," when God created the heavens and the earth, but before Satan tempted Adam and Eve.

"In the beginning." Yes, there was a beginning. Does anyone suppose there is a universe with no Creator? That there are mighty forces with no Cause? That there is infinite wisdom and no source and no Wise One from whom it emanates? Does anyone suppose that there is astronomy without an Astronomer, mathematics ingrained in nature but no Mathematician, the laws of music inherent in the laws of vibration and sound, yet no great Musician? In the beginning there was God.

There was a beginning because now the sun is burning itself out. I do not know how many millenniums of years it will take but since the sun is slowly consuming itself in energy, there was a time when it had to begin and to be charged with the energy it now gives out. And in the beginning there was God.

"In the Beginning God Created the Heaven and the Earth"

There was no earth, but God made an earth. There was no water, but God made water. There was no light, except as Christ Himself is the Light and His light is inherent in deity, but God said, "Let there be light," and there was light.

God made everything out of nothing. That is involved in the word "to *create.*" It is also stated in Hebrews 11:3, "Through faith we understand that the worlds were framed by the word of God, so that things which are seen were not made of things which do appear."

That statement of God in Hebrews 11:3 is important because the believing heart will believe that God created the heavens and the earth, but the man who is an alien from God, who does not know God, whose heart is not enlightened by the Spirit of God, does not see that God created the heavens and the earth. And the creation is a spiritual truth that must be received by faith. There are no witnesses to the creation but God Himself and the angels. There is no reliable record except the record that God Himself has given. So then it is "through faith" that we understand that the worlds were framed by the Word of God and that God made the things that are out of things that were not.

Again, I Corinthians 2:14 tells us, "But the natural man receiveth not the things of the Spirit of God: for they are foolishness unto him: neither can he know them, because they are spiritually discerned."

Christianity, a Religion of Miracles

Here we run smack into the fact of miracles. A miracle is the only possible explanation of the origin of all things. If God did not make matter, where did it come from? If God did not create the germ of life in plants and then in animals, then how did it happen? If God did not set the heavenly bodies in their orbits and with mathematical precisions, balances and counterbalances, set them to running, and if He does not watch over them and keep them in their place, then what explanation do you have for these things?

Does it take faith to believe in a miracle? Yes, but it is not a silly faith like that of the evolutionists who think that things "from inherent forces" grew from dead matter into living cells and then into a mighty tree of plant life and then animal life, culminating in man. That farfetched story is more unbelievable than any fairy tale and one who can swallow all that without a murmur is far more credulous than those who believe that God created the heavens and earth as He said. There is no other logical or believable explanation of this universe except that God created it.

But one who is going to be a Christian has already accepted the fact of miracle when he accepts the fact of God.

The Bible is miraculous, that is, men were moved by the Holy Spirit and gave the exact message God told them to give, without error. That is not natural but supernatural, not ordinary but extraordinary, not human but Divine. The future has been foretold unerringly in hundreds of prophecies in the Bible, and the coming to pass of the prophesied event proves a miraculous inspiration of the prophecy.

Christ is a miracle. He was conceived in the virgin's womb by the Spirit of God, without a human father. He worked miracles in His ministry again and again. He raised the dead. He created matter in feeding the five thousand. He turned water into wine. He stilled the tempest on the sea by a word. Then He rose bodily from the grave and ascended bodily to Heaven. Christ is a miracle.

The new birth is a miracle. That is, one has an actual change in his nature. One has the law of God written in his heart. One now has the Spirit of God dwelling in his body.

One actually becomes a child of God by a miraculous change. He still has the old nature but he now has the new nature.

Answered prayer is a miracle. If God changes the order of things—whether He stops rain or sends rain; whether He permits an accident or prevents it; whether He moves a king or a pauper to act or think a certain way; whether He sends a direct answer to prayer in money or in things or in clear instruction—it is a miracle. It is Divine and not human. It is supernatural and not natural.

And as conversion to Christ is a miracle, it is only the forerunner of another miracle in the bodily resurrection of every Christian that will take place one day.

The Christian religion is a miracle religion. No one need stumble at the statement that "in the beginning God created the heaven and the earth."

They were created! They did not slowly grow. It was not a self-contained process. God may work a series of miracles as He did in creating the earth, the seas, the firmament, the birds, the fishes, the plants, and animals, and man, but a miracle is not itself a process. A bit of protoplasm, with some amino acids and some chemicals, did not of itself become an amoeba. An amoeba did not develop until it was a many-celled animal, and then a mollusk, and then into a higher form. Dogs did not develop into baboons and baboons into apes and apes into men. No, God created things. He made all of them.

GENESIS 1 (cont'd)

Gap Theory Not Scriptural

The theory (1) of original creation in dateless past, (2) of millions of years in which scientists imagine, to provide the fossils, earth strata and coal beds, (3) and then a recent restorative creation of six days on the earth formerly ruined by divine judgment, is not taught in the Bible.

The Scofield Reference Bible, since 1909, has made popular with fundamental Christians what is called the Gap Theory of creation or the "Restoration" Theory. That theory is that Genesis 1:1 tells of an original creation of the earth in the ageless past, that Genesis 1:2 tells of a divine judgment and ruin that came on all creation, lasting for millions or billions of years and accounts for the strata of the earth, the fossils, the coal beds, to fit in with the theories of scientists; and that the rest of Genesis, chapters 1 and 2, tell of a restoration of the ruined earth, with added six days of creation of animals and man.

Scofield Bible Notes on Supposed "Gap" in Creation

On Genesis 1:1, on the word "created" Dr. Scofield has a note as follows:

> But three creative acts of God are recorded in this chapter: (1) the heavens and the earth, v. 1; (2) animal life, v. 21; and (3) human life, vs. 26,27. The first creative act refers to the dateless past, and gives scope for all the geologic ages.

On Genesis 1, verse 2, "the earth was without form, and void. . . ," Dr. Scofield has this note:

> Jer. 4.23-26, Isa. 24.1 and 45.18, clearly indicate that the earth had undergone a cataclysmic change as a result of a divine judgment. The face of the earth bears everywhere the marks of such a catastrophe. There are

not wanting intimations which connect it with a previous
testing and fall of angels. See Ezek. 18.12-15 and Isa. 14.9-
14, which certainly go beyond the kings of Tyre and
Babylon.

Then on verse 3 of Genesis, chapter 1, which says, "And
God said, Let there be light: and there was light," Dr.
Scofield has this following note on page 3:

> Neither here nor in verses 14-18 is an original creative
> act implied. A different word is used. The sense is, made
> to *appear*; made *visible*. The sun and moon were *created*
> 'in the beginning.' The 'light' of course came from the
> sun, but the vapour diffused the light. Later the sun
> appeared in an unclouded sky.

(The above notes are modified in the brand new edition
of the Scofield Bible and the Gap Theory is not given
unqualified endorsement.)

Why the "Gap" Theory Became Popular

If an intelligent Christian, without any previous bias,
would simply read the first chapter of Genesis, he would
believe, as millions of people have believed, that verse 1 and
the rest of the chapter are talking about the same creation,
in the same time. That verse is simply a statement of fact,
which following verses outline in detail, with added detail
about the creation of man in chapter 2.

But people aware of scientific facts and scientific
opinions do not approach the problem of the age of the
earth without a bias. It has been discovered that there are
layers and strata on the earth, and that in these strata or
layers are billions of fossils of plants and animals, and the
coal beds. It has been discovered that on many continents
there are great deposits of sea shells and fossils of sea life.
So scientists who do not believe the Bible and do not believe
in direct creation, have figured out that all life came by
evolution, through natural processes, and that through
millions and millions of years, even billions of years,
perhaps, through natural, gradual processes on this earth,
mountain ranges have been forced up, continents have
sunk under the ocean, ocean beds have risen to be dry land;

and that in these natural processes through many billions of years, plants and animals have been covered and become fossilized, great forests have been covered with soil and rock and have been formed into coal beds, and sea shells and fossils of marine life have been left on the land, even on the highest mountains.

Most unbelieving scientists have now come to believe that these fossil remains, and the changes which are indicated in the surface layers of the earth, were made through countless ages.

It is only fair to say that now hundreds of proved scientists who are Christians do not believe the evolution theory but in direct creation, and have associations, magazines and many books to prove the Bible is scientifically accurate on creation and the flood.

Good Christians, not willing perhaps to accept the theory of evolution instead of direct creation, have sought some explanation of these scientific facts of the fossils, the coal beds. The evidence is that the seas once covered the continents that now are.

So, although the first chapter of Genesis does not discuss plainly two separate periods of creation with a gap of ages between them, Christians formulated the theory that Genesis 1:1 tells about an original creation: "In the beginning God created the heaven and the earth," they say that then a great judgment or cataclysm of destruction came to this earth and that that is mentioned in verse 2. Verse 2 says, "And the earth was without form, and void," and they make that read, "The earth *became* without form and void.'"

Thus they tried to account for the fossils, and tried to pacify scientists who demand millions of years.

So George H. Pember in the book, *Earth's Earliest Ages,* suggested the interpretation that a tremendous age or gap was to be counted after Genesis 1:1. And then, after a cataclysmic judgment of God, which formed the fossils, the coal beds, and the other evidences which scientists claim in the surface layers of the earth, he thought that beginning with Genesis 1:3, God made a new creation of six days. This theory was held also by Franz Delitzsch in Germany and others. It has been made popular by the Scofield Reference Bible.

But Gap Theory Cannot Be Proven by Bible

The attempt to prove the Gap Theory is flimsy. The Scriptures do not teach that there are great ages between Genesis 1:1 and verse 3 and following.

1. To try to make Genesis 1:2 say, "And the earth *became* without form, and void," is a poor translation. "In 1948 at Winona Lake School of Theology, M. Henkel polled twenty leading scholars of the Hebrew language in the United States. They were asked, 'Is there any exegetical evidence for the view that there was a gap between vv. 1 and 2?' Their reply was an emphatic no," according to Prof. Surburg, quoting from the book, *Modern Science and the Christian Faith.*

No, in the first act of creation, God brought matter into being, but it was not yet formed into continents and seas, into plants and animals. It was "without form, and void." Creation was not yet finished. That is the obvious meaning of Genesis 1:1.

2. Dr. Scofield says in his notes on Genesis 1:2,

> Jer. 4.23-26, Isa. 24.1 and 45.18, clearly indicate that the earth had undergone a cataclysmic change as a result of divine judgment.

I believe that that is a serious mistake in exegesis and interpretation. Jeremiah 4:23 says, "I beheld the earth, and, lo, it was without form, and void; and the heavens, and they had no light." But the context clearly indicates that God here speaks of the destruction of Jerusalem and of the nation Judah when they were carried into captivity to Babylon. In the preceding verses Israel is commanded, "For this gird you with sackcloth, lament and howl: for the fierce anger of the Lord is not turned back from us" (vs. 8). Verse 16 says, "Make ye mention to the nations; behold, publish against Jerusalem, that watchers come from a far country, and give out their voice against the cities of Judah." Verse 19 says, "My bowels, my bowels! I am pained at my very heart; my heart maketh a noise in me; I cannot hold my peace, because thou hast heard, O my soul, the sound of the trumpet, the alarm of war." And verse 20 says, "Destruction upon destruction is cried; for the whole land is spoiled: suddenly are my tents spoiled, and my curtains in a moment." And then the earth or the *land* (as the word is often translated) is to be "without form, and void."

And after verse 23, verse 25 says, "I beheld, and, lo, there was no man, and all the birds of the heavens were fled." The people were carried away captive. Verse 27 says, "For thus hath the Lord said, The whole land shall be desolate; yet will I not make a full end." Verse 29 says, "The whole city shall flee for the noise of the horsemen and bowmen; they shall go into thickets, and climb up upon the rocks: every city shall be forsaken, and not a man dwell therein." The destruction mentioned is not some prehistoric cataclysmic judgment on the earth but the destruction of Jerusalem and of the country when Judah was carried captive.

Notice, "and all the cities thereof were broken down. . . ," the statement in verse 26. There were no cities before Genesis 1:2 and this could not mean a cataclysmic judgment on the whole earth, before man was created.

3. Nor does Isaiah 24:1 talk about a prehistoric judgment of God, a cataclysm on the whole earth. Again we find that the destruction mentioned is because of war and trouble which God will bring on the nations. The entire chapter 23 preceding is about the burden of Tyre and its destruction, so the 24th chapter starts on the same theme. Isaiah 24:1 says, "Behold, the Lord maketh the earth empty, and maketh it waste, and turneth it upside down, and scattereth abroad the inhabitants thereof." But the next two verses say, "And it shall be, as with the people, so with the priest; as with the servant, so with his master; as

with the maid, so with her mistress; as with the buyer, so with the seller; as with the lender, so with the borrower; as with the taker of usury, so with the giver of usury to him. The land shall be utterly emptied, and utterly spoiled: for the Lord hath spoken this word." That is a destruction brought by war on a people because of their sins and the priest and people, servant and master, maid and mistress, buyer and seller, lender and borrower, all alike will be carried away in the trouble God will bring them. It seems to be an unworthy subterfuge to pretend that Isaiah 24:1 or that Jeremiah 4:23 talk about a great prehistoric judgment on the whole earth before the creation of man. I do not believe it. The Bible does not sustain it.

Dr. Scofield also makes a reference to Isaiah 45:18, "For thus saith the Lord that created the heavens; God himself that formed the earth and made it; he hath established it, he created it not in vain, he formed it to be inhabited: I am the Lord; and there is none else." But that does not mean, surely, to contradict the statement in Genesis 1:2 that after the first creation of matter it was without form and void. It was not in vain for God then completed His creation.

If the Gap Theory were true, there would still have to be a detailed creation of all plants and animals before the catastrophe that is presumed to have destroyed them, and the Bible does not tell of such creation before Genesis 1:2.

And while the fall of Satan is mentioned in the Bible, the Scriptures nowhere tell of a divine judgment on the whole creation at the time of Satan's fall.

So the Gap Theory cannot be proved from the Bible. And, as we will show next, it is not needed as an explanation of the earth strata and fossils.

Much Evidence That the Flood in Noah's Days Accounts for All Fossils, Coal Beds, and Other Changes in Earth's Surface, for Which Scientists Would Like to Have Millions of Years

The so-called "Gap Theory" of immense ages between

Genesis 1:1 and Genesis 1:3 with a ruined earth of some awful judgment of God, before the six days of creation described in Genesis 1—that theory was formed to try to explain the fossils and layers of the earth which evolutionists say requires millions of years of time.

As we have shown, we do not believe the Gap Theory is taught in the Bible. We believe, rather, that the strata of the earth, the fossils, the coal beds were brought about by the earth-destroying flood of Noah's day described in the Bible and by accompanying and following events. And that awful flood and years of earth convulsions following, surely are a more reasonable explanation of the layers of the earth, the fossils, the coal beds, than the unproved theory of evolution.

Who thinks it reasonable to believe in spontaneous generation, that life without a Creator by the inherent and accidental forces, sprang out of dead matter? Not a single case of the beginning of life has ever been observed nor has man been able to bring it about with all the resources of modern science!

Why is it reasonable to believe the guess that all kinds of plants and animals originated by an evolutionary process, when as I read in a book of science this morning that not one such family or kind has evolved in a million years? Of course that book insisted on billions of years. Why is it reasonable to suppose that animals came from plants, that many-celled animals came from one-celled animals, that vertebrates came from invertebrates, that reptiles came from fish, that birds came from reptiles, that mammals came from birds, and that men came from apes, when not a single link has ever been found between the principal kinds?

The reason people believe in evolution is not that it is reasonable but that it is an excuse for not believing in God and direct creation. So it is natural for the unconverted and unbelieving man.

Why believe that the fossils and coal beds were formed by natural causes following a uniform pattern through the centuries and millenniums and millions of years? No fossils, no coal beds, are now being formed as far as we know, on the earth. "Uniformitarian" geology does not very sensibly explain the mysteries on the surface of the earth.

But when we believe the Bible account of a tremendous flood, with "all the fountains of the great deep broken up," that is, the tidal waves from all the oceans and when "the rain was upon the earth forty days and forty nights" and when "the mountains were covered" and every living thing that had breath died except those in the ark, it is not hard to understand how we have the fossil layers and the coal beds and the strata on the earth.

Remember, Genesis 6:13 says, "And God said unto Noah, The end of all flesh is come before me; for the earth is filled with violence through them; and, behold, I will destroy them with the earth," that is, the people of all the earth and the earth itself, as it then was, were to be destroyed! And Jesus Himself accepted and authenticated the Bible story of the flood. He said:

"And as it was in the days of Noe, so shall it be also in the days of the Son of man. They did eat, they drank, they married wives, they were given in marriage, until the day that Noe entered into the ark, and the flood came, and destroyed them all."—Luke 17:26,27.

Jesus said, "The flood came, and destroyed them all."

A very significant Scripture on this matter is II Peter 3:3-7:

"Knowing this first, that there shall come in the last days scoffers, walking after their own lusts, And saying, Where is the promise of his coming? for since the fathers fell asleep, all things continue as they were from the beginning of the creation. For this they willingly are ignorant of, that by the word of God the heavens were of old, and the earth standing out of the water and in the water: Whereby the world that then was, being overflowed with water, perished: But the heavens and the earth, which are now, by

the same word are kept in store, reserved unto fire against the day of judgment and perdition of ungodly men.''

Notice the Scripture says that scoffers, unbelievers, who walk after their own desires, do not believe there has been any catastrophic change, do not believe what the Bible teaches of the direct creation "that by the word of God the heavens were of old, and the earth standing out of the water and in the water." They do not believe that "the world that then was, being overflowed with water, perished."

Notice that this destruction of the world was so drastic that not only the people, but all the face of the earth as it then was, "perished." And the awful destruction then is likened to the time in the future when another catastrophe will come, when fire shall envelop this planet in "the day of judgment and perdition of ungodly men." Then everything that will burn will burn, everything that will melt will melt. Well, so drastic then was the destruction of the earth by water in the flood.

And it is very significant that God here says that the earth as it now is is a result of two things—direct creation, then the flood! And scoffers deny both the direct creation and a universal flood.

How could such a flood cause the tremendous changes that took place on the face of the earth? The Scripture says that 'all the fountains of the great deep were opened.' In some awful way the waters of the ocean helped cover the land. We know that sometimes volcanic pressure raises an island in the sea, or submerges a bit of coastline. And scientists are all agreed that such changes have happened all over the world. Perhaps then the ocean bottoms were raised to help flood the earth. The great mountain ranges we have now obviously were raised after the flood.

Then "the windows of heaven were opened" and that must mean more than ordinary rain. It rained over the whole earth for the space of forty days, as I understand the Scriptures. And that must mean that there was far more than the average precipitation, and the millions of tons of water that ordinarily held in the vapor of the air were discharged.

Even now, if there is an earthquake on the sea bottom, a tidal wave may rush upon the land doing millions of dollars of destruction and taking many lives. The power of moving water has hurled giant ships to destruction, or has rolled boulders weighing tons before it.

If tidal waves again and again went round the earth, surely the sand, the silt, the carcasses of animals, the uprooted forests would be carried, and then dropped, and then covered by succeeding tides. And then the giant inland seas would begin to break through the soft layers, and so the Grand Canyon could have been formed in the first few years or centuries after the flood. Then volcanic action and internal pressures and changes in the earth could raise the mountain systems as they are today with some of the layers and fossils of sea shells and other fauna, high above their original position.

In the 17th and the early 18th centuries, nearly all scientists believed that the earth strata and fossils were caused by the flood. Hilo, before Christ; St. Augustine, later; Baron Cuvier, in the University of Paris in 1799; Benjamin Silliman, head of the Geology Department of Yale University in 1829; and many other scientists—Williams, Cattcot, Woodward, Granville Penn—held what we call flood geology, believing that the Genesis flood and the adjustment period in the first century or two afterward, are accountable for the geologic conditions of the surface of the earth today.

When most of the scientists were Bible-believing Christians, they believed, of course, in the flood and they could understand and believe what God said about the flood destroying the earth. But when men went away from God, they wanted to leave the Bible out, they wanted to find some natural and not a supernatural source for life on the earth, and so when they discounted God and the Bible, they left off direct creation and left off the flood. But this was with unbelieving men, not an objective and scientific decision but was a subjective decision of men voluntarily refusing to believe the Bible or as II Peter 3:3 says, they are scoffers, walking after their own lusts or desires, and "they willingly are ignorant of, that by the word of God the heavens were of old, and the earth standing out of the water and in the water: Whereby the world that then was, being overflowed with water, perished." A willing ignorance of the Bible led people to turn away from the Bible doctrine of the flood.

But even today there are not wanting many men of science who teach that the strata, fossils, coal beds, etc., are a result of the flood. Overwhelming evidence is given in the book, *The Deluge Story in Stone,* by Byron C. Nelson, Augsburg Press; in *The Flood* by Alfred M. Rehwinkel, Concordia Publishing House; the geology textbooks by Professor George McCready Price; and perhaps best of all by *The Genesis Flood* by Drs. Whitcomb and Morris.

And if you take away the desire to fit in with the scientists' opinions about countless ages, then there is no need to invent a Gap Theory of creation.

No, as far as we can tell from the Bible account, Genesis 1:1 simply states a theme, and the rest of the chapter tells the details of that creation and then more details are given about man in the second chapter.

So, with respect for good men, we do not believe the Gap Theory about creation. Christians should not try to fit their theology to the unproved suppositions of unchristian scientists.

GENESIS 1 (cont'd)

Creation in Six Literal Days, Not Ages

"For in six days the Lord made heaven and earth, the sea, and all that in them is, and rested the seventh day: wherefore the Lord blessed the sabbath day, and hallowed it."—Exod. 20:11.

In Genesis, chapter 1, is a brief outline of the creation of the heavens and the earth. In brief, definite language God tells what happened day by day in six days of creation. The Bible never hints that it is a "poem" or that the language is figurative and allegorical. The simple, honest intent of the Scripture is evidently that thus in six literal days God made the heavens and the earth and then completed them. Genesis 1:1 says "heaven and the earth," but Genesis 2:1 and 4 say "the heavens [plural—all the universe] and the earth."

Infidels and enemies of the Bible would like to say, as Dr. George Buttrick says, that there are "two accounts of the creation and they do not agree" *(The Christian Fact and Modern Doubt,* p. 161). No; in the second chapter of Genesis there follows a detailed explanation of the creation of man, which is stated in Genesis 1:27: "So God created man in his own image, in the image of God created he him; male and female created he them." But God of course wants to expand that statement and tell us more about the creation of man and then of woman, and of their environment, their relation to the animal kingdom, their sin and fall, and the curse and promise involved. So here we do not have two conflicting accounts of creation, but first the bare outline and then the important details, which we need to know. Only flagrant unbelief and wicked bias, such as those of infidels like Tom Paine, Robert Ingersoll and their theological counterparts, would find contradictions here in Scriptures which millions of Bible believers have seen as perfectly harmonious.

I. WHY WE BELIEVE CREATION TOOK SIX LITERAL DAYS

It seems to this writer that there is overwhelming evidence that the account of creation speaks of six literal days in which God made the heavens and the earth, not six ages or eons.

1. Why Not Six Literal Days?

The simple truth is that the only reason people would claim that the days of creation were agelong periods is that they thus try to fit into the theories of unbelieving scientists the speculations and guesses of those who are enemies of the Bible.

Out-and-out unbelievers want to disparage the Bible. They do not accept direct creation as an act of God, so they labor ardently to try to prove that the earth and the universe are billions of years old. The popular idea now is that the universe is about five billion years old.

Some people try to accept evolution as the method of God's creation. They want to put God into it but keep the outline of events about as the speculations of unbelieving scientists would have it. Thus they hope to make the Bible palatable to unbelievers, and hope to have the favor of such men while they are still claiming to be Christians. But nobody reading the Bible ever came to believe in theistic evolution, we would think, until first the idea is put in their minds; then they must try to adjust the Bible to fit the guesses of unbelief.

Some Christian men speak of "progressive creation," indicating there were long ages and that perhaps at the beginning of each age God did a specific act of creation, and thus they try to fit the progressive periods of creation they have imagined, into the schedule manufactured by scientists of unbelief.

Others, like Pember in his book, *Earth's Earliest Ages,*
and many following the Scofield Reference Bible notes,
believe in the "Gap Theory," that millions or billions of
years came between Genesis 1:1 and Genesis 1:2; that the
"original creation" was destroyed by some awful
catastrophe which they think may have been connected
with the fall of Satan; then that a new period of creation
took place as recorded in the six days. Thus they would
explain the fossils and strata of the earth as being the result
of the "original creation."

In the first place, that is not a satisfactory theory either
to unbelievers or to strict Bible believers. It does not fit into
the Bible account of creation itself; it does not satisfy the
speculations of scientists who are enemies of the Bible. But
no one would come to such a conclusion, we suppose, except
in an earnest effort to reconcile the conflicting statements
of the Bible and of unbelieving scientists. But why do men
set unbelievers to judge the Bible? Why accept their
speculations?

2. "Day" and "Night" and "the Evening and the Morning" Indicate Literal Days

One should understand the meaning of the term "day"
in this chapter in its own context. God seems to take
particular pains, in Genesis 1:3-5, to show that He is
talking about literal days.

In literal language, when we say a day we mean a 24-
hour period, generally, in which the earth revolves, with
one period of light and a period of darkness. Or we mean
the period of light itself, the light part of the 24-hour day.

So here God tells, first of all, of the creation of light.
There would have to be light somewhere, in relation to the
earth, so that the revolving of the earth would make a 24-
hour day of light and dark. God says, then, that "God
called the light Day, and the darkness he called Night. And
the evening and the morning were the first day" (Gen. 1:5).
So here is a day which consists of a period of light and a
period of darkness, and this period is called "the first day."

Again, in verse 8, "And the evening and the morning were the second day."

Again, in verse 13, "And the evening and the morning were the third day."

And in verse 19, "And the evening and the morning were the fourth day."

Again, in verse 23, "And the evening and the morning were the fifth day."

And then, in verse 31, God says finally, "And the evening and the morning were the sixth day."

Six periods of light and darkness called days must mean six literal days.

3. Fact That Days Are Numbered Follows Pattern Used Only About Literal Days

It is true that the word "day" can refer to a period of time, like "the day of the Lord," that extended period which will include the return of Christ in glory, the Battle of Armageddon, and the millennial reign on earth. Even in this passage in Genesis 2:4, the Bible speaks of "in the day that the Lord God made the earth and the heavens." Here the word "day" may include the whole period of creation, the whole six days. But we note that in all such figurative and general uses of the term "day" meaning an extended period or epoch, no numeral is ever used.

When Jesus said, "For as Jonas was three days and three nights in the whale's belly; so shall the Son of man be three days and three nights in the heart of the earth" (Matt. 12:40), no one supposes that Jonah was three ages or extended periods in the belly of the whale; and no one supposes that Jesus was in the grave for three extended ages. It is obvious, when the numeral "three days and three nights" is used that it means three literal days and literal nights, or, sometimes more briefly, three literal days.

When the Lord commands in Exodus 12:15, "Seven days shall ye eat unleavened bread; even the first day ye shall put away leaven out of your houses. . . ," no one supposes that the Scripture could mean seven ages, and then the first of seven ages men should put away leaven. When the numeral is used, the term is always literal in the Bible.

In Matthew 17:1 we read, "And after six days Jesus taketh Peter, James, and John his brother, and bringeth them up into an high mountain apart." But there is no possible room for argument that "six days" means six ages. So, according to the common use of language and the Bible pattern everywhere, when the Bible says that "in six days the Lord made heaven and earth" (Exod. 20:11), it means six literal days.

4. When Jesus "Rested on the Seventh Day" and So Blessed and Sanctified It as the Sabbath, It Must Involve a Literal Day

In Genesis 2:1-3 we read:

"Thus the heavens and the earth were finished, and all the host of them. And on the seventh day God ended his work which he had made; and he rested on the seventh day from all his work which he had made. And God blessed the seventh day, and sanctified it: because that in it he had rested from all his work which God created and made."

The Lord refers to that in the Ten Commandments, saying:

"But the seventh day is the sabbath of the Lord thy God: in it thou shalt not do any work, thou, nor thy son, nor thy daughter, thy manservant, nor thy maidservant, nor thy cattle, nor thy stranger that is within thy gates: For in six days the Lord made heaven and earth, the sea, and all that in them is, and rested the seventh day: wherefore the Lord blessed the sabbath day, and hallowed it."—Exod. 20:10,11.

If the day Jesus rested was a literal day, then the six days He worked were literal days. The day He rested was the day He sanctified and set apart as a Sabbath day.

It is true that this Sabbath was not revealed to Israel until Exodus, chapter 16, and was then given as a part of the Mosaic law, but still the Sabbath was a literal day, following the pattern of a literal day in which God rested.

Does anybody suppose that there were six extended ages of creation, each with a period of darkness and a period of light, evening and morning? And then does anybody suppose that there was an extended period like that in which God rested? No, if the Sabbath day was a literal day, then God's day of rest was a literal day, and that means that His days of creation were literal days, too.

5. Order of Events in Creation Themselves Will Fit Literal Days but Not Extended Ages

Let me briefly give one example. In Genesis 1:11, 12 we find that God brought forth grass, herbs, and trees on the earth during the third day. Now if that were an age of perhaps millions of years, how would an earth full of plants, but no animals, live? We now know that God has balanced things so that the plants absorb carbon dioxide and give out oxygen. Then animals absorb the oxygen and give out carbon dioxide. And thus God has balanced plant life and animal life on the earth. How would plants live for many thousands of years in an atmosphere without carbon dioxide?

No, the program of creation by days could not fit long ages. Consider that in Genesis 1:11, 12 we are told, "And God said, Let the earth bring forth grass, the herb yielding seed, and the fruit tree yielding fruit after his kind, whose seed is in itself, upon the earth: and it was so. And the earth brought forth grass, and herb yielding seed after his kind, and the tree yielding fruit, whose seed was in itself, after his kind: and God saw that it was good." That is on "the third day," we are told. But the sun was not created or made to shine until the fourth day and verse 17 says, "And God set them in the firmament of the heaven to give light upon the earth." But if the third day was an age, how could the plants live a whole age with no sun? No plants could live long without the sun. So the third day could not be an age, it must be a literal day.

Grass and herbs, fruit trees and all plants were created on the third day, as we see in Genesis 1:9-12. But fowls, flying creatures, were not created until the fifth day. And creeping and walking animals were not made until the sixth day (vss. 24, 25). But many, many plants—fruits, flowers—can never bear fruit except they are pollenated by insects. How could they live a whole age (if the days of creation were ages of many thousands of years) before any insects were created or any birds or honeybees or other insects? The creation days, as ages, are simply impossible.

GENESIS 1 (cont'd)
The Evolution Fantasy
The Unprovable, Illogical Folly and Faith of Infidels

We have here in Genesis a sensible, logical, divinely inspired account of direct creation, by the hand of God, of this world and everything in it and the universe about us. To intelligent and thinking men, it becomes obvious that the Bible and the theory of evolution are directly contradictory. If the Bible is true, the theory of the unbelieving scientists—that man came from beast ancestry and all animals came from some imaginary one-celled animal and that plants and animals alike came from some common source by a series of amazing circumstances and coincidents, through millions or billions of years—is in direct contradiction to the Bible account. There is no way by which the Bible and the claims of infidel scientists about this matter can be reconciled.

But the Bible is believable. The greatest minds of the ages have found that we who "follow on to know the Lord" (Hos. 6:3), can know that the Bible is true, and that only "the fool hath said in his heart, There is no God" (Ps. 14:1). They have found that Jesus Christ told the truth when He said, "O fools, and slow of heart to believe all that the prophets have spoken" (Luke 24:25).

On the other hand, the theory of evolution is but a fancy, an unproven and unprovable matter of faith by people who do not want a personal God as Creator, do not want to take the Bible as the Word of God, do not want to repent of their sins, be converted and serve God.

First of all, remember that we do not mean development of an individual from a child to a man; we do not mean development of black horses and bay horses and white horses, big horses, little horses, from within a strain of horses. That is not the big claim of evolutionists. All sensible men know that there may be a development within an individual species. There may be variations in a kind, either plants or animals or men. But evolution as an explanation for plants and animals, all the way from the amoeba to mankind, is unscientific, unprovable, is built on a million guesses and it could not be called a scientific conclusion. The word "science" comes from the little Latin word, *scio*, "to know." Science includes known facts and comes to decisions based on actual happenings, on provable and seen experience and experiments. So evolution is not scientific but is a series of guesses.

Consider the vacuum in this evolutionary guess, this faith of infidels!

1. How Can One Explain Matter Without a Creator? How Could Matter Come to Be Without a God?

Those who rule out a personal God have no possible explanation for the origin of matter. "In the beginning God created the heaven and the earth" (Gen. 1:1). If there is not a God, an omnipotent, all-knowing, all-powerful, benevolent Being, a First Cause; then, men cannot even imagine a way for matter to come into existence.

2. How Did Life Come Into Being From Dead Matter?

Years ago ignorant people thought that germs arose spontaneously in water, that maggots came into being spontaneously from spoiled meat, and that otherwise all life more or less originated spontaneously from dead matter. That was the foolish thought of ignorant people. Then Pasteur came along and proved that if water were boiled and every germ killed and then sealed hermetically, it remained without a trace of germs. He proved that life never comes except from life. Since that time, many thousands of scientists in experiments, spending a total of millions of dollars, have tried to create life in the test tube. They have prepared every condition which they conceived would tend to make the origin of life possible. But they have never been able to produce life. Oh, they have boasted that they have found a way to make amino acid, and they thought that was a step in the origin of life. But it didn't live, it cannot live, and every sensible man knows that life does not begin from nothing.

But that, if acknowledged, is a death blow to evolution; so they say that if you give them billions of years, surely someway life could come accidently, though scientists have tried with every possible combination to make life. That is silly, illogical and anti-intellectual. That idea deserves only scorn and laughter from intelligent, cultivated, educated people. Life does not begin spontaneously. It is only one of the wild claims of evolutionists who try to find some way to bypass God. We are indebted to Fred John Meldau for the following quotation:

> Sir Ambrose Fleming, in an address to the members of the Victoria Institute, not only spoke of the origin of matter, but also of the origin of life.
>
> "We (as scientists) have not the smallest knowledge of how empty space first became occupied with the most rudimentary form of matter. Neither have we any conception of how life originated. WE CANNOT IN ANY WAY BRING IT INTO EXISTENCE APART FROM PREVIOUS LIFE. . . ."
>
> Irwin Schroedinger, "Nobel laureate in Physics," and leading atomic scientist, says,
>
> "Where are we when presented with the mystery of life? We find ourselves facing a granite wall which we have not even chipped. . . . We know virtually nothing of growth, nothing of life." (Quoted in the New York Times, in "The Greatest Mystery of All—the Secret of Life," by Waldemar Kaempffert).

(From *Why We Believe in Creation, Not in Evolution.*)

3. Bible Has Set Certain Bounds That Evolutionists Have Never Been Able to Cross

Ten times in the Scriptures we are told that life procreates "after its kind" and "after their kind." Read them over and be impressed.

Genesis 1:11, "God said, Let the earth bring forth grass, the herb yielding seed, and the fruit tree yielding fruit *after his kind*, whose seed is in itself, upon the earth: and it was so"—1.

Verse 12, "And the earth brought forth grass, and herb yielding seed *after his kind*, and the tree yielding fruit, whose seed was in itself, *after his kind*: and God saw that it was good"—2,3.

Verse 21, "And God created great whales, and every living creature that moveth, which the waters brought forth abundantly, *after their kind*, and every winged fowl *after his kind*: and God saw that it was good"—4,5.

Verse 24, "And God said, Let the earth bring forth the living creature *after his kind*, cattle, and creeping thing, and beast of the earth *after his kind*: and it was so"—6,7.

Verse 25, "And God made the beast of the earth *after his kind*, and cattle *after their kind*, and every thing that creepeth upon the earth *after his kind*: and God saw that it was good"—8,9,10.

Here is the honest challenge, foursquare and exactly stated in the Word of God. Plants and animals are made in certain *kinds*. There are some men who say that is the same as species, but the term species is not always defined alike, and with some men it means more than to others. In other words, God did divide created plants and animals into certain kinds and they do not cross from one to another kind.

Some people talk about the "missing link" between man and animal life. Actually, all the links are missing.

There is an infinite variety of detail in each particular kind, even in a one-celled animal. Every single cell of a particular plant or animal carries all the characteristics of that plant and that one kind only.

Scientific people talk about hybrids. They simply mean that from roses you can grow different kinds of roses—red roses, yellow roses, white roses, all the way from the wild single-flowered rose to the tropicana. But they are still roses. They do not cross out of that kind.

I saw the other day in the *National Geographic* where a man had grown horses. One full-grown horse was only fifteen inches high and weighed only twenty-seven pounds. Then there have been giant horses weighing close to three thousand pounds. But, in the first place, that was done by careful selection by men; it did not come naturally through chance as evolutionists think the animal kinds came to be; and in the second place, they were horses. I mean they had all the features of horses—looks, limbs, color, etc., of horses.

Mendel's laws were not known by Darwin, but that monk Mendel, through generation after generation of breeding, found that the plants and animals reproduce after certain known laws and that every variation is caused by a regrouping of the genes already present, and is not new but is a part of the inheritance of the plant. So it is with animals. Variations are simply a regrouping of factors, genes already present, never new.

For example, my wife and I have gray eyes. Both of us have some brown-eyed folks in our families, so two of our girls have brown eyes instead of gray! That is not a new development; it is what we carried already in our genes, and some of those things will come out in their descendants, of course.

How men have tried to get away from this and to prove that there is no gap between kinds!

In North Texas years ago Colonel Goodnight, who had a big ranch, set out to cross cattle and buffaloes. Cattle have the best beef in the hindquarters. Buffaloes have the best beef in the front quarters. So he thought he could cross them and make better beef all around. But it turned out that the "cataloes" which he developed were sterile as far as reproducing themselves. They could be bred back only to become buffaloes or cattle. They could not continue a strain of "cataloes."

The bison or buffalo are in the same family of animals, so interbreed. At last after many years of experimentations Mr. D. C. Basalo of Tracy, California, has succeeded where Col. Goodnight failed and crossed cattle with the buffalo. The cross is called "Beefalo." So donkeys, horses and zebras, of the same family, may interbreed, though there are difficulties. But these still bring forth only "after their kind."

In Archer County, Texas, years ago I knew a merchant and farmer with scientific interests and attitudes who set out to desperately try to cross sheep and goats and to cross pigs with other animals. But he found it impossible. The chromosomes are different. Every cell in each of these animals is distinctly its own kind of a cell and carries the characteristics which will be reproduced in descendants. He couldn't cross that boundary.

In West Texas we raised horses and mules. You can breed a mare to a jack, a male donkey, and produce mules, but the mules are sterile. They cannot reproduce. You see, God has a law people cannot get around.

Things reproduce after their kind. Scientists look at a few bones among fossils and they decide they can trace down the "descent of the horse." Well, they find some animals with some similar kinds of bones, from the size of a dog on up to the size of a horse; and some of these animals have three toes and some four, but the horse has one. Strangely enough, they think that one descended from the other, though they found the fossil of one in one continent and the other in another continent! And at the same time, there were horses like those today and their bones found in the same strata among the fossils, of their supposed ancestors! Foolish! But they pretend they have thus found the descendant of a horse from one kind of three-toed horse to a one-toed horse. They have found nothing of the kind. They have imagined that but they find no evidence that the one turned into the other. Oh, we can have different size horses and different color horses, but they are horses, they have the nature of horses and that never changes. Horses don't turn into cows, sheep don't turn into goats, quails do not turn into chickens, turtles do not turn into fish, and corn does not turn into cotton. One who is not impressed with this fact so clearly evident in all animal life and plant life is certainly biased and ignorant.

But this same great gap between different kinds is found

in all the fossil beds of the world. It astonished Darwin; it has astonished all the others that sought for a connection. Oh, first they said that when later we found more fossils, we would find connecting links. They were never found. Out of multiplied millions of fossils there are no connecting links between one kind and another.

It is not intelligent to be an evolutionist. It is only a sign of the fancy and the kind of religious faith of an infidel who doesn't want the God of creation. A theory based on imagination and guessing without facts is not defensible.

Is this fact that there are no intermediary forms between kinds among animals a recognized fact among scientists? Oh, yes, it is known to scientists everywhere, even to evolutionists and to their chagrin. In *Why We Believe in Creation, Not in Evolution*, Fred John Meldau quotes many scientists acknowledging this utter failure to find evidence of transformation of one species into another:

> Dr. Etheride, speaking of the British Museum, said, "In all this great museum there is not a particle of evidence of transmutation of species."
>
> Professor T. H. Morgan said, "Within the period of human history we do not know of a single instance of the transformation of one species into another" (p. 43, *Evolution and Adaptation).*
>
> Yves Delage, renowned biologist, said, "If one take his stand on the exclusive ground of facts . . . the formation of one species from another has not been demonstrated at all."
>
> Darwin himself confessed, "Not one change of species into another is on record." "We cannot prove that a single species has been changed (into another)" (Vol. 1, p. 210; *My Life and Letters).*

No reputable scientist ever claims to find fossils showing the gradual development of one species of a kind into another. This is the despair of avowed evolutionists. It is the reason many scientists now say evolution cannot be proved and many are turning to believe in direct creation.

In the book, *Is Evolution Proved?* Douglas Dewar quoted Sir J. William Dawson, F. R. S., of McGill

University (Toronto), a trained geologist. Professor Dawson said in his day:

> "The evolutionist doctrine is itself one of the strangest phenomena of humanity, but that in our day a system destitute of any shadow of proof . . . should be accepted as a philosophy, and should enable adherents to string upon its thread of hypotheses our vast and weighty stores of knowledge is surpassing strange.

In a truly monumental work (published in 1954) by Dr. Heribert-Nilsson, Professor of Botany at the University of Lund, Sweden, he gives the results of his life's studies in genetics and other subjects. Speaking of fossil flora, he says,

> "If we look at the peculiar main groups of the fossil flora, it is quite striking that at definite intervals of geological time they are ALL AT ONCE and QUITE SUDDENLY THERE; and, moreover, in full bloom in all their manifold forms. . . . Furthermore, at the end of their existence (if they are now extinct) they do not change into forms which are transitional towards the main types of the next period: such are entirely lacking. This all stands in as crass a contradiction to the evolutionary interpretation as could possibly be imagined. There is not even a caricature of an evolution."

(Quoted from *Why We Believe in Creation, Not in Evolution*, by Fred John Meldau.)

4. Fossil Beds, Coal Beds, and Strata of Earth Could Not Have Come About Through Evolutionary Process

The evolutionists have had to retreat from so many arguments trying to prove evolution, but their greatest argument in these days is probably based on the fossil beds. They think that earlier animals were in a lower strata of the earth and that they developed into more advanced kinds and these are presented in some other later strata of the earth, etc. This is an artificial decision, of course, because often what they think is the lowest strata is on top of what they call a more recent strata. Then they rate the fossils themselves by the artificial time clock they have already set up. And having guessed about the strata and the earth, they now guess about the animals and plants coming in the age they think that represents. It is a circular reasoning that is not scientific and, of course, is not really factual.

There are several striking things that perturb and distress and trouble the evolutionists about this. In the first place, there are literally thousands and thousands of square miles when some of the so-called lower strata overlay the so-called higher strata. They think that one great section was slid over another section, etc., etc. They make all kinds of excuses that are not sensible, not mechanically and physically possible.

Byron C. Nelson calls attention in *The Deluge Story in Stone* to this fact:

> In one section of the earth, comprising part of Montana, Alberta and British Columbia, an "upside-down" condition ("Algonkian" and "Cambrian" on top of "Cretaceous") *covers 7,000 square miles.*

Nelson made a special study of this enormous area which modern geologists tried to suppose was turned upside-down and that the younger strata was now on the bottom. But, worse yet, no fossil beds are now being formed. Fossils can only be formed when an animal or plant is covered quickly and put under pressure and thus is preserved. Now, if a fish dies in the water, it swells up and floats and the decay is eaten by the other fish and creatures in the water. If a cow dies on the prairies, her body is picked by vultures and wolves or foxes and the bones lie there and finally decay. As a boy in the cattle country of Texas, I used to take a little wagon out on the prairie and collect bones of cattle, long dead, and sell them for fertilizer. Fossils in the sense of the fossil beds, found and depended upon by the evolutionists, are not being made today. They could not be made without a giant cataclysm. The coal beds are not being made today. They could not be made without the covering of great forests by waves and layers of mud and debris, put under great pressure and thus preserved and pressed and turned into carbon as coal.

The fossil beds where millions of fishes are found encased in the soil or perhaps the soil has sometimes turned to stone, doesn't happen today in any place we know of. In the fossil beds were the mammoths (giant, woolly elephants); thousands of them were covered over and became fossils in Siberia and Alaska. Nothing like that happens anywhere in the world today as far as we know. In certain areas fossils are found massed in great numbers. One cannot imagine any place in the world today where that kind of fossil making is being done. Go to the Painted Desert and to the great areas of fossilized trees, now turned into silica but with all the color and shape of trees; that kind of work is not going on anywhere in the world today. Only a giant cataclysm like the flood can explain the fossils. It does not fit with the evolutionary theory, millions of years of common, ordinary day-by-day routine life on this earth.

Where do you suppose anywhere in the world enough fishes and plant life are covered over and put under giant pressure to be making petroleum today?

5. Scientists Cannot Agree on Any Mechanics of Evolution—How It Is Supposed to Work

It is now fifty-four years since I graduated from the university, taught in college and then went to do graduate work in the University of Chicago. In these years I have seen a continual retreat as scientists had to admit the failure of their arguments for evolution, a failure of the so-called "proofs."

Evolutionists who do not want to believe in God grasp at straws to prove an unprovable theory that gets more and more unbelievable as more scientific truth comes to light and as reasonable men consider their foolish arguments.

In my boyhood the great argument of how evolution came about was by acquired characteristics. We were told that giraffes grew such long necks, no doubt, because in times of drouth and famine only the giraffes with the longer necks could reach the highest trees and eat the leaves and so they did not die and others did and so we grew a race of long-necked giraffes! Now every scientist worthy of the name in all the world knows that acquired characteristics are not passed on to the next generation.

Multiplied thousands of generations of fruit flies and other insects have been bred to check.

There are remarkable evidences in life, that acquired characteristics are not inherited.

For example, for many hundreds of years it has been the custom to cut off the tails of sheep. The general public doesn't know it, but the sheep men know that a sheep's tail grows into a big blob of fat, gets in the way, doesn't make any more mutton and so it is customary to cut off the tails of baby sheep. After hundreds and hundreds of generations sheep still grow tails.

From the days of Moses, Jews have been taught to circumcise boy babies, and they still do. But the circumcision is not inherited. There is never any hint that this acquired characteristic is passed on to descendants.

Acquired characteristics are not inherited. And evolutionists now know that.

Another pet argument of the evolutionist was that sexual selection had a part in the progress from one kind to another. We are told that no doubt originally men had hair like their supposed ape ancestors, but that the female liked better men with less hair and so they wouldn't mate with hairy men and thus gradually the hair was bred off! But they have retreated from that. Evolutionists now do not believe that argument.

In more recent years, after the failure of other explanations of evolution, now scientists are saying that evolution takes place by mutations. A few years back they were saying that there were tiny mutations, changes, and that a multitude of these small changes eventually took one from one class to another, of one kind to another, and bridged that gap. However, how would all the mutations, each one only one case in hundreds of thousands—how would these tiny mutations happen often enough and in the same direction in successive individuals, to grow an ear where there wasn't an ear or to turn jellyfish into a vertebrate, or to turn a reptile into a mammal! That would be miraculous accident upon miraculous accident and a million times to make one important change. Now scientists have pretty well given up the idea of tiny mutations. And so they now talk about great mutations, a leap at one time into another kind. However, in the real evidence they find no good proof. The simple truth is that mutations are nearly always harmful. In fact, as far as we can tell they are always harmful. A mutation is a kind of deformity. It may be caused by X-ray or by some accident, but it is not helpful.

For example, a mother may have the measles while she is carrying a baby and that may mean the baby will be deaf or deformed. That is a mutation but not a helpful one.

Under some circumstances of pressure or a blow, someway there is an injury to a little one, so that a child is born without an arm. I know a man who was born with only small fragments of arms and legs, no hands or feet. Was that an improvement? Obviously not. It was a genuine handicap. Yesterday's paper pictured a dog with six legs! To depend on mutations to explain the theory that from nothing to matter and then from dead matter to life and then from vegetable to animal and then from one kind to another and from some far off imaginary ape ancestor to man—that is not believable to a sensible person. It is a fantasy, it is a faith without facts to support it.

It is not a faith in God but faith in a heathen theory without God and a preference for no God.

6. Science Keeps Finding Evidences That Life as We Have It Today Has Been Same From Beginning

For example, in amber they have found embedded many long centuries or millenniums ago some mosquitoes. But those mosquitoes are exactly like mosquitoes today.

They find coral in the oldest possible strata, as scientists count it, but that coral is just like coral today.

Scientists had found the bones of a coelacanth and they

said that was a kind of fish that died out millions of years ago and became extinct, and then, behold, from deep in the Indian Ocean somebody brings up a coelacanth and since that time some others have been found from the bottom of the sea. Webster's Dictionary says, "Coelacanth, any of several primitive ganoid fishes, possibly ancestors to land animals: so called because of their hollow spines: they were long believed to be extinct, but several living specimens have been found in recent times." They do not live near the surface of the water and so are not frequently found, but that is no sign that they have changed into any other form or that they have disappeared.

7. Unbelieving Scientists Have Made All Kinds of Claims About Savage Early Men or Cave Men

Some are called "Neanderthal men." However, men were surprised to find that when skulls were measured they had the same brain capacity of men today and had every evidence of being just as intelligent and complete in mind and body as men today. It is very probable, actually, that they were men who lived in caves for a time after the flood and when all the cities had been destroyed and when the confusion of languages scattered people around the whole earth. Some would live in caves before houses and cities were built. So in West Texas and New Mexico and Kansas men built "dugouts" and "soddy" houses, with blocks of adobe mud and with poles and brush and hay on top and covered with dirt. Oh, but those were soon outgrown and outlived as men got ways to build modern homes. The Neanderthal men were simply men.

Out in Nebraska a scientific man named Cook found a tooth. It had to be a human tooth! From it he made a description of the early apeman of hundreds of thousands of years ago. Ah, with what imagination and guesses an infidel faith is built! A man with no faith in God can manufacture so much "scientific evidence"! Alas, after being acclaimed by scientists everywhere as a remarkable evidence of the evolution of man, the tooth was found to be simply the tooth of a peccary, a wild pig. I think some of them are still found living in Mexico.

The Eoanthropus man, and what a find! A jaw, a few teeth, a bit of a skull! Obviously, to infidel Charles Dawson of Piltdown, England, it must be the remains of an apeman! The English paleontologist Sir Arthur S. Woodward decided that the bones were of a now-extinct type of man, which he called Eoanthropus (dawn man) and which also became known as Piltdown man. Today we all know that Eoanthropus was a deliberately planned hoax—a hoax that deceived the world's leading anthropologists for forty years, because they wanted to be fooled! It was discovered that the teeth had been filed down to simulate apes' teeth, colored to appear aged. There was no Piltdown man. There went another "proof."

Illusioned scientists and gullible followers have manufactured "apemen" in museums and pictured them in textbooks, with receding foreheads like an ape, with "orbital ridges" above the eyes, like apes are supposed to have. They are pictured with hairy bodies like apes. And manufactured from what? Oh, from a leg bone, or a part of a jaw or a skull fragment or a tooth or two! And the rest all filled out with plaster of Paris and painted. They are wicked, dishonest fakes pictured in the textbooks, some are presented in museums. They represented only the hopes and imaginations of the infidels who put them out to deceive high school young people and a gullible public. Shame, shame!

I saw a picture widely published showing a primitive man with a tail! It was a "bushman" I think, from Australia and there he was in a natural picture with a tail. Didn't that plainly prove that man came from monkeys? But many scientists remembered that the higher apes, chimpanzees, gorillas, orangutans do not have tails! Then the picture was found to be a fake; the tail was artificially fastened on to the poor bushman for the picture! No primitive men had tails.

8. Man Was Supposed to Have Invented Writing Only a Few Centuries Before Christ

Infidels and their wolves in sheep's clothing liberals said that Moses could not have written the Pentateuch because writing had not been invented then! Oh, but, alas, the code of Hammurabi was discovered and archaeologists learned of the library of Babylon in the days of Sargon, a thousand years before Nebuchadnezzar!

And now we learn that in Ur of the Chaldees, home of Abraham, and before he left, there was a library there. Yes, there was pictograph writing and hieroglyphic writing on clay tablets and engraved on stone, and, no doubt, written on parchment and skins, that was written and read by sons and grandsons of Noah! We remember that Mizraim, said to be a son of Ham and the first historical king of Egypt, had his reign and his descendants copied down.

There is no proof in the world of evolution.

9. A High Civilization From Very Beginning of Ancient History

The oldest accounts in the world are of the civilization in Egypt. There is much evidence that from the very beginning of known history, the people who had brought learning and civilization that people knew before the flood, building cities, writing, skilled in music and use of metals, that culture appears in the archeology of the very first Egyptian dynasties.

Dr. Harry Rimmer in the book, *Dead Men Tell Tales*, says:

> Strangely, in view of the consistent demands of the evolutionary school, we find no evidence of human evolution in the land of Egypt. More than this, the doctrine that man began with a brutish intellect and gradually developed his high and peculiar culture, is refuted by the evidences from this country. In fact, the contrary is strikingly the case. Instead of proving a process of evolution, the history of man as found in the archeology of Egypt is a consistent record of degeneration.

The eminent Sayce, one of the ablest archeologists in the whole history of that great science, expressed his wonder and amazement at the high stage of culture met with in the very earliest records of the Egyptian people. Other authorities, such as Baikie, have written voluminously upon this subject. It had been hoped that when excavators finally reached undisturbed tombs of the first dynasty, they would find themselves in the dawn of Egyptian culture. It was our fortunate privilege to be at Sakkara a year ago when the first dynasty was uncovered. It was our privilege to keep a close check and watch upon all that was done at that time, and the conclusions and postulations of hopeful theorists were utterly shattered in such discoveries as were made.

Indeed, we can no longer start Egyptian culture with the beginning of the dynastic ages. Through the first tombs, we peer back into an older preceding culture that dazzles and amazes the human understanding. Instead of finding the dawn of a developing humanity, we see mankind already in the high noon of cultural accomplishments. Instead of nomadic dwellers in shaggy tents, we look upon works of enduring stone. Instead of brutish, Egyptian ancestral artifacts, we find a pottery culture that is really superb. It almost seems that the further back we go into Egyptian antiquity, the more perfect was their culture and learning.

Again Dr. Rimmer has an interesting comment on the "so-called Stone Age" in Egypt:

There are many anomalies and mysteries in this so-called stone age in Egypt. In the museum at Cairo there will be found some of the most remarkable specimens of stone flaking to be seen on the face of this earth. Others may be seen in the British Museum, in the various exhibits of Egyptian culture. One of these knives is equipped with two points, and all of them are equally sharpened on both edges. In the author's own gatherings from the various stone cultures of mankind, there are something over 25,000 artifacts. We have seen every important collection of stone implements in the present world, but these specimens from ancient Egypt are unquestionably the most magnificent types of stone culture we have ever been privileged to observe.

The significant and startling fact is that these stone knives have handles of beaten gold. At once we are impressed with the anomalous fact that the stone age was thus synonymous with an age of metal. Furthermore, it was an artistic age. The golden handles on these stone weapons are engraved with scenes common to the life of the people. On one side of the stone dagger with the double points, there is a sailing vessel typical of the pleasure craft that were common to all ages of Egyptian life. On the raised deck of this boat, dancing maidens were entertaining the circle of spectators. This work was not crude and brutish, but showed a high development of the engraver's art. The reverse side of the handle was even more interesting in that it contained, in beautifully incised characters, the cult sign of the owner.

So in this same age when some people used stone tools, others in the same culture used metals and they had a written language and art.

It has been a great joy to go to the National Museum in Cairo. I have been delighted at beautiful, exquisite relics from the tombs of the Pharaohs, gold scarabs and pins, and other beautiful ornaments that indicated the highest culture.

Again Dr. Rimmer says:

If there is one voice that can be heard in archeology, and one lesson that can be specifically learned, it is the certainty of the fallacy of the theory of evolution. Egypt, as elsewhere, shows us no dim, brutish beginning, but a startling emergence of this people in a high degree of culture.

CONSIDER OTHER CLAIMS OF EVIDENCE FOR EVOLUTION

Evolutionists years ago claimed that a baby conceived in his mother's womb followed all the pattern of so-called evolution from a one-celled animal up to man. There were stages in which they thought that fetus represented a fish, with "gill slits" and then on through other stages up to the state of man. It was a silly thought. Actually, when a sperm united with the cell sent forth by the female ovary—in that single cell all that would develop was already contained definitely. Already all the things that make a man or woman were tied up in there and would not be changed. If anybody thought that fetus at any time looked like some other animal, he would be foolish, because actually that little one knows where he is going. Even the color of eyes and hair, general size and brain capacity and musical capacity and other such matters are already tied up in that cell and only God Himself could put that miracle together. No, a fetus does not reproduce steps of evolution.

There is a great argument because of similarity, that since an ape has arms and legs and so has a man, and with a backbone, the one must be descended from the other. Even a bird has wings to take the place of arms, and so the bird and men came from the same source, they say.

The simple truth is that all that proves is that there is a good reason for birds to have wings and feet and good reason for man to have arms and legs and hands and feet, and Almighty God did it that way.

I sit now in a chair with four legs. Before me is a table with four legs. Does that prove that the chair was descended from the table or that the table was descended from the chair? No, it simply shows that for stable equilibrium the four legs are a convenient way to make chairs and tables. This example does not show that the chair descended from the table or vice versa, it simply shows that the carpenters and furniture builders have the same general idea of what is sensible and easy and safe in building furniture.

Similarity! What does it prove? Some years ago America airlifted some military supplies to Pakistan, north of India. Great cargo planes flew in to the airport and a big door was let down in the tail and out of the belly of that great freight-carrying airship man drove a jeep and then a man drove another jeep and then another and then another. A wise father of Pakistan stood there with his son and he gravely explained to the son: The big animal has given birth to some little ones. And now those little ones will grow wings and grow big like the other. He thought the jeeps were simply descended from airplanes and would grow into airplanes themselves. That was a leap in the dark, fanciful, imaginative argument that similarity means evolution, or that one descends from the other. Well, jeeps had rubber-tired wheels, so did the big plane; so the man leaped to a conclusion that was not sensible. Similarity is no proof of evolution.

Population figures show the present population would have come in some four thousand years since the flood, not in 300,000 years!

WHY, THEN, DO MEN BELIEVE IN EVOLUTION? The answer is simply because they want to. Like the men after the flood, described in Romans 1, they "do not like to retain God in their knowledge."

"And even as they did not like to retain God in their knowledge, God gave them over to a reprobate mind, to do those things which are not convenient."—Rom. 1:28.

They are like those scoffers who walk after their own lusts that II Peter 3:3-9 tells us of:

"Knowing this first, that there shall come in the last days scoffers, walking after their own lusts, And saying, Where is the promise of his coming? for since the fathers fell asleep, all things continue as they were from the beginning of the creation. For this they willingly are ignorant of, that by the word of God the heavens were of old, and the earth standing out of the water and in the water: Whereby the world that then was, being overflowed with water, perished: But the heavens and the earth, which are now, by the same word are kept in store, reserved unto fire against the day of judgment and perdition of ungodly men. But, beloved, be not ignorant of this one thing, that one day is with the Lord as a thousand years, and a thousand years as one day. The Lord is not slack concerning his promise, as some men count slackness; but is longsuffering to us-ward, not willing that any should perish, but that all should come to repentance."

Jesus said, "And this is the condemnation, that light is come into the world, and men loved darkness rather than light, because their deeds were evil. For every one that doeth evil hateth the light, neither cometh to the light, lest his deeds should be reproved. But he that doeth truth cometh to the light, that his deeds may be made manifest, that they are wrought in God" (John 3:19-21).

Men do not believe in evolution because they are convinced against their will; they believe in evolution because they want some way to explain things without God, without a God who demands judgment, a God who sends Christ-rejecting sinners to Hell.

Does anybody in the world know of any example of evolution actually taking place today? They do not. Does anybody find in the fossil record intermediary links between the different kinds of plants and animals? They do not. There are no intermediate forms. Each kind in the fossil beds springs forth entirely new and separate. Is there anywhere in the world today where things that evolutionists claim happened before are happening now? Are there fossil beds being made? Are forests being buried and made into coal? Are tremendous quantities of animal matter and vegetable matter being made into petroleum now? They are not. Men who do not want God have a faith, not in the Bible or in Christ, but a faith in man's wisdom, a faith in a manmade system of doctrine, which cannot be proven.

And even the theistic evolutionist is a strange creature. His scientific opinions do not satisfy the unbelieving scientists. His twisting and misuse of the Scriptures and unbelieving and throwing discredit on plain statements of Scripture do not please Christians. The truth is that the so-called theistic evolutionist is trying to keep his standing with the scientific infidels and so he compromises convictions about the Bible to please ungodly men.

Go back and read it again. Ten times God said that plants and animals were to bring forth only "after his kind" and "after their kind" and all scientific evidence in the world goes to prove that that is exactly how it is today.

————

GENESIS 1 (cont'd)

The Six Days of Creation

VERSES 1-5:

IN the beginning God created the heaven and the earth.

2 And the earth was without form, and void; and darkness *was* upon the face of the deep. And the Spirit of God moved upon the face of the waters.

3 And God said, Let there be light: and there was light.

4 And God saw the light. that *it was* good: and God divided the light from the darkness.

5 And God called the light Day, and the darkness he called Night. And the evening and the morning were the first day.

We have discussed Genesis 1:1, "In the beginning God created the heaven and the earth." It was well to do so. But we should understand that actually that is a part of a discussion in the first five verses, all about the first day of creation. So after a bit we will come back to discuss this chapter, divided up into the six-day periods of creation.

First Day of Creation

Some good men think that verse 1 simply gives a statement something like a general headline or summary and then that following that there are the details of creation. That could be interpreted so. I think rather, however, here in verses 1 to 5, all are included in what was done on the first day. The earth itself was brought forth "without form and void"—that is, the material, the matter of the earth itself was created. So a potter or a sculptor might first have the block of stone or the lump of clay from which some beautiful thing would be formed, but first it is just the unformed material.

There was "darkness. . .upon the face of the deep. And the Spirit of God moved upon the face of the waters" (vs. 2). Oh, what wonderful things God had in mind. What a marvel of joy God had in making the things which He later pronounced so good!

Then God said, "Let there be light and there was light." Do you mean light before there was any sun? Yes, I do. Someone says that in our solar system all light is from the sun.

Years ago Professor John R. Sampey, later president of Southern Baptist Seminary, in discussing this matter, said:

> The fact that the creation of the sun is placed in the fourth day is proof that we do not have in this chapter a strictly scientific account of the events sketched; for no modern scientist would place the creation of the sun after that of the earth. While the scientist must admire much in this sketch of the creative process as anticipating some of the views of modern students of nature, he would not interpret the Hebrew story as a cold and scientifically accurate account of the order of events. It is a popular account with the emphasis on the religious element, attention being drawn to the Divine activity throughout the story. The long creative process is compressed within the limits of a week of days. The author evidently wished to put emphasis on the observance of the Sabbath.—From page 51 of *The System Bible Study*.

But Dr. Sampey was mistaken. In the first place, the scientists' thought that all light and energy comes from the sun is simply not true. Genesis 1:3 and 4 shows that God created light, and that this light was some way positioned in relation to the earth so that day and night followed one another as the earth revolved toward that light.

No, all light is really from God and God may use the sun for a time to dispense light, but God is not bound to that limitation. Revelation 21:23,24 tells about the heavenly Jerusalem. "And the city had no need of the sun, neither of the moon, to shine in it: for the glory of God did lighten it, and the Lamb is the light thereof. And the nations of them which are saved shall walk in the light of it: and the kings of the earth do bring their glory and honour into it." Ah, the city lighted without any sun or moon! You will remember that Christ is "the light of the world" (John 8:12).

John 1:4,5 says, "In him was life; and the life was the light of men. And the light shineth in darkness; and the darkness comprehended it not." Shining now into this dark world, Jesus is called "The bright and morning star" (Rev. 22:16). But when He comes in glory to reign, then He will be "the Sun of righteousness" (Mal. 4:2). Even in nature there is sometimes light created by decaying vegetable matter, or light from the insects as the "lightning bug" or the firefly, or like the glowworm. There is no need to shake up the order of events as God gives them here. God said, "Let there be light: and there was light." Does it appear from the first day of creation that this earth is the center of God's creation? I think so. Not the sun, which is physically the center of our planetary system and not the giant North Star, many light years away; not Betelgeuse. The earth was made first and then the sun and moon made to serve the earth! Oh, you see, God had in mind to make men. Before the foundation of the world it had already been decided. Man should be made in the image of God, made with the will to choose right or wrong. And already Christ had surrendered Himself to die for sinners and pay for our sins so that, in the mind and plan of God, He was the "Lamb of God, slain from the foundation of the world."

An elephant is bigger than a man but not as important as a man. A mountain, a planet, a sun may be bigger than a man but not as important in God's sight as a man made in God's image, with an immortal soul to be redeemed with the blood of Christ, to praise God forever!

VERSES 6-8:

6 And God said, Let there be a firmament in the midst of the waters, and let it divide the waters from the waters.

7 And God made the firmament, and divided the waters which *were* under the firmament from the waters which *were* above the firmament: and it was so.

8 And God called the firmament Heaven. And the evening and the morning were the second day.

Second Day of Creation

Take to heart the Word of God. Here a strange thing is said and the meaning may not at once be obvious. There is a firmament, that is, the heavens above the earth, including all the air space and where the birds fly. But this firmament was made to separate between two great volumes of water. God "divided the waters which were under the firmament from the waters which were above the firmament."

Down on earth, the waters under the heavens were gathered together into the seas, but above the firmament the waters were not gathered together, but evidently they were in vapor form and surrounding this earth was a great blanket of water vapor. The sun could shine through, but some of the infrared rays and others that might harm were filtered out, and the whole earth was somewhat insulated so that the climate would be even. The result was, the whole earth was like a hothouse with moderate climate.

Now scientists are astonished that in Siberia, in the deadly cold where in the short days of summer, a willow sprout can grow but two inches before it is overwhelmed by the deadly cold of another winter—there they found the frozen carcasses of many, many mammoths, the woolly elephants that populated the region, and multiplied thousands of these mammoths have left their bones and their tusks, enough to make commerce for the nations for long years. What a strange thing! And some of these quick-frozen woolly elephants, or mammoths, were perfectly preserved when found. And in their mouths and in their stomachs were undigested tropical plants and grasses and flowers such as now could not possibly grow in the Arctic regions. So it is found in Alaska, also. What does it mean? It must mean, surely, that in the days before the flood the whole earth once had a tropical climate protected by that great envelope or canopy of water vapor which covered the earth.

Since the flood in Noah's days we have had no such canopy of water vapor. But the planet, Saturn, has rings around it and scientists have now discovered that those are rings of ice. They are far enough above the planet, they turn with the planet, and the centrifugal force counteracts the gravity so they do not fall. So it was, no doubt, with the great layer of water vapor above the earth until the time of the flood. Note, God speaks here of the waters that were under the firmament and the waters that were above the firmament. God is planning some great things here in the second day.

VERSES 9-13:

9 ¶ And God said, Let the waters under the heaven be gathered together unto one place, and let the dry *land* appear: and it was so.

10 And God called the dry *land* Earth; and the gathering together of the waters called he Seas: and God saw that *it was* good.

11 And God said, Let the earth bring forth grass, the herb yielding seed, *and* the fruit tree yielding fruit after his kind, whose seed *is* in itself, upon the earth: and it was so.

12 And the earth brought forth grass, *and* herb yielding seed after his kind, and the tree yielding fruit, whose seed *was* in itself, after his kind: and God saw that *it was* good.

13 And the evening and the morning were the third day.

Third Day of Creation

Now God is molding this earth into the habitation of man. So the water vapors under the firmament, that is, the fog and vapor that covered the earth under the skies are now condensed and gathered together into seas and the dry land appears. So now there are the land and the seas.

Now then, the earth is ready to bring forth the "grass and herbs and fruit trees and all kinds of plants." Will you notice that God does not say that He made some seeds and put them in the earth that they might some day grow into great trees. No, no. He made the herbs. He made the grass, made the fruit trees already "yielding fruit after his kind." God made trees.

We know now that the rings in the tree are somewhat the record of periods of rainfall and then rest. The tree would grow in the summertime, the periods of rain; then in periods of drought or of quietude it would not grow. So the rings usually represent years and sometimes big rings represent very wet years of good growth and small rings may represent times of drought. But God made some trees complete. Did they have rings? I have no doubt they did. If God made a tree, He made it to look like a tree. It had the appearance of age though it had not grown. This earth was already beautiful with plants and, no doubt, some trees had fruit on them in this tropical world God had prepared by the end of the third day.

VERSES 14-19:

14 ¶ And God said, Let there be lights in the firmament of the heaven to divide the day from the night; and let them be for signs, and for seasons, and for days, and years:

15 And let them be for lights in the firmament of the heaven to give light upon the earth: and it was so.

16 And God made two great lights; the greater light to rule the day, and the lesser light to rule the night: *he made* the stars also.

17 And God set them in the firmament of the heaven to give light upon the earth,

18 And to rule over the day and over the night, and to divide the light from the darkness: and God saw that *it was* good.

19 And the evening and the morning were the fourth day.

Fourth Day of Creation

Some way, from some fixed light, God marked off the day. You see the Lord does not have a sundown and a sunrise to know when a day is gone. And we have no men keeping a calendar here. It is God who keeps a calendar and so now three days are gone before He makes the sun and the moon and the stars. You may be sure that time is the managed, controlled servant of God, and since God had selected the unit of time as a day, He starts with that and then later God puts His clock in the sky so men can keep account of the days by the revolution of the earth toward the sun and around and toward the sun again. Again I remind you the earth was more important to God than a sun. It was no great thing for God to reach a hand out into the limitless expanse and suddenly create a sun. He could do that as easily as He multiplied the loaves and fishes when He fed the five thousand. Ah, but it was not the yearning of heart, not the holy joy of creation and not the outgoing of love that He had when He made man. So God put the earth here for men and the earth is more important in God's account than the sun, moon, and stars.

Already there was light. Now God centered light in the sun and some in the stars and reflected light on the moon. And physically the sun is to rule the day and the moon the night.

Heathen people have sometimes worshiped the sun. Oh, but how much better to worship the God who made the sun—the benevolent, loving God who provided growth for plants and animals and all the good things that grow physically on the earth. And how we need the sun!

And how dark night would be if there were never a moon or stars! Oh, yes, and so God "saw that it was good." Everything God made was good, until man sinned and brought a curse upon it.

VERSES 20-23:

20 And God said, Let the waters bring forth abundantly the moving creature that hath life, and fowl *that* may fly above the earth in the open firmament of heaven.

21 And God created great whales, and every living creature that moveth, which the waters brought forth abundantly, after their kind, and every winged fowl after his kind: and God saw that *it was* good.

22 And God blessed them, saying, Be fruitful, and multiply, and fill the waters in the seas, and let fowl multiply in the earth.

23 And the evening and the morning were the fifth day.

Fifth Day of Creation

And now there is animal life on the earth. First in the seas. One can hardly imagine the millions of kinds of life that are in the sea. "God created great whales." He did not

create baby whales alone and let them grow into great
whales. He did not simply multiply some eggs and let the
fowl hatch out of the eggs. To the old question, "Which
came first, the hen or the egg?" God's answer is here, that
God made the hen. You see, it is not an incipient beginning
of life that God has here, but completely, every living
creature in the water and every winged fowl, after their
kind.

And God gave the command to the multitudinous
animals of the sea and the fowls of the heaven that they
should "be fruitful and multiply, and fill the waters in the
seas, and let fowl multiply in the earth."

Why did God create animals in the sea, and fowls of the
air before He made other creeping things and cattle? I do
not know. I should think probably that God delighted to
create first the simple and then the complex. I should think
that He delighted to make the little one-celled animals
with the intricate pattern in the invisible parts that now
amaze men, before He put cells together to make many-
celled animals. I should think that He found it interesting
to make coldblooded fish before he made warmblooded
animals. And it may well be that the fowl were more
necessary for the pollination of flowers and the spread of
the seeds of plants than were animals and so God created
fowls before animals. He had a good reason and when we
learn to enter into the marvelous thoughts of God we will
see how fitting it was.

VERSES 24-27:

24 ¶ And God said, Let the earth
bring forth the living creature after
his kind, cattle, and creeping thing,
and beast of the earth after his kind:
and it was so.

25 And God made the beast of the
earth after his kind, and cattle after
their kind, and every thing that
creepeth upon the earth after his
kind: and God saw that *it was*
good.

26 ¶ And God said, Let us make
man in our image, after our likeness:
and let them have dominion over the

fish of the sea, and over the fowl of the air, and over the cattle, and over all the earth, and over every creeping thing that creepeth upon the earth.

27 So God created man in his *own* image, in the image of God created he him; male and female created he them.

Sixth Day of Creation

And now God comes to the climax and crowning day of His creation. Now God makes living creatures, cattle, creeping things, beasts of the earth. It may be that here God is deliberately making a contrast between man and beast. No one feels that a man and a fish are necessarily close kin. Some very foolish people would make man the descendant of some ape-like creature. Ah, but when they are all made, then God made man, then God put man to have dominion over all these others. No beast is to rule; man is to rule because man is not like the beast. He is made in the image of God.

There is an uncrossable gulf made here between man and beast. Man is made in the image of God and in His likeness. Ah, men may make musical instruments and write songs. Men may make languages and create poetry and literature. Men may build the most intricate machinery and master learning, not only anatomy and astronomy, but chemistry and electricity, and no one has yet imagined the length to which man may go in control of the things God has put here on earth. But no ape did ever write a song, nor ever sing one. No ape ever wrote a book or read one. An ape cannot even drive a nail. No animal in the world can think about eternity and salvation in God. Ah, man is made in the image of God. Man has a conscience. Man can think, can seek God, can see Him in nature, yes, and even by God's help, in the Bible.

GENESIS 1 (cont'd)

Creation Was Complete and Perfect

The theory of the evolutionists is that man is good and getting better; that he has climbed up from savagery and even from the animal creation. That is not what the Bible teaches and is not true. That is, the evolutionists would like to think that things were imperfect and through inherent forces animals and plants have fitted themselves with their environment, have grown more complex and more advanced through the centuries. That is not the picture painted in the Bible. The Bible speaks of a perfect creation and of a man, made in the image of God, who in the perfect Garden of Eden fell into sin and so brought ruin on a race of sinners.

So God's creation was complete and perfect and beautiful.

1. Again and Again "God Saw That It Was Good"

Note these wonderful statements about the creation:

Genesis 1:4, "And God saw the light, that it was good."

Genesis 1:10, "And God called the dry land Earth; and the gathering together of the waters called he Seas: and God saw that it was good."

Genesis 1:12 (concerning grass and herbs and trees), "And God saw that it was good."

Genesis 1:18 (concerning the sun, moon, and stars), "And God saw that it was good."

Genesis 1:21 says that after the creation of whales and living creatures and all animal life, "And God saw that it was good."

Genesis 1:25, after the creation of all earthly living creatures and animals, "And God saw that it was good."

And then, climaxing it all, Genesis 1:31: "And God saw every thing that he had made, and, behold, it was *very good.*"

Each step in creation was complete and right and perfect.

2. That Meant That Without Waiting for Development, Earth and Life on Earth Was Already Well Adjusted

There were trees on the earth, bearing fruit, though they had never blossomed; they were created already mature, no doubt, some of them.

The trees had rings like the annual rings the trees have today, though they had not gone through the summers and winters that now make those rings in the trees.

The soil had humus just as if there had been the decay of plant life and vegetable life through long years, to make top soil. But it was already there in good working order.

There were already seas and dry land, and there were already rivers in well-established beds, as we are told in Genesis 2:10-14. God did not take centuries of rain falling and running off a flat earth to erode riverbeds. They were there to start with.

It seems likely that salt was already in the sea water, and some fishes and sea life that require salt water had that environment to start with, without waiting for the rivers to leach out salt from the earth.

I think that there were baby animals that had never been born, just created as babies. I think that there were cows heavy with calves, and mares heavy with foals, which had never conceived. They were created already heavy with young.

We suppose Adam had a navel. He had never had an umbilical cord connecting him to a placenta in the mother's womb, as his children would have. But he was created to look and be as other men would be.

The sun, moon, and stars were created. But no doubt the starlight was created when the stars were created. The sunshine did not need to wait about eight minutes to get to the earth ninety-three million miles away. The great galaxies of stars of some light years away did not have to wait for the light years before they could be seen by the eyes of the first man and the first woman. If God can make a sun, He can make sunshine at the same time.

You see, we need to adjust our thinking to direct creation, the supernatural miracle of God, who prepared this earth perfectly and declared that it was good, even very good! Scientists have sometimes foolishly supposed that this earth had to start with nothing finished, nothing completed, and so they would like to measure the age of rocks as billions of years. There is a kind of lead which is found, the result of the decay of radium. But who would say that God would not have some of that kind of lead in the original creation? The earth was already in working order, and it did not need to wait for the results of natural processes. The natural processes began, but the apparent results of natural processes were created, too, in many, many cases.

VERSE 28:

28 And God blessed them, and God said unto them, Be fruitful, and multiply, and replenish the earth, and subdue it: and have dominion over the fish of the sea, and over the fowl of the air, and over every living thing that moveth upon the earth.

Large Families Are to Be Blessed of God

On the sixth day of creation there are two short verses given about the cattle and creeping things created on that day, all the land animals except fowls and all creeping things, perhaps insects that could not fly. God does not need to give more space to that. But verses 26 to 28 give the details that man is made in the image of God and is to have dominion. Then there followed some detailed instructions. Here the Scripture says that man is to "be fruitful and multiply and replenish the earth, and subdue it: and have dominion. . . ." You see, man is at the top and so there must be particular instructions to him.

Here the Scripture commands man to be fruitful and multiply. Animals do not need that command. They reproduce after their kind. They follow inbuilt instinct and have times and seasons for mating and always with mutual consent. No rules are needed that animals should reproduce after their kind.

But man chooses and plans and is somewhat master of his own fate. Man needs instruction so God adds the command that he is to be fruitful and multiply and replenish the earth.

Dr. Scofield in the Scofield Reference Bible had already committed himself to the "gap theory" that the earth had once been populated, at least with animals, and so the man and woman in Eden were responsible to replenish the earth with a new order—man. He thought that the earth which had been once made wasted and void by some great cataclysm in Satan's rebellion, and the animals and plants largely destroyed, must now be repopulated and he thinks the command is to repopulate the earth once made barren. But "replenishing" is needed all the time, since men die and their places are to be filled by others.

But this command to be fruitful and multiply, and replenish the earth—would that be as much the duty of men today as in Adam's time? Now, they speak of population explosion and food shortages and so some people insist that people should try to limit their families to one or two children, but that is foreign to the teaching and the spirit all the way through the Bible.

After the flood, God gave similar instructions very strong and plain. In Genesis 9:7 He said, "And you, be ye fruitful, and multiply; bring forth abundantly in the earth, and multiply therein."

Psalm 127:3-5 says, "Lo, children are an heritage of the Lord: and the fruit of the womb is his reward. As arrows are in the hand of a mighty man; so are the children of the youth. Happy is the man that hath his quiver full of them: they shall not be ashamed, but they shall speak with the enemies in the gate." Children, then, are a rich heritage, they are a reward from God. And happy or blessed is the man who has many of them that Scripture says.

Again, Psalm 128 tells that the man who fears the Lord and walks in His ways, it will be well with him. This is the blessing he shall have, "Thy wife shall be as a fruitful vine by the sides of thine house: thy children like olive plants round about thy table. Behold, that thus shall the man be blessed that feareth the Lord" (Ps. 128:3,4). So children are a special blessing and reward from God.

It is probable that the ceremonial laws, restricting the marriage relationship to certain times, probably somewhat spaced the birth of children within reasonable bounds. But there is never any indication in the Bible that married people ought to seek not to have children. The only case we recall in the Bible where anyone sought to prevent conception of a child, is, of course, the case of Onan in Genesis 38:9; he did not want to raise up seed to his brother by taking his brother's wife and God killed him.

In how many, many cases do we learn from Sarah, from Rebekah and Hannah, and Rachel and Leah and Elisabeth, that for a woman not to have children was accounted a great calamity! Children are an heritage of the Lord. They are a reward of God's love for parents who walk uprightly. And when they are reared for God they are not a curse, but a blessing.

It is true that a child reared without discipline, without character, and without God can bring to his mother shame. We do not suggest anyone would do well to raise children to take dope, to be school dropouts, to be hippies and rebels and criminals and godless. No, but children well reared are always blessed of God and a blessing to the world as well as to the family.

Susannah Wesley had nineteen children. Number thirteen was John Wesley, the founder of Methodism. Number seventeen was Charles Wesley who wrote six thousand hymns, many of them among the greatest. Does anyone now wish that Susannah Wesley had had fewer children?

The late Dr. Bob Jones, Sr., was the eleventh child of his mother. If she had had only ten, there would have been no preacher in the family. Did she have too many?

It is true that in heathen countries where they do not know God, where abject poverty rules, their own lack of enlightenment, their idolatry and heathen ways, make misery and poverty. Many, many children are born to want in such countries. It is still true that if people serve the Lord acceptably they could have His blessing on their families. There is no reason why Christian people in the civilized nations should leave all the heathen races and depraved or illiterate or criminal classes to furnish the population for tomorrow. Oh, what great blessings God can make of a family of godly children to the world!

The Population Problem

Dr. Henry Morris, a noted scientist, says, "It can be shown, in fact, that if the population continued to increase at the rate of 2% per year, in less than 700 years there would be one person for every square foot of the earth's surface. Obviously, the present growth rate cannot continue indefinitely.

"Nevertheless, many creationists find such arguments unconvincing. Since the evidence for a purposeful Creator of the world and mankind is exceedingly strong, the creationist can be confident that the world God made for man is large enough and productive enough to accomplish His purpose. That purpose will surely have been consummated before the population exceeds its divinely-intended maximum.

"According to the Biblical record of creation, immediately after the first man and woman were created, God instructed them as follows:

" 'Be fruitful and multiply, and replenish [literally, 'fill'] the earth, and subdue it' (Gen. 1:28). Essentially the same commandment was given to the handful of survivors of the great Flood (Gen. 9:1). Since man has not yet come anywhere near to *filling* the earth (the total population currently averages less than one person for every 400,000 square feet of land area), even to its maximum feasible 'carrying capacity,' it seems unlikely that the earth has yet reached its optimal population, as far as the purposes of the Creator are concerned."

He continued, "Even apart from Biblical revelation, however, there is no good reason for alarm over population. The earth is quite able to support a much larger population than it now possesses. Even with the present status of technology (available water for irrigation, potentially arable land, modern methods of soil treatment and improved crop yields, etc.), authorities estimate that the earth's reasonable 'carrying capacity' is about 50 billion people. Future advances in technology (solar energy, saline conversion, etc.), may well increase this still more.

"Thus, even at the present annual increase of 2%, it will still be 135 years before this maximum population will be reached. However, in order for this population to be achieved, modern technological knowledge will have to be employed worldwide, in the underdeveloped countries as well as in the developed nations. In turn, experience in the latter shows that population growth rates tend to drop off as a society's technology increases. Revelle comments on this as follows:

" 'Here we are faced with a paradox: attainment of the earth's maximum carrying capacity for human beings would require a high level of agricultural technology, which in turn calls for a high level of social and economic development. Such developments, however, would be likely to lead to a cessation of population growth long before the maximum carrying capacity is reached.' "

Dr. Morris calls attention to the fact that although population is now increasing at the rate of 2% a year, the average for four thousand years since the flood would not have been more than one-half of 1%. And that is one of the evidences that mankind has been on the earth only a few thousand years, certainly not much over six or seven thousand years as Bible chronologies testify.

But cannot Christians believe that God who made the earth and made man on the earth, and commanded man to be fruitful, to multiply and replenish the earth, has His own plan so that when men do right, God's resources will never be too little?

What a blessing it is to have children given in answer to prayer, reared in the nurture and admonition of the Lord, and won to Christ and dedicated to His service!

VERSES 29-31:

29 ¶ And God said, Behold, I have given you every herb bearing seed, which *is* upon the face of all the earth, and every tree, in the which *is* the fruit of a tree yielding seed; to you it shall be for meat.

30 And to every beast of the earth, and to every fowl of the air, and to every thing that creepeth upon the earth, wherein *there is* life, *I have given* every green herb for meat: and it was so.

31 And God saw every thing that he had made, and, behold, *it was* very good. And the evening and the morning were the sixth day.

Man and Beast Before the Fall Had Vegetable Diets Only

Nothing was said about carnivorous animals then. It may be that after the fall the animals began to be carnivorous. I do not know. The question is not mentioned again until after the flood, then God said in Genesis 9:3,4, "Every moving thing that liveth shall be meat for you; even as the green herb have I given you all things. But flesh with the life thereof, which is the blood thereof, shall ye not eat." After the flood men began to eat flesh. They may have done so before, most likely men did not. It is possible that animals had become carnivorous.

We know that in the Kingdom Age "the lion shall eat straw like the ox" (Isa. 11:7).

Man's mastery over all created things on earth was enlarged later to include meat for food.

No Conflicting Accounts
of Creation in
Genesis

Brief Statement of Creation Followed by
Detailed Explanation

Here we have in the first verse in the Bible, "In the beginning God created the heaven and the earth." That is not the end of the story, it is simply a statement of the general, tremendous fact. The earth itself, and heaven around it—the matter—is brought into being. And the rest of chapter 1 continues the details of the creation on the first day.

Then in Genesis 1:26 and 28 God briefly tells of the creation of man as the climax of the sixth and final day of creation. The second chapter tells of the seventh day in which God rested and that God had plans about the Sabbath for the future. Then Genesis 2:7 tells of the creation of Adam as a separate individual, while in verses 21 to 25 He tells of the creation of Eve and of the two happily married.

There are not two different accounts of creation. There are not two differing accounts of the creation of man. One states the fact, then later more details are given of the same creation.

Dr. Scofield and others would take verse 1 out of God's account of the first day, and suppose between it and verse 2, there were illimitable ages. That, we think, is not justified. Unbelievers would like to make two conflicting accounts of creation in chapters 1 and 2. That is artificial, unscholarly and wrong. There is one grand, perfect, inspired account and must be taken as God's perfect Word.

Unconverted liberals, counting themselves wise enough

to pass judgment on the Bible, make some very foolish and unscholarly and unreasonable statements. For example, in the *Interpreter's Bible Commentary,* concerning Genesis 1:1 we read,

> Chs. 1-2 contain two accounts of the creation of the world by God. According to the first (1:1-2:4a), man was created, male and female (1:26-27), after the creation of plants (1:11-12) and animals (1:20-25); according to the second (2:4b-25), man was created first (2:7), then the trees (2:9), and finally woman (2:21-22). In view of these discrepancies, to say nothing of the differences of style and feeling so obvious as to need no detailed enumeration here, the two stories cannot come from the same hand. The first is basically from P, the second from J2; both of them bear the marks of having been elaborated by writers other than their original authors.

And what is the purpose of this infidel and foolish judgment? The purpose is to try to promote the Graf-Wellhausen theory, that silly infidel teaching now so discredited by Allis and Robert Dick Wilson of Princeton and Dr. Melvin Grove Kyle, and other scholars. He says, "The two stories cannot come from the same hand. The first is basically from P, the second from J2; both of them bear the marks of having been elaborated by writers other than their original authors."

George A. Buttrick, the general editor of the Interpreter's Bible, did not write that comment above, but in his book, *The Christian Fact and Modern Doubt,* he states the same thing on page 161: "There are two accounts of the creation and they do not agree. Similarly there are two accounts of the Flood. . . ."

But I am reminded that the Bible says, "Through faith we understand that the worlds were framed by the word of God, so that things which are seen were not made of things which do appear" (Heb. 11:3). One who does not have the faith of a born-again child of God will not understand the creation. It is not surprising that the unregenerate heart, coming in spiritual pride to the Bible, will not understand it, for we are plainly told, "but the natural man receiveth not the things of the Spirit of God: for they are foolishness unto him: neither can he know them, because they are spiritually discerned.''

Down through the centuries the most intelligent Christians have seen and agreed. Ellicott's *Commentary on the Whole Bible* says about Genesis 1 and 2, ''The two verses go together, and form a general summary of creation, which is afterwards divided into its several stages.'' Or as Alexander Maclaren puts it, ''The revelation which it gives is the truth, obscured to all other men when it was given, that one God 'in the beginning created the heaven and the earth.' That solemn utterance is the keynote of the whole. The rest but expands it.''

I read those verses before I was ten years old and I understood that there was no discrepancy: first the simple facts were told and then the expanded details. I read it again after forty years an editor, after a college degree in language and literature, after years of study and teaching and preaching and with millions of copies of my books in circulation, and it still says what it said before and means the same. The alleged discrepancy was not discovered by scholarship but claimed by the unregenerate, unbelieving heart not enlightened by the Holy Spirit and thus at enmity with God and with the Bible.

There is good evidence that chapter 2 is simply an expansion of the creation story in chapter 1.

For example, verse 7 says, ''And God made the firmament, and divided the waters which were under the firmament from the waters which were above the firmament: and it was so.'' What waters? There has not been any creation of water, unless that is included in that general verse 1.

And verse 9 says, ''And God said, Let the waters under the heaven be gathered together unto one place, and let the dry land appear: and it was so.'' What dry land? But what land is there, wet or dry? Not any unless it was created in verse 1. Actually the chapter as a whole tells the same story as uncounted millions have read it and understood it:

"Through faith we understand that the worlds were framed by the word of God, so that things which are seen were not made of things which do appear" (Heb. 11:3).

GENESIS 2

VERSES 1-3:

THUS the heavens and the earth were finished, and all the host of them.

2 And on the seventh day God ended his work which he had made; and he ²rested on the seventh day from all his work which he had made.

3 And God blessed the seventh day, and sanctified it: because that in it he had rested from all his work which God created and made.

GOD RESTED ON SEVENTH DAY

We think God set apart the number seven for some spiritual meaning and not only the day of the week.

The number seven is built into life processes in nature in a number of ways. Chicken eggs hatch out in twenty-one days—three times seven. Turkey eggs hatch out in four weeks—four times seven. Some little birds, we think, hatch in one week. A woman's menstrual period is usually each four weeks, or twenty-eight days.

In ceremonial law, the seventh day Saturday was a Sabbath of rest. The seventh year every Jewish field was to lie fallow, resting untilled. Then after seven times seven years—forty-nine years—the fiftieth year was to be a year of jubilee. In that year land was to go back to the original owners. Bondslaves taken among Jews for money were to be released. The feast of unleavened bread was for seven days, beginning with the Sabbath of rest and ending with the Sabbath of rest (Exod. 12:14-16).

Peter asked Jesus, 'Should we forgive one penitent who wronged us seven times?' 'No, till seventy times seven,' Jesus said (Matt. 18:22). That probably meant beyond numbering. So seven has some divine flavor.

The Meaning of the Weekly Sabbath

In the weekly Sabbath, the six days of labor when man is to "do all thy work" pictured man living a perfect life. Then the Sabbath day pictured a Heaven which he had earned by his righteousness. That, of course, is law and not grace. That plan failed by man's failure and sin, so no one ever earned Heaven. Romans 10:5 says, "For Moses describeth the righteousness which is of the law, That the man which doeth those things shall live by them." But fallen, sinful man has never been able to keep the law. "By the works of the law shall no flesh be justified" (Gal. 2:16). But the law shows what righteousness ought to be, and so a man ought to be perfect all his life and ought to be fit for Heaven. He is not.

But does God have no picture of Heaven in the ceremonial law except as one should earn it? Oh, yes. When God gave the passover lamb, He gave the plan of salvation by the atoning blood of Jesus. So the very night that the Jewish family had the blood on the door and ate the passover lamb, picturing Christ our Perfect Sacrifice, they entered into a high annual Sabbath, that day of "holy convocation" in which "no manner of work shall be done in them, save that which every man must eat." The Christian, trusting in Christ, enters into his heavenly rest here now and the seven days of unleavened bread picture us feasting on Christ day by day, and then a great Sabbath at the end pictures Heaven. In Hebrews 4:9 we learn, "There remaineth therefore a rest to the people of God," and that word *rest* is the Greek word for Sabbath. So, instead of a salvation earned by works now, I have a salvation I have already received. I am already a child of God. I already "received the atonement" when I trusted Christ.

That annual Sabbath, when they ate the passover lamb, was that "high sabbath" that followed the day of preparation when Jesus was crucified.

Weekly Sabbath Ceremonial Law for Jews, Not for Us

There are some remarkable, scriptural facts not generally known about the Sabbath. First, though God sanctified the Sabbath day, He did not let it be known to mankind for hundreds of years! He did not tell Adam about it. Noah never heard of it. It was never mentioned to

Abraham or Isaac or Jacob! The first time God ever mentioned the Sabbath to men or gave commands about it is in Exodus 16. The heavenly manna was given to Israel for six days and they were told that the seventh day was the Sabbath and they were not to gather on that day (Exod. 16:23-30).

So in Nehemiah 9:13,14 we are told:

"Thou camest down also upon mount Sinai, and spakest with them from heaven, and gavest them right judgments, and true laws, good statutes and commandments: And madest known unto them thy holy sabbath, and commandedst them precepts, statutes, and laws, by the hand of Moses thy servant."

God first made known the holy Sabbath to Jews when they were gathered in the wilderness near Mount Sinai.

The second point not generally known is that this was a particular covenant between God and Israel and nobody else.

"And the Lord spake unto Moses, saying, Speak thou also unto the children of Israel, saying, Verily my sabbaths ye shall keep: for it is a sign between me and you throughout your generations; that ye may know that I am the Lord that doth sanctify you. . . . Wherefore the children of Israel shall keep the sabbath, to observe the sabbath throughout their generations, for a perpetual covenant. It is a sign between me and the children of Israel for ever: for in six days the Lord made heaven and earth, and on the seventh day he rested, and was refreshed."—Exod. 31:12,13,16,17.

But one may insist, "The Sabbath command is in the Ten Commandments." Yes, it is, but remember, the Ten Commandments are addressed primarily to Israel. "And God spake all these words, saying, I am the Lord thy God, which have brought thee out of the land of Egypt, out of the house of bondage. Thou shalt have no other gods before me" (Exod. 20:1-3). That is addressed to Israel.

The Ten Commandments are repeated again in Deuteronomy 5:

"And Moses called all Israel, and said unto them, Hear, O Israel, the statutes and judgments which I speak in your ears this day, that ye may learn them, and keep, and do them. The Lord our God made a covenant with us in Horeb. . . . I am the Lord thy God, which brought thee out of the land of Egypt, from the house of bondage. Thou shalt have none other gods before me."—Deut. 5:1,2,6,7.

It is not surprising that in the Ten Commandments the Lord brought in a ceremony which pictures salvation and going to Heaven.

The third scriptural fact not generally known about the Sabbath is that we are commanded in Colossians 2:16,17, "Let no man therefore judge you in meat, or in drink, or in respect of an holyday, or of the new moon, or of the sabbath days: Which are a shadow of things to come; but the body is of Christ." He has just said before those verses that the handwriting of ordinances of the law was nailed to the cross and therefore they are no longer binding. Now no Christian is to be judged in meat or drink, in respect of an holyday, or of the new moon or the Sabbath days in those things which were commanded in the ceremonial law to Israel, for those things were "a shadow of things to come; but the body is of Christ." They were ceremonial.

That means that the Sabbath was never given to anyone but Israel. It was a special covenant between God and Israel. There is not a single command for anybody *before Mount Sinai* to keep the Sabbath. There is not a single command in *the New Testament* for anybody to keep the Sabbath. Sabbath-breaking is not even mentioned in the list of sins in the New Testament. The Jewish Sabbath is ceremonial law.

Christians have the Lord's day voluntary, not legal. It is primarily a day of worship, while the Jewish Sabbath was primarily a day of physical rest.

We should remember also these words in Genesis 2:2,3, that God rested on the seventh day, blessed it and sanctified the Sabbath. That was not written down until Moses wrote it as described, we think, in Exodus 24:3-8.

As that sign of the Sabbath:

"Speak thou also unto the children of Israel, saying, Verily my sabbaths ye shall keep: for it is a sign between me and you throughout your generations; that ye may know that I am the Lord that doth sanctify you. Ye shall keep the sabbath therefore; for it is holy unto you: every one that defileth it shall surely be put to death: for whosoever doeth any work therein, that soul shall be cut off from among his people. Six days may work be done; but in the seventh is the sabbath of rest, holy to the Lord: whosoever doeth any work in the sabbath day, he shall surely be put to death. Wherefore the children of Israel shall keep the sabbath, to observe the sabbath throughout their generations, for a perpetual covenant. It is a sign between me and the children of Israel for ever: for in six days the Lord made heaven and earth, and on the seventh day he rested, and was refreshed."—Exod. 31:13-17.

Certain it is that a day of rest is good. But the Lord's day is not the Sabbath. Christians honor it as a reminder of the resurrection of Christ and as a day of worship as well as voluntary rest.

VERSES 4-6:

4 ¶ These *are* the generations of the heavens and of the earth when they were created, in the day that the LORD God made the earth and the heavens,

5 And every plant of the field before it was in the earth, and every herb of the field before it grew: for the LORD God had not caused it to rain upon the earth, and *there was* not a man to till the ground.

6 But there went up a mist from the earth, and watered the whole face of the ground.

No Rain Before the Flood!

Before the flood we understand that the sunlight filtered through the canopy of vapor "above the firmament." It made some difference in warming the air somewhat in the daytime and thus it evaporated and soaked up more of the water from the river and sea. Then a little cooler in the night it would condense as dew or be in a mist or fog, a vapor, so the ground was watered without any rain.

We are sure there was some movement of the sea in tides caused by the moon then as now. There was some moderate moving of air because of changes in temperature. But all this was very moderate. We suppose there were no violent winds in the balanced climate, so near equilibrium, and there was no rain.

The Scriptures say there was no rain until at the time of the flood. Then, when the great mass of water vapor above had been condensed in rain and the climate had entirely new adjustments, there were more extremes of cold and heat. There would be storms and rain now. So God gave the rainbow, then visible after the flood for the first time, sun shining through the rain, as a sign there would be no more world-destroying flood (Gen. 9:8-17).

VERSE 7:

7 And the Lord God formed man *of* the dust of the ground, and breathed into his nostrils the breath of life; and man became a living soul.

How Man Was Made

Before, God stated in Genesis 1:27 that "God created man in his own image"; now He gives some details of how the body and spirit of the man came into being. "The Lord God formed man out of the dust of the ground." I can imagine with what infinite detail He made each molecule, the cells of every organ, adjusted them together, planned the strength, the texture, the color, the glands, every tiny magnificent detail in the million wonders of a human body. God formed man out of the dust of the earth! Here there is no foolish talk about a man's struggle up through the centuries, trying to climb out of beasthood into manhood. God formed man.

Then God breathed into his nostrils the breath of life and he became a living soul—a soul destined for Heaven or Hell, to live forever somewhere.

Man in the image of God? That means that man has an immortal soul. That soul goes on forever! That man is a spiritual being, conscious of right and wrong. Not only so, but man was intended to walk in the presence of God and commune with God and have eternal fellowship with God. Alas, that sin ever broke that fellowship and communion. But Christ has purchased back those who will trust Him; and man, born again, is destined to dwell in the presence of God and rejoice in Him forever. Man is made in the image of God.

It is interesting to see that the male is made in the image of God more specifically than the woman. In I Corinthians 11 we are told that men and women are not to be alike. A woman is to have long hair for her glory. It is a covering, a veiling, indicating woman's submission to her husband or father. "For a man indeed ought not to cover his head, forasmuch as he is the image and glory of God: but the woman is the glory of the man" (I Cor. 11:7). How foolish and senseless to suppose that man, made in the image of God, developed from beasts! The gulf is infinite and impassable between man and all animal creation.

So man is to have dominion over the earth, over the plants and the animals. Yes, and although man did not always know so, man is to have dominion over the air and space as far as he can conquer it. We think this symbolic of the time when born-again Christians will come back to reign with Christ on the earth.

VERSES 8-14:

8 ¶ And the LORD God planted a garden eastward in Eden; and there he put the man whom he had formed. 9 And out of the ground made the

LORD God to grow every tree that is pleasant to the sight, and good for food; the tree of life also in the midst of the garden, and the tree of knowledge of good and evil.

10 And a river went out of Eden to water the garden; and from thence it was parted, and became into four heads.

11 The name of the first *is* Pison: that *is* it which compasseth the whole land of Hăv-ĭ-läh, where *there is* gold;

12 And the gold of that land *is* good: there *is* bdellium and the onyx stone.

13 And the name of the second river *is* Gī-hŏn: the same *is* it that compasseth the whole land of Ethiopia.

14 And the name of the third river *is* Hĭd-dĕ-kĕl: that *is* it which goeth toward the east of Assyria. And the fourth river *is* Eû-phrā-tēṣ.

Trees in Eden

God planted a garden "eastward in Eden." Eastward from where? Perhaps eastward from the Sinai Peninsula where Moses wrote this down by divine inspiration in Exodus 24:4.

We can be sure that none of the characteristics of the land, rivers, valleys, mountains, remained after the flood as they were before. Yet it may well be that the general area was distinguishable. Somewhere in that general area was the Garden of Eden. Mount Ararat, where the ark rested after the flood, is designated.

It is interesting that God "planted a garden." God took particular delight in preparing the vegetation that would please men. Every plant that would be needed and useful, every plant that would be enjoyed—the texture, the taste, the color, the fragrance—every detail a loving God thought out and put there for man to enjoy in the Garden of Eden.

We need not think that in some careless way God allowed the details to work themselves out. Jesus told us that He notes the fall of every sparrow. Even the wild flowers, the lilies of the field, were colored by the Lord Jesus, although they are so profuse that today the flowers bloom sweetly and then in a day they are dried and burned in the oven. But God knows.

Psalm 65:9-13 tells us how God waters the earth and looks after the details. And Psalm 104:11-14 tells us:

"They give drink to every beast of the field: the wild asses quench their thirst. By them shall the fowls of the heaven

have their habitation, which sing among the branches. He watereth the hills from his chambers: the earth is satisfied with the fruit of thy works. He causeth the grass to grow for the cattle, and herb for the service of man: that he may bring forth food out of the earth. . . ."

Gray's "Elegy in a Country Churchyard" says:

> **Full many a gem of purest ray serene**
> **The dark unfathom'd caves of ocean bear;**
> **Full many a flower is born to blush unseen,**
> **And waste its sweetness on the desert air.**

Oh, what infinite capacity for beauty and for attention has our Creator who made and sustains all things.

There were trees in Eden. There was the Tree of Life. Man could eat freely of that. I suppose that it had some marvelous quality that was a vitamin or enzyme for every need of the body. There was an antibody for every infection. There was an antidote for every disease in the marvelous Tree of Life.

We will see it again once in resurrected bodies when we gather near the City of Gold and by the "pure river of water of life, clear as crystal, proceeding out of the throne of God and of the Lamb," and we will find in the midst of the street in Heaven and "on either side of the river" the Tree of Life which bears "twelve manner of fruits," new fruit every month, "and the leaves of the tree were for the healing of the nations." Oh, after Adam and Eve sinned, an angel with a flaming sword kept them from the Tree of Life lest they eat and live forever in their sin.

Rivers in Eden

One river went out of Eden to water the Garden. It is very likely that the Garden of Eden was subirrigated, that is, water soaked through the soil and spread so that everywhere plants could get all the nourishment they needed. There "went up a mist from the earth, and watered the whole face of the ground."

But that one river went out and divided into four heads:

Pison, Gihon, Hiddekel and Euphrates. The names are interesting. Gihon was the name of that pool that runs along south of the city wall of Jerusalem. It is the place where Solomon was crowned king. Other names here are familiar—Euphrates, Assyria, Ethiopia. I do not believe that any of the land or cities or rivers before the flood were left as they were after the mighty convulsions that destroyed the whole earth in the flood and in the years following. But it is quite likely that men carried over these names from before the flood into the civilization that followed, and so Assyria became a nation, and Ethiopia, and the river was called the Euphrates River. We need not be surprised if that be so, because in America we have New York after York in England, and how many, many other cities are named for some loved place in the old countries! That indicates there was no break in the civilization from before the flood and after.

Before the flood they knew gold, bdellium and onyx stone and valued them.

VERSES 15-17:

15 And the LORD God took the man, and put him into the garden of Eden to dress it and to keep it.

16 And the LORD God commanded the man, saying, Of every tree of the garden thou mayest freely eat:

17 But of the tree of the knowledge of good and evil, thou shalt not eat of it: for in the day that thou eatest thereof thou shalt surely die.

What Kind of Tree Was the Tree of the Knowledge of Good and Evil?

We do not know. Was there some inherent quality in the fruit of that tree itself that caused people to know good and evil? I think not. The Lord did not have to have it here, and obviously it was here as a testing and a proof for man. I think the very act of disobedience was the sin. It was not that the fruit itself was sinful, except it was forbidden. Man sinned when he chose that which would make him wise in matters of the world, of sinful things and knowledge about things which he ought not know or care about.

Some people have thought that the sin of Adam and Eve in the Garden of Eden was sex sin. That is foolish. God had already told them they were married. They were to multiply and replenish the earth. Their holy relationship as husband and wife did not displease God. But in eating the forbidden fruit they disobeyed God. More than that we do not know about this "tree of knowledge of good and evil."

VERSES 18-22:

18 ¶ And the LORD God said, *It is* not good that the man should be alone; I will make him an help meet for him.

19 And out of the ground the LORD God formed every beast of the field, and every fowl of the air; and brought *them* unto Adam to see what he would call them: and whatsoever Adam called every living creature, that *was* the name thereof.

20 And Adam gave names to all cattle, and to the fowl of the air, and to every beast of the field; but for Adam there was not found an help meet for him.

21 And the LORD God caused a deep sleep to fall upon Adam, and he slept: and he took one of his ribs, and closed up the flesh instead thereof;

22 And the rib, which the LORD God had taken from man, made he a woman, and brought her unto the man.

"It Is Not Good That the Man Should Be Alone"

There was, it is true, a shade of loneliness in Paradise as the man went about his duty and his pleasure in the Garden of Eden. There was a sense of incompleteness. Oh, it was intangible, to be sure. There was no foreboding, no sense of loss, no grief. Rather, there was a glad expectancy. God, who had revealed a million wonders and joys to him, had something more to give! Adam had delighted in every animal. The giraffe had bent his long neck down for the man to scratch his head around the stub horns. The spotted leopard had rubbed against his leg and purred. As soon as he sat down, a squirrel scampered up to his knee and offered a nut, and a parakeet lit on his shoulder and playfully nibbled his ear. When Adam slept in a shady bower on rose petals or soft grasses, a puppy nestled at his feet. But there was a sense of eager expectancy. There was a better companionship than this, though Adam did not know what it was he looked for.

He went about his work in dressing the garden and keeping it. But as he pruned the grapevines and trained them and the trumpet vines and Virginia creeper over graceful arbors near a babbling brook, there was no one to admire his work. He dressed the garden carefully and kept it and found fresh delight in every fruit and flower. But there was no one to taste with him the first ripe peaches or mangoes or figs or melons.

When he ran or swam or leaped with the inexhaustible energy of perfect manhood, sinless youth, and godlike health, it seemed there should be someone to run with him, or to laugh at his leaps, or admire his skill.

It was wonderful that God came into the garden and He and Adam talked together in sweet and intimate converse. But when he was nearly bursting with the wonder of God's love and wisdom, the animals could not understand what he wanted to say. Even in the perfection of creation thus far, God had something to add. Without woman, a man could never be in love. Without a wife, he could never be a husband or a father. Without a queen, he could never be a king.

I. MARRIAGE IN PARADISE

Thus, Scripture tells us that the man was not made for the woman but the woman for the man. We are told that the man "is the image and glory of God: but the woman is the glory of the man" (I Cor. 11:7).

Do I, then, believe the Bible account, that God formed man out of the dust of the earth and breathed into his nostrils the breath of life? And that God put Adam into a deep sleep and took from his side a rib and from it formed a woman? Of course I do! So it is in divine revelation, and

nobody else but God knows what happened and could tell it
right. And God has told it in His infallible Word. Is, then,
the story of creation a myth, a bit of poetry with some
spiritual meaning? Oh, no! It is fact, eternal and certain
truth. It is clothed in language of poetry and beauty, but it
is surely fact, as certain and literal as the birth and
crucifixion and coming of the Saviour.

Why do men with "a wicked heart of unbelief" desire to
prove that man came from beast instead of from God? Why
depend upon ugly and perverted guesses, when we have
divine revelation?

But we are Christians and so we believe the Bible, and
direct creation is not too hard nor too wonderful for the
God we know.

Now God brought the beautiful woman to the noble and
perfect man. It was love at first sight. Both were perfect, so
neither had ought to fear in loving the other completely.
The first charm, the thrill of first meeting and instant
infatuation could not do less than grow and grow and grow
in perfect love. There could be no fear and no harm, for God
made them for each other and He gave them to each other.

Oh it was heavenly! And Paradise was complete when
Adam took his bride into his arms!

Six times I have walked down the long church aisle on
gleaming white muslin, strewn with rose petals, and the
sweet bride on my arm, with wedding train and veil and
orange blossoms, was my daughter. When the question
came, "Who giveth this woman to be wedded to this man?"
six times I have answered. How beautiful the bride! How
happy the dreams and plans for the young couple's home
and life together!

I wonder, Did God, who regularly appeared in the garden
in some manifestation in which He could walk and talk
and be seen and felt—did God lead Eve gently through the
flowers and present her, with her fast beating heart and
with first love blushing in her cheeks, to Adam in some
sweet vale of Eden?

However it was, God Himself presided and was Witness,

Father, Mother and Friend at this wedding. God Himself performed the first marriage ceremony for Adam and Eve in the Garden of Eden.

1. Marriage Beautiful and Holy

Ah, I am glad that the first marriage took place before sin ever came into the world! Now we can know that God planned the human heart, character and body for love, marriage, companionship, home and children! The only institution that man brought as he stumbled, sad and guilty, out of the Garden of Eden after sin came in was marriage and the home. The angel with the flaming sword blocked the way back into Eden, but thank God, He allowed Adam and Eve to come out together! Marriage, then, is a divine institution, properly called "holy matrimony."

We read that "marriage is honourable in all, and the bed undefiled: but whoremongers and adulterers God will judge" (Heb. 13:4). It is in marriage that man is most like God; and wives are commanded, "Wives, submit yourselves unto your own husbands, as unto the Lord. For the husband is the head of the wife, even as Christ is the head of the church: and he is the saviour of the body. Therefore as the church is subject unto Christ, so let the wives be to their own husbands in every thing" (Eph. 5:22-24).

The relationship of husband and wife is likened unto the relationship of Christ and the church. So the husband is commanded, "Husbands, love your wives, even as Christ also loved the church, and gave himself for it" (Eph. 5:25).

Marriage, then, is older than the church, older than the Mosaic law, older than any sacrifice, older than any religious rite or duty. And the institution of marriage and home is more important than the church, is more important than government or school, and older than either.

Then is it wrong that a young man should feel the same stirrings that must have moved in Adam's heart and body, and long for a companion, beautiful and loving and good?

Is it wrong that a man should look upon a young woman, not made like a man but made as complement and helper and partner and comforter to man—and love her and feel a need for her? Ah, no! God planned it so.

People have often thought a teenage girl silly when she fell so desperately in love with some youth or man, so much in love that she would leave father and mother and go to a far country with him; so much in love that she would go with him into poverty, toil, responsibilities of wifehood and motherhood. That love and attraction, too, has sometimes been so unrestrained that a girl has given her heart to a scoundrel or vagabond whom she loved not wisely but too well, and trusted where she should not have trusted, and let love overmaster reason and sometimes let love overmaster purity and right. Many such girls, out of love, have gone wrong and have been left with their shame.

Ah, love should be guarded, should be controlled by reason and convention, perhaps, certainly by wisdom, purity, and righteousness. But love is not wrong! Men and women were made to learn to love each other and to want each other and to give themselves to each other.

That unrest of the sex instinct, that rising of desire, that sense of physical need in sex matters that men feel, is not wrong! It is holy and good, so holy that it ought to be guarded with manhood's character and faithfulness and with spiritual devotion. Sex natures of a man and woman are meant for holy uses, and so the perversion of sex is all the more wicked, all the more certain to bring heartbreak, all the more certain for punishment from God.

It is not wrong that the human body should grow hungry and long for food, but it is wrong for people to take or plan to take somebody else's food. It is not wrong that noble, good men as well as others not so good, should feel some compelling hunger for love and mating, but it is wicked that any man should defile what does not belong to him and so make mockery of God's blessing and make bitter God's cup of sweetness.

Let us rejoice in that marriage came right out of the

Garden of Eden and from the hand and presence of God. As far as we can tell, a happy Christian home on this earth can come nearest of all to the Paradise of God if God blesses the home with righteousness, love, forbearance and contentment.

VERSES 23-25:

23 And Adam said, This *is* now bone of my bones, and flesh of my flesh: she shall be called Woman, because she was taken out of Man.

24 Therefore shall a man leave his father and his mother, and shall cleave unto his wife: and they shall be one flesh.

25 And they were both naked, the man and his wife, and were not a-shamed.

2. In Eden the Marriage Was Perfect Fulfillment

People sometimes say that certain marriages "were made in Heaven." In one sense that is true of all legitimate marriages, because God Himself puts His authority where society and government pronounce a marriage. It may be that some men and some women are not fitted for each other and the marriage is not wise; but it is nevertheless a legal marriage, accepted on earth and in Heaven and so bound by the laws of God as well as the laws of man.

But there is a sense, too, in which no marriage on earth is now quite heavenly. It is said that "love is blind." That only means that young love must overlook many defects and flaws to be as rapturous and compelling as love sometimes is.

But in the Garden of Eden two people were perfect and sinless, loving and good.

We are told: "And Adam said, This is now bone of my bones, and flesh of my flesh: she shall be called Woman, because she was taken out of Man. . . . And they were both naked, the man and his wife, and were not ashamed" (Gen. 2:23,25).

There was no disillusionment in that marriage. Eve did

not find herself shocked by hearing Adam snore, find him falling into fits of temper. Adam did not find that Eve had been reared as a spoiled brat and wanted her own way about everything, or that she could not cook! No, the limitations, the disappointments, the inevitable compromises and adjustments that must be made to frailty in human character were not a part of that perfect, lovely marriage in Eden!

Both Adam and Eve knew that the marriage was forever, "And Adam said, This is now bone of my bones, and flesh of my flesh." He took her to his heart for all the years ahead and she was a part of him, and he a part of her. They were one in such perfect understanding, in such perfect agreement, in such perfect enjoyment of each other's fellowship and ideas and company, as poor, sinning mortals now never attain!

"And they were both naked, the man and his wife, and were not ashamed." Oh, after sin came in they felt in their guilty hearts they had much to hide. They could not trust themselves nor others; their deepest emotions and needs must be covered because of the constant threat and frailty and guilt of which they were conscious. But before sin in the Garden of Eden, just as the innocent baby does not tempt and is not tempted by his nakedness nor embarrassed by it nor ashamed, so Adam and Eve in perfect love and perfect union lived in happy marriage.

3. How Perfect Was Environment and Setting for Home in Paradise!

Since in the Garden of Eden there was no sin but perfect holiness and innocence, there was perfect health. These two who felt perfectly at home in God's presence and were not ashamed before His holiness, had the glorious health that can only come where there is no sin. I believe that Adam's body was like ours will be at the resurrection, a body like Jesus had after His resurrection. I am not one of those who believe that in the resurrection we will have ghostly bodies without blood. It is true that "flesh and

blood cannot inherit the kingdom of God" (I Cor. 15:50).
That simply means that natural, unregenerate men cannot
enter Heaven. It does not mean that they will not have
blood. I believe that God made Adam and Eve with perfect
bodies to start with, and if they were perfect, then, surely
our perfect resurrection bodies will be like those in the
Garden of Eden.

The resurrection body of Jesus digested foods, and so
shall ours. Then we need the liquids in the body, and I
would suppose that God's beautiful plan, having the blood,
which is the life of the flesh to carry on the life processes,
would be ours in glorified bodies even as it was true in the
perfect bodies of Adam and of Eve.

Remember that God's creation plan was not wrong. But
now it has become fallen and tainted and corrupted.

The perfect health and strength and youth of Adam and
Eve was maintained constantly as they ate, not only of all
the other pleasant fruit God provided, but of "the tree of
life also in the midst of the garden." They were forbidden
to eat of "the tree of knowledge of good and evil," but they
were not forbidden to eat of the tree of life. In fact, they
were explicitly told that "of every tree of the garden thou
mayest freely eat: But of the tree of the knowledge of good
and evil, thou shalt not eat of it. . ." (Gen. 2:16,17).

After sin had come in and they were driven outside the
garden, it was for an express intention: "Lest he put forth
his hand, and take also of the tree of life, and eat, and live
for ever" (Gen. 3:22). God would not have men with a taint
of sin in their hearts and blood, alienated from God, to live
in this flesh forever. But in Eden before sin came in the
perfect health and youth and marvelous strength was
maintained always as they ate whenever they wished of the
Tree of Life as well as of the other fruit in the garden.

Oh, when Paradise is regained, when God plants again
this poor, fallen and cursed earth and makes it anew a
Garden of Eden, and when God Himself makes His
tabernacle with men on the renovated earth, then we are
told, in John's inspired vision, "And he shewed me a pure

river of water of life, clear as crystal, proceeding out of the throne of God and of the Lamb. In the midst of the street of it, and on either side of the river, was there the tree of life, which bare twelve manner of fruits, and yielded her fruit every month: and the leaves of the tree were for the healing of the nations" (Rev. 22:1,2).

So again, in glorified bodies as pure and innocent as Adam's and Eve's, we will live in God's Eden made new and we will drink of that pure river of water of life and we will eat of the Tree of Life with its twelve manner of fruits. Then our bodies will know the eternal healing of the leaves of the Tree of Life which are "for the healing of the nations."

We are not to suppose that Adam and Eve lived as savages. No, a man in perfect touch with God, the Source of all wisdom; a man with mind unchained or perverted by sin, would know far more than any man knows today. In Genesis 4:17-22 we learn that in Adam's lifetime men not only had fire and offered sacrifices, but Cain built a city; Jubal "was the father of all such as handle the harp and organ"; and Tubal-cain was "an instructor of every artificer in brass and iron." There was no "Stone Age" in the Garden of Eden. Man was not climbing upward from brute beast through the silly myth of evolution, but man came direct from the hand of God and with the wisdom and genius of God about him. All the heathen people in the world came from those who after the flood turned their hearts away from God and God gave them over to a reprobate mind and they entered into heathen darkness and idolatry and uncleanness. But Adam was far more intellegent than any man today, and we may be sure that about them they had every comfort and convenience in the perfect environment of Eden.

And best of all, the associations in the garden were with God and angels. God would come every day and walk in the cool of the day with Adam. They talked and had sweetest fellowship. All Adam needed to know he could ask. Best of all, he delighted in the fellowship and had no guilt of conscience, no sense of his own weakness or failure to make him turn away from that sweet fellowship—until the awful day when Adam found he had sinned and felt his sinful wickedness was naked and uncovered before God! Oh, that first home in Eden was a home with wonderful surroundings!

After God had made woman and brought her to Adam, we read,

"And Adam said, This is now bone of my bones, and flesh of my flesh: she shall be called Woman, because she was taken out of Man. Therefore shall a man leave his father and his mother, and shall cleave unto his wife: and they shall be one flesh. And they were both naked, the man and his wife, and were not ashamed."

II. SCRIPTURAL IMPLICATIONS OF WEDDING IN EDEN

There are certain scriptural implications here which one should note about this marriage in the Garden of Eden.

1. Husband and Wife Become One

Of course, Eve was literally of Adam's flesh and bone and blood. But in marriage we are taught that the blood and the lives unite and blend in their children and they should come to have such heart unity that spiritually they are "of one flesh." The husband and wife often come to look alike, to think alike, to eat the same food, have the same habits, want the same thing. The need of a man and a woman for each other is so deep-seated in their nature, they each could compensate for the weakness and the need of the other. They should count themselves one.

They were both naked and were not ashamed. Godly love and faithfulness when men and women commit themselves each to the other for a lifetime make it so a husband and wife do not need to hide from each other.

First Corinthians 7:3-5 tells us that there is no restraint, no curb from God on the lovemaking intimacies of a husband and wife. Marriage is thus intended to be a lifelong matter. A man is to leave all others to cling to his wife. A "man shall leave his father and his mother, and shall cleave unto his wife." In the marriage ceremony, when a man takes a wife and vows that he is "forsaking all others" and when the wife takes such a vow, too, they are only agreeing to what God has written into the very institution of marriage. Marriage is for better or for worse, for richer, for poorer, until death ends it.

That means that there can be no proper divorce unless the marriage has already been ruined by persistent adultery, that is, fornication, which makes it impossible for love and respect and cooperation. When God gave marriage in Eden, He made no provision for divorce.

This was a monogamous marriage and so although later God sometimes permitted a man to take two wives, the pattern set here in Eden, the proper, perfect pattern, is for one man and for one woman.

2. Eve Was the Mother of All Living, Adam Said

That means that there was not a tribe of apes that grew gradually, more and more humanlike, and thus that a race of men descended from a race of animals. No. Everybody on the earth is descended from Eve. So it is after the flood as Genesis 9:19 tells us, "These are the three sons of Noah: and of them was the whole earth overspread." Everybody in the world is descended from Noah's three sons. All the black people, all the white people, all the yellow races, all the brown races—all the way from the bushmen of Australia, the pygmy of African forests, the slant-eyed Mongolians, or the people in the American Congress or British Parliament—all are descended from Eve. She was the mother of all living and all are descended from Noah and his sons. Scientifically, people know that that is true, all the races are fertile when they interbreed. They are all of the same species.

GENESIS 3

NOW the serpent was more subtil than any beast of the field which the LORD God had made. And he said unto the woman, Yea, hath God said, Ye shall not eat of every tree of the garden?

2 And the woman said unto the serpent, We may eat of the fruit of the trees of the garden:

3 But of the fruit of the tree which *is* in the midst of the garden, God hath said, Ye shall not eat of it, neither shall ye touch it, lest ye die.

4 And the serpent said unto the woman, Ye shall not surely die:

5 For God doth know that in the day ye eat thereof, then your eyes shall be opened, and ye shall be as gods, knowing good and evil.

6 And when the woman saw that the tree *was* good for food, and that it *was* pleasant to the eyes, and a tree to be desired to make *one* wise, she took of the fruit thereof, and did eat, and gave also unto her husband with her; and he did eat.

THE SERPENT IN EDEN

The relationship between man and animals in Eden was very, very close and sweet before sin came in. Nature is not accursed. Man is beset by storms, flood, lightning, heat and cold. He is attacked by disease germs. Most animals fear him, and many a beast would kill man. But we believe that the microbes which are now dangerous disease germs were once innocent and healthful microbes. We believe that in Eden the roses had no thorns. We believe that before sin came in there were no convulsions of nature to threaten man or harm him.

God sometimes helps men to break down the barrier so that men and animals can understand each other. So He had two of every kind of animal march into the ark Noah built. So He had the unbroken colt of a donkey walk sedately down the streets of Jerusalem amid the cheering, praising throng, with the Lord Jesus seated upon his back in the triumphal entry into Jersualem. And so in the Kingdom Age we are told, "The wolf also shall dwell with the lamb, and the leopard shall lie down with the kid; and the calf and the young lion and the fatling together; and a little child shall lead them. And the cow and the bear shall feed; their young ones shall lie down together: and the lion shall eat straw like the ox. And the sucking child shall play on the hole of the asp, and the weaned child shall put his hand on the cockatrice' den'' (Isa. 11:6-9).

1. The Snake That Talked

It is no myth, it is not simply fanciful poetry that Satan entered into a serpent and the serpent talked to Eve.

Now snakes are under a curse. God has put antipathy between snakes and men. The snake is a type of Satan and of evil. But originally it was not so. Then "the serpent was more subtil than any beast of the field which the Lord God had made,'' more intelligent and closer to man than horse or dog or chimpanzee.

Dr. Scofield says:

> The serpent, in his Edenic form, is not to be thought of as a writhing reptile. That is the effect of the curse (Gen. 3.14). The creature which lent itself to Satan may well have been the most beautiful as it was the most "subtle" of creatures less than man. Traces of that beauty remain despite the curse. Every movement of a serpent is graceful, and many species are beautifully coloured. In the serpent, Satan first appeared "as an angel of light" (II Cor. 11.14).

Did snakes regularly talk to men in the Garden of Eden? I do not know. I entered a home in Phoenix, Arizona, and was startled to hear a clear voice say, "Well, can't you say hello?" It was as clear as any human speech, but it was a Myna bird. My dog Flicka could not talk, but she gave very clear evidence of memory, of conscience, of jealousy, of love, of joy and shame; she knew the meaning of scores of words, possibly hundreds. She loved music. Before the curse that put thorns on the roses and put weeds in the field and set nature against man, animals might have talked. And when God had a donkey to reprove Balaam, He may have for a moment simply freed that donkey from the curse which is on nature. I do not know. But Eve did not seem surprised when the serpent spoke. She may have been so accustomed to the intelligence of the serpent that his words did not surprise her.

2. Satan in the Serpent

If we read carefully Isaiah 14:4-17 we will find that the king of Babylon is here set up as a type not only of the Antichrist himself who will come, but of Satan, the great and final Antichrist. In verse 12 we find that Satan was originally "Lucifer, son of the morning," an archangel of God, and that he fell by his rebellion in trying to exalt himself above God and be equal with God. The Scofield Bible note on this passage says:

> "Verses 12-14 evidently refer to Satan, who, as prince of this world-system (see 'World,' John 7.7; Rev. 13.8, note), is the real though unseen ruler of the successive world-powers, Tyre, Babylon, Medo-Persia, Greece, Rome, etc. (see Ezk. 28.12-14). Lucifer, 'day-star,' can be none other than Satan. This tremendous passage marks the beginning of sin in the universe. When Lucifer said, 'I will,' sin began. See Rev. 20.10, note. See other instances of addressing Satan through another. Gen. 3.15; Mt. 16.22,23."

Again in Ezekiel 28:13-15 Satan is addressed through the king of Tyre. And God says:

"Thou hast been in Eden the garden of God; every precious stone was thy covering, the sardius, topaz, and the diamond, the beryl, the onyx, and the jasper, the sapphire, the emerald, and the carbuncle, and gold: the workmanship of thy tabrets and of thy pipes was prepared in thee in the day that thou wast created. Thou art the anointed cherub that covereth; and I have set thee so: thou wast upon the holy mountain of God; thou hast walked up and down in the midst of the stones of fire. Thou wast perfect in thy ways from the day that thou wast created, till iniquity was found in thee."

So Lucifer, the angel of God, fell and became Satan, the enemy of God.

Then in the Garden of Eden Satan entered into a serpent, the brilliant, intelligent animal, to tempt Eve and to cause sin among mankind. And as an eternal memorial to that wicked thing, God now calls Satan "the dragon, that old serpent, which is the Devil, and Satan" (Rev.

20:2). He is a dragon or a great reptile; he is the serpent. And as a reminder to mankind, God put a curse on serpents and enmity between men and snakes. And a snake is now cursed to crawl on the ground.

3. Satan the Enemy of God and Man

What eternal frustrations must ferment in the bosom of Satan! What haunting memories of those days when he was in intimate fellowship with God! How lonely Satan must be now that he hates God, now that he has no more sweet communion with the pure angels, now that he cannot delight in the creation God made but rather hates it and wishes to destroy it!

When Satan looked on the purity and happiness of man and woman in the garden, I do not wonder that he hated them. It is said that "misery loves company." Those who have not, hate those who have. Those who are poor hate those who are rich. Those who are ignorant hate those who are wise. The unbelieving hate those who walk in sweet and simple faith. And so Satan was tormented with the urge to ruin the happiness in Eden, to frustrate the plan of God, to besmirch all that was beautiful and holy in mankind.

When Satan saw how God walked in the garden in the cool of the day and how sweet was the conversation that Adam and Eve had with God, he determined to break that fellowship. When he saw how tenderly Adam loved and cared for and made happy his wife, he longed to make every husband a brute, to make every wife a shrew!

I know there is a personal Devil. I know he hates the children of God and would do us evil. I know that he resists the Gospel and takes away the gospel seed out of the heart of the hearer when he can. I know that when God says to the poor sinner, "Today is the day of salvation," Satan whispers in the other ear, "Not now. Wait until you have had your fling. Wait until you have had a good time. Wait until you feel like it." I say, I know there is a personal Devil, the enemy of Christ, the enemy of the Gospel and my own hateful enemy. I know that when I go to rescue souls from the burning, that I go to snatch the lamb from the mouth of the lion. I know that ". . . we wrestle not against flesh and blood, but against principalities, against powers, against the rulers of the darkness of this world, against spiritual wickedness in high places" (Eph. 6:12).

One preacher said to me, "Brother Rice, you talk as if the Devil is a person and that he constantly opposes the Gospel and threatens the happiness and usefulness of Christians and would even take their lives. You act as if the Devil were a constant menace. Why," he said, "the Devil never bothers me that way."

I replied, "If you twisted the Devil's tail as much as I do, if you pulled out of his hand drunkards and harlots and infidels, old men and women as well as young people and children, the Devil would bother you." Ah, yes, we ought to be reminded that "the devil, as a roaring lion, walketh about, seeking whom he may devour" (I Pet. 5:8). And we ought to "put on the whole armour of God," for the constant warfare (Eph. 6:11).

So Satan entered into the serpent and tempted the first woman to sin.

4. How Satan Planned This Temptation

We should learn from the manner of Satan's temptation through the serpent and be always on guard against his methods.

First, Satan came as a friend. Since the serpent was the most intelligent beast of all God had created, until God put a curse on the snake, no doubt Adam and Eve had been about that charming and intelligent creature a good bit. And Satan came professing to offer a way of happiness and wisdom. The Scripture says about false teachers: "For such are false apostles, deceitful workers, transforming themselves into the apostles of Christ. And no marvel; for Satan himself is transformed into an angel of light. Therefore it is no great thing if his ministers also be transformed as the ministers of righteousness; whose end shall be according to their works" (II Cor. 11:13-15). So

Satan himself does not come with horns and hoofs and pitchforks, but he comes as a good friend. He comes in the form of a beautiful and attractive woman. It may be with smiles and tears and love, as in the case of Delilah with Samson. Or he comes in the form of a cultivated, scholarly gentleman, as modernists and unbelievers in Christ and the Bible come. He comes in the guise of the scholarly professor who would lead you into "truth," he says, while he breaks down your faith in God and the Bible. So Satan, in Eden, came to the woman as a friend, seeking, he said, to show her how to be happy and wise!

Oh, how that old lie of Satan has deceived and damned its millions! Satan promises happiness, but in the bottom of the cup of nectar is gall and bitterness! All Satan's apples have worms. All Satan's promises are lies. All Satan's good times end in heartbreak. All Satan's scholarship leads to the darkness of eternal night, with blinded mind, perverted heart, soul estranged from God.

Satan started with a question, "Hath God said?" Unbelief and sin always start with a question about the Word of God, some denial of God's authority. Did God really say it? Is the Bible really the infallible Word of God? And so unbelievers deny the story of Jonah, while Satan means that to be a denial of Christ's resurrection, of which it is the prophetic type. And so-called scientists by their guesses and theories deny the direct creation of mankind in the image of God, but Satan means it to turn people from the second creation, the new birth. Men affirm that the moral standards of the Bible are only relative and temporary and not, perhaps, suited to this enlightened age, but really Satan means thus to lead people on the road to broken hearts, broken homes, diseased bodies, tainted minds and at last to Hell. Mark you, when you hear anybody questioning the Word of God, you should listen for the hiss of the serpent. You should see the leering eyes of Satan behind it.

All Christianity stands or falls with the Bible. The deity of Christ, the truth about Heaven and Hell and the new birth, and every promise of God hinges on whether or not the Bible is really God's infallible Word. So Satan starts to break down faith in the Word of God. He said to the woman, "Yea, hath God said, Ye shall not eat of every tree of the garden?"

Then Satan in the serpent followed with outright denial, "And the serpent said unto the woman, Ye shall not surely die: For God doth know that in the day ye eat thereof, then your eyes shall be opened, and ye shall be as gods, knowing good and evil" (Gen. 3:4,5).

Others have called attention to the fact that Satan here brought the threefold temptation mentioned in I John 2:16: "For all that is in the world, the lust of the flesh, and the lust of the eyes, and the pride of life, is not of the Father, but is of the world."

When Satan got the woman to gazing upon the forbidden fruit, "And when the woman saw that the tree was good for food, and that it was pleasant to the eyes, and a tree to be desired to make one wise, she took of the fruit thereof, and did eat, and gave also unto her husband with her; and he did eat" (Gen. 3:6). Now that she has opened herself to sin by looking longingly at the tree and the forbidden fruit, her fleshly nature craves the taste—"the lust of the flesh." And it appears to be good for food, "The lust of the eyes." And the crowning touch of the temptation is Satan promises her that it will make her like God and she will know good and evil. "Pride of life"!

Well, if there is anything she wants, it is to be wise. Oh, to be scholarly! To have learning and wisdom! That has led many a professor into infidelity. It has ruined many an ambitious college student. It has turned fundamental institutions into hotbeds of infidelity all through these years. That pride of the heart that wants to be known as wise and scholarly!

And those so-called "liberal" churchmen with "an evil heart of unbelief" as the Bible calls it, say that fundamentalists, Bible believers, are reactionary, that they are obstructionists, that they oppose science, that they are ignorant. No, Sir Winston Churchill believed the Bible and said so. He was not ignorant. Woodrow Wilson, president of Princeton University, then governor of New Jersey, and then President of the United States, was not an ignorant man nor an opponent of science and learning. He was a simple Bible believer, and in the Red Cross Testament given me as a soldier in World War I, President Woodrow Wilson made an earnest appeal that every soldier should personally take Christ as Saviour. No, no, the Bible believers like Machen and Robert Dick Wilson, and W. B. Riley and E. Y. Mullins were not ignorant and unlearned men, though they were simple Bible believers. One who listens to that tomfoolery has been led astray by the serpent and by the pride of his wicked heart that wants the favor of an ungodly world!

So Satan led the woman to sin, and she gave of the forbidden fruit to her husband and he did eat. Then both found themselves naked before God, not only physically naked, but far worse—with guilty consciences and perverted minds and now under the gaze of an angry God whose rule they had broken and whose command they had disobeyed and whose love they had betrayed!

God gives us this sad story in

VERSES 7-13:

7 And the eyes of them both were opened, and they knew that they *were* naked; and they sewed [7]fig leaves together, and made themselves a-prons.

8 And they heard the voice of the LORD God walking in the garden in the cool of the day: and Adam and his wife hid themselves from the presence of the LORD God amongst the trees of the garden.

9 And the LORD God called unto Adam, and said unto him, Where *art* thou?

10 And he said, I heard thy voice in the garden, and I was afraid, because I *was* naked; and I hid myself.

11 And he said, Who told thee that thou *wast* naked? Hast thou eaten of the tree, whereof I commanded thee that thou shouldest not eat?

12 And the man said, The woman whom thou gavest *to be* with me, she gave me of the tree, and I did eat.

13 And the LORD God said unto the woman, What *is* this *that* thou hast done? And the woman said, The serpent beguiled me, and I did eat.

1. The Woman First Went Wrong, Then the Man

Many a preacher has won the smiles of the women to whom he preached by saying that Adam blamed Eve for his sin and that men have been blaming women ever since. Well, it is true enough that all of us, men and women, have a tendency to excuse our sins and to blame others for them. But in truth that charge hardly fits the case with Adam and Eve.

So it is really true as Adam said, Eve first "took of the fruit thereof, and did eat," and then she "gave also unto her husband with her; and he did eat" (Gen. 3:6).

2. Eve Was Deceived, Adam Was Not

An enlightening commentary is given on this fact in I Timothy 2:11-15:

"Let the woman learn in silence with all subjection. But I suffer not a woman to teach, nor to usurp authority over the man, but to be in silence. For Adam was first formed, then Eve. And Adam was not deceived, but the woman being deceived was in the transgression. Notwithstanding she shall be saved in childbearing, if they continue in faith and charity and holiness with sobriety."

Here we find that "Adam was not deceived, but the woman being deceived was in the transgression."

Satan convinced Eve that God's Word was not true! He convinced her that she would not really die if she ate of the forbidden fruit. He convinced her that she would become wise like God. Eve was deceived by Satan speaking through the serpent.

No doubt there is a reason why Satan chose to speak first to the woman. Adam was a man, and he was made to be head of the wife, stronger in body, more logical in mind, more responsible spiritually. Woman was made to be subject to her husband, to be a helper to her husband, to be the joy and comfort of her husband, a helper, a mate. In I Peter 3:7 the husbands are commanded to give "honour unto the wife, as unto the weaker vessel." And so Satan began his temptation with the weaker vessel. He deceived the woman and she fell into sin.

Then in that passage in I Timothy, chapter 2, God makes clear that this is why He does not want a woman to "usurp authority over the man, but to be in silence," as far as leadership in Christian services are concerned. The woman is not to be over the man in her home. The woman is not to usurp authority over the man as a teacher or preacher in the church. The woman is the weaker vessel. She was deceived by Satan when Adam was not deceived. So women are not to be put in places of authority and responsibility where they are likely to lead men astray, being themselves deceived.

It is a remarkable thing how many false cults have grown up around women. I think of Mrs. White the so-called "prophetess" of the Seventh-Day Adventist movement; I think of Mrs. Mary Baker Eddy, the founder of Christian Science. I think of the Fox sisters who started the way of spiritism, teaching people to get in touch with demons. Even the false religion of Romanism goes more and more wrong as it exalts Mary instead of Christ. And so in Revelation 17 the great harlot, the woman, pictures the perverted state church that will arise in the time of the Antichrist. And this wicked woman is not only a harlot but "the mother of harlots" or false religions.

So God forbids women to have leadership and authority over a man, particularly in spiritual matters. And He uses the reminder that Eve was deceived, but Adam was not deceived.

3. Why Then Did Adam Follow Eve in Sin?

Adam did not believe what Satan said. He believed that he would surely die. God had said it and Adam was not deceived about that. Doubtless he did not quite realize fully all that was involved in the physical death, the spiritual death involved in his disobedience. But he was not deceived. He still believed God.

Adam did not believe that the forbidden fruit would

make him wise like God. Oh, there is a wisdom which is not good and not sweet and not helpful. Some wicked things a Christian ought not to be acquainted with, ought not to mention favorably. It is true that to sin gives some acquaintance with sin, but it gives no true wisdom and does not make a man like God. And Adam was not deceived. He still believed what God said instead of what Satan said.

I think even that Adam was not tempted by the attractive color and odor of the fruit; that is not why Adam sinned.

Why, then, did Adam sin? When Eve ate of the forbidden fruit, he ate also. When Eve sinned, he sinned also.

Ah, you may be sure that Satan knew what he was doing when he used Eve to reach Adam! And down through the centuries, Satan has been using the woman, who was meant for her beauty and holiness, meant for pleasure and comfort and encouragement, meant for companionship and holy inspiration, to lead man into sin. So he did in the case of Adam and Eve.

I believe that Adam loved his wife as no other man has ever loved a woman. We are commanded, "Husbands, love your wives, even as Christ also loved the church, and gave himself for it" (Eph. 5:25). I ought to do that but I do not, I cannot. I am so sinful and frail that I cannot be as good as Jesus Christ about anything, certainly not about that.

But Adam was perfect and sinless. Up to that time Adam had constant contact with God. He loved his wife as one ought to love his wife. And no one, I suppose, can conceive of how his heart was torn when he considered whether he would let his wife go on into death and ruin away from God, and leave him alone in the Garden of Eden, or whether he should go with her into sin.

A man's love for his wife may be one of the highest and holiest influences in his life. Or it may be used of Satan to lead a man wrong. I knew a man who, with an aching heart, stayed, with fruitless ministry, in a fine home he had prepared for his wife because he had made her a vow that he would never ask her again to follow him up and down the land in evangelism or in a change of pastorates. I know men who keep their good jobs and fine income instead of going into the ministry or to the mission field, because they cannot bear to give their wives less that the wives want and seem to need.

So Adam made his choice and went with Eve. He took of the fruit, too, and ate it. It may be he wept as he ate it, I do not know. Or it may be he was so blinded by love for his wife that he rushed headlong into the sin. I do not know. Only we are told that Adam was not deceived. He knew what he did. He sinned, not like the poor, blinded, lighthearted woman, but like a strong man with an open mind who knew what he was doing. And so Adam sinned and came into death and ruin, and brought the whole human race with him into ruin.

I do not mock Adam. He is the father of us all. I do not blame him more than I blame all of us who sin. I only want to remind you that Satan will use the holiest and best in your life to lead you from God and from the right.

Satan uses the good to lead you away from the best. Satan uses patriotism and love of mother and father, or love of wife and children, or the respect of your friends, or the appeal of learning and education, to lead men away from God and the Bible and obedience and righteousness. So Satan used Eve to lead Adam into sin.

It may well be that here we have a reminder that Jesus, the second Adam, went into death for all of us, even as Adam went into death for his wife. I do not mean that Jesus ever sinned, but He who knew no sin became sin for us that we might become the righteousness of God in Him. Jesus, who had a right to remain in the Paradise of God, walked out of it, and down the stately stairs of Glory to be born in the stable, to take on Himself the form of a servant, to die like a criminal, in order that we might be won to Him, His bride.

And so Adam, when he walked into death and out of the presence of God, may have pictured the Lord Jesus as He said good-by to Heaven and took on Himself our blame and our human frailty, and took at least the blame for our sins, and even let God the Father turn His face away from Him on the cross, that He might bear our sins and pay our debt and redeem us to God!

VERSES 12,21:

12 And the man said, The woman whom thou gavest *to be* with me, she gave me of the tree, and I did eat.

21 Unto Adam also and to his wife did the LORD God make coats of skins, and clothed them.

I. HOW WOMEN HAVE INFLUENCED MEN THROUGH THE AGES

Eve was the first woman. She is called "the mother of us all" and "the mother of all living." So Eve is a type of every woman, good and bad. Her influence on Adam was good and bad. And so down through the years women have had tremendous influence on their husbands for right or wrong, for good or bad.

Let every man consider with deep gratitude how God has made good women, Christian women to be a blessing and an uplift through the centuries, and rejoice in whatever good God has sent his way through mother or wife or sister or daughter or friend.

1. Thank God for Christian Mothers!

Paul very wisely reminded Timothy of his noble, believing mother and his grandmother. He was inspired to write the young preacher: "When I call to remembrance the unfeigned faith that is in thee, which dwelt first in thy grandmother Lois, and thy mother Eunice; and I am persuaded that in thee also" (II Tim. 1:5).

Timothy had had a heathen father, a Greek, as we learn from Acts 16:1, and unlike Timothy's mother who "believed," the Scripture says. But that godly mother Eunice and that godly grandmother Lois had unfeigned faith, and had taught it to Timothy from babyhood.

The charming story of Hannah and how she prayed with such holy concern and devotion for a boy to serve the Lord is told in I Samuel, chapter 1. The child was conceived and born in prayer and after she had loved him and trained him and taught him for a season, then she took him to the Temple, and said, "As long as he liveth he shall be lent to the Lord." Oh, we would have more Samuels if we had more Hannahs!

Consider the amazing story of how John the Baptist was born after Zacharias and Elisabeth had prayed for a child perhaps thirty years or more. Read Luke 1:13-17, and I think you will be convinced, as I am, that they had long prayed for a boy who would never touch drink, for a lad who would be filled with the Holy Ghost, for a lad who would be a mighty soul winner. They had in mind, no doubt, one who would be bold and faithful after the pattern of the Spirit-filled Elijah. And that is exactly what God gave them. And I do not doubt that the ironlike character of John the Baptist, his godly simplicity and unworldliness, came largely from the influence and prayers of Elisabeth, the mother who prayed so many years that she might hold a baby in her arms and rear him for God!

My own mother died before I was six years old, yet I could never measure the impact of her life and testimony on me. She gave me to God when I was born and wanted me to be a preacher. She called me her "preacher boy." She taught me to sing Christian songs. She made all of us promise to meet her in Heaven. On her deathbed my mother rejoiced in the Lord and asked us all to sing, "How Firm a Foundation." Thank God for Christian mothers!

2. Many Men Have Been Greatly Blessed With Christian Wives Who Influenced Them for Good

Many a godly woman has invited me to eat meals in her home, or to be a guest for longer than that. So one day when Elisha the prophet passed by "a great woman" in Shunem "constrained him to eat bread," and so it came to pass that hereafter he often came by for meals. And this good woman "said unto her husband, Behold now, I perceive that this is an holy man of God, which passeth by us continually. Let us make a little chamber, I pray thee, on the wall; and let us set for him there a bed, and a table, and a stool, and a candlestick: and it shall be, when he cometh to us, that he shall turn in thither" (II Kings 4:9,10).

And so a godly woman influenced her husband to make a prophet's chamber for Elisha. Oh, how glad he was later when because of the prophet's intercession God gave a son, and then in answer to the prophet's prayers the son was raised from the dead. That was a good woman, a praying woman. It may be that the term "great woman" referred to her large size or it may refer to the breadth of her mind and her great sympathetic heart. But she was a great woman in God's sight, a woman of prayer and faith, a benediction to her husband and her son, and of course to the prophet of God.

And then there is the charming story of Abigail, the wife of Nabal the Carmelite. Her churlish husband despised David, was not grateful for the watchcare that kept his flocks from the wolves and thieves, and would not share food and blessing with David and his band of hungry men. But while Nabal was drunken Abigail took food supplies and rushed to meet David ere he could bring destruction on all the household. She knew that God had anointed David to be king, that if he sinned in this matter he would later regret it. She saved her husband's life and property, and saved David from sin. She said a good word for the Lord. Later she became the wife of David.

Oh, if Pilate had only listened to his wife who pleaded with him not to condemn Jesus to death! Pilate rose early, was called by the Jews to come to the judgment seat to try Jesus. His wife slept later, but had a terrifying dream in which God revealed to her that Jesus was the Saviour, that He was innocent; so "when he [Pilate] was set down on the judgment seat, his wife sent unto him, saying, Have thou nothing to do with that just man: for I have suffered many things this day in a dream because of him" (Matt. 27:19).

I do not know if Pilate's wife was saved, but I believe that she was. She was more spiritually approachable, more alert to the voice of God than her husband. She pleaded with him to do right.

How many men have gone to Hell because they did not listen to the pleading of a good wife who urged them to turn from sin and be saved. How many lost men will meet the tears of their wives at the judgment, and their tears are part of God's testimony against them and a witness to God's compassion for sinners.

3. Good Women Have Been Blessing to Countless Other Men Through Centuries

Womankind was meant to be a blessing and the sweet influence of a woman's character, her smile, counsel, faith, Christian devotion have been a blessing to multitudes.

We must remember that good women came from Galilee with Jesus and with the apostles "and ministered unto him of their substance." Some of the women who followed Jesus are named in the Bible: Mary Magdalene and another Mary, and the wife of Zebedee, the mother of James and John. There was Joanna the wife of Chuza, Herod's steward. Some good woman no doubt wove that seamless garment that Jesus wore until His crucifixion. Good women gave the money that bought food for Jesus and for the apostles. And Mary anointed Him with an alabaster box of ointment costing three hundred pence.

Paul, too, had great occasion to thank God for the help and influence of Christian women. There was Phoebe and Priscilla and "Mary, who bestowed much labour on us," and the sister of Nereus and the mother of Rufus, "His mother and mine," Paul said in Romans 16. And Paul, writing to Philippians, pleaded with them, "Help those women which laboured with me in the gospel. . ." (Phil. 4:3).

On foreign mission fields and at home as teachers and assistants, as typists, secretaries, Sunday school teachers, Christian women have upheld the arms of good men who serve the Lord. Eve is the mother of all the good women who brought blessing to men.

4. Women Who Have Been a Curse to Men

When Eve took of the forbidden fruit and offered it to Adam, and he, undeceived, but loving his wife and not wanting to displease her, not wanting to lose her, sinned with her, Eve was the type and picture of many a woman who has been a curse to the man she loved and to other men.

We think of Delilah, who entertained Samson in the valley of Sorek. We are told that Samson loved her. But the Philistines bribed her to entice Samson that she might discover the source of his strength and rob him of his power. And as Samson lay with his head in her lap, she caressed him and joked with him and pleaded and wept, and thus she betrayed him into the hands of his enemies. She learned the secret of his power. When he slept she had his hair cut off. The Philistines took him and bound him and blinded him and put him to grinding at the mill like a donkey. O Samson, the wrong kind of love can lead a man to ruin!

There was Jezebel, wife of King Ahab of Israel. It was wrong for Ahab to marry Jezebel, the daughter of Ethbaal, king of the Zidonians. She worshiped Baal and she was a wicked, heartless woman. I think there is no doubt she loved Ahab and wanted him to be happy. So when Ahab coveted Naboth's vineyard, and Naboth would not sell nor trade, and when Ahab mourned over his disappointment, Jezebel told him she would get for him the vineyard. So she wrote letters that led to the public accusation and stoning of Naboth as a blasphemer and traitor. She led Ahab on to the worship of Baal, on to murder, and finally to disaster and the judgment of God. And the dogs gnawed the bones of Jezebel and then they licked the blood of Ahab in payment for their sin against Naboth. So Jezebel, wicked queen, led her husband to sin and ruin.

We think of Herodias, the wicked wife of King Herod. King Herod had met his brother's wife and fallen in love with her. He put away his own wife and married his brother's wife and took her with him to rule over Galilee. John the Baptist warned King Herod plainly, "It is not lawful for thee to have thy brother's wife." Therefore "Herodias had a quarrel against him, and would have killed him; but she could not" (Mark 6:18,19).

So Herodias had a plan. On Herod's birthday, he made a feast for many of his lords. Herodias trained her daughter Salome to dance before King Herod. Perhaps she had not on many clothes. She appealed to the king. He promised her anything she would ask, even to the half of his kingdom and made an oath to that effect.

Then Salome ran to her mother Herodias and came back with the demand, "I will that thou give me by and by in a charger the head of John the Baptist." Ah, Herod, no doubt you went to Hell because of wicked Herodias. John preached to you, and you were convicted. Then you heard John again and again because you knew he was a man of God. Yet you were living in sin with your brother's wife. She led you on to do evil. She led you to hate the preacher. She led you to kill him.

Herodias is the type of all the women who have led their husbands into sin and led the men they loved into sin.

Eve, when you turned and offered the forbidden fruit to Adam, you were bringing a curse on all the world. And countless millions of other wives have by their love and their beauty enticed their husbands to follow them in sin.

After Paul was arrested at Jerusalem and was kept in prison at Caesarea, Paul was brought before Governor Felix twice. The second time we are told:

"And after certain days, when Felix came with his wife Drusilla, which was a Jewess, he sent for Paul, and heard him concerning the faith in Christ. And as he reasoned of

righteousness, temperance, and judgment to come, Felix
trembled, and answered, Go thy way for this time; when I
have a convenient season, I will call for thee. He hoped also
that money should have been given him of Paul, that he
might loose him: wherefore he sent for him the oftener, and
communed with him."—Acts 24:24-26.

Felix and Drusilla sat together before Paul and as Paul
reasoned and preached boldly concerning righteousness
and temperance and the coming judgment, we are told that
Felix trembled! He hoped to be saved. He would send for
Paul at a more convenient time.

We are not told that Drusilla trembled. Here is a strange
sight. The man, the influential governor of the province,
sits and trembles before Paul as Paul talks to him about
righteousness and rebukes him for his intemperance and
warns him of the coming judgment for sinners. Felix
trembled and his wife beside him may have covered her
yawn with a fan or turned her face away. She may have
looked with scorn. I do not know. She may never have said
a word; only surely God meant us to understand that
though Felix trembled, his wife did not.

Felix was so near the kingdom. He was conscious of his
sins. He trembled at the thought of coming judgment. He
promised to hear Paul again and he hoped to be saved, no
doubt. But he did not hear him again. And I fear, yea, I
verily believe that Drusilla held Felix' soul in her hand that
day.

If Drusilla had turned and said, "Felix, let's trust the
Lord now! Paul is right! We need forgiveness," I have no
doubt that Felix would have been saved. But Drusilla did
not say the word. She did not join him in his trembling
conviction. She did not encourage his interest in his soul.

Many a woman will give an account to God for an
unsaved husband, the woman who did not care enough to
speak or the woman who herself went on in her worldly
way.

Dr. Torrey or Dr. Chapman, I think, tells of a man who
had a lovely Christian wife. And so on her birthday he said,

"What can I give you for your birthday? I want to give something that will make you happy. You have been such a good wife and I should like to show my love. What do you want?"

And as they sat before the fire, she is reported to have said, "There is only one thing that I want more than everything else and if you would give me that, I would be happy."

And he answered, "Tell me what it is. If I can I will do it."

"The thing I want most of all," she said, "is that you would turn to Christ and take Him as your Saviour and go with me to Heaven."

We are told that he said, "Surely I could not deny a request like that from one who has been such a good wife as you have been." And so he trusted the Saviour to go with his wife to Heaven.

Oh, in so many, many revival campaigns and in so many homes I have seen a godly wife plead with her husband to be saved and I thank God that many millions of men have been won to Christ because they listened to godly wives. I hope one who hears me today, if you be unsaved, and if it be a wife or a daughter or a mother or any woman who loves you dearly, I hope you will let that woman's love and kindness turn your heart to Christ today.

II. THE CURSE AT THE GATE OF EDEN

There is a theme that runs throughout the Bible, that sin must be punished, that men reap what they sow, that man must answer to an angry God in judgment. That theme began in Paradise itself, before woman was ever created. There in that beautiful land in the Garden of Eden God said, "But of the tree of the knowledge of good and evil, thou shalt not eat of it: for in the day that thou eatest thereof thou shalt surely die" (Gen. 2:17).

Well, both woman and man ate of the forbidden fruit. And now on them the solemn warning takes effect, "Thou shalt surely die."

Note that God did not say that they would eventually die. That was true. Eventually the body would become completely dead, the heart would stop beating, the senses would dwell there no more: but that is not first and foremost what God said or meant. The death that God promised would happen immediately—"In the day that thou eatest thereof."

VERSES 14,15:

14 And the LORD God said unto the serpent, Because thou hast done this, thou *art* cursed above all cattle, and above every beast of the field; upon thy belly shalt thou go, and dust shalt thou eat all the days of thy life:

15 And I will put enmity between thee and the woman, and between thy seed and her seed; it shall bruise thy head, and thou shalt bruise his heel.

1. First, the Curse on the Serpent

The serpent was the most intelligent of all animals. Now he is the most cursed. Then the serpent enjoyed the fellowship of Adam and Eve in the Garden of Eden until Satan possessed him and used him as a tool for sin. Now there is enmity between man and the snake more than between man and any other beast.

Now the serpent must crawl in the dust. I think likely that before the curse the snake was not poisonous, that he walked upon legs like other animals and that the snake was winsome and beautiful. Now God has forever put the symbol, the accursed serpent, to show that the earth itself is under a curse because of sin, and to remind us that Satan himself, the old master serpent and dragon, will be put in the bottomless pit one day! The snake becomes a symbol of sin for all mankind to see, and of the judgment of God on sin.

VERSE 16:

16 Unto the woman he said, I will greatly multiply thy sorrow and thy conception; in sorrow thou shalt bring forth children; and thy desire *shall be* to thy husband, and he shall rule over thee.

2. What Did Sin Bring Upon Womankind?

Woman's sorrows are multiplied. Often her marriage will bring trouble. The children given for blessing may bring heartache.

Woman's conception was greatly multiplied. Once, no doubt, women were not troubled with the menstrual cycle, conception was not possible except at long intervals, but now God says, "I will greatly multiply thy sorrow and thy conception."

We can well believe that if Adam and Eve had remained perfect and sinless in the Garden of Eden and if Eve had there borne children, that it would have been without pain, without danger and without sorrow. Now woman has pain and sorrow and trouble in childbirth.

However, there is blessed comfort in I Timothy 2:15 speaking of the curse upon womankind because "the woman being deceived was in the transgression." But the Scripture says, "Notwithstanding she shall be saved in childbearing, if they continue in faith and charity and holiness with sobriety."

It appears, too, that the woman's subjection to her husband is now part of the trial which comes because of sin.

I do not believe it was any burden or trouble for Eve to obey a perfect husband, one who was as holy as God, one who loved her as Christ would love the church, one who would make any sacrifice to please her or help her. It is true that even in the garden she was a helper and assistant. Man was not created for the woman but the woman for the man. But now that subjection, which in the Garden of Eden was blessed and happy, becomes a burden to many women.

Now a woman is commanded to "submit yourselves unto

your own husbands, as unto the Lord," (Eph. 5:22) that is, as if he were Jesus Christ, but the husband is a long way from being Jesus Christ! Now the woman is commanded to be subject to her husband even if he is unsaved and will not hear the Word of God (I Pet. 3:1,2).

Oh, among a sinful race of people all authority may seem hateful. The prodigal son hates the rule of his good father, and goes into the far country. The workman hates his boss, and defies his authority. The citizen hates the speed laws, and tries to avoid the income tax. I say, in a world of sinful people, authority becomes hard and bitter.

Even when the authority is wholly right and good, the rebellious hearts of sinful men and women find authority unhappy. That is why men everywhere want to find some other explanation of the universe instead of direct creation by a God to whom they must give an account. That is why infidels want to find flaws in the Bible. Consciously or subconsciously they do not want to be accountable to the law of God and to meet in judgment the God of vengeance and the Christ they will not love and trust.

Now the woman is a sinner, so she must be subject to her husband. Now men are sinners everywhere, so there must be human government. Now children are born with tainted, wicked hearts, so parents must discipline their children.

VERSES 17-20:

17 And unto Adam he said, Because thou hast hearkened unto the voice of thy wife, and hast eaten of the tree, of which I commanded thee, saying, Thou shalt not eat of it: cursed *is* the ground for thy sake; in sorrow shalt thou eat *of* it all the days of thy life;

18 Thorns also and thistles shall it bring forth to thee; and thou shalt eat the herb of the field;

19 In the sweat of thy face shalt thou eat bread, till thou return unto the ground; for out of it wast thou taken: for dust thou *art*, and unto dust shalt thou return.

20 And Adam called his wife's name Eve; because she was the mother of all living.

3. The Curse on the Ground

Adam's life is now to be a life of toil and sweat. In the Garden of Eden there were no weeds and the fruit and berries and grain and nuts and melons grew in rich profusion the year round. There were no beasts of prey. There was no blight of insect. There was no crowding of weeds. But now the ground is to bring forth thorns and thistles, and only by constant labor is man to be able to make the ground produce as it should. Now there will be thorns on the roses. Now insect pests will be the enemy of man. Now drought and floods and shriveling heat will threaten all of man's efforts to grow food and clothes and provide homes and tools and comforts.

I do not mean that God cursed the ground because He hated man. I am saying that God cursed the ground because man needs to work. Now that man is by nature wicked and sinful, only a shortened life and the burden of toil can keep man from orgies of sin.

4. Physical Death Is Part of Curse

God said to Adam, ". . .till thou return unto the ground; for out of it wast thou taken: for dust thou art, and unto dust shalt thou return" (Gen. 3:19). So that day Adam began to die. There had never before been a tired wrinkle in his face. There had never been a gray hair, never been a decayed tooth. He had never had a headache. He had never felt his joints stiff.

That night perhaps when Adam came in from his first weary toil, he may have started to put his arm about Eve to caress her and comfort her, and perhaps she shoved him away. She has become fretful; she is not well. She has become a sinner, as has Adam.

Can you imagine how Adam sought for some medicine to relieve the first headache pains? Can you imagine his distress when food for the first time became indigestible? And when Eve tried to gather fruit for their food or vegetables from their garden and found herself stung by a nettle or scratched by a thorn—do you suppose she felt how awful it was to have the whole world cursed because of sin and to have death begun in her body?

Oh, we may be sure that all these pains and sorrows, all the hospitals, all the crying babies, all the sad funeral processions, all the tearful good-bys in the world were brought about because Adam and Eve sinned.

5. Now Adam and Eve Are Spiritually Dead

Heretofore Adam had run gladly to meet God when He came to walk in the garden, and followed Him eagerly when the Lord went away in whatever human manifestation He may have appeared. But now when God came, after Adam is conscious of the guilt of sin, he runs and hides himself in the trees and bushes and God runs after him calling, "Adam, Adam!" Now Adam is not at home in the presence of God. He turns his face away. It has become true with Adam and with Eve, as it is true now of every unregenerate sinner in the world:

"He that believeth on him is not condemned: but he that believeth not is condemned already, because he hath not believed in the name of the only begotten Son of God. And this is the condemnation, that light is come into the world, and men loved darkness rather than light, because their deeds were evil. For every one that doeth evil hateth the light, neither cometh to the light, lest his deeds should be reproved. But he that doeth truth cometh to the light, that his deeds may be made manifest, that they are wrought in God."—John 3:18-21.

It is still true that "every one that doeth evil hateth the light, neither cometh to the light, lest his deeds should be reproved." Adam is already a sinner. Adam is already unfit for the presence of God. Adam is headed for judgment, and so is Eve.

Oh, I am certain that as Adam and Eve went weeping outside the garden and the angels of God pushed them along, and as an angel with a flaming sword was put at the gate to see that they never again could set foot within that holy precinct, they wept.

Did they go back near, sometime, to see if they could catch a glimpse of the Tree of Life, before that Tree of Life was transplanted back into the heavenly Jerusalem and before the Garden of Eden was taken over by the tangle of a cursed earth and cursed plants and cursed animals?

And now Adam and Eve are become the parents of a race of sinners. The taint is in the blood. The curse is on every cell of their bodies. The curse will be on every child they shall bring forth and every descendant down through the millenniums.

Far later when David came face to face with the shocking discovery that he was an adulterer and a murderer, he wept and said, "Behold, I was shapen in iniquity; and in sin did my mother conceive me" (Ps. 51:5). He did not mean that there was anything wrong in proper marriage and the reproduction of children. He meant that every child ever born bears a taint of an accursed father and cursed mother who bear in their bodies the ruin of Adam and Eve's sin.

And so Romans 5:12 says: "Wherefore, as by one man sin entered into the world, and death by sin; and so death passed upon all men, for that all have sinned."

I do not say that an unaccountable child, a baby, is condemned to Hell. I do not believe that. I believe that ". . . as in Adam all die, even so in Christ shall all be made alive" (I Cor. 15:22). I believe that the dear Lord Jesus has paid for all of Adam's sin and that no one goes to Hell because of the inherited taint of sin. I think little children are kept safe until they come to know right from wrong and come to choose sin for themselves and then they must personally turn to Christ and be born again or go to Hell. But it is a fact, nevertheless, that "they go astray as soon as they be born, speaking lies" (Ps. 58:3) and that every child born has the taint of sin inbred.

Adam and Eve went on in a world where trouble is. Among briars and thorns they set out to dig the ground and grow food. God blessed them with a child and Eve hugged it to her heart and said, "I have gotten a man from the Lord."

But that first child born turned out to be a murderer, Cain. And Cain was not a murderer because he got into bad company down in some pool hall, or in some juvenile gang. Cain did not turn out to be a murderer because, like the two famous Chicago murderers Loeb and Leopold, they were taught in school godless evolution and that man is a beast. No, Cain turned out to be a murderer because he had a sinful nature just as every murderer to be born after him, and every child who did not actually commit murder born after him, would be a sinner by nature.

Oh, I am sure angels wept over the ruin of a fallen world. They must have looked on with great pain as the Garden of Eden was eventually dismantled, the Tree of Life was taken away, and that which was once the Paradise of God on earth became some jungle of briars and thorns, of wild beasts and poison snakes. They must have looked down on men and women laboring, sweating, sinning, weeping, growing old and dying, and wept! Oh, the heart of God surely did weep, as Jesus wept over Jerusalem. And so all good men ought to weep over the ruin that has come upon a race turned away from God!

I hear prattle of Bible teachers who talk about how men are getting so bad "in these last days." They foolishly forget that man is by nature incurably wicked, that "the heart is deceitful above all things, and desperately wicked: who can know it?" (Jer. 17:9). They forget that man is a depraved, fallen creature by nature, dead in trespasses and in sins. Death has passed upon all men for that all have sinned!

Now unless God has some way to save poor, fallen, wicked sinners, man can never live in the Paradise of God again, man can never walk and talk in happy fellowship with God again. Unless God has some way to save people not worth saving and to change people and make them good when they are by nature wicked, then man will never again eat of the Tree of Life, and walk beside the river of life, and know peace and joy again that is eternal.

III. BLESSED REDEMPTION FOR FALLEN MAN

Ah, that was a sad couple after they had eaten of the forbidden fruit and suddenly saw themselves naked and recognized they were sinners and felt alienated from God and afraid of God whom they had wronged and disobeyed! Now they are lost sinners and they will act like sinners.

1. Fig Leaf Aprons for Naked Sinners

We are told, "And the eyes of them both were opened, and they knew that they were naked; and they sewed fig leaves together, and made themselves aprons" (Gen. 3:7).

Well, fig leaves make a very puny covering. When I was a boy we tried to make garments of grape leaves and oak leaves, pinning them together with straws. But they soon got brittle and fell apart.

Ever since Adam and Eve made themselves aprons of fig leaves, men have been making flimsy coverings for their sin, flimsy and unsuccessful efforts to hide their sins from God.

I do not wonder that God says about man's efforts at righteousness that "all our righteousnesses are as filthy rags. . ." (Isa. 64:6). And God said, "Can the Ethiopian change his skin, or the leopard his spots? then may ye also do good, that are accustomed to do evil" (Jer. 13:23).

The heathen tries to appease an angry God with incantations or the offering of a chicken or the rites of the witch doctor. The Romanist would have men seek to cover their naked wickedness before God with masses and prayers and penance and candles and by abstaining from meat or confessing to a priest. The lodge man seeks to subdue his passions, to do good to his fellow man, to be a good husband and father, and thus to be received into the Elysian fields by the Grand Architect of the universe.

And many who turn to Christ still think they must "hold out faithful," think they are "on probation" and they must make their own mended garments and fig-leaf aprons while, as they think, they are "on probation." Oh, poor, sinful man seeks in vain to hide his sin from God or to hide himself from judgment by his homemade covering!

Adam and Eve were conscious of the frailty and failure of their garments. When God saw them in fig-leaf garments, Adam explained why he had hid himself. Even so, "And he said, I heard thy voice in the garden, and I was afraid, because I was naked; and I hid myself." Even with his fig-leaf garments he was naked. And the sinner with all his foolish and failing attempts to cover his sin is still naked before God, shamefully exposed in his sinfulness.

2. First Blood Shed in Universe Was Because of Sin

But God loved His erring creatures. And God had planned before the world began a way of mercy, a way of pardon, a way back to Paradise.

So in the presence of the startled and shamed man and woman, God killed innocent animals and then He made "coats of skins, and clothed them" (Gen. 3:21). As far as we know, up to this time there had never been a drop of blood shed. As far as we know until sin came in there had never been a beast of prey. We suppose that the lion then ate straw like the ox, as he will do again in the Kingdom Age. And man had been free to eat all the vegetables and fruits, but as far as we know, had never eaten flesh. Now God killed innocent animals. Their blood flowed out as a witness against man's sin. But far more, it pictured that God will have a Lamb whose blood will be poured out on Calvary to pay for sin.

Long later Abraham said to his son Isaac, "My son, God will provide himself a lamb for a burnt-offering" (Gen. 22:8). Ah, God will never let man forget that He has plans, that He has One who is coming to pour out His blood and pay for man's sin.

That is why by faith Abel, the prophet of God, offered a more excellent sacrifice because it pictured a coming Saviour. That is why all the bloody sacrifices of the Old Testament. That is why John the Baptist cried aloud with holy exaltation, when standing by the banks of Jordan he pointed out the Saviour, "Behold the Lamb of God, which taketh away the sin of the world" (John 1:29).

God made coats of skins for Adam and Eve. Their nakedness is covered. It is not covered by any of their own works nor any of their own merits. The innocent has died that the wicked might be covered. Animals that did not sin have died that man who did sin could have his sin covered; and so it is that Jesus came to die and was counted a sinner and bore our sins in His own body on the tree, so that all of us might have the blessed covering for our sins.

David understood that and was inspired to write: "Blessed is he whose transgression is forgiven, whose sin is covered. Blessed is the man unto whom the Lord imputeth not iniquity. . ." (Ps. 32:1,2).

I am sure that Adam and Eve understood that God was making a way of salvation for them, for He told them about the seed of the woman, but more of that later.

Now Adam and Eve can say, "I will greatly rejoice in the Lord, my soul shall be joyful in my God; for he hath clothed me with the garments of salvation, he hath covered me with the robe of righteousness. . ." (Isa. 61:10).

I think that God meant the same thing when He put those coats of skin around poor, naked, shivering, shamefaced Adam and Eve, and when He took the seamless robe off the dear Lord Jesus when they nailed Him to a cross. Jesus took off the seamless robe of righteousness so we could wear it.

3. "Seed of the Woman" Promised

Back in Genesis 3:15 God had said to the serpent, "And I will put enmity between thee and the woman, and between thy seed and her seed; it shall bruise thy head, and thou shalt bruise his heel."

This is the first clear promise of the coming of the Saviour. Surely God means the same here as He did in Isaiah 7:14, "Behold, a virgin shall conceive, and bear a son, and shall call his name Immanuel." The Seed of the woman is the Son of the virgin.

In Jeremiah 31:22 God promised backsliding Israel,

". . . for the Lord hath created a new thing in the earth, A woman shall compass a man." It is not promised that a man and woman shall mate and a son be born, but the promise is that a new thing entirely, that a woman will bring forth a man child without a human father. That is the same as God promised Eve, when He mentioned the Seed of the woman.

Jesus is the Son of Adam. He is the Seed of Abraham and the Seed of David. He is the Seed of the woman, too, the Son of the virgin. He is thus the "only begotten Son of God," that is, the only child of God who was physically begotten of God without a human father. All of us who are saved are spiritually born of God, but only Jesus was physically and literally begotten of God and so without a human father. And so Jesus is the Seed of the woman that was promised to shame-faced Adam and Eve after they had sinned.

And, oh, I would say to every poor sinning man and woman in the world, that the only remedy God has for any of us is that we look to the Lord Jesus Christ and let His righteousness take the place of our sinfulness. Let God count us righteous for Jesus' sake even as He counted Jesus a sinner and let Jesus die on the cross! God would clothe us with the garments of salvation and with the robe of righteousness, even as He covered Adam's and Eve's nakedness with garments of skins from innocent animals.

4. Oh, the Road to Paradise Again Is Open!

"The seed of the woman shall bruise the serpent's head," says the Scripture. Many have supposed that that meant Christ's crucifixion. No, it means more than that. It is true that the garments of skin picture the crucifixion and the righteousness of Christ which is imputed to us when we trust Him, because He bore our sin on the cross. But the time when Christ will bruise the serpent's head points to the Second Coming, and not only to the first. For in Romans 16:20 we are told, "And the God of peace shall bruise Satan under your feet shortly. . . ."

Oh, the victory over Satan—Adam and Eve will never know it completely until they can have glorified, sinless bodies again. They will never know it completely until God rules on this earth through Christ, as He ruled in the Garden of Eden and walked and talked with them in perfect happiness and righteousness. Adam and Eve will never know again all the blessedness that is promised to them until Satan is bound and put in the bottomless pit and then that God shall make a new Heaven and a new earth and plant the Garden of Eden again upon this earth.

Oh, that happy day when the desert shall blossom as the rose! That day when "the eyes of the blind shall be opened, and the ears of the deaf shall be unstopped. Then shall the lame man leap as an hart, and the tongue of the dumb sing" (Isa. 35:6).

And in that happy day "sorrow and sighing shall flee away."

And then beyond the millennial age, better yet—when the new Heaven and the new earth are made perfect and when the tabernacle of God is with men and when the river of life shall flow from underneath the throne of the Lord Jesus and when the trees of life will bloom and bear fruit each month on each side of the river of life! Oh then, Adam and Eve will have Paradise restored. And so will all of us who put our trust in the dear Lord Jesus.

Thank God, He has a way of restoring Paradise and Eden for all those who come under the blood. The blessed "Seed of the woman" is the way of present salvation and future blessedness for all who trust in Him.

Come then, poor sinner, to the throne of mercy! O shamed sinner, conscious of your guilt and nakedness before God, do not run away! And do not depend upon the fig-leaf garments of your own shabby righteousness! But come for mercy confessing your sin and trusting in the blood of Jesus Christ!

Through the first Adam death came upon the whole race. But through Christ, the second Adam, man is offered salvation and eternal life and eternal happiness in the Paradise of God!

LET CHRIST COVER YOUR NAKEDNESS NOW

I have earnestly, and with love and tears and prayer, worked on this chapter for days in a hotel room in Denver. Now the best I know I have shown how man is by nature a poor, wicked sinner and how each one of us needs mercy and forgiveness. I have showed you how God loves sinners and has provided a way of salvation. He gave His only Begotten Son to die and suffer the torments of the cross and the shame of a criminal's death in order that you and I might enjoy the blessings of sonship with God the Father. Oh, there is salvation for you if you will take it!

And now I want scores of you to decide for Christ and write and tell me so. Are you tired of sin? Do you honestly in your heart turn to Christ today for mercy? Then trust Him now. Take Him into your heart as your own personal Saviour! Depend upon Him and take the salvation He offers freely! And then when you can honestly say yes to Christ and depend upon Him for forgiveness and salvation, I beg you write out the decision form below, and mail it to me today. May God put it in the hearts of scores to turn and be saved now.

Dr. Curtis Hutson
P. O. Box 1099
Murfreesboro, Tennessee 37130

Dear Dr. Hutson:

I have read from Dr. Rice's Genesis commentary about Adam and Eve and their fall, their sin, and how God in loving mercy made coats of skin to cover their nakedness and promised the coming Saviour that they could trust. I confess that I, too, am a poor, lost sinner who needs saving. I am tired of sin. I want God to forgive me. Today I turn my heart to Him for mercy. I believe that Jesus Christ died on the cross and wants to save me. So here and now I turn my heart to Jesus Christ. I trust Him to forgive my sins and save my soul.

This moment I depend on Him and claim Him as my own personal Saviour. I will confess Him before men and will set out to live for Him now. Please send me a letter of encouragement as I now start out to live for Christ whom I am trusting as my own personal Saviour.

Signed_____

Address_____

_____

GENESIS 4

AND Adam knew Eve his wife; and she conceived, and bare Cain, and said, I have gotten a man from the LORD.

CAIN, FIRST CHILD, UNBELIEVER, MURDERER

Cain was the first child ever born into this world! Ah, Adam and Eve had looked forward to the time. God had commanded them to "multiply, and replenish the earth." But God had promised that the Seed of the woman should bruise the serpent's head and he shall bruise His heel (Gen. 3:15). Now Eve held in her arms the little one and nursed him at her breast. Ah, how glad she was. "I have gotten a man from the Lord," she said. It may be that she really thought "THE man from the Lord." It may be she hoped that this would be the Redeemer promised who would bruise Satan's head and bring redemption.

Eve had pain and anguish as she had had uncomfortable days and nights in the time of pregnancy and sorrow and pain and blood in the birth of the child. That was the heritage from the fall. And yet, how little did she know that the curse on the whole world is in that little baby boy born that day! He is born with the taint of sin in him. He will be a murderer.

Cain did not go wrong through the influence of the boys down at the pool room. There were no evil companions to lead him in sin. He had the taint, the poison in his blood, and so does every child ever born. Every child born is potentially a murderer. Every girl born is potentially a harlot. "They go astray as soon as they be born, speaking lies" (Ps. 58:3).

Oh, Cain had in him what Paul found in himself:

"For that which I do I allow not: for what I would, that do I not; but what I hate, that do I. If then I do that which I would not, I consent unto the law that it is good. Now then

it is no more I that do it, but sin that dwelleth in me. For I know that in me (that is, in my flesh,) dwelleth no good thing: for to will is present with me; but how to perform that which is good I find not. For the good that I would I do not: but the evil which I would not, that I do. Now if I do that I would not, it is no more I that do it, but sin that dwelleth in me. I find then a law, that, when I would do good, evil is present with me."—Rom. 7:15-21.

Even Paul, saved, converted, had still the old carnal and tainted nature.

How many godly parents have discovered to their dismay this awful downward trend in the children. So Manasseh, wicked more than the heathen about him, did not follow his godly father Hezekiah (II Kings 21; II Chronicles 33). So Eli, godly man, will have wicked sons. Samuel's sons will not follow him. D. L. Moody's sons chose to run with modernists and liberals. Billy Sunday's children brought him shame. I do not excuse Adam and Eve, and I do not excuse other men whose children have gone wrong. But let every man who brings a child into the world know that it must take strict discipline and punishment for sin and godly teaching and earnest soul-winning effort to keep the child you love from turning out to be a Cain in morals and religion.

VERSES 3,5,6,7:

3 And in process of time it came to pass, that Cain brought of the fruit of the ground an offering unto the LORD.
5 But unto Cain and to his offering he had not respect. And Cain was very wroth, and his countenance fell.
6 And the LORD said unto Cain, Why art thou wroth? and why is thy countenance fallen?
7 If thou doest well, shalt thou not be accepted? and if thou doest not well, sin lieth at the door. And unto thee *shall be* his desire, and thou shalt rule over him.

Cain's Humanist Religion

"Cain brought of the fruit of the ground an offering unto

the Lord." He did not believe in blood atonement. He probably was not willing to humble himself, confess himself a wicked sinner needing an atonement. His was a liberal kind of religion who could believe in a God but not in a virgin-born Saviour who would die for the sins of the world, and a miraculous change that God would make in the believing heart, making him a child of God. Cain is mentioned twice in the New Testament. First John 3:12 says, "Not as Cain, who was of that wicked one, and slew his brother. And wherefore slew he him? Because his own works were evil, and his brother's righteous."

"His own works were evil," that is, he was a wicked man. We do not know the details of his wickedness, but it is always true that the so-called liberal in doctrine is also wicked in heart. One cannot have the righteousness of God without having Christ. And to reject Christ and His blood atonement is usually because already one has rejected the moral standards of God and has chosen to sin. Jude tells us of those filthy dreamers who "defile the flesh, despise dominion, and speak evil of dignities," and said, "But these speak evil of those things which they know not: but what they know naturally, as brute beasts, in those things they corrupt themselves. Woe unto them! for they have gone in the way of Cain. . . . These are spots in your feasts of charity, when they feast with you, feeding themselves without fear: clouds they are without water, carried about of winds; trees whose fruit withereth, without fruit, twice dead, plucked up by the roots" (Jude 8,10-12).

Wicked people rebelling against authority, against divine revelation, go in the way of Cain. Cain was not a good man. He was wicked in life and in religion he was a humanist, a liberal; in other words, an unbeliever.

Dr. Scofield, in the note on Jude 11, says, "Cain (cf. Gen. 4.1), type of the religious natural man, who believes in a God, and in 'religion,' but after his own will, and who rejects redemption by blood. Compelled as a teacher of religion to explain the atonement, the apostate teacher explains it away."

Cain was angry when God would not receive his sacrifice of good works and God said, "If thou doest well, shalt thou not be accepted? and if thou doest not well, sin lieth at the door. And unto thee shall be his desire, and thou shalt rule over him." And Dr. Scofield calls attention to the fact that sin lieth at the door or "sin-offering." "In Hebrew the same word is used for 'sin,' and 'sin-offering,' thus emphasizing in a remarkable way the complete identification of the believer's sin with his sin-offering (cf. John 3.14 with 2 Cor. 5.21)."

Cain could have had mercy. A sin offering was ready if he had wanted to acknowledge the need for a blood atonement and his faith in the coming Messiah. He, too, could have offered a lamb, but he did not. He was still a rebel against God, a deliberate unbeliever.

VERSE 8:

8 And Cain talked with Abel his brother: and it came to pass, when they were in the field, that Cain rose up against Abel his brother, and slew him.

Cain the Murderer

Abel was righteous, a godly man. He was not killed for any crime against Cain. No, Cain, because his works were evil and his heart was wicked, hated his prophesying, believing brother. It was a matter of antireligious hate. It was a persecution for Christian faith and belief, when Cain killed his brother Abel.

VERSES 9-12:

9 ¶ And the LORD said unto Cain, Where is Abel thy brother? And he said, I know not: Am I my brother's keeper?

10 And he said, What hast thou done? the voice of thy brother's blood crieth unto me from the ground.

11 And now art thou cursed from the earth, which hath opened her mouth to receive thy brother's blood from thy hand;

12 When thou tillest the ground, it shall not henceforth yield unto thee her strength; a fugitive and a vagabond shalt thou be in the earth.

A Curse on Cain

The blood of Abel cried out against Cain. Yes, the shameful excuse, "Am I my brother's keeper?" was lying subterfuge.

When Moses said to the tribes of Reuben and Manasseh, "But if ye will not do so, behold, ye have sinned against the Lord: and be sure your sin will find you out" (Num. 32:23), that is a general law, not only applying to those tribes that would settle on the east side of Jordan but to sin everywhere. The Word of God in Galatians 6:7,8, is, "Be not deceived; God is not mocked: for whatsoever a man soweth, that shall he also reap. For he that soweth to his flesh shall of the flesh reap corruption; but he that soweth to the Spirit shall of the Spirit reap life everlasting."

God has made a universe in which sin cannot get by. The ground itself cried out about the blood of Abel. "The stars in their courses fought against Sisera," the enemy of Israel (Judges 5:20). Nature is aligned to bless the righteous, and so if the little children had ceased to praise the Lord Jesus in His triumphal entry, even the rocks would have cried out (Luke 19:40).

When Christ returns in glory, all the trees of the field shall clap their hands (Isa. 55:12).

So we read those curses and blessings in Deuteronomy 28, and we see that the ground itself in its fruit-bearing is cursed or blessed by the actions of men. And in Malachi 3:10 the Jews were told, "Bring ye all the tithes into the storehouse, that there may be meat in mine house, and prove me now herewith, saith the Lord of hosts, if I will not open you the windows of heaven, and pour you out a blessing, that there shall not be room enough to receive it." I say, God controls nature and causes it to react against sin and for the righteous.

There has been a terrible progressive curse on the land of Palestine. That which was once flowing with milk and honey, now, by countless wars and invasions, has had the land shorn of its forests and the topsoil has eroded. So the rainwater flows away, is not retained and the rainfall itself has become less and less. Cities once prosperous are now buried in a desert of sand on the Arabian Desert. Where once were the giant civilizations of Babylon and Assyria and Nineveh and the cities of Baalbek and Jeresh and Petra, are now desolate. Sin brings a curse even on the ground. And God made Cain know that. He said, "When thou tillest the ground, it shall not henceforth yield unto thee her strength; a fugitive and a vagabond shalt thou be in the earth."

Innocent Blood Brings Curse Upon Land

This was one of the reasons God had the children of Israel and Judah taken captive to far off Babylon. In II Kings 24:1-4 we read:

"In his days Nebuchadnezzar king of Babylon came up, and Jehoiakim became his servant three years: then he turned and rebelled against him. And the Lord sent against him bands of the Chaldees, and bands of the Syrians, and bands of the Moabites, and bands of the children of Ammon, and sent them against Judah to destroy it, according to the word of the Lord, which he spake by his servants the prophets. Surely at the commandment of the Lord came this upon Judah, to remove them out of his sight, for the sins of Manasseh, according to all that he did; And also for the innocent blood that he shed: for he filled Jerusalem with innocent blood; which the Lord would not pardon."

Note this came upon Judah "for the innocent blood that he shed: for he filled Jerusalem with innocent blood; which the Lord would not pardon." How, then, can America escape the judgment of God when nearly a million of the innocent unborn are slain every year in America with the approval of the law and the approval of liberal churchmen and society! The blood cries out of the ground to the Lord.

13 And Cain said unto the LORD, My punishment *is* greater than I can bear. 14 Behold, thou hast driven me out this day from the face of the earth; and from thy face shall I be hid; and I shall be a fugitive and a vagabond in the earth; and it shall come to pass, *that* every one that findeth me shall slay me.

15 And the LORD said unto him, Therefore whosoever slayeth Cain, vengeance shall be taken on him sevenfold. And the LORD set a mark upon Cain, lest any finding him should kill him.

The Mark of Cain

What was the mark on Cain? I do not know. Perhaps some physical mark or scar or identification. We are not told what it was. It was not a matter of race. No race on the earth is more descended from Cain than others for everybody in the world descended from Noah, after the flood.

Later God will establish human government. Now there has been no recognized government to put Cain to death and no one is authorized to do it. He goes away from the presence of God and godly people, into the land of Nod. He knows that men will despise him as a murderer. They will not be allowed to kill him because of the mark that is upon him.

---

16 ¶ And Cain went out from the presence of the LORD, and dwelt in the land of Nod, on the east of Eden.

Cain Must Get Away From the Lord

"Cain went out from the presence of the Lord." He had married, no doubt, one of his sisters, or a niece. Adam had lived, after Seth was born, "eight hundred years: and. . .begat sons and daughters" (Gen. 5:4). The race was young. There were not the accumulated curses on individuals brought by individual sin. So in those early centuries Abraham could marry his half-sister and Jacob his cousins, Leah and Rachel, without harm. But later inbreeding by those who are close kin would multiply the chances of retardation and physical handicaps. But in this case the only way for Cain and Seth to marry was with their own sisters.

VERSES 2 and 4:

2 And she again bare his brother Abel. And Abel was a keeper of sheep, but Cain was a tiller of the ground.

4 And Abel, he also brought of the firstlings of his flock and of the fat thereof. And the LORD had respect unto Abel and to his offering:

ABEL THE RIGHTEOUS, GOD'S FIRST HERO

Adam and Eve both knew the Gospel. In their nakedness, they were conscious of their sin, and God had covered them with garments of skin, symbolizing the righteousness of Christ, to cover wicked sinners. And God had promised them: "I will put enmity between thee and the woman, and between thy seed and her seed; it shall bruise thy head, and thou shalt bruise his heel," referring to the crucifixion of Christ. And we may be sure that they, who had talked to God so intimately before their sin, and had been instructed and treated with such loving grace after their sin—they knew certain great spiritual truths. But it is neither Adam nor Eve who is named as righteous, or as witnessing, or as suffering as a Christian, or as acting by faith.

It is Abel who is called "the righteous"—Abel, the prophet of God, Abel, the man who "by faith" in the coming Saviour "offered a more excellent sacrifice." Abel was God's first hero.

In that divine gallery of heroes of the faith given in Hebrews 11, Abel is mentioned first: "By faith Abel offered unto God a more excellent sacrifice than Cain, by which he obtained witness that he was righteous, God testifying of his gifts: and by it he being dead yet speaketh."

Jesus calls Abel "righteous Abel" (Matt. 23:35). Jesus named him as the first of the prophets (Luke 11:51). And we are told in I John 3:12 that Abel's works were righteous. And Hebrews 12:24 reminds us of the witness of the blood of Abel. So Abel, in the fallen race of men after the Garden of Eden, was God's first hero.

1. Abel Early Got Acquainted With Awful Fact of Sin

Let us suppose that two little boys, a year or two different in age, play beside a small stream. Nearby is a valley they have been strictly forbidden to enter. For a short while, an angel with a flaming sword had stood at the entrance lest Adam and Eve should return and eat of the Tree of Life and live forever as sinners! Suppose Cain said to his brother, "I would like to see what is there. Mother always weeps when it is mentioned."

"But Dad says we must never go there: we have no right there. God forbids it," says Abel, the younger lad.

Nevertheless, let us suppose, they creep to a ridge overlooking the valley and look down upon it. Now there is no Tree of Life. We suppose it has been transplanted in Heaven, where the trees of life will be on each side of the river of water of life, and will bear fruit every month, and their leaves will be for the healing of the nations; but they are gone from Eden now. So is the tree of the knowledge of good and evil. And what was once an ideal park has become a tangle of briars. The flowers are crowded with weeds. The animals are not friendly. There is poison oak and snakes lurk in the grasses. Man's sin ruined Eden.

I do not know whether it was thus that Abel came to know how awful was the sin that brought the curse on the race, but he knew it! And perhaps Abel had prevailed on Adam to tell the sad story of happy days of close fellowship with God now gone, and sin that had driven them from the Garden and cursed the earth with briars and thorns and brought the gray to Adam's temples and the tears that often came to Eve, and the arrogant self-will in the heart of his brother Cain.

But Abel had heard the Gospel. He knew about the Saviour. Perhaps one day when Mother Eve buttoned the handsewn garments on little Abel she told him of the garments of skin that God Himself had prepared to cover the awful, shamed nakedness of the sinning parents. And surely Eve and Adam knew, and so they would have told Abel, that it pictured a great spiritual truth that not by works of righteousness but by the covering of Christ's own righteousness could one be accepted of God and be good in His sight.

And Abel and Cain had heard the story, the curse and the promise, that came when Adam and Eve were expelled from the Garden. The ground was cursed, and now it would grow briars and weeds easier than corn and beets and cabbage. Mother Eve must now look to Adam and he should rule over her. Woman's conception and sorrow in childbirth were greatly increased. But God had promised that some "seed of the woman" should crush the serpent's head, (and that old serpent pictured Satan) and the serpent should bruise His heel. That is, Christ would suffer all the torments of the damned for poor sinners but would triumph and come forth from the grave, and Satan would eventually be conquered and cast over into Hell. Abel must have known that. That much had been clearly revealed to Adam and Eve.

But he knew more. God had not left His creatures without instructions. Already He had taught them to give a lamb for an offering, picturing the coming Lamb of God. We know that Job, and Abraham, Isaac, and Jacob all offered such sacrifices before the Mosaic law was given, and God taught His people thus about the coming Saviour.

And God had given some instructions about righteous living, too. Jesus had called Abel righteous. And I John 3:12 says Abel's works were righteous. That meant that such moral evils as lying and stealing, covetousness, adultery, murder, had been marked as sins; and Abel knew that code and earnestly tried to live by it. And when Cain killed his brother Abel, Cain knew that he had sinned, and he feared "that every one that findeth me shall slay me." The details of God's revelation are not recorded. We are told in Acts 14:17 that God "left not himself without witness, in that he did good, and gave us rain from heaven, and fruitful seasons, filling our hearts with food and gladness." And already the moral law was implanted in the hearts of men, their conscience "accusing or else excusing" them.

So somewhere in those early years Abel, knowing himself to be a sinner, and learning that God had provided a sacrifice, a Saviour, put his trust in the Saviour who was to come, the "seed of the woman" who should bruise the serpent's head, and as a token of this faith in the coming Christ, he offered a lamb for a sacrifice "of the firstlings of his flock." And so it was "By faith Abel offered unto God a more excellent sacrifice than Cain, by which he obtained witness that he was righteous, God testifying of his gifts: and by it he being dead yet speaketh" (Heb. 11:4). And we are told, "And the Lord had respect unto Abel and to his offering" (Gen. 4:4).

Dr. Scofield, in his notes, wisely says, "Abel's offering implies a previous instruction (cf. Gen. 3:21), for it was 'by faith' (Heb. 11:4), and faith is taking God at His word. . . ."

Abel was not saved by offering a sacrifice any more than a present-day Christian is saved by taking the Lord's Supper. The sacrifice was simply a token, a confession of faith in the coming Saviour, just as taking the Lord's Supper in remembrance of Christ's death is properly a token, a confession of faith in the Saviour who died for us.

It is important to see that Abel was saved exactly as we are. So Acts 10:43 says about Jesus, "To him give all the prophets witness, that through his name whosoever believeth in him shall receive remission of sins." Remember that Abel was himself a prophet, the first of the prophets, according to Jesus, in Luke 11:51, and this is the Gospel he believed and witnessed to, with all the prophets. He knew no other plan of salvation than Jesus and faith in Him!

So Abel would have as much right to claim to be Christian as any believer in Christ today. He was saved by trusting in Jesus, not relying upon his works. Cain was rejected because the sacrifice of the fruit of the ground which Cain brought was a profession that he was relying upon the results of his own works and his own righteousness, and it did not please God.

When John the Baptist saw Jesus by the River Jordan and proclaimed: "Behold the Lamb of God, which taketh away the sin of the world," he was talking about the same Lamb of God that Abel believed in and looked forward to.

2. Abel the Prophet of God

How intrigued and moved I was when I first paid close attention to what Jesus said in Luke 11:47-51:

"Woe unto you! for ye build the sepulchres of the prophets, and your fathers killed them. Truly ye bear witness that ye allow the deeds of your fathers: for they indeed killed them, and ye build their sepulchres. Therefore also said the wisdom of God, I will send them prophets and apostles, and some of them they shall slay and persecute: That the blood of all the prophets, which was shed from the foundation of the world, may be required of this generation; From the blood of Abel unto the blood of Zacharias which perished between the altar and the temple: verily I say unto you, It shall be required of this generation."

Through the centuries God has been sending prophets, and all these prophets up to the time of Christ, if they were faithful, were hated by those who heard them and were in some sense forerunners of the Saviour Himself. And so Israel, so greatly blessed in being the chosen people through whom the prophets and the Scriptures came, and through whom the Saviour came, must bear responsibility for "the blood of all the prophets, which was shed from the foundation of the world." When you see that all this must come upon the generation that crucified the Saviour, you find inevitable the coming destruction of Jerusalem and the dispersion of the Jews around the world!

And we read that when God speaks of "the blood of all the prophets, which was shed from the foundation of the world" would be required of the generation that crucified the Saviour, we read that that succession of prophets for which they must pay, goes all the way "from the blood of Abel unto the blood of Zacharias which perished between the altar and the temple. . . ."

But the impressive thing is that Abel himself was one of those mighty prophets who suffered for Christ and were hated and rejected for Jesus' sake and thus in some sense were forerunners of the Saviour.

To be a prophet means to speak for God, in the power of the Holy Spirit. That is made clear in a number of Scriptures. In Acts 2:17,18 Peter quotes from Joel, chapter 2: "And it shall come to pass in the last days, saith God, I will pour out of my Spirit upon all flesh: and your sons and your daughters shall prophesy. . . . And on my servants and on my handmaidens I will pour out in those days of my Spirit; and they shall prophesy."

Acts 10:43 tells us that the prophets all give witness to Christ and that one who believes and trusts in Him is saved.

In I Corinthians 14:23 and 24, Paul was inspired to say that if all spoke with foreign languages, "and there come in those that are unlearned, or unbelievers, will they not say that ye are mad? But if all prophesy, and there come in one that believeth not, or one unlearned, he is convinced of all, he is judged of all." A prophet might speak to a congregation, and sometimes did, but sometimes to an individual. The prophecy may involve foretelling the future but not necessarily so. A prophet is one who speaks for God in the power of God. So Hebrews 1:1 tells us that "God. . .at sundry times and in divers manners spake in time past unto the fathers by the prophets."

Thus when we learn that Abel was a prophet, we know that he was a man who spoke for God in the power of the Holy Spirit.

We may be sure then that Abel preached about the Christ that he trusted in. It was by faith that he offered the sacrifice of a lamb, picturing the coming Saviour. As a prophet, he surely witnessed about that faith. No doubt he urged upon Cain his need for forgiveness and cleansing, his need for a blood atonement. No doubt he rebuked Cain for his self-righteousness in depending on his own works.

And we need not be surprised that Abel was only the first of a long line of prophets, hated, abused, murdered, slandered, and ostracized because they pressed upon people the claims of Christ, the need to be born again, and the power of the Holy Spirit insisted upon.

VERSES 16-22:

16 ¶ And Cain went out from the presence of the LORD, and dwelt in the land of Nod, on the east of Eden.

17 And Cain knew his wife; and she conceived, and bare Enoch: and he builded a city, and called the name of the city, after the name of his son, Enoch.

18 And unto Enoch was born Irad: and Irad begat Mĕ-hū́-jael: and Mĕ-hū́-jael begat Mĕ-thū́-sā-ĕl: and Mĕ-thū́-sā-ĕl begat Lā́-mĕch.

19 ¶ And Lā́-mĕch took unto him two wives: the name of the one was Adah, and the name of the other Zĭĺ-lăh.

20 And Adah bare Jā́-băl: he was the father of such as dwell in tents, and *of such as have* cattle.

21 And his brother's name *was* Jū́-băl: he was the father of all such as handle the harp and organ.

22 And Zĭĺ-lăh, she also bare Tu-bal–cain, an instructer of every artificer in brass and iron: and the sister of Tubal–cain *was* Nā́-ă-măh.

EARTH BEFORE THE FLOOD

". . . The world that then was, being overflowed with water, perished."—II Pet. 3:6.

There was a great civilization, with millions of people perishing in the flood.

A tropical climate, with lush vegetation covering the Arctics and all the world.

Water vapor above the earth filtered the sunlight, and men lived hundreds of years.

There was no rain until after the flood; the ground was watered by dew and mist.

Unbelieving scientists and those who follow them ignorantly believe that there was only a local flood, not the worldwide flood clearly pictured in the Bible where all the tops of all the mountains and the whole earth were covered. These unbelieving scientists do not believe that the earth is only six thousand or seven thousand years old, that God created the earth in six literal days as the Scripture plainly says, and that plants and animals were all created to bring forth only "after their kind," as God says ten times in the first chapters of the book of Genesis.

Unbelievers are taught that the earth is billions of years old, that everything on the earth just happened by process of evolution, that plant and animal life all came from an accidental spontaneous generation where life came into being! (What a whopper!) They believe that all the bacteria, all the worms, insects, fishes of the sea, the birds, the animals, the apes and then man—all progressed; also that modern man thus has such an animal ancestry, by chance in a world without God. They believe that through hundreds of thousands of years men have been on the earth. They believe first there were ape-like creatures, then developed more, until eventually they reached the modern kind of man. They believe that men lived in trees, then in caves, like animals; then eventually there came the Old Stone Age and New Stone Age, then the Bronze Age, then finally the Steel Age. After savagery, eventually barbarism and modern and civilized man. All this is manufactured and untrue. The simple truth is, man in a wonderful civilization was destroyed in the flood and some parts of mankind have carried on that civilization ever since with increasing use of gadgets and literature but with the high type civilization from the days of Adam down to Noah, and from Noah down to Abraham, and to New Testament times, and to the present.

The Scripture says in II Peter 3:3-7:

"Knowing this first, that there shall come in the last

days scoffers, walking after their own lusts, And saying, Where is the promise of his coming? for since the fathers fell asleep, all things continue as they were from the beginning of the creation. For this they willingly are ignorant of, that by the word of God the heavens were of old, and the earth standing out of the water and in the water: Whereby the world that then was, being overflowed with water, perished: But the heavens and the earth, which are now, by the same word are kept in store, reserved unto fire against the day of judgment and perdition of ungodly men."

You will note the Scripture here says that some wicked people "willingly. . .ignorant," scoff at the Bible truth that man was created by the hand of God, that the flood came and changed the whole face of the earth. But, it is true and one day in another giant catastrophe at the time of the great white throne judgment out in space this world will perish again by fire, that is, everything that fire can burn will be burned, then God will make it into a new earth with new heavens.

Meantime, let us see what kind of an earth it was before the flood. You will marvel as you study, I think.

1. A Great Civilization Before the Flood, Not a Race of Savages

Consider the civilization before the flood. Men even then tilled the ground and kept domestic animals. Genesis 4:3,4 says, "And in process of time it came to pass, that Cain brought of the fruit of the ground an offering unto the Lord. And Abel, he also brought of the firstlings of his flock and of the fat thereof. And the Lord had respect unto Abel and to his offering."

So already when man came out of the Garden of Eden he had been commanded to have dominion over all the earth, and mankind set out at the first to do that. Flocks and herds were under Abel's care. Cain was the tiller of the ground.

But do you suppose that as people increased, all the population lived as wandering barbarians? No, for Genesis

4:17 says, "And Cain. . .builded a city, and called the name of the city, after the name of his son, Enoch." There were farms and cities, shepherds and artisans.

Genesis 4:20 says, "And Adah bare Jabal: he was the father of such as dwell in tents, and of such as have cattle." So there were herdsmen then who lived in tents and followed flocks. But verse 21 tells us, "And his brother's name was Jubal: he was the father of all such as handle the harp and the organ." Do you mean that civilization even then had a musical scale? That they had instruments of music? Oh, yes. And I would suppose that the harps were stringed instruments as they are now, and the organ was a wind instrument.

But they had manufacturing also, for Genesis 4:22 says, "And Zillah, she also bare Tubal-cain, an instructer of every artificer in brass and iron." So they smelted copper, probably mixed with tin, as it is today, to make it into bronze. They smelted the iron and used it for tools and weapons here in the first days of the human race before the flood. That was in the lifetime of Adam and of Cain and Cain's children.

Then before the flood there were cities, there were factories, there were tools of iron, there was engraving of precious stones and jewels.

In the great museum in Cairo, Egypt, we saw very finely engraved things of gold and instruments that went back to the oldest civilization we have since the flood. We suppose that Mizraim, who first started to build up Egypt after the flood, had inherited through Noah and his sons the arts and knowledge of the pre-flood civilization. Mizraim, son of Ham, born soon after the flood (Gen. 10:6) is a historical figure, we think the first king of Egypt. *Halley's Bible Handbook* says under FROM FLOOD TO ABRAHAM (*This Period in Egyptian History*):

> 1st Dynasty. Menes (Mena), first historical king, consolidated various tribes, and united Upper and Lower Egypt. Conquered Sinai, and worked its turquois mines. His name is identified by some scholars with Mizraim, the son of Ham. He may have been about contemporary

with Nimrod; while Nimrod was laying the foundations of Imperialism among the small states of Babylonia, Menes was doing the same in Egypt. His tomb has been found at Abydos, and in it a vase of green glaze with his name. This dynasty had 9 kings (p. 96).

2. Many Millions of People Before the Flood

How many people were there before the flood? Well, according to the genealogies given in the Bible, the flood came over sixteen hundred years after Adam was expelled from the Garden of Eden. It was about that much time between the day that Noah came out of the ark, with already one generation advantage and before the Babylonian captivity of Judah. So then surely there would be as many people alive at the time of the flood as there were in the whole earth at the time of the Babylonian captivity, with all the nations of Egypt, Assyria, China, India and the others mentioned in Scripture. There were millions of people. Now the truth is that since before the flood people lived to such advanced ages and had such long childbearing years, it is very likely there were far more people than that. Adam lived "nine hundred and thirty years and begat sons and daughters," we are told. So the earth may have been as well populated before the flood as it was about the time of Christ. Millions of people died in the flood. They were civilized people. They had cities and artisans, tools of iron, musical instruments, were builders, farmers, herdsmen.

Evidences of Civilization

Pember, in the book, *Earth's Earliest Ages,* said on pages 202-204:

And in that age, when, instead of being cut off at threescore and ten or fourscore, men lived on for nearly a thousand years, their immense accumulation of knowledge, experience, and skill, must have advanced science, art, and the invention and manufacture of all the appliances of a luxurious civilization, with a rapidity to us almost inconceivable.

* * *

And doubtless many of the mighty labours accomplished by the earliest descendents of Noah may be considered to have sprung from reminiscences of pristine grandeur, and fragments of lore, handed down by forefathers who had passed a portion of their existence in the previous age of human glory and depravity. Such may have been the daring conception of a literally cloud-capped tower; the stupendous and splendidly decorated edifices of Babylon and Nineveh; and the wondrous structure of the first pyramid, involving as it apparently does, an accurate knowledge of astronomical truth which would seem to have been at least on a level with the vaunted advances of modern science. For all these great efforts, be it remembered, were in progress during the lifetime of Shem, and probably in that of his brothers also.

Nor must we forget recent discoveries in regard to the primeval civilization on the Accadians, "the stunted and oblique-eyed people of ancient Babylonia," whose very existence was unknown to us fifty years ago. Their language was dying out, and had become a learned dialect, like the Latin of the Middle Ages, in the seventeenth century before Christ. And yet so great had been their intellectual power that the famous library of Agane, founded at that time by Sargon I., was stocked with books "which were either translated from Accadian originals, or else based on Accadian texts, and filled with technical words which belonged to the old language." A catalogue of the astronomical department, which has been preserved, contains a direction to the reader to write down the number of the tablet or book which he requires, and apply for it to the librarian. "The arrangements," says Sayce, "adopted by Sargon's librarians must have been the product of generations of former experience." Could we have a stronger proof "of the development of literature and education, *and of the existence of a considerable number of reading people in this remote antiquity*"?

People foolishly try to have man climbing out of animal background to the Old Stone Age and a New Stone Age, an Age of Bronze and Age of Iron. All that is human manufacture, without truth. The simple truth is, there are areas in heathendom in the world today. There men are not climbing out of ape-hood; they are places where wicked men have regressed into savagery and ignorance just as

Romans, chapter 1 tells that many did after the flood. In some areas there may be Stone Ages today and men may live in caves. That is not the history of the human race. That is regression, not progress.

If there had been only one valley of people killed in the flood, why would God cover the whole earth in a catastrophe that would destroy everything on the face of the earth? No, there were millions of people then. And there was a high degree of civilization.

3. A Tropical Climate Before the Flood

Modern scientists have been amazed to find in Alaska and in Siberia even up within the Arctic Circle, frozen remains of many mammoths—a kind of hairy elephant. There were many, many thousands of these carcasses found frozen solid, besides the bones of thousands more. And the tusks of these hairy elephants have been commerce through all the world for years. And in the frozen mouths and stomachs of some of these elephants have been found undigested tropical plants and flowers that now never grow within a thousand miles of that frozen area! Here is evidence of all kinds of tropical plants and tropical weather in Siberia, an area where now in the short sunlit days of summer even little willow twigs grow no more than two inches!

Also, in the Arctic regions and in the Antarctic regions, it is found that there are great coal beds under the earth. What can that mean? That means that at one time there were great forests there, a tropical kind of forests. These were covered by layers of soil the world over by tidal waves of the flood and made the coal beds of the earth.

How can you explain these tropical climates near the North Pole and the South Pole? Evidently there has been a tremendous change. We must believe that the "world that then. . .perished" was a different world than what we have today. What a difference!

I think we find the key in the Bible account of creation

itself. Back in Genesis 1:6-8 God says:

"Let there be a firmament in the midst of the waters, and let it divide the waters from the waters. And God made the firmament, and divided the waters which were under the firmament from the waters which were above the firmament: and it was so. And God called the firmament Heaven. And the evening and the morning were the second day."

Here is a strange thing. The firmament—the heavens above us, the air where the birds fly—was "in the midst of the waters." There were some waters "above the firmament" and some below. And verse 9 says, "And God said, Let the waters under the heaven be gathered together unto one place, and let the dry land appear: and it was so."

It appears that there were two great areas of water—some down just above the earth, under the firmament (that is, the heavens around us), and another great layer of transparent water vapor above the air space (not clouds, above that) and above the earth. The firmament was thus between these two great collections of water. Then God collected together the vapor that was down on the earth as water into the seas. So we suppose that the great layer of water vapor was above the earth, probably high above it, and probably moving with the earth, so there would be no reason for it to fall. That water vapor covered the earth and insulated the earth in some sense. The sun would shine through, but some infrared rays would be filtered out.

We know now that a satellite can be shot out into space, and after it reaches a certain height, then travels about eighteen hundred miles an hour, it can stay up in space and the centrifugal force balances the pull of gravity and it stays there, it does not fall to the earth. So if God had a great area of water vapor above the earth and traveling with the earth so it would not be pulled down by gravity as rain, it would stay there. The evidence is that it did stay there through the years before the flood.

Scientists tell us now that those great rings about the

planet Saturn are of ice. They travel with the planet and they are frozen. However, if it were in water vapor and not condensed, the sun could shine through with some filtering and bring its blessed results to plant and animal life. But there would be some change.

There would be no storms, hurricanes, no rainfall. The air would be nearly saturated with water, and a mist or a dew would water the ground, and there would be no reason for rain. So it was, we suppose, before the flood.

We are told in Genesis 2:5,6: ". . . for the Lord God had not caused it to rain upon the earth, and there was not a man to till the ground. But there went up a mist from the earth, and watered the whole face of the ground."

After the flood, then it began to rain. There had been a great change. So in Genesis 9:13 God told Noah He would set a rainbow in the cloud, a token that there would be no more such a flood of waters to destroy the earth. There was no rainbow, because no rain, before the flood, we understand.

Earth's Climate, Before and After the Flood

Here we give part of an article from the *Bible-Science Newsletter* for July, 1975. It is part of an address before the Bible Science Conference in Swanwick, England, in April, 1975, by Bruce F. Baker of Thornton, Heath, Surry, England.

> The earth's climate, for all its apparently unpredictable and often destructive behavior, can be regarded as a machine of which each working part is reasonably well understood. The interrelationship between the parts, however, is so complex that the slightest variation in one part has considerable repercussions in the performance of the whole.
>
> The Biblical data concerning its working parts and performance in the period before and immediately after the Flood, is found in Genesis 1:6-7, 2:5-6,10, 3:8, 8:1,22, 9:13-15.
>
> An initial survey raises doubt as to whether such a climate machine could really function, apparently without rain or rainbows. While accepting that the

description given is quite different from our present climatic experience, it is the purpose of this paper to demonstrate that such is inevitable, bearing in mind the different model of the climate machine which is described in Genesis. No machine as delicately balanced as this can have its parts modified without giving a very different performance.

Climate Before the Flood

We begin by noting a part unique to the machine before the Flood, namely, "the waters which were above the firmament" (expanse). If the canopy so formed above the expanse of the atmosphere were in the form of water vapor, then it would be invisible, and being only 60 percent of the weight of air and unable to condense due to the absence of suitable particles, there would be no problem with it remaining there.

It is true that no trace of it is to be found today. Surely, however, its end can be pinpointed to Genesis 7:7-11 when "the windows of heaven were opened" and 40 days of continuous torrential rain fell, for that was no ordinary rainstorm.

The consequences of this new part lying between the machine's energy source (the sun) and the rest of the working parts are profound for the overall performance, e.g.:

1. Temperature

The effect would be rather like a house-owner insulating his loft, for although the canopy would reflect some heat from the sun, the prime difference would be to effectively retain the heat of the earth's atmosphere.

This likens the canopy to a greenhouse which lets in most of the sun's heat but holds most of the heat emitted from the soil. The overall effect in both the greenhouse and the earth's atmosphere below the canopy is to raise the temperatures of the entire space. With a water vapor canopy, therefore, we would have a world of subtropical temperatures from pole to pole.

2. Atmospheric Pressure and Winds

* * * * *

In a world of even temperatures there would be very little pressure variation. In other words, before the Flood there was a planet devoid of strong winds.

* * * * *

3. Rain

Winds are sponges that soak up moisture. The moisture

is only wrung out as the air is cooled, perhaps by rising up over mountains or over cold masses of air that have drifted from the poles. Before the Flood, however, there were no strong winds to soak up moisture, no high mountains, and no cold poles to create cold air masses.

* * * * *

Before the Flood the temperature of the atmosphere did not drop rapidly with height, as today, since the canopy would be trapping the heat. Thus, our bubble of air would hardly get off the ground before it had cooled to the temperature of its warm surroundings. At this point it would sink back to the ground before clouds and rain could form. The canopy, therefore, ensures that every method of producing rain (and rainbows) was cut off. "The Lord God had not caused it to rain upon the earth" nor "put his bow in the clouds when he massed them together."

The only method of wringing out the water content from the air would be to cool it by contact with a cool earth. This, no doubt, occurred after sunset during the "cool of the day" when a ground mist and dew must have formed. Thus the moisture, which could not escape vertically or horizontally, would return to the ground from which it had been evaporated. The supply of water to plants would, therefore, be like that to a plant in a sealed bottle, where lack of watering does not bring about drought.

Genesis 2:5-6 may confirm this mist, although the "rising up continually" and "watering" are more suggestive of springs which presumably were present anyway as the source of the large river "that went out of Eden to water the garden."

Climate After the Flood

1. Temperature

The collapse of the canopy was like smashing all the panes of the greenhouse, that is, it produced a great loss of heat. Up till now, the fact that the equator had always been heated more effectively than the latitudes nearer the poles (due to the higher angle of the sun concentrating the heat) had been masked by the canopy redistributing the heat. Now the full impact of whatever the angle of the sun happened to be at different latitudes would be felt.

Despite the appearance of clouds to reflect some heat,

we can imagine that daytime temperatures would now rise at the equator. On the other hand, latitudes nearer the pole would be appreciably colder. Heat would no longer be transferred from the equator. Neither would there be much to trap the heat emitted from the earth's surface since the two most effective absorbers of it, water vapor and carbon dioxide, would be greatly reduced: the former by loss of the canopy and the latter by burial of vast quantities of living things under the Flood sediment. Accentuating the drop in temperature in the early years would be the abundant volcanic dust in the air ejected during the volcanic activity associated with the Flood. This would reflect the sun's heat. Only when this settled and when life began to establish itself again, thus raising carbon dioxide levels, would an improvement take place. Even today, 20 percent of the world that once could support agriculture before the Flood, is too cold for farming.

2. Wind

The new temperate contrasts created the winds and these, given a twist by the earth's rotation, are the cause of our cyclones and the force behind our ocean currents. Both winds and ocean currents redistribute heat over the earth but not nearly so effectively as the canopy did before them.

3. Rain

The new strong winds would soak up the moisture of the enlarged oceans and, rising up over the new mountains and now cold polar air masses, would release their contents. Elsewhere, warm air pumped up into the atmosphere by rising warm air currents, would produce heavy downpours.

The colder temperatures would ensure that much of the moisture fell as snow especially in the early years after the Flood. Thus the northern continents and Antarctica were smothered in snow which the cooler summers failed to melt. As layer upon layer was added, the snow was compressed to ice and in a very short time the continental ice sheets were formed.

Since rain became the chief source of water supply and since it is carried by moving and rising air, deserts arose after the Flood in those areas where saturated air was unable to reach or rise. Thus, another 20 percent of our planet was lost to agriculture.

Did Climate Before Flood Inhibit Decay and
Fermentation and Partly Explain
Enormous Ages?

In the same chapter we find that Noah began to be an husbandman, planted a vineyard, drank the wine and was drunken. I do not know, but it is very possible that Noah had never known about alcoholic liquor. It is possible that grape juice did not ferment so quickly before the flood as afterward, and that Noah was surprised when he got drunk. At any rate, we know that there was a difference. Now there was rain. Now the sun could come down with infrared rays and others that cause aging. Now there would be deserts and swampland. Now there would be tropic and arctic areas. Now there would be winter and summer. But before the flood, we would suppose that there was not this difference in the climate. No doubt that as in Alaska and in Siberia and at the South Pole there were tropical plants and forests and animals we now find in the Tropics, it was so over the whole earth, protected as it was by the great layer of water vapor.

And surprisingly, men lived to enormous ages before the flood. Adam lived 930 years and begat sons and daughters. Methuselah lived 969 years and died in the year of the flood. The ages are amazing. Even Noah was 600 years old when the flood came and he lived many years afterward. But then the ages of mankind began to decline. Abraham lived only 175 years, Jacob 147 years, and Joseph 110 years. At David's time the customary old age was "threescore years and ten" (Ps. 90:10). Some Christian men who are scientists think that the sun's rays, shining through water vapor above the air, filtered out the infrared rays and others that have an aging effect on men. So we need not be surprised that there were giants in the days before the flood and sometimes in these centuries immediately following. And we need not be surprised to find the fossils of great dinosaurs, saber-toothed tigers, and mammoths and other animals larger in size than their counterparts today. No doubt there were better health and longer life before the flood.

VERSES 23,24:

23 And Lā́-mĕch said unto his wives, Adah and Zĭl-láh, Hear my voice; ye wives of Lā́-mĕch, hearken unto my speech: for I have slain a man to my wounding, and a young man to my hurt.

24 If Cain shall be avenged sevenfold, truly Lā́-mĕch seventy and sevenfold.

No Death Penalty Until After Flood

God would not allow anyone's vengeance on Cain because human government was not set up. Later, after the flood, the Lord plainly commanded Noah, "Whoso sheddeth man's blood, by man shall his blood be shed" (Gen. 9:6). Later this was incorporated in the Mosaic law (Exod. 21:12). In the New Testament Jesus plainly affirmed the right of the government to put criminals to death in the case of Pilate and some rebels in Luke 13:1-5. And Romans 13:3,4 says that the ruler "is the minister of God to thee for good. . .for he beareth not the sword in vain: for he is the minister of God, a revenger to execute wrath upon him that doeth evil."

VERSES 25,26:

25 ¶ And Adam knew his wife again; and she bare a son, and called his name Seth: For God, *said she*, hath appointed me another seed instead of Abel, whom Cain slew.

26 And to Seth, to him also there was born a son; and he called his name Enos: then began men to call upon the name of the LORD.

The Birth of Seth

Seth was born, we suppose, after Cain killed Abel and Seth took Abel's place, we suppose not only in the mother's love, but as a godly man. Seth then married and had a son named Enos. No doubt Seth married one of his sisters. No doubt Cain did. "Then began men to call upon the name of the Lord." That would mean, we think, that now clustered around Seth and with his descendants, people developed systematic habits of prayer and sacrifices like those of Abel, and conscious enjoyment of God's fellowship.

GENESIS 5

THE GENEALOGIES FROM ADAM TO NOAH

THIS *is* the book of the generations of Adam. In the day that God created man, in the likeness of God made he him;

2 Male and female created he them; and blessed them, and called their name Adam, in the day when they were created.

3 ¶ And Adam lived an hundred and thirty years, and begat *a son* in his own likeness, after his image; and called his name Seth:

4 And the days of Adam after he had begotten Seth were eight hundred years: and he begat sons and daughters:

5 And all the days that Adam lived were nine hundred and thirty years: and he died.

After Abel had been slain and when Adam was 130 years old, God gave him another son, Seth. Seth was "after his image." The son looked like the father. Then Adam lived 800 years more and "begat sons and daughters." How much of this time was spent in the Garden of Eden before sin came in and they were cast out, I do not know. Here begins a godly line, under Seth, taking Abel's place, and an ungodly line of men, headed by Cain.

Notice in each line there is an Enoch and there are other similar names, but out of Cain's children there seemed to have been none that pleased God. Outstanding among the men of this generation is Enoch, the seventh from Adam in Seth's line who "walked with God and was not, for God took him." That is, when he was 365 years old, he was translated, taken to be with God without dying.

In Jude 14 we are reminded of the first prophecy ever given to man of the second coming of Christ, as far as we have any scriptural record. Enoch then was a prophet, though no other details of his prophecy are given. Methuselah, Enoch's son, is famous because he reached the astounding age of 969 years—lacking only 31 years reaching a thousand years! If you read carefully, you can prove by the 5th chapter that Methuselah died in the year of the flood. He was not in the ark, and he may have died in the flood. If so, it would show that he paid no attention to the prophecies of his godly father Enoch, nor to the preaching of his grandson, Noah; for it seems clear that all who died in the flood were *unbelievers*.

VERSES 6-32:

The Family of Seth

6 And Seth lived an hundred and five years, and begat Enos:

7 And Seth lived after he begat Enos eight hundred and seven years, and begat sons and daughters:

8 And all the days of Seth were nine hundred and twelve years: and he died.

9 ¶ And Enos lived ninety years, and begat Cā-ĭ-nǎn:

10 And Enos lived after he begat Cā-ĭ-nǎn eight hundred and fifteen years, and begat sons and daughters:

11 And all the days of Enos were nine hundred and five years: and he died.

12 ¶ And Cā-ĭ-nǎn lived seventy years, and begat Mă-hăl-ă-lêèl:

13 And Cā-ĭ-nǎn lived after he begat Mă-hăl-ă-lêèl eight hundred and forty years, and begat sons and daughters:

14 And all the days of Cā-ĭ-nǎn were nine hundred and ten years: and he died.

15 ¶ And Mă-hăl-ă-lêèl lived sixty and five years, and begat Jared:

16 And Mă-hăl-ă-lêèl lived after he begat Jared eight hundred and thirty years, and begat sons and daughters:

17 And all the days of Mă-hăl-ă-lêèl were eight hundred ninety and five years: and he died.

18 ¶ And Jared lived an hundred sixty and two years, and he begat Enoch:

19 And Jared lived after he begat Enoch eight hundred years, and begat sons and daughters:

20 And all the days of Jared were nine hundred sixty and two years: and he died.

21 ¶ And Enoch lived sixty and five years, and begat Mĕ-thū-sĕ-lǎh:

22 And Enoch walked with God after he begat Mĕ-thū-sĕ-lǎh three hundred years, and begat sons and daughters:

23 And all the days of Enoch were three hundred sixty and five years:

24 And Enoch walked with God: and he *was* not; for God took him.

25 And Mĕ-thū-sĕ-lǎh lived an hundred eighty and seven years, and begat Lā-mĕch.

26 And Mĕ-thū-sĕ-lǎh lived after he begat Lā-mĕch seven hundred eighty and two years, and begat sons and daughters:

27 And all the days of Mĕ-thū-sĕ-lǎh were nine hundred sixty and nine years: and he died.

28 ¶ And Lā-mĕch lived an hundred eighty and two years, and begat a son:

29 And he called his name Noah, saying, This *same* shall comfort us concerning our work and toil of our hands, because of the ground which the LORD hath cursed.

30 And Lā-mĕch lived after he begat Noah five hundred ninety and five years, and begat sons and daughters:

31 And all the days of Lā-mĕch

were seven hundred seventy and
seven years: and he died.

32 And Noah was five hundred
years old: and Noah begat Shem,
Ham, and Jā-phĕth.

Note the Ages of Men in This Chapter

Adam lived 930 years, Seth lived 912 years, Cainan 910
years, Jared 962 years, Methuselah 969 years. Yes, we are
to believe that they were literal years. Some one suggested
that maybe the writer meant months. That would mean
five-year-old boys having children when a man listed as
sixty-five years old had a son. No, the enormous life and the
strength of men before the flood were inherited from a
perfect creation and growing in a world that was then
protected, we suppose, by that vapor of "waters which were
above the firmament" (Gen. 1:7) so that some of the
infrared rays did not shine through and thus people did not
age as fast. So men lived to enormous ages. There is a
declining strength in the race which is according to the
second law of thermodynamics of science that strength and
efficiency decrease and disorganization instead of
organization comes naturally. Things run down. And we
must remember that the giant mammoths—the saber-
toothed tiger, giant sloths and hippopotami and
rhinoceroses and such animals—whose fossils are found
now from animals that died in the flood—indicated the
enormous strength in life before the flood and, no doubt,
are partly the explanation of giants that came on the earth
then and shortly after the flood.

Count the years from Adam to the flood. Count the life of
each man until the son named here is born, and you will
find the years add up from Adam to Noah, in this chapter,
to 1,556 years. Then there was another hundred years until
the flood came (Gen. 7:6), so from the creation of Adam to
the flood, according to this genealogy, was 1,656.

We do not suppose that exact ages to the month and the
day are intended, but surely this is intended to be an
accurate and divinely inspired genealogy of the time from
Adam to the flood.

This genealogy is repeated, going all the way back from

Heli, the father-in-law of Joseph and so the father of Mary, to Adam, in Luke 3:23-38. This genealogy is also repeated in I Chronicles 1:1-4.

It is possible that for good reasons God might in some genealogies leave out one unworthy person, but still the genealogies are intended to be taken at face value, and there is no reasonable way for a Bible believer to suppose that it was much longer than the 1,656 years from the creation until the flood. And the time from the flood down to the time of Christ is also pretty carefully revealed in the Scriptures. We do not guarantee that Bishop Ussher, in his chronology, was accurate to the day or the month or even to a particular year, but if the Bible is to be taken at literal face value, his chronology is generally reliable and based upon actual figures in the Scripture.

In the midst of this genealogy there is a miracle. "Enoch walked with God: and he was not; for God took him" (vs. 24). We believe that Enoch was simply taken to Heaven alive, as was Elijah. And in Jude is a marvelous revelation not anywhere else recorded: "And Enoch also, the seventh from Adam, prophesied of these, saying, Behold, the Lord cometh with ten thousands of his saints, To execute judgment upon all, and to convince all that are ungodly among them of all their ungodly deeds which they have ungodly committed, and of all their hard speeches which ungodly sinners have spoken against him" (Jude 14,15). So Enoch was a prophet of God and walked with God and God took him. What a bright spot in the genealogy!

Lamech was evidently a spiritual, godly man. When his son was born "he called his name Noah, saying, This same shall comfort us concerning our work and toil of our hands, because of the ground which the Lord hath cursed." Since Lamech lived, after Noah was born, 595 years, he lived during the time the ark was in process of building and, while the judgment of God waited, five years after his death the flood came.

This Is the History of the Godly Line of Seth

We notice that Adam lived 800 years and begat sons and daughters. No more of them are named after Seth. Seth begat Enos. He probably had many other children, but they are not named, and so through the whole list only one son is named for this is a line down to Noah and then we go from Noah down to Abraham, Isaac, and Jacob and the tribe of Judah and David down to Christ.

But men lived to enormous ages and in these 1,600 years millions of people were born and lived to cover the earth, no doubt. Millions of people died in the flood, and there was a reason why the flood must cover the whole earth and destroy the earth with its burden of a race of sinful men, except Noah and his family.

When Noah was 500 years old, Shem, Ham, and Japheth were born. We do not suppose they were triplets but perhaps a year or two apart. God is using a simple, round number. A like statement is in Genesis 11:26, "And Terah lived seventy years, and begat Abram, Nahor, and Haran."

GENESIS 6

AND it came to pass, when men began to multiply on the face of the earth, and daughters were born unto them,

2 That the sons of God saw the daughters of men that they *were* fair; and they took them wives of all which they chose.

PRECEDING THE FLOOD

Intermarriage of Children of Seth With Wicked Descendants of Cain

There are several indications that the "sons of God" were of the godly line of Seth. In Genesis 4:25,26 we learn that about Seth Eve said, "For God, said she, hath appointed me another seed instead of Abel, whom Cain slew." And then the next verse shows us about Seth's son, "Then began men to call upon the name of the Lord." I take it that Seth was righteous like Abel whose place he took, and that it was through Seth and his descendants that "then began men to call upon the name of the Lord."

Also, as we read through Genesis, chapter 5, we find that the godly men, including Enoch who walked with God and was translated, and Noah, were descendants of Seth. So we take it these were godly, righteous people.

Also, throughout the Bible and Christian literature, saved people are called "sons of God," or "children of God," so we would suppose that the descendants of Seth here are godly people, like those named in chapter 5, and were called "sons of God."

On the other hand, Cain was a wicked man, and although his descendants are named in chapter 4, nothing is said about any of them serving the Lord. So they are not sons of God but were natural, fleshly sons of men; and so good Bible students are pretty well agreed that here the "sons of God" refer to the line of Seth, and the "daughters of men" refer to those natural, unconverted women that the sons of God married and led the world into backsliding and sin.

Not the Marriage of Angels With Men but Saved Men With Ungodly Women

Dr. Scofield says,

> Some hold that these "sons of God" were the "angels which kept not their first estate" (Jude 6). It is asserted that the title is in the O. T. exclusively used of angels. But this is an error (Isa. 43.6). Angels are spoken of in a sexless way. No female angels are mentiond in Scripture, and we are expressly told that marriage is unknown among angels (Mt. 22.30). The uniform Hebrew and Christian interpretation has been that verse 2 marks the breaking down of the separation between the godly line of Seth and the godless line of Cain, and so the failure of the testimony to Jehovah committed to the line of Seth (Gen. 4.26).

Matthew Henry says about this verse:

> Mixed marriages (v. 2) *The sons of God* (that is, the professors of religion, who were called by the name of the Lord, and called upon that name), *married the daughters of men*, that is, those that were profane, and strangers to God and godliness. The posterity of Seth did not keep by themselves, as they ought to have done, both for the preservation of their own purity and in detestation of the apostasy. They intermingled themselves with the excommunicated race of Cain: *They took them wives of all that they chose*. But what was amiss in these marriages? (1.) They chose only by the eye: *They saw that they were fair*, which was all they looked at. (2.) They followed the choice which their own corrupt affections made: they took *all that they chose*, without advice and consideration. But, (3.) That which proved of such bad consequence to them was that they *married strange wives, were unequally yoked with unbelievers*, 2 Cor. vi. 14. This was forbidden to Israel, Deut. vii. 3,4. It was the unhappy occasion of Solomon's apostasy (1 Kings xi. 1-4), and was of bad consequence to the Jews after their return out of Babylon, Ezra ix. 1,2. Note, professors of religion, in marrying both themselves and their children, should make conscience of keeping within the bounds of

profession. The bad will sooner debauch the good than the good reform the bad. Those that profess themselves the children of God must not marry without his consent, which they have not if they join in affinity with his enemies.

Martin Luther says,

By "sons of God" Moses means the male descendants of the patriarchs who had the promise of the blessed Saviour. In the New Testament they are called the believers, who call God their Father and by Him are called His children. The Jews foolishly explain this expression to designate evil spirits from whom came the generation of the ungodly.

H. C. Leupold says,

Here now is the natural sequence of thought: after the Cainites were observed to be going in one definite direction in their development, and the Sethites, too, were seen to be going in an entirely different direction, and these two streams of mankind were strictly keeping apart because they were so utterly divergent in character, now (ch. 6) the two streams begin to commingle, and as a result moral distinctions are obliterated and the Sethites, too, become so badly contaminated that the existing world order must be definitely terminated.

The interpretation of some that the "sons of God" here who married "the daughters of men" were angels is not reasonable nor logical. If angels neither marry nor are given in marriage but are sexless creatures, then they have neither the capacity nor the desire for sex. Since the angels do not reproduce angels, it is foolish to suppose that they could reproduce men. And if angels were to take on the form of men and thus be miraculously allowed to marry with human beings, it would take a miracle of God, which surely He would never allow, since it would be sin. And if these were angels of God, and in some strange way that one time in the history of the world mated with people, then what was the lesson and what the benefit to us for it to be in the Bible? But since these "sons of God" were evidently of the godly line of Seth and are marrying the daughters of the wicked line of Cain, the pungent and important lesson is for all of us.

For Saved to Marry the Unconverted Is Disastrous

Marriage is the most intimate of all human relationship and in some sense has more to do with the spirit of man than any other relationship. Oh, then, what sin when like marries unlike, when the righteous marries the wicked.

Going into the land of Canaan, the children of Israel were plainly commanded that when they came among the Hittites, the Girgashites, the Amorites, the Canaanites, the Perizzites, the Hivites, and the Jebusites, "Neither shalt thou make marriages with them; thy daughter thou shalt not give unto his son, nor his daughter shalt thou take unto thy son. For they will turn away thy son from following me, that they may serve other gods: so will the anger of the Lord be kindled against you, and destroy thee suddenly" (Deut. 7:3,4). That admonition is repeated more than once to the children of Israel. They were not to marry heathen people.

Solomon sinned in marrying heathen women. First Kings 11:1-8 says:

"But king Solomon loved many strange women, together with the daughter of Pharaoh, women of the Moabites, Ammonites, Edomites, Zidonians, and Hittites; Of the nations concerning which the Lord said unto the children of Israel, Ye shall not go in to them, neither shall they come in unto you: for surely they will turn away your heart after their gods: Solomon clave unto these in love. And he had seven hundred wives, princesses, and three hundred concubines: and his wives turned away his heart. For it came to pass, when Solomon was old, that his wives turned away his heart after other gods: and his heart was not perfect with the Lord his God, as was the heart of David his father. For Solomon went after Ashtoreth the goddess of the Zidonians, and after Milcom the abomination of the Ammonites. And Solomon did evil in the sight of the Lord, and went not fully after the Lord, as did David his father. Then did Solomon build an high place for Chemosh, the abomination of Moab, in the hill that is before Jerusalem,

and for Molech, the abomination of the children of Ammon. And likewise did he for all his strange wives, which burnt incense and sacrificed unto their gods."

One cannot take fire in his bosom and not be burned.

To have fellowship in spiritual matters with the wicked is so often forbidden in the Bible. Psalm 1:1 says, "Blessed is the man that walketh not in the counsel of the ungodly, nor standeth in the way of sinners, nor sitteth in the seat of the scornful."

Second Corinthians 6:14-18 says:

"Be ye not unequally yoked together with unbelievers: for what fellowship hath righteousness with unrighteousness? and what communion hath light with darkness? And what concord hath Christ with Belial? or what part hath he that believeth with an infidel? And what agreement hath the temple of God with idols? for ye are the temple of the living God; as God hath said, I will dwell in them, and walk in them; and I will be their God, and they shall be my people. Wherefore come out from among them, and be ye separate, saith the Lord, and touch not the unclean thing; and I will receive you, And will be a Father unto you, and ye shall be my sons and daughters, saith the Lord Almighty."

So heretofore there was one group of people who seemed to keep themselves somewhat separate from the ungodly descendants of Cain. But now they intermarry, the sons of God with the daughters of men. And so there seems to have been no one left but Noah to stand firmly, plainly alone in this heathen, godless world.

VERSE 3:

3 And the LORD said, My spirit shall not always strive with man, for that he also *is* flesh: yet his days shall be an hundred and twenty years.

God's Spirit Will Not Always Strive

The blessed Spirit of God strove with these men before

the flood to repent, to return to God. First Peter 3:18-20 tells us, "Christ. . .by the Spirit: By which also he went and preached unto the spirits in prison; Which sometime were disobedient, when once the longsuffering of God waited in the days of Noah, while the ark was a preparing, wherein few, that is, eight souls were saved by water." So Christ was in the saving business in the Old Testament, and the Holy Spirit was warning men then as now.

We do not wonder that Jesus gave the solemn warning about that blasphemy against the Holy Spirit which has no forgiveness. Surely He did not mean simply saying certain blasphemous words but a blasphemous heart like those Pharisees who saw the miracles of Jesus and hated Him and must have known He is all He claimed to be, but they turned their wicked hearts away and thus they resisted and blasphemed the Holy Spirit that convicted them. Jesus "knew their thoughts" and it was their thoughts He rebuked.

An unpardonable sin? Yes, and even today, no doubt, the Spirit calls and calls. But a heart may become so set against God and so become no longer amenable to His sweet insistence and thus pass beyond the time he can ever be saved. God does not change, but when it is no longer possible that one be saved, the Spirit of God quits His calling: "My spirit shall not always strive with man," the Scripture says.

"Yet his days shall be an hundred and twenty years" means, I think, that soon these enormous ages—800, 900 years—will be cut down, limited, in a few generations, declining immediately after the flood, until in David's day threescore and ten years was a normal old age. God had Moses write this down (Exod. 24:4) and Moses died at 120.

VERSES 4-7:

4 There were giants in the earth in | those days; and also after that, when

he sons of God came in unto the daughters of men, and they bare *hildren* to them, the same *became* mighty men which *were* of old, men *of* renown.

5 ¶ And God saw that the wicked-**ness** of man *was* great in the earth, **ind** *that* every imagination of the houghts of his heart *was* only evil continually.

6 And it repented the LORD that he had made man on the earth, and it grieved him at his heart.

7 And the LORD said, I will destroy man whom I have created from the face of the earth; both man, and beast, and the creeping thing, and the fowls of the air; for it repenteth me that I have made them.

God Determines to Destroy the World

There were giants in the earth in those days. The enormous strength of original mankind, with no taint in the blood until centuries of sin weakened mankind, was enormous, so the long ages of 800-900 years and more before the flood. And so the enormous size of some of the men. So note also the same conditions on the earth probably protected by the canopy of water vapor so that aging infrared rays could not come through, and with the pleasing climate, resulted in the enormous mammoths whose bodies are found, now destroyed in the flood, and such beasts as the saber-toothed tiger, the giant sloths and the dinosaurs. I am saying there were giants in the earth.

Down in Texas, embedded in the stone bottom of a river, the small Paluxy River near Glen Rose, were found the footprints of a man, near the footprint of a dinosaur, both made in the mud which was soon covered again and became stone. The man's foot was eighteen inches long and he must have been eight or nine feet high. That was a man, no doubt, soon after the flood.

And no doubt there were lingering traces of the giants down through the centuries. Some were among the Philistines, like Goliath and his family. Some were the Anakims and one was the giant king Og of Bashan whose bedstead was nine cubits in length and four cubits in width (Deut. 3:11).

There were giants in the earth in those days.

It may be also that when the separated line of Seth gave up the separation and intermarried with the sons of Cain that there was a new vigor in the race because of the cross. Stockmen find now that to cross Shorthorn and Hereford cattle gives a new vigor and strength and so prize calves at the fat stock show are sometimes so crossed. At any rate there were giants and famous men of might and war before the flood.

But the wickedness of man! Note how terrible. It was "great in the earth." Not only so but "every imagination of the thoughts of his heart was only evil" and "only evil," and that "continually." Oh, was there not a single heart turning to God? No. Noah preached for a hundred years without a convert except his wife, his three sons and their wives. Now there must come judgment.

"It repented the Lord that he had made man on the earth, and it grieved him at his heart." Oh, the grief of God as He looked on the race of men He had made and said, "It was good." Now sin has ruined the handiwork of God. Now man who was made to honor God and love Him has become the enemy of God, enslaved by sin and so perverted that there are no good thoughts, no good intentions, no repenting, no righteousness. They must be destroyed.

God must start over with Noah and his family alone on the earth.

Some have been shocked that God would destroy the millions of people by the flood, at one time. But what is the difference between all dying now and dying bit by bit through another fifty years or so, or a hundred? For "it is appointed unto men once to die, but after this the judgment" (Heb. 9:27). "The wages of sin is death." Like it or not, when Adam and Eve sinned they became dead in trespasses and in sin and death passed on the whole human race. And now whether all die en masse at one time or whether they die separately, it does not change the fact. Sin brings death and death is at the judgment of God.

Would you say that God ought not have anything to say about when this death should come on sinners? That would be foolish.

And we remember that every person's breath is in the

hand of God and Jesus said, "Fear not them which kill the body, but are not able to kill the soul: but rather fear him which is able to destroy both soul and body in hell" (Matt. 10:28).

Remember how God destroyed Pharaoh and his army. Remember how God brought a great plague of fiery serpents on Israel because of their bitter complaining against God and Moses, in Numbers 21:5-9. Remember how Dathan and Abiram, because of their wicked rebellion, had the ground open and they fell bodily into the pit!

Remember that the Lord Jesus, in Luke 13:1-5, voiced His approval when Pilate, representing the government acting for God, put to death the rebel Galileans and that when the wall fell on those wicked men at Jerusalem, Jesus counted that the act of God, as it was. And He said, "Except ye repent, ye shall all likewise perish."

In our time God has put the death penalty for murder and certain other crimes in the hands of the government and He says, "Rulers. . .beareth not the sword in vain: for he is the minister of God, a revenger to execute wrath upon him that doeth evil" (Rom. 13:3,4).

But think of all the little unaccountable children who died suddenly in the flood. Well, then, remember the death of the firstborn children among the Egyptians on the passover day in Egypt. Was that bad? How much better for a little one, unaccountable, and kept by God's mercy from Hell until he becomes accountable—how much better for the little one to go to Heaven now instead of to live and become a well-taught enemy of God, certain for Hell. The greatest mercy that could happen to these children was to die now and go to the arms of a loving God before they were accountable sinners. For remember the Scripture says in I Corinthians 15:22, "For as in Adam all die, even so in Christ shall all be made alive." No one goes to Hell because of the taint of inherited sin but only for his own sin.

But if these had lived to become accountable, they would have chosen to sin as does every person in the world when he comes to know right from wrong. Yes, it was the mercy of God that babies should die in the flood instead of living to be vicious sinners and then go to Hell.

And it is a reminder of the wickedness of these people that in a hundred years of preaching, with the power of the Holy Spirit as Christ preached to them through Noah, not one was saved.

They must be destroyed.

VERSES 8-13:

8 But Noah found grace in the eyes of the LORD.

9 ¶ These *are* the generations of Noah: Noah was a just man *and* perfect in his generations, *and* Noah walked with God.

10 And Noah begat three sons, Shem, Ham, and Jā-phĕth.

11 The earth also was corrupt before God, and the earth was filled with violence.

12 And God looked upon the earth, and, behold, it was corrupt; for all flesh had corrupted his way upon the earth.

13 And God said unto Noah, The end of all flesh is come before me; for the earth is filled with violence through them; and, behold, I will destroy them with the earth.

Godly Noah Alone in a Godless Race

But Noah "found grace in the eyes of the Lord." What a strong character he must have been to resist the pull of the whole race! Note the way he is described here: he was a "just man." He was "perfect in his generations," that is, all through his life. Not sinless, but the term "perfect" means completely sold out to God, upright or sincere. And like it was said of Enoch, "Noah walked with God." Noah is one of the heroes of the faith mentioned in Hebrews 11:7, and what a godly man he was standing alone in the midst of a gainsaying world, believing God when all the rest of the world denied Him, making that giant oceanliner of a boat inland where people thought it could never float. The faith and the separated godliness of Noah pleased God greatly and Noah "became heir of the righteousness which is by faith," we are told in Hebrews 11:7.

And I Peter 3:18-20 tells us that when Noah preached to the people it was Christ preaching through the Spirit.

Those people who heard the Gospel, by Noah, could have been saved and Noah himself trusted in the great Saviour whom he had not seen but whom he preached.

Notice that where wickedness increases, violence increases. As the schools in America turn away from the Bible and direct creation and teach the folly of atheistic evolution and as the Bible is forbidden and as prayer is forbidden in the schools, so immorality and adultery become widespread and the murder of unborn infants is now legalized and defended. You need not be surprised at the flood of lawlessness and crime increasing on every hand. So was the violence before the flood and God said, "The earth is filled with violence through them; and, behold, I will destroy them with the earth." Notice that the destruction is not only to be for the race but "for the earth." That is the world that then was with its cities, its rivers, its mountains, its forests, its wild beasts, its oceans—all this was to be utterly destroyed with a kind of cataclysmic flood that would not only cover all the mountains in the earth with water but with tidal waves flowing thousands of feet of debris and mud over cities and forests and animals being buried in these layers and with volcanoes and earthquakes and glaciers, following for months after the flood. God would destroy all the earth that then was or as I Peter 3:6 says, "Whereby the world that then was, being overflowed with water, perished," along with the people of it.

VERSES 14-22:

14 ¶ Make thee an ark of gopher wood; rooms shalt thou make in the ark, and shalt pitch it within and without with pitch.

15 And this *is the fashion* which thou shalt make it *of:* The length of the ark *shall be* three hundred cubits, the breadth of it fifty cubits, and the height of it thirty cubits.

16 A window shalt thou make to the ark, and in a cubit shalt thou finish it above; and the door of the ark shalt thou set in the side thereof; *with* lower, second, and third *stories* shalt thou make it.

17 And, behold, I, even I, do bring a flood of waters upon the earth, to destroy all flesh, wherein *is* the breath

of life, from under heaven; *and* every thing that *is* in the earth shall die.

18 But with thee will I establish my covenant; and thou shalt come into the ark, thou, and thy sons, and thy wife, and thy sons' wives with thee.

19 And of every living thing of all flesh, two of every *sort* shalt thou bring into the ark, to keep *them* alive with thee; they shall be male and female.

20 Of fowls after their kind, and of cattle after their kind, of every creeping thing of the earth after his kind, two of every *sort* shall come unto thee, to keep *them* alive.

21 And take thou unto thee of all food that is eaten, and thou shalt gather *it* to thee; and it shall be for food for thee, and for them.

22 Thus did Noah; according to all that God commanded him, so did he.

The Enormous Ark

How big was the ark? It was 300 cubits long, 50 cubits wide, 30 cubits high. A cubit was originally intended to be the measure of a man's forearm to the tip of his fingers. Ordinarily that will be 18 to 27 inches. The cubit varied because there was no standard measurement put away in Washington, D. C., by which all the yardsticks were made as now. It may have been more before the flood, when men were larger and taller, when many were giants—the cubit might have been much longer. It was three stories high and if a cubit was only eighteen inches, the three stories would be about fifteen feet high. It would be 450 feet long and 45 feet wide. But with a few inches longer to the cubit, it would have been twice as big in volume. It had a window (or windows) near the top which could be opened (Gen. 8:6).

And Noah was to have some of every living thing of all flesh in the ark, "Two of every sort." They were to be male and female, fowls and cattle and creeping things. And he was to take of clean beasts by sevens, possibly to provide animals for the sacrifice of Noah later after the flood.

Of course, we must expect miracles in connection with this matter. The flood itself was miraculous. And God, no doubt, put it in the hearts of animals to come two and two into the ark and to be subject to Noah. All kinds of food was stored and they had a hundred years to get it ready and no doubt they did.

Since there would only need to be one pair of dogs to provide the 104 kinds of dogs we have now, perhaps that would include the wolves also which interbreed with dogs.

It may be there would only be one pair of the cat family for lions and tigers and leopards and mountain lions are all cats and we know that some of them, perhaps all of them, can interbreed. These varieties could come from a single stock. There would only need to be two horses and from them would come all the thoroughbreds, the giant Percheron and Clydesdale, the Arabians and the Shetlands and other ponies.

Wise men have figured out that there would be abundant space for all the animals necessary in the ark and feed could be preserved for them. It is possible, of course, that God would set out to preserve them, could have bears and some other animals go into their winter sleep, hibernation. However God wanted to handle it He did and miraculously He saved alive two of every kind of animal.

Some of them have since become extinct as have most of the dinosaurs (we have left, of course, crocodiles, alligaters, and giant lizards) of the same general family. But we can believe what God says here.

Oh, what a hundred years' preparation building that giant boat and gathering up the food and preparing for the time!

GENESIS 7

THE WORLD WAS DESTROYED IN A FLOOD AND MORE THAN A YEAR OF VOLCANOES, EARTHQUAKES AND TIDAL WAVES

VERSES 1-9:

AND the LORD said unto Noah, Come thou and all thy house into the ark; for thee have I seen righteous before me in this generation.

2 Of every clean beast thou shalt take to thee by sevens, the male and his female: and of beasts that *are* not clean by two, the male and his female.

3 Of fowls also of the air by sevens, the male and the female; to keep seed alive upon the face of all the earth.

4 For yet seven days, and I will cause it to rain upon the earth forty days and forty nights; and every living substance that I have made will I destroy from off the face of the earth.

5 And Noah did according unto all that the LORD commanded him.

6 And Noah *was* six hundred years old when the flood of waters was upon the earth.

7 ¶ And Noah went in, and his sons, and his wife, and his sons' wives with him, into the ark, because of the waters of the flood.

8 Of clean beasts, and of beasts that *are* not clean, and of fowls, and of every thing that creepeth upon the earth,

9 There went in two and two unto Noah into the ark, the male and the female, as God had commanded Noah.

The Flood That Was to Cover the Whole World

Noah was now 600 years old. It had been one hundred years since "Noah begat Shem, Ham, and Japheth" (Gen. 5:32), and we suppose that long since Noah had been warned about the flood in the 6th chapter. Noah had "righteousness which is by faith," for II Peter 2:5 says, "And spared not the old world, but saved Noah the eighth person, a preacher of righteousness, bringing in the flood upon the world of the ungodly." Noah was "a preacher of righteousness."

It was by faith that Noah built the ark and entered that galaxie of saints recorded in that Hall of Fame in Hebrews 11:7: "By faith Noah, being warned of God of things not seen as yet, moved with fear, prepared an ark to the saving of his house; by the which he condemned the world, and became heir of the righteousness which is by faith."

But in those days, "when once the longsuffering of God waited in the days of Noah, while the ark was a preparing," Christ, through the Holy Spirit in Noah, was preaching to these people who are now those "spirits in prison" (people in Hell). But it was Noah who preached in the power of the Holy Spirit and thus preached Christ to them (I Pet. 3:19,20). Noah, then, had the same anointing of the Spirit that Elijah, Elisha, and Moses had, and the same fullness of the Spirit that was given in the New Testament to John the Baptist and to others at Pentecost and beyond. So Noah, a saved man with the Spirit of God upon him, preached the Gospel and for, we suppose, a hundred years with nobody saved save his own family.

Noah alone, with his family, went into the ark. With them went a great mass of animals that God had moved so that they came, two and two, male and female. Of clean beasts that would be used for sacrifice, they came in by sevens, and fowls of the air by sevens. Of course, this was miraculously controlled.

They went into the ark seven days before the rain began. There that great oceanliner kind of boat sat out on the dry ground. No doubt the foolish and wicked who had heard Noah's preaching all these years mocked at it, as, no doubt, they had mocked at his building such a ship which they thought would never reach the water.

And for the unsaved multitude on the earth, life went on as usual. "They were eating and drinking, marrying and giving in marriage, until the day that Noe entered into the ark, And knew not until the flood came, and took them all away." When Noah and family went into the ark, they still did not repent, they still did not believe, they still scoffed. They were still wicked, Christ-rejecting, God-hating sinners. Then suddenly the flood came and took them all away (Matt. 24:38,39). Just as sudden and unexpected will be the second coming of Christ!

Again God tells how certain and how complete will be the

destruction: "Every living substance that I have made will I destroy from off the face of the earth." No land animals and I suppose no birds and no creeping things or insects (Gen. 7:21) would be left alive outside. This was to be a total destruction of life on the earth. More than that, it was to be a destruction of the earth itself as it then was, its civilization, its cities, its men. Even the rivers and mountains and plains and seas, as the world had been before the flood, were to be destroyed.

VERSES 10-16:

10 And it came to pass after seven days, that the waters of the flood were upon the earth.

11 ¶ In the six hundredth year of Noah's life, in the second month, the seventeenth day of the month, the same day were all the fountains of the great deep broken up, and the windows of heaven were opened.

12 And the rain was upon the earth forty days and forty nights.

13 In the selfsame day entered Noah, and Shem, and Ham, and Jā'-phĕth, the sons of Noah, and Noah's wife, and the three wives of his sons with them, into the ark;

14 They, and every beast after his kind, and all the cattle after their kind, and every creeping thing that creepeth upon the earth after his kind, and every fowl after his kind, every bird of every sort.

15 And they went in unto Noah into the ark, two and two of all flesh, wherein is the breath of life.

16 And they that went in, went in male and female of all flesh, as God had commanded him: and the LORD shut him in.

Whence Came the Water to Cover the Earth?

The flood began "in the six hundredth year of Noah's life, in the second month, the seventeenth day." Note the elements of the flood. First, "All the fountains of the great deep [were] broken up." We suppose that "the great deep" means the oceans. The convulsion, the catastrophe with which God is to destroy the earth, will include the breaking up of all the natural boundaries of the oceans and seas. Now then volcanic activity, earthquakes and other things will cause tidal waves to sweep over the land. Mountains will rise, volcanoes will spew out the lava, covering thousands of square miles of ground, the bottoms of the sea will fall and rise, tidal waves around the earth will wash across the highest mountains, will cover the greatest forests, will cover the bodies of the slain animals with great layers of earth, one kind and another, as the waters wash back and forth. The earth is in convulsion.

Meantime, the "windows of heaven were opened." We suppose that there had never been rain before but "there went up a mist from the earth, and watered the whole face of the ground" (Gen. 2:6). But now the rain came.

Not only rain but evidently there was also a vast overhead reservoir of water released. In the creation God said, "Let there be a firmament in the midst of the waters, and let it divide the waters from the waters. And God made the firmament, and divided the waters which were under the firmament from the waters which were above the firmament: and it was so" (Gen. 1:6,7). The firmament was air above, but even above that was a great mass of waters—"waters which were above the firmament."

We suppose that a great mass of water vapor above the air where the birds fly, like the icy rings that, we are told, still turn as satellites around the planet Saturn, was above the earth. But now Scripture says that "the windows of heaven were opened. And the rain was upon the earth forty days and forty nights."

Now that canopy of water, invisible water vapor above the earth, was turned loose. We suppose that now there would not be enough moisture in the air for it to rain solidly over the whole earth for any extended period of time. But in the flood that water that had been suspended above the earth came down in rain, rain, rain, for forty days and nights!

God repeats here about the entrance to the ark. Verse 16 says, "And they that went in, went in male and female of all flesh, as God had commanded him: and the Lord shut him in." I would suppose that great ark stood open for the seven days. That is an invitation of mercy to those who rejected mercy all those years. I suppose they had

committed the unpardonable sin in that they had so set
their hearts against God that they now could not be moved.
They had become so settled in their rejection of Christ that
they felt no conviction, no turning of repentance. Long ago
they had turned away for good. But the unpardonable sin
does not change God; it changes sinners. It does not close
the offer of mercy; it simply makes the man who commits
that sin unable to want mercy, unable to turn for mercy; he
has passed the place of forgiveness and the opportunity is
gone forever.

". . .and the Lord shut him in" (vs. 16). God gave
instructions about the building of the ark. He forewarned
Noah and his family about it. The ark is built. They are
instructed to enter the ark; they do. God Himself shut the
door! What a picture of salvation! The ark pictures Christ,
the "ark of safety." One who is in Christ is safe. Jesus said,
"My sheep hear my voice, and I know them, and they
follow me: And I give unto them eternal life; and they shall
never perish, neither shall any man pluck them out of my
hand. My Father, which gave them me, is greater than all;
and no man is able to pluck them out of my Father's hand"
(John 10:27-29).

It would be utterly impossible for Noah to save himself in
this great flood. It took an ark, God's ark. God had shut the
door. God had to preserve that great vessel as it moved on
the waters, as it plunged in the convulsive tidal waves that
went around the world. But it was well made and they were
perfectly safe there. So is one who puts his trust in Christ.
There may be doubts and fears, but God is faithful. He
keeps His own.

John 5:24 says, "Verily, verily, I say unto you, He that
heareth my word, and believeth on him that sent me, hath
everlasting life, and shall not come into condemnation; but
is passed from death unto life."

> Safe in the arms of Jesus,
> Safe on His gentle breast,
> There by His love o'er-shaded,
> Sweetly my soul shall rest.

VERSES 17-24:

17 And the flood was forty days upon the earth; and the waters increased, and bare up the ark, and it was lift up above the earth.

18 And the waters prevailed, and were increased greatly upon the earth; and the ark went upon the face of the waters.

19 And the waters prevailed exceedingly upon the earth; and all the high hills, that *were* under the whole heaven, were covered.

20 Fifteen cubits upward did the waters prevail; and the mountains were covered.

21 And all flesh died that moved upon the earth, both of fowl, and of cattle, and of beast, and of every creeping thing that creepeth upon the earth, and every man:

22 All in whose nostrils *was* the breath of life, of all that *was* in the dry *land*, died.

23 And every living substance was destroyed which was upon the face of the ground, both man, and cattle, and the creeping things, and the fowl of the heaven; and they were destroyed from the earth: and Noah only remained *alive*, and they that *were* with him in the ark.

24 And the waters prevailed upon the earth an hundred and fifty days.

The Whole World Covered With the Flood

Some people have supposed it was a local flood and that one valley was flooded. No, no! The Scripture plainly says, "And the waters prevailed exceedingly upon the earth; and all the high hills, that were under the whole heaven, were covered." That has to mean the whole world. And the Scripture says that "the mountains were covered." And if it were simply a flood in one valley, then how could that flood continue covering the hills and the mountains in that valley for six months without flowing away? No, it was more than that; it covered the whole world! Only someone who wants to make concessions to infidels and try to please the would-be scientists and their unbelief would say that this was only a local flood.

Besides that, in these more than sixteen hundred years of life on the earth there would be millions of people, and they were to be destroyed, all but Noah and his family. Besides that, the Scripture says, "And every living substance was destroyed which was upon the face of the ground, both man, and cattle, and the creeping things, and the fowl of the heaven; and they were destroyed from the earth: and Noah only remained alive, and they that were with him in the ark" (vs. 23). So no honest Bible believer can take it as less than what it is expressly said to be—a worldwide flood covering the whole world.

The waters were "fifteen cubits upward" above the mountains. Suppose we say a cubit would be 23 or 24 inches; then the highest mountains were covered with 30 feet of water. Not a giraffe, not an elephant could reach above that highest mountain to get breath. Every living thing in the world that had breath died except those in the ark.

It may be that "the fountains of the great deep" of Genesis 7:11 meant that great quantities of water had been held in caverns under the earth. I rather think that it simply means that the great canopy of water vapor above the earth now descended in a mighty rain, and so the earth had more water on it than it had ever had before. And the mountains were covered.

Then the problem, What went with all the water? Where would it flow to? You will find that Noah stayed in the ark for more than a year. And no doubt the ocean basin sank, giant ranges of mountains reared their heads, and so God made room in the oceans for the water and it drained away. Meantime, earthquakes and floods and convulsion of the earth continued for long months, more than a year, including the flood and the aftereffects that went with the flood.

Verse 12 says, "And the rain was upon the earth forty days and forty nights." Verse 17 says, "And the flood was forty days upon the earth; and the waters increased, and bare up the ark, and it was lift up above the earth." Evidently the flood increased after the rain stopped. But there was another source besides rain. Genesis 7:11,12 says, "In the six hundredth year of Noah's life, in the second month, the seventeenth day of the month, the same day were all the fountains of the great deep broken up, and the windows of heaven were opened. And the rain was upon the earth forty days and forty nights."

"The great fountains of the deep were broken up" may

mean that because of great earthquakes and volcanic action, the rising of mountain ranges, the sinking of the sea floor, that the waters of the seas rushed around the earth sweeping all before it in great tidal waves. But it also may mean that some water had been kept within the depths of the earth, and now this was brought out to add to the waters of the rain and the seas.

But it seems clear also that now the waters from above, the great volume of water vapor that had enveloped the earth and insulated it, fell to the earth. We believe that now, the water vapor canopy was removed and the North and South Poles, without any sunlight for six months out of the year, were suddenly frozen with a great cold of outer space. And whatever of the water fell there was snow or turned instantly into ice, so the great ice caps of the North and South Poles were formed. I think, too, that was the cause of the "Ice Age," and that great ice caps pressed down and the ice, spread out in glaciers over the northern parts of the world, covered the land and we think the Antarctica. At any rate, we do not believe there were successive Ice Ages many thousands of years ago. More likely, over 4,500 years ago the Ice Age began and in a few years the glaciers melted back further and further toward the north.

But the water had covered the whole earth. The Lord had said, "For yet seven days, and I will cause it to rain upon the earth forty days and forty nights; and every living substance that I have made will I destroy from off the face of the earth" (Gen. 7:4). The whole earth is involved. And again the Scriptures tell us, "And the waters prevailed exceedingly upon the earth; and all the high hills, that were under the whole heaven, were covered. Fifteen cubits upward did the waters prevail; and the mountains were covered" (Gen. 7:19,20).

GENESIS 8

VERSE 1:

AND God remembered Noah, and every living thing, and all the cattle that *was* with him in the ark: and God made a wind to pass over the earth, and the waters asswaged;

"God Remembered Noah"

In this author's book, *"And God Remembered. . .,"* is a sermon on this subject:

"And God Remembered Noah" (Gen. 8:1); "God Remembered Abraham" (Gen. 19:29); "God Remembered Rachel" (Gen. 30:22); Hannah, "And the Lord Remembered Her" (I Sam. 1:19); "And God Remembered His Covenant," "His Mercy," "His Promises" (Exod. 2:24; Exod. 6:5; Ps. 105:8; Ps. 106:45; Ps. 98:3; Ps. 105:42); "He Remembereth That We Are Dust" (Ps. 103:14); "He Will Remember Their Iniquity" (Hosea 9:9); "Great Babylon Came in Remembrance Before God" (Rev. 16:19).

How wonderful that God never forgets His own! The man who obeyed God's command about the ark is perfectly safe. He may be sure that God will see the thing through. God does not repent of His promises. God does not welsh on His obligations. God remembers His own.

Oh, it was a stormy sea on which that ark floated, but Noah and his family were perfectly safe. They were never out of the eye of God nor out of the mind of God. And in due season God would bring Noah out.

It may have seemed strange that for some seven months after the flood subsided, Noah must remain in the ark. God had other things to do in this terrible destruction of "the world that then was," which perished in the flood (II Pet. 3:6).

Does someone have a promise of God? Then call it to God's attention. He will remember, He will honor His word. Faith is believing that God will do what He said He would, and risking Him to do it. God remembered Noah! And, oh, my heart rejoices that He remembers me. I am His child. "He that spared not his own Son, but delivered him up for us all, how shall he not with him also freely give us all things." God remembers His own.

So "God made a wind to pass over the earth, and the waters asswaged." We may suppose that the winds now are unusual because before the flood, when there was a canopy of water vapor above the firmament and the earth had some hothouse conditions and tropical temperatures even in the Arctic and Antarctic regions, there were no violent winds. So God particularly mentions the wind here as He mentions the rain.

VERSES 2-5:

2 The fountains also of the deep and the windows of heaven were stopped, and the rain from heaven was restrained;

3 And the waters returned from off the earth continually: and after the end of the hundred and fifty days the waters were abated.

4 And the ark rested in the seventh month, on the seventeenth day of the month, upon the mountains of Ararat.

5 And the waters decreased continually until the tenth month: in the tenth *month*, on the first *day* of the month, were the tops of the mountains seen.

1. The Ark at Rest on Mount Ararat

God stopped the downpour of rain. Evidently the canopy that once was above the earth is now all descended and is in the ocean of water that covers the mountains. And the fountains of the deep are stopped. Mighty tidal waves, we suppose, are stopped. Those waves have taken hundreds of feet of soil to cover every forest and cover the bodies of millions of beasts that were drowned. Even on the highest mountains there will be found sea shells. So the increase of the waters for the time being is stayed and restrained. And now, after this, that is after 150 days, "the waters were abated." It had rained forty days and nights, but the waters had prevailed "an hundred and fifty days" (Gen. 7:24). Now the waters begin to decrease until the tenth month, four or five months after the rain has ceased to fall, the tops of the mountains are seen at last. What goes with the water? Ocean basins no doubt are sinking to make room for it, and the tops of the mountains appear.

The ark settled down upon one of the very highest mountains, Mount Ararat.

VERSES 6-14:

6 ¶ And it came to pass at the end of forty days, that Noah opened the window of the ark which he had made:

7 And he sent forth a raven, which went forth to and fro, until the waters were dried up from off the earth.

8 Also he sent forth a dove from him, to see if the waters were abated from off the face of the ground;

9 But the dove found no rest for the sole of her foot, and she returned into him into the ark, for the waters were on the face of the whole earth: then he put forth his hand, and took her, and pulled her in unto him into the ark.

10 And he stayed yet other seven days; and again he sent forth the dove out of the ark;

11 And the dove came in to him in the evening; and, lo, in her mouth was an olive leaf pluckt off: so Noah knew that the waters were abated from off the earth.

12 And he stayed yet other seven days; and sent forth the dove; which returned not again unto him any more.

13 ¶ And it came to pass in the six hundredth and first year, in the first month, the first day of the month, the waters were dried up from off the earth: and Noah removed the covering of the ark, and looked, and, behold, the face of the ground was dry.

14 And in the second month, on the seven and twentieth day of the month, was the earth dried.

2. A Year and Seventeen Days in the Ark!

Do you suppose that Noah was anxious? He was shut up for a year. From seven days (Gen. 7:4) before the second month and the seventeenth day of the 600th year of Noah's life (Gen. 7:11), down to the second month and the twenty-seventh day of the month of the 601st year (vss. 13,14), Noah was in the ark. That is a year and seventeen days!

After the tenth month the tops of the mountains were seen. Forty days more and Noah opened the window of the ark and sent forth the raven. Then he sent forth the dove and the dove returned, showing that the earth was still mainly covered with water. Then another seven days and he sent forth the dove again and it brought an olive leaf. Ah, green things are sprouting up from the debris, and some olive tree, washed away no doubt but now with its roots in the mud, starts to bring forth green leaves and so with other living plants in all the world. And in seven days more the dove was sent forth and stayed away.

In nearly eleven months Noah removed the covering and "behold, the face of the ground was dry." Now, in the second month of the 601st year, on the twenty-seventh day, the earth is dry, and God tells Noah to come forth and all the living things with him.

How long did this flood continue? In Genesis 7:24 we are told, "And the waters prevailed upon the earth an hundred and fifty days." After that, Genesis 8:2 tells us, "The fountains also of the deep and the windows of heaven were stopped, and the rain from heaven was restrained." Then we are told, "And the waters returned from off the earth continually: and after the end of the hundred and fifty days the waters were abated" (Gen. 8:3). I suppose that meant the waters began to recede. Then a month and a half later, "The ark rested in the seventh month, on the seventeenth day of the month, upon the mountains of Ararat" (Gen. 8:4). "And the waters decreased continually until the tenth month: in the tenth month, on the first day of the month, were the tops of the mountains seen" (Gen. 8:5).

Forty days went by, then Noah sent out a raven and sent forth a dove twice and eventually, ". . .It came to pass in the six hundredth and first year, in the first month, the first day of the month, the waters were dried up from off the earth: and Noah removed the covering of the ark, and looked, and, behold, the face of the ground was dry. *And in the second month, on the seven and twentieth day of the month, was the earth dried*" (Gen. 8:13,14). Now after a year and seventeen days, Noah came out of the ark!

Evidently then, the catastrophe was not only one sudden

flood but continued a year and seventeen days (Gen. 7:6; 8:14) of flood and then the things that went with it. No doubt much of the volcanic and earth trembling and changing continued for years!

George Frederick Wright, in The International Standard Bible Encyclopaedia, gives the following:

"NOAH'S LOG BOOK"

Month	Day		Number of days
2	17	All enter the ark; God shuts the door. Rains fall. Floods pour in from sea. Ark floats. Ark sails swiftly..............................	40
3	27	Rain stops. Floods keep pouring in and water rising................	110
7	17	Ark touches bottom on top of high mountains and stays there. Waters stop rising. Water stationary.........................	40
8	27	Waters begin to settle. Settle fifteen cubits in....................	34
10	1	Ark left on dry land. Waters continue to settle. Noah waits.....	40
11	11	Noah sends out a raven. It returns not. Waters settle. Noah waits.............................	7
11	18	Noah sends out a dove. It returns. Waters settle. Noah waits.............................	7
11	25	Noah sends out dove again. Dove brings an olive leaf just grown. Waters settle. Noah waits.........	7
12	2	Noah sends out dove again. It returns not. Waters settle. Noah waits.............................	29
1	1	Noah removes covering, looks all around. No water can be seen. Ground dries up. Noah waits......	56
2	27	God opens the door, and says, "Go forth." Total time of flood....	370

Dr. Wright, in the same article, says:

Owing to the comparatively brief duration of the Noachian Deluge proper, we cannot expect to find many positive indications of its occurrence. Nevertheless, Professor Prestwich (than whom there has been no higher geological authority in England during the last cent.) adduces an array of facts relating to Western Europe and the Mediterranean basin which cannot be ignored (see *Phil. Trans. of the Royal Soc. of Lond.,* CXXIV [1893], 903-84; *SCOT,* 238-82). Among these evidences one of the most convincing is to be found in the cave of San Ciro at the base of the mountains surrounding the plain of Palermo in Sicily. In this cave there was found an immense mass of the bones of hippopotami of all ages down to the foetus, mingled with a few of the deer, ox and elephant. These were so fresh when discovered that they were cut into ornaments and polished and still retained a considerable amount of their nitrogenous matter. Twenty tons of these bones were shipped for commercial purposes in the first six months after their discovery. Evidently the animals furnishing these bones had taken refuge in this cave to escape the rising water which had driven them in from the surrounding plains and cooped them up in the amphitheater of mountains during a gradual depression of the land.

Similar collections of bones are found in various ossiferous fissures, in England and Western Europe, notably in the Rock of Gibraltar and at Santenay, a few miles S. of Chalons in central France, where there is an accumulation of bones in fissures 1,000 ft. above the sea, similar in many respects to that in the cave described at San Ciro, though the bones of hippopotami did not appear in these places; but the bones of wolves, bears, horses and oxen, none of which had been gnawed by carnivora, were indiscriminately commingled as though swept in by all-pervading currents of water. Still further evidence is adduced in the deposits connected with what is called the rubble drift on both sides of the English Channel and on the Jersey Islands. Here in various localities, notably at Brighton, England, and near Calais, France, elephant bones and human implements occur beneath deep deposits of unassorted drift, which is not glacial nor the product of limited and local streams of water, but can be accounted for only by general waves of translation produced when the land was being reelevated from beneath the water by a series of such sudden earthquake shocks as cause the tidal waves which are often so destructive.

3. Mountain Ranges Formed, Earthquakes, Volcanoes Changed Face of Earth

Where did all the waters go? With water enough to cover the whole earth, where did it go? Now there is not enough water in the seas to cover the whole earth, with the surface as it now is; but something happened. Mountain ridges were raised up. From the bowels of the earth volcanoes spouted thousands of square miles of lava, covering the ground. Evidently the basins of the seas were lowered and the water retreated from covering the mountains and from the land as God had set a bound for it.

This mighty movement of the seas retreating from the flood to fill the lowered ocean basins is wonderfully recorded in Psalm 104:5-9:

"Who laid the foundations of the earth, that it should not be removed for ever. Thou coveredst it with the deep as with a garment: the waters stood above the mountains. At thy rebuke they fled; at the voice of thy thunder they hasted away. They go up by the mountains; they go down by the valleys unto the place which thou hast founded for them. Thou hast set a bound that they may not pass over; that they turn not again to cover the earth."

The waters covered the whole earth "as with a garment: the waters stood above the mountains." God set the bounds of the seas so that "they turn not again to cover the earth."

Perhaps inspired Nahum referred to these days at the close of the flood and after, when he said about the Lord, "The mountains quake at him, and the hills melt, and the earth is burned at his presence, yea, the world, and all that dwell therein" (1:5).

God made room in the oceans for all the waters that covered the earth in the flood. As Psalm 33:7 says, "He gathereth the waters of the sea together as an heap: he layeth up the depth in storehouses."

Evidently ancient people had memories and oft-told traditions of the year of the flood and the catastrophes that followed for several years. That is revealed in Psalm 46:1-3: "God is our refuge and strength, a very present help in trouble. Therefore will not we fear, though the earth be removed, and though the mountains be carried into the midst of the sea; Though the waters thereof roar and be troubled, though the mountains shake with the swelling thereof. Selah."

Isaiah has the Lord saying, "Behold, at my rebuke I dry up the sea, I make the rivers a wilderness: their fish stinketh, because there is no water, and dieth for thirst" (Isa. 50:2). Here we can see the vast inland sea in America (now the great plains next to the Rocky Mountains) when the ocean bed was lowered, when the plains were raised up, and the waters broke through the mud layers left by the flood (layers that would soon become stone), and carved out violently the Grand Canyon of the Colorado River. The shorelines of that and of other ancient seas are now discernible in some places. The fish would die and stink. Do modern geologists insist there were no worldwide catastrophe but only uniformitarian natural processes as we now see them? The Bible contradicts them.

There is abundant physical evidence of great volcanic action and earthquakes. Can you imagine the rising from the sea in a short time, the Rocky Mountain range in North America, and the Andes in South America, and the enormous tidal waves it would send around the world? So we may be sure that the volcanoes, the earthquakes that passed over the earth (Gen. 8:1) had a catastrophic effect upon the face of the earth.

Remember that the Scripture says that by the flood, "the world that then was, being overflowed with water, *perished*" (II Pet. 3:6). It is not simply that some men perished, it is not that civilization was wiped out, but the cities themselves were washed away, the rivers and mountains and valleys were changed. Not a single human monument to that race that had turned against God was left. If there were inscriptions, monuments and buildings, they were destroyed. The enormous force of the waters and the turmoil of volcanoes and earthquakes during that flood can only be imagined. At least, suffice it to say that the great forests were covered with layers of mud, then the waters washing back brought more trees and brush and then covered them, perhaps, with another layer of mud of another color making coal beds of the forests. Animals collected in certain areas and were overwhelmed by the floodtide, then buried in the mud; so the fossil beds of the world were formed. We now find sea shells on top of mountains. We now find fossils deep in the earth. Much of that, we suppose, occurred while Noah's ark sat seven months and three days on Mount Ararat (Gen. 8:4, 14).

The coal beds are simply the remains of the giant forests that covered the earth in the tropical climate before the flood.

We do not find many fossils of men before the flood. It may well be that Pekin Man, Heidelburg, Neanderthal men, some of the so-called Early Men found sometimes in caves or as rivers washed the dirt off debris, were people before the flood.

God did not intend for there to be much memorial left to that race of men that He determined to blot out. Not a building, not a single monument to the achievements of men, are left of that age and that civilization. That race, that world perished! Its people, its animals, its cities, its buildings, its roads, its monuments, its books, its culture, its artifacts—all perished as far as we know.

We would expect that men, more intelligent than animals, would be the last to be overwhelmed by the flood. They would run to the mountains. They would take to their boats. If Noah could build a giant ocean-liner-type boat, we may be sure other people had boats, too. And those who were drowned would soon bloat and float on the surface and their bodies would be decayed or eaten by the animals of the sea. So not many fossils of men before the flood are found.

In his tremendous book, *Worlds in Collision,* page 20, Velikovsky says,

> Occasionally, also, during mining operations, a human skull is found in the middle of a mountain, under a thick cover of basalt or granite, like the Calaveras skull of California.
>
> Human remains and human artifacts of bone, polished stone, or pottery are found under great deposits of till and gravel, sometimes under as much as a hundred feet.

There is no explanation for such finds except by the flood and the tremendous convulsions that changed the face of the whole earth in the flood period.

4. Note Again the Scriptures That Suggest Some World Changes Taking Place During and Following Flood

If the waters covered the whole earth, even the tops of the mountains, it is obvious that some change had to be made in the face of the earth so that the earth would not remain all covered. It is said that even now if the land of the world were all level, the waters would cover the earth nearly two miles deep! In the days before the flood Noah evidently lived where the mountain ranges were few and relatively small. The seas were shallow. The waters within them could be contained well enough as long as the great floods of water up above the air ("waters above the firmament," Scripture calls them), did not descend. But when the waters above fell and the whole earth was inundated and covered, then there had to be some arrangements to accommodate those waters.

In the first place, there would need to be deeper seas. Evidently there needed to be a rising up of mountains to balance that. So there is no doubt that now volcanoes spewed out from the heart of the earth and many, many thousands of square miles of lava, the great chains of mountains reared themselves in the sky, and the ocean bottoms sunk so they could contain the waters and leave the continents dry. These great catastrophic changes took place perhaps during the flood and during the year that Noah was in the ark and perhaps some of them continued years afterward.

Let me remind you again that this is indicated in the Scriptures. Yes, the Scriptures indicate that even mountains and hills were moved, shaken, washed away in this tremendous wash of tidal waves around the earth during the time of the flood. We think that Psalm 46:1-3 speaks of that time with reassurance for men:

"God is our refuge and strength, a very present help in trouble. Therefore will not we fear, though the earth be removed, and though the mountains be carried into the midst of the sea: Though the waters thereof roar and be trouble, though the mountains shake with the swelling thereof."

Men knew that that happened! Can you imagine the roaring of the troubled waters and the mountains shaking and swelling and some mountains being cast into the midst of the sea? There is no other time in human history, as far as we know, when that would fit except in the time of the flood and following. But in the midst of that, God remembered Noah and his family and brought them safely from the trouble. And here the sweet assurance is that God will again care for His people in any time of great disaster.

Isaiah 64:3 mentions the time when "the mountains flowed down at thy presence." When would that be except at the time of the flood and following?

God then formed new boundaries for the sea bed as the sea bottoms were lowered still and great mountains reared up out of the water. Job said, "As the waters fail from the sea, and the flood decayeth and drieth up" (Job 14:11). Evidently Job, who wrote long before the Pentateuch, had heard the reports and there was a racial memory of the great events of the time of the flood. So the Scriptures visualize the flood of waters retreating down into its newly enlarged basins and God setting new boundaries and coasts for the sea.

Psalm 104 exalts a mighty God "with honour and majesty" and speaks of His world. Verses 5 to 9 say:

"Who laid the foundations of the earth, that it should not be removed for ever. Thou coveredst it with the deep as with a garment: the waters stood above the mountains. At thy rebuke they fled; at the voice of thy thunder they hasted away. They go up by the mountains; they go down by the valleys unto the place which thou hast founded for them. Thou hast set a bound that they may not pass over; that they turn not again to cover the earth."

Note that Scripture says the waters once stood above the mountains. That was in the days of the flood, surely, and there God covered the earth with the deep as with a garment. But at God's rebuke, the waters fled, retreating into the deeper basins now prepared and to the new limits God had set. They set a bound for them that they might not pass over and turn again to cover the earth. Surely God is talking here about the flood and the catastrophic events during and following it.

Most of the layers of rocks were laid down by flood waters. Some of the layers are lava poured out of volcanoes or out of fissures in the earth. But that water, rushing with tidal waves here and there and great agitation of the flood waters, took the mud of one area and washed it over another vast area. Then as the tides seemed to subside, they would then start back and another kind of soil would be washed over that area. Forests would be covered, the green trees and vegetation would finally be submerged, and these all turned into layers of coal. The dead animals were covered here, there and everywhere.

We suppose these layers in the ground would have been laid approximately level but with the sinking of ocean basins and the rising of mountains and with the earthquakes and convulsions, sometimes the ground would be squeezed together, raising mountains, and those layers would be curved. For example, on Highway I-24 between Murfreesboro and Nashville, the highway cuts through some hills. The layers are arched. When these layers of mud and soft dirt were pressed together in waves, then they hardened into stone and the waves are still there.

During that time of the flood and after, we suppose that there was a great sea in the American midwest. Scientists find remnants of a shoreline. In those days, before the mud and sand had hardened into stone, like concrete, that inland sea broke through and began to run out in what is now the Columbia River and so in the soft layers it washed out what is now the Grand Canyon. Now the layers are turned to stone. But it did not take long for the waters to break through and the great inland sea was drained, before the layers were hardened as they now are.

5. Changes and Convulsions of Earth Probably Continued Some Years

We are sure that great changes continued in the surface of the earth following the flood. There is evidence, acknowledged by all scientists, that there was a time when the great land bodies of the earth were connected and that men and animals and plants from some central area spread out to cover the world. Genesis 9:19 says, "These are the three sons of Noah: and of them was the whole earth overspread." All the races on the earth are descended from these three sons of Noah. That is also stated in Acts 17:26, that God "hath made of one blood all nations of men for to dwell on all the face of the earth, and hath determined the times before appointed, and the bounds of their habitation." So God planned that the world should be overspread by the sons of Noah in the different races of mankind, and God evidently planned the distribution.

We are told how God deliberately brought confusion of tongues at the tower of Babel so men would be scattered, with different languages, over the earth. In Genesis 10:25 we read, "Unto Eber were born two sons: the name of one was Peleg; for in his days was the earth divided." Peleg was the great, great grandson of Shem and may have been born 130 or 200 years after the flood. And in Peleg's days the earth was divided. The word "earth" here is the Hebrew word *eretz,* the same word as in Genesis 1:1 and used everywhere for the literal earth. It does not mean the world system or the population. So it may well mean that the continents were separated by seas in the days of Peleg *130 to 200* years after the flood.

We need not be surprised that the old earth had not settled down after such terrible convulsions; so down through the centuries the earth still trembles with earthquakes, volcanoes still spue out lava to cover great areas. Vesuvius covered the two Italian cities of Pompeii and Herculaneum in the year 79 A. D. Every now and then some new island rises from the sea or another one disappears. The coast of Texas near Houston has sunk eleven feet in recent years. Recent earthquakes in Nicaragua and Bangladesh are illustrations. In the giant upheavals, the earth was crushed together to form mountains, that and the sinking of the seas have left faults and fissures, and slowly the earth settles.

Traditions of many races indicate that the surface of the earth has changed greatly at various times soon after the flood.

For example, the *Encyclopaedia Britannica* says:

> Atlantis, Atalantis or Atlantica, a legendary island in the Atlantic ocean. Plato in the *Timaeus* describes how Egyptian priests, in conversation with Solon, represented the island as a country larger than Asia Minor with Libya, situated just beyond the Pillars of Hercules. Beyond it lay an archipelago of lesser islands. Atlantis has been a powerful kingdom nine thousand years before the birth of Solon, and its armies had overrun the Mediterranean lands, when Athens alone had resisted. Finally the sea overwhelmed Atlantis, and shoals marked the spot. In the *Critias* Plato adds a history of the ideal commonwealth of Atlantis. It is impossible to decide how far this legend is due to Plato's invention, and how far it is based on facts of which no record remains. Mediaeval writers, receiving the tale from Arabian geographers,

believed it true, and had other traditions of islands in the western sea, the Greek Isles of the Blest (*q.v.*), or Fortunate Islands; the Welsh Avalon, the Portuguese Antilia (*q.v.*) or Isle of Seven Cities, and St. Brendan's island, the subject of many sagas in many languages. All except Avalon were marked in maps of the 14th and 15th centuries, and formed the object of voyages of discovery; St. Brendan's island until the 18th century. Somewhat similar legends are those of the island of the Phaeacians (Homer, *od.*), the island of Brazil (*q.v.*), of Lyonnesse (*q.v.*), the sunken land off the Cornish coast, of the lost Breton city of Is, and of Mayda or Asmaide, the French *Isle Verte* and Portuguese *Ilha Verde* or "Green Island." The last appears in many folk-tales from Gibraltar to the Hebrides and until 1853 was marked on English charts as a rock in 44 degrees 48' N. and 26 degrees 10' W. After the Renaissance attempts were made to rationalize the myth of Atlantis. It was identified with America, Scandinavia, the Canaries or Palestine. Ethnologists saw in its inhabitants ancestors of the Guanchos, the Basques or the ancient Italians. Even in the 17th and 18th centuries the credibility of the legend was seriously debated, and sometimes admitted, even by Montaigne, Guffon and Voltaire.

It is true that legends are often exaggerated and are sometimes colored by men's imagination and various oft-told tales. Still, the legends about countries that once appeared in the ocean and now are sunken are so many that we feel sure there must be some basis for them. Of course it was not 9,000 years before, and such figures would be inaccurate, but this is only an indication that once all the continents were joined and some lands then appeared which later disappeared in the sea, and all known historical facts about the world as it is today can be included in the less than 5,000 years since the flood. But we are to remember that "the world that then was, being overflowed with water, perished."

6. Mammoths and the Ice Age in New World

The mammoth was a woolly elephant. Many, many thousands of them, millions we suppose, fed on the tropical growth around the earth before the flood. Many thousands of their frozen carcasses and massive graveyards of their bones and tusks are all along the Arctic ice, especially in Siberia. We suppose that those in that area died instantly and many were frozen solid before decay could come, when the canopy or "water above the firmament" as the Bible calls it, fell on the earth to help cause the flood. The poles would have known the tremendous cold then, as now, when exposed to the cold of outer space after the insulating cover of the great layer of water vapor which was above the earth was removed.

Volcanic activity, so great at that time, would fill the air with dust particles so increasing snowfall. The water falling in the flood would have been snow or would have frozen at the poles, and no doubt that accounts for a large part of the icecaps a mile or two miles thick at the two poles. That ice, spreading out under pressure, would run down to certain areas, as far as into the United States in some places and as far as northern European countries. So glaciers were formed and moved. And that is all there was to the Ice Age. It melted back rapidly each summer, perhaps advancing a little in winter, with the climate about like it is now: and now the permanent ice and the glaciers remain largely either very close to Arctic or Antarctic areas or on mountains where the snow still falls to make massive glaciers.

At the time of the flood there are, we think, two factors that changed the Arctic and Antarctic regions from moderately warm climate and dense vegetation such as covered practically the whole earth at that time, into a frigid country. These two factors evidently brought the intense cold at the poles and snow that packed into the icecaps and glaciers of the so-called "Ice Age." This intense cold is the reason that many thousands of mammoths were suddenly frozen solid even with tropical vegetation in their mouths and stomachs, as has been found true in Siberia and similar finds in Africa.

These two factors are first the breaking down of a great canopy of water vapor which had a greenhouse effect and made a moderate and subtropical climate over the whole earth. And second it involved the sudden loss and change of carbon dioxide in the air, when the millions and millions of animals on the earth, supported by dense vegetation many times more abundant than is possible today, all died in the flood and could not breathe out carbon dioxide. It is thought that an increase of carbon dioxide in the air makes much more effective radiation heat from the sun and a decrease in carbon dioxide would decrease the effect of solar radiation and so temporarily decrease the temperature throughout the whole earth. In *The Genesis Flood,* by Henry M. Morris and John C. Whitcomb, Jr., is this statement:

> Dr. Gilbert Plass, of the Office of Advanced Research of Aeroneutronic Systems, Inc., has studied the effect of carbon dioxide probably more intensively than any other individual. He says:
>
> "Calculations show that a 50-percent decrease in the amount of carbon dioxide in the air will lower the average temperature of the earth 6.9 degrees Fahrenheit. We can be reasonably sure that such a sharp drop in temperature would cause glaciers to spread across the earth."
>
> Plass also gives corresponding quantitative data for the effect of heavier concentrations of CO_2 in producing warm climates; for example, he calculates that if the carbon dioxide content were quadrupled, and in balance with the carbonates on the earth's surface and in the oceans, then the earth's average temperature would be 12.5 degrees Fahrenheit higher than at present.

The quotations from Dr. Plass are taken from the *Scientific American* for July, 1959.

"Cave Men," "Stone Age" Men
After the Flood

What about cave men and the pictographs, writings and drawings in some of the caves? They very probably are the results of the dispersion after the flood.

You may be sure that after the Tower of Babel, when the languages of all the people were confused and they were scattered out everywhere to fill the earth, they would take whatever shelter they could for a time. Down through the years people who needed quick shelter would live in caves.

In my boyhood in West Texas, I visited one family down by the Wichita River who lived in a cave. They hoped to be able to buy a little place and own a home later. Meantime, they lived in a cave. They were not Stone Age savages.

The many, many pioneers who moved out in West Texas or Kansas or New Mexico and built "dugouts," that is, a kind of a half cellar in the ground covered over with poles and then dirt, were not heathen people. Those who built "soddies" (sod houses), or adobe houses out of mud bricks in New Mexico, Colorado, and Arizona were not Stone Age people.

The simple truth is that people up to the flood had a high state of civilization. After the flood there is in some areas much evidence of a high degree of civilization.

Mizraim is thought to have been Menes, the first king in Egypt, whose grave was found in 1897. He was the son of Ham who came through the flood. And the Egyptian records (that is such a dry country and so parchments and monuments would often be preserved) are among the oldest we have. Civilization goes back to the sons of Noah, back to the flood.

Infidels in the past have sometimes said that Moses could not have written the Pentateuch because Moses could not read nor write. They supposed men, evolving from beasts, had not learned a written language! That was silly and ignorant. Since that time we have found the Code of Hammurabi long before Abraham, in that area, and even the town, Ur of the Chaldees, from which Abraham came, has been identified and it had a library.

The very ancient jewelry and works in gold, silver, bronze, etc., in Egypt indicate a very high degree of civilization that must have flourished soon after the flood.

Even in Old Mexico and in Peru, there is amazing evidence that the Aztecs and other early inhabitants of South America and Mexico knew things about astronomy and mathematics and such matters that most people now do not know.

There have been degenerate people on every continent. There always will be. Romans 1 tells how people after the flood who did not like to retain God in their knowledge were turned over to reprobate minds and heathendom and sex sin and idolatry. But since the flood mankind has had an unbroken chain of good civilizations despite those who went on in heathendom, ignorance, and savagery.

The mammoths, we think, died out soon after the flood. The mammoth was a hairy elephant, and elephants, I am told, eat as much as one-fifth of their weight in green stuff a day! You can soon see that after the flood one pair of mammoths might get along for a time, but when they began to multiply on the earth where the forest had been covered and made into coal and where they had to depend on new sprouting trees and grass and forest growths, mammoths would not find many areas of the world where they would have plenty to eat. Even now elephants are pretty well confined to certain parts of Africa, India and Southeast Asia where there are enormous forests and almost unlimited green stuff for them to eat. We are not surprised that the mammoths soon died out. The last ones died, no doubt, sometime after the flood.

Dinosaurs Soon Became Extinct After the Flood

And what about the dinosaurs? It is now evident that the dinosaurs were on earth when men were here. In Texas they have discovered a print of a dinosaur in the stone river bed and nearby the giant naked footprint of a man's foot. It is about eighteen inches long, indicating the man was very large. This is in the Paluxy River, near Glenrose, Texas, and actual photographs are available.

Then there were dinosaurs on the earth after the flood for a short time. The Chinese have had traditions of "dragons" and before they knew about the fossil remains of dinosaurs that have been found today they were pictured very much like what the reconstructed dinosaurs looked like.

The Bible speaks a number of times of "dragons." These Scriptures may well have meant the dinosaurs.

But again remember that the dinosaurs were great lumbering beasts. Like many other beasts that were prolific before the flood, the larger ones became extinct. We suppose that in the new world, after the flood, with a limited area of tropical climate and without any great rain forests at once for their feed, dinosaurs had a hard time and gradually the larger ones of the group became extinct. Many other species have become extinct, some in modern times.

You know that crocodiles and alligators are of the same general family. And the *National Geographic* magazine tells of a certain remnant of dinosaurs, giant lizards big enough to eat a deer, on an island of the Indian Ocean. But the great bodied dinosaurs would not fit in this new world and without enough food it seems they soon became extinct.

And that didn't happen millions of years ago but only since the flood, it now seems certain.

Dinosaurs Since the Flood

Dr. John C. Whitcomb, Jr., in his book, *The Early Earth*, page 132, has this important statement:

> The dinosaurs ("terrible lizards") flourished especially during the period from Adam to the Flood because of the warm and humid climate that characterized the entire pre-Flood world. They did not become extinct *before* Adam, for he was given dominion over *all* the kinds of animals (Gen. 1:28). This has been confirmed by the remarkable discovery of human footprints in the same rock layers with the footprints of dinosaurs (cf. Whitcomb and Morris, *The Genesis Flood*, Presbyterian and Reformed Publishing Co., 1961, pp. 172-176). In the broader sense of the term *dinosaur*, we may say that they are not yet extinct. On the island of Komodo in Indonesia, about a thousand huge dragon lizards still survive, some of them attaining a length of ten feet and a weight of over three hundred pounds (*National*

Geographic Magazine, Dec., 1968). And surely the twenty-foot crocodile would qualify as a "terrible lizard"! Since reptiles attain sexual maturity long before their full growth is reached, we need not assume that huge and therefore old individuals represented their kind on Noah's ark. After the Flood, reptilian dinosaurs found themselves confined to a comparatively narrow belt near the equator, and thus in most cases became extinct during the subsequent centuries of desperate struggle for existence against the more versatile and adaptable mammals.

SOME LESSONS GOD GIVES US FROM THE FLOOD

See again that Scripture in II Peter 3:3-7:

"Knowing this first, that there shall come in the last days scoffers, walking after their own lusts, And saying, Where is the promise of his coming? for since the fathers fell asleep, all things continue as they were from the beginning of the creation. For this they willingly are ignorant of, that by the word of God the heavens were of old, and the earth standing out of the water and in the water: Whereby the world that then was, being overflowed with water, perished: But the heavens and the earth, which are now, by the same word are kept in store, reserved unto fire against the day of judgment and perdition of ungodly men."

1. Wicked Unbelievers Will Scoff at Creation and Flood

God says that scoffers who walk after their own lusts will laugh at the idea of Christ's return. They believe in "uniformitarian" geology, not that there were great catastrophies like the flood, but that things were going on as now, with the gradual changing for millions of years. Why? Because they are scoffers. They are walking after their own wicked desires. They do not want to believe the Bible, they do not want to be accountable to God, they do not want to repent. So scoffers turn away from what the Bible teaches about creation and about the flood. They are "willingly ignorant." They have a bias of mind.

So although they now know that spontaneous generation is impossible, they think things must have begun that way millions of years ago, instead of being by direct creation. Although they find no missing links between species or kinds, they still believe there must have been some such. Already the great claims of the evolutionists about acquired characteristics being inherited are all proven false. And Mendel's laws, now agreed upon, clearly show that only what is in the genes in a plant or animal can reproduce, and that the varieties are always there already and that they really do reproduce only "after their kind," as the Bible says.

Scientific people know the first and second laws of thermodynamics. The first is that things are not growing into and developing into more than they were. There can be no change in matter-energy except by direct intervention of God. The second law says that there is a constant regression, a wearing out, a running down of machinery, an increase in disorder. All scientists know this happens regularly in machinery and in plants and animals. The universal tendency is down, not up.

Horses running wild, without man's care in breeding, become mustang ponies. Only man's care produces thoroughbreds or Tennessee Walkers or Standardbred horses or giant Clydesdales.

Fine roses left to nature return to scrubby wild roses. Nature, left alone, runs downhill, not up. The idea of evolution from simple to complex, from beast to man, violates the second law of thermodynamics, a recognized scientific law.

But if the world is running down, somebody had to start it! Life, energy, matter did not start themselves. Evolution cannot explain creation. Yet men, because of their evil lust, want to believe in evolution, want to believe that the fossils did not come from the flood but through millions of years without God.

2. World Will Perish Again but by Fire

Another lesson we must remember is that there will be

another destruction of the world. Second Peter 3:10, 11 says:

"But the day of the Lord will come as a thief in the night; in the which the heavens shall pass away with a great noise, and the elements shall melt with fervent heat, the earth also and the works that are therein shall be burned up. Seeing then that all these things shall be dissolved, what manner of persons ought ye to be in all holy conversation and godliness."

The heavens shall pass away with a great noise. The elements shell melt with fervent heat. The earth and the works therein shall be burned up. Everything that fire can destroy on this earth will be destroyed. And that will be in "the day of judgment and perdition of ungodly men," II Peter 3:7 tells us.

So when the great white throne judgment takes place as described in Revelation, chapter 20, and while all the redeemed are there to witness, and the unsaved are there to face judgment out in space, and Christ is on a great white throne from which the heaven and earth have fled away, then God will destroy this earth with all that fire can destroy. Then we find that God makes all this into a new heaven and a new earth. Then God can keep His promise to Abraham that the seed of Abraham will inherit the land given them. Then it will be true that "the meek shall inherit the earth."

You will note, then, that this destruction of the earth by fire is to take place after the rapture, after the return of Christ in glory to reign for a thousand years, and at that time the last great white throne judgment out in space.

VERSES 15-19:

15 ¶ And God spake unto Noah, saying,
16 Go forth of the ark, thou, and thy wife, and thy sons, and thy sons' wives with thee.
17 Bring forth with thee every liv-

ing thing that *is* with thee, of all flesh, *both* of fowl, and of cattle, and of every creeping thing that creepeth upon the earth; that they may breed abundantly in the earth, and be fruitful, and multiply upon the earth.

18 And Noah went forth, and his sons, and his wife, and his sons' wives with him:

19 Every beast, every creeping thing, and every fowl, *and* whatsoever creepeth upon the earth, after their kinds, went forth out of the ark.

3. Out Into a Totally Different World!

Noah comes forth to this devastated world. It is not the same world. The rivers, the mountains are not the same. No cities are left. No men are left, only those animals that he brings out of the ark, but they are to spread abroad and breed abundantly and multiply in the earth. God is starting over with a race of mankind in the world which He made.

VERSES 20-22:

20 ¶ And Noah builded an altar unto the LORD; and took of every clean beast, and of every clean fowl, and offered burnt offerings on the altar.

21 And the LORD smelled a sweet savour; and the LORD said in his heart, I will not again curse the ground any more for man's sake; for the imagination of man's heart *is* evil from his youth; neither will I again smite any more every thing living, as I have done.

22 While the earth remaineth, seedtime and harvest, and cold and heat, and summer and winter, and day and night shall not cease.

Noah Builds an Altar

Noah built an altar. How blessed that now God starts again with people who love Him and would serve Him. Although up to this time men have never eaten flesh but only vegetables (Gen. 1:29, 30) and there were no carnivorous animals, yet Abel had offered animal sacrifices, and so Noah offers animal sacrifices, too. This is before the ceremonial law, but even then Abel and Noah understood that the sacrifice represented Christ, the Lamb of God who would come and die.

Those who were saved in Old Testament times were saved by faith in the Saviour who would come. Dimly it may be they saw, but by faith they did see that God would provide a Sacrifice, even as Abraham had told Isaac, "My son, God will provide himself a lamb for a burnt-offering" (Gen. 22:8). It was by faith that Abel offered a sacrifice (Heb. 11:4). Now we know that Noah, looking forward to the coming Saviour, offered sacrifices that pleased God. Today we take the Lord's Supper, the memorial supper picturing the death of Christ for us. The sacrificial lamb meant the same to Noah, although the Sacrifice pictured was in the future.

And how it pleased God! How long He had been grieved at the wickedness of godless sinners; now God's man offers a sacrifice and his heart opens to the Lord's mercies and blessings, and God is pleased at this.

So God makes a promise: No more will the whole earth be destroyed by a flood of water. And "while the earth remaineth, seedtime and harvest, and cold and heat, and summer and winter, and day and night shall not cease." That may mean there were some changes in the seasons by the flood, but there will be none hereafter.

There is a foolish saying that ignorant people sometimes think is in the Bible, that "the time will come when you can't tell the summer from the winter except by the budding of the leaves." No, God has set the earth on its course around the sun and the tilt of its axis that makes summer and winter and the seasons not change, the seedtime and harvest; God has given His word for that.

Will you see that in verse 21 God knows the pitiful weakness in mankind. We are reminded of Psalm 103:8-17:

"The Lord is merciful and gracious, slow to anger, and plenteous in mercy. He will not always chide: neither will he keep his anger for ever. He hath not dealt with us after our sins; nor rewarded us according to our iniquities. For as the heaven is high above the earth, so great is his mercy toward them that fear him. As far as the east is from the west, so far hath he removed our transgressions from us. Like as a father pitieth his children, so the Lord pitieth them that fear him. For he knoweth our frame; he remembereth that we are dust. As for man, his days are as

grass: as a flower of the field, so he flourisheth. For the wind passeth over it and it is gone; and the place thereof shall know it no more. But the mercy of the Lord is from everlasting to everlasting upon them that fear him, and his righteousness unto children's children."

So here the Lord reminds Himself of man: ". . .for the imagination of man's heart is evil from his youth." But God's mercy is determined.

GENESIS 9

AND God blessed Noah and his sons, and said unto them, Be fruitful, and multiply, and replenish the earth.

2 And the fear of you and the dread of you shall be upon every beast of the earth, and upon every fowl of the air, upon all that moveth *upon* the earth, and upon all the fishes of the sea; into your hand are they delivered.

3 Every moving thing that liveth shall be meat for you; even as the green herb have I given you all things.

Noah in the New World

In Genesis 1:28 Adam and Eve had been commanded, "Be fruitful, and multiply, and replenish the earth, and subdue it: and have dominion over the fish of the sea, and over the fowl of the air, and over every living thing that moveth upon the earth." Now that command is repeated to Noah and his sons: "Be fruitful, and multiply, and replenish the earth." Again I remind you that the earth has to be replenished continually. Men die. The command was not only to Adam and to Noah but to all of us. "Marriage is honourable in all, and the bed undefiled." "Lo, children are an heritage of the Lord: and the fruit of the womb is his reward" (Ps. 127:3). Verse 7 repeats the command with more emphasis.

And now "the fear of you and the dread of you shall be upon every beast of the earth" (vs. 2). It may be that before the flood animals were not afraid of men. No man had ever killed animals except to kill the domestic sheep, we suppose, lambs as a sacrifice. Men ate vegetables. There were no carnivorous beasts, and I suppose animals would not be especially afraid of man, as now they do not much fear men where men have never been before. But now the fear of man is on beasts and now men are to eat meat. Now carnivorous animals will eat other animals.

Some people think that a vegetable diet is more suitable. God does not think so. The Scripture says, ". . .eat such things as are set before you" (Luke 10:8), and again the Lord commands, "For every creature of God is good, and nothing to be refused, if it be received with thanksgiving: For it is sanctified by the word of God and prayer" (I Tim. 4:4,5).

Now even the ceremonial restrictions which are given to the Jews are not binding on New Testament Christians. Colossians 2:16,17 says, "Let no man therefore judge you in meat, or in drink, or in respect of an holyday, or of the new moon, or of the sabbath days: Which are a shadow of things to come; but the body is of Christ."

There was a ceremonial meaning in the ceremonial law, but not a moral command for Christians.

VERSES 4-6:

4 But flesh with the life thereof, *which is* the blood thereof, shall ye not eat.

5 And surely your blood of your lives will I require; at the hand of every beast will I require it, and at the hand of man; at the hand of every man's brother will I require the life of man.

6 Whoso sheddeth man's blood, by man shall his blood be shed: for in the image of God made he man.

Death Penalty for Murder

Before the flood we do not suppose there was any organized human government, and God had not put it in the hands of men to execute the death penalty. Cain was allowed to go with a mark upon him so no one would kill him in vengeance for his slaying of Abel. But now there will be a rule of human government: "Whoso sheddeth man's blood, by man shall his blood be shed." There is the death penalty here for murder.

This rule is carried over into the ceremonial law and expanded. Exodus 21:12-17 says,

"He that smiteth a man, so that he die, shall be surely put to death. And if a man lie not in wait, but God deliver him into his hand; then I will appoint thee a place whither

he shall flee. But if a man come presumptuously upon his neighbour, to slay him with guile; thou shalt take him from mine altar, that he may die. And he that smiteth his father, or his mother, shall be surely put to death. And he that stealeth a man, and selleth him, or if he be found in his hand, he shall surely be put to death. And he that curseth his father, or his mother, shall surely be put to death."

Here is the death penalty for first-degree murder. Here is the death penalty for a man who strikes his father or mother or for kidnapping. The Lindbergh law was in the Bible first. One who even curses his father or mother should be put to death. Yet the same ceremonial law provides for leniency in a second-degree murder where one had not intended murder.

That command is enlarged and repeated in Leviticus 20:10, "And the man that committeth adultery with another man's wife, even he that committeth adultery with his neighbour's wife, the adulterer and the adulteress shall surely be put to death." And for sodomy and other such perversions, the death penalty was given in the ceremonial law also.

In the New Testament, Romans 13:1-4 repeats this teaching:

"Let every soul be subject unto the higher powers. For there is no power but of God: the powers that be are ordained of God. Whosoever therefore resisteth the power, resisteth the ordinance of God: and they that resist shall receive to themselves damnation. For rulers are not a terror to good works, but to the evil. Wilt thou then not be afraid of the power? do that which is good, and thou shalt have praise of the same: For he is the minister of God to thee for good. But if thou do that which is evil, be afraid; for he beareth not the sword in vain: for he is the minister of God, a revenger to execute wrath upon him that doeth evil."

So the ruler represents God, is a minister of God who bears not the sword in vain, ". . .for he is the minister of

God, a revenger to execute wrath upon him that doeth evil."

Jesus taught the same thing in Luke 13:1-5:

"There were present at that season some that told him of the Galileans, whose blood Pilate had mingled with their sacrifices. And Jesus answering said unto them, Suppose ye that these Galileans were sinners above all the Galileans, because they suffered such things? I tell you, Nay: but, except ye repent, ye shall all likewise perish. Or those eighteen, upon whom the tower in Siloam fell, and slew them, think ye that they were sinners above all men that dwelt in Jerusalem? I tell you, Nay: but, except ye repent, ye shall all likewise perish."

A curse is on the land that does not execute the murderer. A curse is on the land where innocent blood is shed and not avenged. The captivity of Judah was partly because of innocent bloodshed. Second Kings 24:3 and 4 says:

"Surely at the commandment of the Lord came this upon Judah, to remove them out of his sight, for the sins of Manasseh, according to all that he did; And also for the innocent blood that he shed: for he filled Jerusalem with innocent blood; which the Lord would not pardon."

What about the nearly one million innocent unborn murdered every year in America? No wonder American blood stained the soil of Korea and Vietnam! God must have vengeance for innocent blood shed.

VERSE 7:

7 And you, be ye fruitful, and multiply; bring forth abundantly in the earth, and multiply therein.

Command to Multiply Repeated

In Genesis 1:28 God blessed Adam and Eve, "And God

said unto them, Be fruitful, and multiply, and replenish the earth, and subdue it: and have dominion over the fish of the sea, and over the fowl of the air, and over every living thing that moveth upon the earth." So God again repeats here instructions to Noah and to his sons, after saying the same thing in verse 1. Note the added emphasis, ". . . bring forth abundantly." Big families please God.

VERSES 8-17:

8 ¶ And God spake unto Noah, and to his sons with him, saying,

9 And I, behold, I establish my covenant with you, and with your seed after you;

10 And with every living creature that *is* with you, of the fowl, of the cattle, and of every beast of the earth with you; from all that go out of the ark, to every beast of the earth.

11 And I will establish my covenant with you; neither shall all flesh be cut off any more by the waters of a flood; neither shall there any more be a flood to destroy the earth.

12 And God said, This *is* the token of the covenant which I make between me and you and every living creature that *is* with you, for perpetual generations:

13 I do set my bow in the cloud, and it shall be for a token of a covenant between me and the earth.

14 And it shall come to pass, when I bring a cloud over the earth, that the bow shall be seen in the cloud:

15 And I will remember my covenant, which *is* between me and you and every living creature of all flesh; and the waters shall no more become a flood to destroy all flesh.

16 And the bow shall be in the cloud; and I will look upon it, that I may remember the everlasting covenant between God and every living creature of all flesh that *is* upon the earth.

17 And God said unto Noah, This *is* the token of the covenant, which I have established between me and all flesh that *is* upon the earth.

Rainbow Given

We wonder which of the eight left alive on the earth—Noah, his wife, Shem, Ham, Japheth and their wives—was the first one to see the beautiful rainbow in the skies! We understand there had been no rain before the flood. In Genesis 2:5,6 the Lord says, "And every plant of the field before it was in the earth, and every herb of the field before it grew: for the Lord God had not caused it to rain upon the earth, and there was not a man to till the ground. But there went up a mist from the earth, and watered the whole face of the ground." Now that hothouse-like canopy covering the earth above the firmament is gone. Now the semitropical climate of the whole earth has been changed; there are Arctic Zone, Temperate Zone and Tropic Zone. Now there is rain to water the earth. And with rain comes the rainbow. God takes this occasion to make a great pledge or covenant with mankind, and the rainbow is a visible, repeated reminder of that pledge. Never again will there come a flood to destroy the whole world.

The rainbow is mentioned again in Revelation 10:1, "I saw another mighty angel come down from heaven, clothed with a cloud: and a rainbow was upon his head. . . ." That angel is to declare that time shall be no longer, but in the midst of that prophecy God reminds us of His covenant. He will care for His own. And when time, as we know it, is no longer, Christ Himself shall reign over the whole earth in a millennial reign.

Should we not think when we see the rainbow in the cloud and when the sun is shining through the drops of water and is refracted into the colors of the rainbow, that God means all things for good to those that love Him? He remembers His covenant with us.

VERSES 18-29:

18 ¶ And the sons of Noah, that went forth of the ark, were Shem, and Ham, and Jā´-phĕth: and Ham *is* the father of Cā´-nă-ăn.

19 These *are* the three sons of Noah: and of them was the whole earth overspread.

20 And Noah began *to be* an husbandman, and he planted a vineyard:

21 And he drank of the wine, and was drunken; and he was uncovered within his tent.

22 And Ham, the father of Cā´-nă-ăn, saw the nakedness of his father,

and told his two brethren without.

23 And Shem and Jā´-phĕth took a garment, and laid *it* upon both their shoulders, and went backward, and covered the nakedness of their father; and their faces *were* backward, and they saw not their father's nakedness.

24 And Noah awoke from his wine, and knew what his younger son had done unto him.

25 And he said, Cursed *be* Cā´-nă-ăn; a servant of servants shall he be

unto his brethren.

26 And he said, Blessed *be* the LORD God of Shem; and Cā́-nă-ăn shall be his servant.

27 God shall enlarge Jā́-phĕth, and he shall dwell in the tents of Shem;

and Cā́-nă-ăn shall be his servant.

28 ¶ And Noah lived after the flood three hundred and fifty years.

29 And all the days of Noah were nine hundred and fifty years: and he died.

Drunken Noah: the Curse on Canaan

Everybody in the world is descended from these three sons of Noah (vs. 19). How strange that Noah got drunk! Some suggest that possibly Noah did not know the result of fermented wine. It is interesting that in all the discussion of the terrible wickedness and violence in the world before the flood, drunkenness is never mentioned. There was murder, for Cain killed Abel. "And God saw that the wickedness of man was great in the earth, and that every imagination of the thoughts of his heart was only evil continually" (Gen. 6:5). Genesis 6:11 says, "The earth also was corrupt before God, and the earth was filled with violence." Verse 12 says, "Behold, it was corrupt; for all flesh had corrupted his way upon the earth." And verse 13 says, "The earth is filled with violence."

Things were different before the flood. Men lived to enormous ages—up to more than nine hundred years. Animals, whose fossils we find buried under the layers deposited by the flood, were much larger than similar animals today. We suppose, then, that just as that canopy of vapor, "the waters which were above the firmament," may have shut out some of the infrared rays of the sun and diminished the aging effect, just so bacteria was restrained, food did not spoil as soon, and fruit juice did not ferment as readily.

Now in the new earth Noah planted a vineyard and drank wine and was drunken. Let us charitably suppose that he was not accustomed to the quickly fermented wine and now learns sadly the effect of alcoholic drink.

Noah, drunken, lay naked in his tent. Liquor takes away the normal restraints and inhibitions. Those who tarry at the wine are warned, "Thine eyes shall behold strange women, and thine heart shall utter perverse things. Yea, thou shalt be as he that lieth down in the midst of the sea, or as he that lieth upon the top of a mast." Hence Habakkuk 2:15,16 tells us the woe on those who get others to drink and uncover themselves:

"Woe unto him that giveth his neighbour drink, that puttest thy bottle to him, and makest him drunken also, that thou mayest look on their nakedness! Thou art filled with shame for glory: drink thou also, and let thy foreskin be uncovered: the cup of the Lord's right hand shall be turned unto thee, and shameful spewing shall be on thy glory."

We read that backslidden Israel "sat down to eat and to drink, and rose up to play" (Exod. 32:6). Their hilarious and drunken revelry, dancing around the golden calf, was heard by Moses and Joshua as they came down from Mount Sinai (Exod. 32:18,19) and in verse 25 below we find, ". . .Aaron had made them naked unto their shame among their enemies." Drinking and nakedness go together. Noah learned it sadly.

Ham saw the nakedness of Noah in the tent and he told his two brothers. Perhaps he joked about it. At any rate, Shem and Japheth took a garment and, taking heed to hide their faces, they covered the nakedness of their father.

Later there would be very strict commands among the Jews not to observe the nakedness of father or mother or others of close kin (Lev. 18:6-17). The instructions clearly say, "None of you shall approach to any that is near of kin to him, to uncover their nakedness," and the father, the mother, the sister and others are mentioned. Here there has been no written law except the law that is written in the heart. In that conscience which accuses or excuses, the law of God written in the heart (Rom. 2:14-16)—even heathen people have some sense of modesty, and sensible people know that nudity leads to lust and adultery. Those who do not have a sensitive heart about temptation are not strong to resist sin.

In the case of a son seeing his own naked father, there is not a temptation to adultery but there is a lack of respect, a lack of that godly fear which children should have for their fathers. So Noah pronounced a curse on Ham's son because of Ham's disrespect in this matter.

What was that curse? It is not given in great detail. Canaan should be servant to his brethren. The Canaanites were among those who held the land of Canaan when the children of Israel came from Egypt and drove them out. We are not told that the curse of Canaan was on the other descendants of Ham. We do not know that it was to continue for many generations as a racial matter. It does seem that in the history of the world certain races of men have more often been subject to others, and that the children of Japheth and those of Shem have been more often conquerers and rulers.

Noah lived 350 years after the flood. Then Abram was born two years after Noah died. And Shem, who lived 502 years after the flood, lived nearly as long as Abraham.

GENESIS 10

NOW these *are* the generations of the sons of Noah, Shem, Ham, and Jă-́phĕth: and unto them were sons born after the flood.

2 The sons of Jă-́phĕth; Gomer, and Magog, and Mă-́dâi, and Jă-́văn, and Tubal, and Mĕ-́shĕch, and Tī-́răs.

3 And the sons of Gomer; Ăsh-kĕ-́năz, and Rī-́phăth, and Tō-găr-́măh.

4 And the sons of Jă-́văn; Elishah, and Tär-́shĭsh, Kĭt-́tĭm, and Dō-́dă-nĭm.

5 By these were the 'isles of the Gentiles divided in their lands; every one after his tongue, after their families, in their nations.

Descendants of Japheth

Dr. Scofield's notes lists these sons of Japheth as follows:

Gomer, "Progenitor of the ancient Cimerians and Cimbri, from whom are descended the Celtic family."

Magog, "From Magog are descended the ancient Scythians, or, Tartars, whose descendants predominate in the modern Russia. See Ezk. 38.2; 39.6; Rev. 20.8."

Madai, "Progenitor of the ancient Medes."

Javan, "Progenitor of those who peopled Greece, Syria, etc."

Tubal, "Tubal's descendants peopled the region south of the Black Sea, from whence they spread north and south. It is probable that Tobolsk perpetuates the tribal name. A branch of this race peopled Spain."

Meshech, "Progenitor of a race mentioned in connection with Tubal, Magog, and other northern nations. Broadly speaking, Russia, excluding the conquests of Peter the Great and his successors, is the modern land of Magog, Tubal, and Meshech."

Tiras, "Progenitor of the Thracians."

Dr. Scofield says,

From these seven sons of Japheth are descended the *goyim,* or Gentile, nations, trans. "heathen" 148 times in the A. V. The name implies nothing concerning religion, meaning simply, non-Israelite, or "foreigner."

The Scripture says that by these descendants of Japheth, "were the isles of the Gentiles divided in their lands." So originally, we would suppose, the term Gentiles referred particularly to the sons of Japheth and not including the descendants of Ham. Later, no doubt, the term is used of all non-Jews. For example, Paul was "the apostle of the Gentiles" (Rom. 11:13; Gal. 2:8). Does that mean that he was an apostle only to the descendants of Japheth and not to the sons of Ham, the Canaanites, the Egyptians, the Philistines and others descended from them? I doubt it. Romans 3:29 says that God is 'the God of the Jews and Gentiles.' Certainly that does not mean to exclude the rest of the human race. I would suppose Gentiles here mean all non-Jews.

We think that the judgment of the nations mentioned in Matthew 25:32 would mean all non-Jews. It is not likely that all the Gentiles mentioned in Acts 9:15; 13:47; 13:42; Acts 15:12; 22:21; 28:28, to whom Paul preached, were descended from Japheth and none of them from Ham.

We notice that Japheth had seven sons. The descendants of only two of these are named: of Gomer are named four sons; of Javan are named four sons. The genealogy is not carried further with the other sons of Japheth.

VERSES 6-20:

6 ¶ And the sons of Ham; Cush, and Mĭz′-rā-ĭm, and Phut, and Cā′-nă-ăn.

7 And the sons of Cush; Seba, and Hăv′-ĭ-läh, and Sabtah, and Rā′-ă-mäh, and Săb-tĕ′-chäh: and the sons of Rā′-ă-mäh; Sheba, and Dedan.

8 And Cush begat Nĭm′-rŏd: he began to be a mighty one in the earth.

9 He was a mighty hunter before the Lord: wherefore it is said, Even as Nĭm′-rŏd the mighty hunter before the Lord.

10 And the beginning of his kingdom was Babel, and Ĕr′-ĕch, and Accad, and Calneh, in the land of Shī′-när.

11 Out of that land went forth Asshur, and builded Nĭn′-ĕ-vēh, and the city Rē′-hŏ-bōth, and Calah,

12 And Rē′-sĕn between Nĭn′-ĕ-vēh and Calah: the same *is* a great city.

13 And Mĭz′-rā-ĭm begat Ludim, and Ăn′-ă-mĭm, and Lĕ-hā′-bĭm, and Năph-tû′-hĭm,

14 And Păth-rû′-sĭm, and Căs-lû′-hĭm, (out of whom came Phĭl′-ĭs-tĭm,) and Căph′-tō-rĭm.

15 ¶ And Cā′-nă-ăn begat Sidon his firstborn, and Heth,

16 And the Jĕb′-ū-sīte, and the Amorite, and the Gĭr′-gă-sīte,

17 And the Hivite, and the Arkite,

and the Sinite,

18 And the Ãr-vă-dīte, and the Zĕm-'ă-rīte, and the Hamathite: and afterward were the families of the Cã-nă-ăn-ītes spread abroad.

19 And the border of the Cã-nă-ăn-ītes was from Sidon, as thou comest to Gerar, unto Gaza; as thou goest,

unto Sodom, and Gō-mŏr-'răh, and Admah, and Zĕ-bō-'ĭm, even unto Lasha.

20 These *are* the sons of Ham, after their families, after their tongues, in their countries, *and* in their nations.

Descendants of Ham

Four sons of Ham are named. That does not necessarily require that Ham had no other sons or that Japheth had no other sons than the seven who are named. The daughters are not named. For the purpose God had in mind, these are named and the other descendants are not all listed.

Cush had sons: Seba, Havilah, Sabtah, Raamah, Sabtechah; but **verse 8 also says,** "Cush begat Nimrod."

Mizraim is thought to be the Menes, beginning the first dynasty of kings in Egypt, listed in secular history. And Nimrod, a son of Cush, was king, we suppose, at Babel, and so in his great strength and energy, a mighty hunter. He was famous. Did he hunt the great dragons (dinosaurs) and other great animals, after the flood?

Nimrod had a kingdom beginning at Babel. So we think the tower of Babel was built in his lifetime, possibly within 100 years or 130 years of the time after the flood.

Seven sons of Mizraim are mentioned, dwelling principally in Africa and in the border country occupied by the Philistines.

Canaan, son of Ham, begat Sidon. Note the country involved, from Tyre and Sidon up in what is now Lebanon, including the Jebusites, original dwellers in Jerusalem, the Amorites and others that lived in the land of Canaan.

Note the list in verse 19—the Canaanites dwelt all the way from Sidon down the coast to Gaza, then over to Sodom and Gomorrah and Admah and Zeboim, the four towns destroyed in the time of Lot for their sins.

It would appear that big families spread out to make separate nations. In verse 20—". . . after their families, after their tongues, in their countries, and in their nations." Many families, many tongues or languages, a number of countries and nations. Does that mean that the confusion of tongues at Babel took place during the time of these grandsons of Ham and the great-grandsons of Noah?

Also, verse 31, speaking of Shem, says, "These are the sons of Shem, after their families, after their tongues, in their lands, after their nations." So we would suppose the confusion of tongues occurred during the lifetime of the people here mentioned.

VERSES 21-32:

21 ¶ Unto Shem also, the father of all the children of Eber, the brother of Jā́-phĕth the elder, even to him were *children* born.

22 The children of Shem; Elam, and Asshur, and Är-phăx́-ăd, and Lud, and Aram.

23 And the children of Aram; Uz, and Hul, and Gḗ-thĕr, and Mash.

24 And Är-phăx́-ăd begat Salah; and Salah begat Eber.

25 And unto Eber were born two sons: the name of one *was* Peleg; for in his days was the earth divided; and his brother's name *was* Joktan.

26 And Joktan begat Almodad, and Sheleph, and Hā-zär-mā́-vĕth, and Jerah,

27 And Hă-dôr-́ăm, and Ū́-zăl, and Diklah,

28 And Obal, and Ă-bĭm-́ā-ĕl, and Sheba,

29 And Ṓ-phĭr, and Hăv́-ĭ-läh, and Jobab: all these *were* the sons of Joktan.

30 And their dwelling was from Mḗ-shă, as thou goest unto Sephar a mount of the east.

31 These *are* the sons of Shem, after their families, after their tongues, in their lands, after their nations.

32 These *are* the families of the sons of Noah, after their generations, in their nations: and by these were the nations divided in the earth after the flood.

Sons of Shem

The descendants of Shem will be counted more important than the sons of Japheth and Ham because here we get into the ancestral line of Abraham, Isaac, Jacob, and the Jews.

Genesis 5:32 says, ". . .and Noah begat Shem, Ham, and Japheth." Shem is named first, but here we learn in verse 21 that Shem was "the brother of Japheth the elder." So Shem was listed as more important in the genealogical tables, although he was born after Japheth and possibly after Ham.

Note the genealogy here of Shem, Arphaxad, Salah, Eber. Compare that with the genealogy in Luke, chapter 3, where Cainan is listed as a son of Arphaxad, but not listed here. Other names were spelled differently. Remember, they had been taken from the Hebrew into the Greek language for the New Testament. And some men doubtless were called by more than one name. It is possible that some son, not important, is omitted and that God skipped to the grandson for His own reasons that we do not know. In the genealogy of Abraham in the next chapter, verses 10 to 26, the list is given: Shem, Arphaxad, Salah, Eber, Peleg, Reu, Serug, Nahor, Terah, and Abram.

"The Earth Divided" and Land Bridges Between the Continents Disappear

Genesis 10:25 says, "And unto Eber were born two sons: the name of one was Peleg; for in his days was the earth divided; and his brother's name was Joktan."

In Peleg's day "the earth was divided." The word for earth is *erets* in the Hebrew. The same word is used when God "created the heaven and the earth." It is the physical earth that was divided, not the people, at the confusion of tongues, we think.

All the air-breathing land animals died in the flood save those that were in the ark. That means that all the animal population of the earth now descended from those that came out of the ark. How did they get to the Americas, to Australia, and great islands of the sea? It is evident that once all the continents were connected and animals and men spread to all the earth after the flood and then the earth was divided.

We remember that the flood and accompanying convulsions lasted more than a year. Then for long after that there were gigantic movements, earthquakes, volcanoes, floods. Ocean bottoms sank, mountain ranges rose, thousands of cubic miles of lava were spewed out of

GENESIS

the heart of the earth in volcanoes, the surface of the earth would shrink and so shriveled into waves, and the newly laid layers of earth caused by the gigantic tidal waves that swept continents and mountains, covered forests with mud, and so laid the strata of the earth, the fossils, the coal beds. All these, then rather plastic and soft, were wrinkled so that we find now, after it has turned to stone, the strata are sometimes in waves or broken and up-tilted. When the sea bottoms sank to make room for the waters that covered every mountain of the earth during the flood, it is likely that later some of the surface connections between the continents would sink, too, and did.

But another mighty factor was the covering up of these land bridges with water. Immediately following the flood and one of the results of the flood, no doubt, were giant ice caps that appeared in the Northern and Southern Hemispheres.

Patten, in his book, *The Biblical Flood and the Ice Epoch*, page 111, says:

> It has been established, from the direction of ice flows, studies of gradients, distances, and other related data, that there were several nodes of ice on the Canadian Shield. It has further been established that the depth of ice at these nodes was between 15,000 and 17,000 feet.
>
> In the Southern Hemisphere, a comparable circumstance apparently existed. In 1958, an ice core was taken on the Antarctic Ice Cap near Byrd Station. Drilling commenced at an elevation of 5,000 feet above sea level. The thickness of the ice sheet was 10,000 feet, and the drill went through solid ice all the way. This means that ice is not only situated 5,000 feet above sea level in the Antarctic Region; it is also resting on terra firma some 5,000 feet below sea level. How is this explained?

He refers to the book by Dolph Earl Hooker, *Those Astounding Ice Ages.*

Note that the ice goes even 5,000 feet below sea level in the Antarctic.

On page 114 Dr. Patten says:

> The diameter of the breadth of the ice mass was

between 5,000 and 5,200 miles. The area it covered was about 17,000,000 square miles. It is equal to all of the land surface in the Western Hemisphere, including both Americas and their offshore islands. Or, on the other hand, it is equal to the continent of Asia in its entirety.

This was the area involved in the Northern Hemisphere. Presumably a nearly equal amount of ice descended in the Southern Hemisphere also.

He continues to say, "The ice was approximately 3 miles deep in its central nodes, and it feathered out toward the edges. On the basis of conic volumes, the volume of the ice in the Northern Hemisphere is estimated at about 6,000,000 cubic miles. Probably a like amount was deposited in the Southern Hemisphere."

Then he says, "Thus the estimate of the ice involved in the Ice Epoch in both hemispheres is between 12,000,000 and 14,000,000 cubic miles."

But there are only about 138,000,000 square miles of oceanic surface, so 12,000,000 or 14,000,000 cubic miles of water, if it were taken out and put back into the ice cap as it was, would cause that the ocean surface would everywhere be more than 500 feet lower than it is now, and the continental shelves around the continents would be dry land and great areas now covered with water would be dry. There would be land then between Alaska and Russia, and between Australia and Asia would be a great land passage. Very likely, also, there would be connections between the United States and Europe and between South America and Africa. Very likely the enormous mass of water melting from the ice cap caused the ocean bottom to sink more and land bridges be covered.

Certain it is that all the land animals now in the world descended from those in the ark and all the earth was once accessible to the migration of men and animals.

GENESIS 11

AND the whole earth was of one language, and of one speech.

2 And it came to pass, as they journeyed from the east, that they found a plain in the land of Shī-när; and they dwelt there.

3 And they said one to another, Go to, let us make brick, and burn them throughly. And they had brick for stone, and slime had they for morter.

4 And they said, Go to, let us build us a city and a tower, whose top *may reach* unto heaven; and let us make us a name, lest we be scattered abroad upon the face of the whole earth.

5 And the LORD came down to see the city and the tower, which the children of men builded.

6 And the LORD said, Behold, the people *is* one, and they have all one language; and this they begin to do: and now nothing will be restrained from them, which they have imagined to do.

7 Go to, let us go down, and there confound their language, that they may not understand one another's speech.

8 So the LORD scattered them abroad from thence upon the face of all the earth: and they left off to build the city.

9 Therefore is the name of it called Babel; because the LORD did there confound the language of all the earth: and from thence did the LORD scatter them abroad upon the face of all the earth.

Descendants of Noah

These descendants of Noah scattered widely over the world. Remember, they had enormous energy and longevity, descended from the men before the flood. Noah lived 350 years after the flood (Gen. 9:28). Shem lived 502 years after the flood (Gen. 11:10,11). Several of these men in the ancestry of Abraham, after the flood, lived 400 years. Some of them had been far to the east and as they returned, came to the country later called Babylon. There they determined to "build us a city and a tower." They wanted a great center so they would not be scattered. No doubt also they thought about some mighty place of refuge in case of another flood.

Nimrod, descended from Ham and Cush, "was a mighty hunter before the Lord" (Gen. 10:9), and he made a kingdom beginning at Babel (vs. 10). A mighty hunter? In the land where out of the ark had come saber-toothed tigers, "dragons" or dinosaurs, and mighty animals that had now come to fear man, and had scattered over the world and multiplied—a man could make him a great name as a bold and mighty hunter. So Nimrod became a king and gathered around him the multitude. They wanted a center and imagined great things in their own human wisdom. God saw the evil imaginings of their hearts and brought upon them the confusion of tongues. God's intent was to people the earth with different nations and languages. Paul was inspired to say at Athens that God ". . .hath made of one blood all nations of men for to dwell on all the face of the earth, and hath determined the times before appointed, and the bounds of their habitation" (Acts 17:26).

Foolish, infidel scientists would like to think that men evolved from beast ancestry and lived in trees and then lived naked in caves, then gradually developed speech and languages, then began to cultivate the ground. No, all this is from civilized people with a high degree of civilization before the flood. Later, many of these people, scattered in all the world, will lapse into heathendom and be turned over to their own wicked ways and ignorance, as we learn in Romans, chapter 1. But well-defined languages were among civilized races of people scattered out from the tower of Babel to cover the world. Perhaps some of the ancient ziggurats of Babylon were patterned after this tower of Babel.

Babylon: Growth of the Great City and Nation

This Babel was evidently the genesis of the great city and kingdom of Babylon. In this area were the great kingdoms of Nineveh, Assyria, and Babylon. Here were evidences of great civilization. Under **Babylonia,** the *Encyclopaedia Britannica* says:

> No flint weapons or other remains of a palaeolithic or true neolithic culture have been found in Babylonia or Assyria, and it is doubtful whether the river valleys were ever inhabited by men unacquainted with the use of metal.

There was no "Stone Age" there. Remember, this was soon after the flood.

Under **Archaeology of the Early Sumerian Period,** the *Encyclopaedia Britannica* says:

> According to the dynastic lists of Sumerian kings, the 1st dynasty after the Flood ruled at Kish, and from excavations there some early works of art have been recovered. Fragments of frieze, consisting of white limestone bas-reliefs on a background of slate, show a king slaughtering his enemies, and men engaged in tending cattle and dairy work. These reliefs appear to be earlier than the series found at Tall al'Ubaid, 4m. W. of Ur, which are certainly dated to the time of the 1st dynasty of Ur, the 3rd dynasty after the Flood; but the series from there, consisting of shell (*tridacna squamosa*) and limestone bas-reliefs on a background of a bituminous mixture, are in exactly the same technique and serve to show the earliest form of this kind of work.

Under **HAMMURABI,** the *Encyclopaedia Britannica* says:

> HAMMURABI, 6th king of the Amoritic or West Semitic dynasty of Babylonia, reigned 43 years, 2067-2025 B.C. and is one of the most illustrious figures of ancient history.

Later that same article says,

> Henceforth Babylon was to be the political and intellectual centre of West Asiatic history right down to the Christian era. His name is particularly associated with the great law code promulgated for the use of the courts throughout the empire.

That was the famous Code of Hammurabi.

So written language was well established long before this time. That article says,

> Hammurabi is generally identified with Amraphel, king of Shinar, who with Arioch of Ellasar, Cheodorla'omar of Elam and Tidal, king of Goiim, invaded Canaan in the days of Abraham.

Remember, Abraham was from Ur of the Chaldees, and Ur had a library and evidences of civilization, according to archaeologists.

Babylon thus has come to typify strong, worldly, godless government. And the book of Revelation seems to refer to

Rome, to be the center of the world empire of the Antichrist, as spiritual Babylon.

Civilization in Job's Day

The book of Job is the oldest book of the Bible. In it there is no mention of the Mosaic law, circumcision, priesthood, the tabernacle, the Sabbath, nothing about the sojourn in Egypt. It must have been written about the time of the patriarchs. Of course we regard it as the verbally inspired Word of God.

But Job speaks of the organ and harp (Job 30:31). Job 29:6 says, ". . .and the rock poured me out rivers of oil." That sounds like petroleum, though it is not likely they had any refining then. But they dug out and refined silver, gold, iron and brass, in common use (Job 28:1,2). Precious stones are mentioned: onyx, sapphire, crystal, coral, pearls, rubies and topaz (Job 28:16-19). It is evident that Job, a few generations after the flood, was in a great, well-established civilization that knew music, all the principal metals, precious stones and such matters. It was not a "Stone Age."

In Job also there seems to be some memory of the great convulsions that took place on the earth following the flood. Inland seas and lakes broke out and washed out rivers and flowed to the ocean. Job 28:4 says, "The flood breaketh out from the inhabitant; even the waters forgotten of the foot: they are dried up, they are gone away from men." Job 28:9-11 says, "He putteth forth his hand upon the rock; he overturneth the mountains by the roots. He cutteth out rivers among the rocks; and his eye seeth every precious thing. He bindeth the floods from overflowing; and the thing that is hid bringeth he forth to light."

We remember that that is divinely inspired and so it has full meaning. Job knew about the floods and the rising of mountains and the cutting of streams through the layers laid down by the flood.

VERSES 10-30:

10 ¶ These *are* the generations of Shem: Shem *was* an hundred years old, and begat Är-phăx-ăd two years after the flood:

11 And Shem lived after he begat Är-phăx-ăd five hundred years, and begat sons and daughters.

12 And Är-phăx-ăd lived five and thirty years, and begat Salah:

13 And Är-phăx-ăd lived after he begat Salah four hundred and three years, and begat sons and daughters.

14 And Salah lived thirty years, and begat Eber:

15 And Salah lived after he begat Eber four hundred and three years, and begat sons and daughters.

16 And Eber lived four and thirty years, and begat Peleg:

17 And Eber lived after he begat Peleg four hundred and thirty years, and begat sons and daughters.

18 And Peleg lived thirty years, and begat Rē-ū:

19 And Peleg lived after he begat Rē-ū two hundred and nine years, and begat sons and daughters.

20 And Rē-ū lived two and thirty years, and begat Serug:

21 And Rē-ū lived after he begat Serug two hundred and seven years, and begat sons and daughters.

22 And Serug lived thirty years, and begat Nā-hôr:

23 And Serug lived after he begat Nā-hôr two hundred years, and begat sons and daughters.

24 And Nā-hôr lived nine and twenty years, and begat Terah:

25 And Nā-hôr lived after he begat Terah an hundred and nineteen years, and begat sons and daughters.

26 And Terah lived seventy years, and begat Abram, Nā-hôr, and Haran.

27 ¶ Now these *are* the generations of Terah: Terah begat Abram, Nā-hôr, and Haran; and Haran begat Lot.

28 And Haran died before his father Terah in the land of his nativity, in Ur of the Chăl-dēēs.

29 And Abram and Nā-hôr took them wives: the name of Abram's wife *was* Sâr-ā-ī; and the name of Nā-hôr's wife, Milcah, the daughter of Haran, the father of Milcah, and the father of Iscah.

30 But Sâr-ā-ī was barren; she *had* no child.

Ancestry of Abram

God now begins the story of Abram, Isaac, Jacob, and the nation Israel. The stream of divine revelation will now carry this nation and its contact with other nations of the world down to the time of Christ.

Notice the enormous age of some of these. Shem lived after the flood 502 years, but that meant a total of only about 600 years, while Noah had lived 950 years (Gen. 9:29). There is a decreasing life span from Noah. Abram lived 175 years (Gen. 25:7,8). Isaac lived 180 years (Gen.

35:28). Jacob lived 147 years (Gen. 47:28). Joseph lived 110 years (Gen. 50:26).

But to understand the vigor with which the descendants of Noah set out to cover the world and populate it, it is well to remember the enormous vitality and strength of those men! Abram is ten generations from Noah. Ur of the Chaldees in the time of Abram was a civilized city. It had a great library, so people could read and write. Abraham is still called Abram, Sarah is here called Sarai; her name will be changed to Sarah. And Sarah is barren and will be barren until she is ninety years old!

Verse 26 says, "And Terah lived seventy years, and begat Abram, Nahor, and Haran." We do not suppose they were triplets but born in succession.

Compare verse 26, "And Terah lived seventy years, and begat Abram, Nahor, and Haran," with Genesis 5:32, "And Noah was five hundred years old: and Noah begat Shem, Ham, and Japheth." Again three are listed together but were not born together. And again the most important one is mentioned first, Shem, although from Genesis 10:21 we find that Japheth was "the elder." Even so here Abram, the most important son, is named first, but that would not necessarily mean he was born first. He may well have been the younger. Terah may have been seventy years old when Nahor was born and Abram born many years later. If Abram had been born when Terah was seventy years old, that would make a conflict in other dates.

Infidels have insisted that the evolution of mankind in civilization had not progressed far enough for Moses to write the Pentateuch. So the Graff-Wellhausen theory arose that the Pentateuch was a patchwork from many sources, including oral tradition, and prepared by a "redactor" or editor pretending to be Moses, about the time of the captivity! They said that Moses could not write and so could not have written the Pentateuch.

The wish was father to the thought, but the unbelievers have been shamed by the facts as they have appeared. Even

in Abraham's day, Hammurabi had his written code of
laws widely distributed and they doubtless copied laws two
hundred years before.

Dr. Joseph Free in *Archaeology and Bible History* gives
the following:

> Abraham's father, Terah, lived in Ur of the Chaldees in
> Southern Mesopotamia. Here Abraham grew up and
> spent his younger days. As a result of the archaeological
> excavations conducted at Ur in recent years (1922-34) by
> C. Leonard Woolley, a great deal is now known about this
> city; in fact, the whole background and environment of
> Abraham can now be pictured. The type of house of the
> Abrahamic period was well illustrated at Ur. An average
> dwelling measured forty by fifty-two feet, and had a side
> yard fifteen feet wide. The lower walls were built of
> burned brick, the upper of mud brick, and the whole wall
> was usually plastered and whitewashed. An entrance
> lobby led into the central court, on which all the rooms
> opened. On the lower floor were located the servants'
> room, the kitchen, the lavatory, the guest chamber, and
> also a lavatory and wash place reserved for visitors. In
> addition, there was a private chapel at the back of the
> house. Thus all the first floor was utilized for the servants
> and guests. The second floor housed the family, providing
> five rooms for their use. The entire house of the average
> middle-class person had from ten to twenty rooms.

> Other discoveries at Ur showed that education was not
> lacking in the days of Abraham. In one part of the
> excavations a school was found, and the nature of the
> curriculum was evidenced by the clay tablets which were
> discovered. Here the young scholars learned to write the
> cuneiform signs, as they were demonstrated by the
> schoolmaster on a flattened lump of soft clay. They also
> had reading lessons, which consisted mostly of hymns.
> Other clay tablets showed that in arithmetic they learned
> the multiplication and division tables, and as they
> progressed, they were subjected to working at square and
> cube roots. When the results of this part of the excavation
> are reviewed one finds that four thousand years ago, in
> the days of Abraham, the pupils had the same "reading,
> writing, and 'rithmetic" as their modern counterparts
> struggle with today.

> Even evidence of the far-reaching extent of the
> commerce of that day was revealed when a bill of lading of

about 2040 B.C. was unearthed. It showed that a ship had come up the Persian Gulf to Southern Mesopotamia after a two-year cruise. The cargo included copper ore, gold, ivory, hard woods for the cabinetmaker, and diorite and alabaster for making statuary. Several of these imported materials would have come from quite distant lands.

We are reminded again that Abraham, only ten generations from Noah, knew the civilization, the cities, the work in metals, in music and government, carried over from before the flood. Shem was still alive. He had lived before the flood.

How Old Is the Earth: How Long Ago the Flood?

It is customary for liberal historians to ignore the Bible and announce as though it were a scientific fact that it was 10,000 years ago that there was an Ice Age on earth or that four successive Ice Ages occurred beginning perhaps 20,000 or more years ago.

So, they have set dates for different events, the reign of various ancient kings and certain world movements based on an elaborate series of estimates and guesses. For example, in Byblos, the village in Lebanon from which we get the word "Bible" and which some call the oldest village in the world, we were told it had a civilization over 7,000 years ago.

Some estimate that the old Stone Age lasted so long, the New Stone Age so long, the Copper or Bronze Age so many years or centuries, the Iron Age, etc. Actually, the different stages of culture have varied in every general area. For example, there was no old Stone Age at the same time around the whole world. The beginning of the use of iron did not happen simultaneously around the world. Some heathen races even now use no iron. Some of them, not even bronze or copper. Some have used metals ever since the flood and before.

These liberal unbelievers in the Bible do not tell us that all these supposed dates are guesswork based on human reasoning and estimates. For example, how long would it probably take for certain heathen races to develop a language? How long to develop, then, written words? How many centuries they guess did it take for certain kinds of pottery to be supplanted by a different style. All this by guessing, by estimates. Then by stretching out Manetho's list of dynasties in Egypt (written by an Egyptian heathen priest about 250 B.C.—a thousand or two thousand years after these occurred) they try to place historic events and persons parallel to those dynasties. That list, however, is treated as if it were one consecutive list of kings when actually in a number of cases two or more reigned at the same time in various parts of Egypt. Then, where the length of a reign is not given as it usually is not in Manetho's list, they estimate how long was each reign. Was it 20 or 30 years?

Thus, by guessing these would-be scientists ignore the Bible, which is by far the most reliable of all ancient records, to make a fairy tale of a chronology of supposed dates. Velikovsky estimates historians have thus added at least 600 years to the true chronology of ancient Egypt and thus to other countries where there is some relation or connection.

The Genealogy From Adam to the Flood

In Genesis 5 we have a detailed genealogy from Adam through the godly line of Seth to Noah and the flood. Counting the age of each man when the son was born and adding 600 years, Noah's age when the flood came (Gen. 7:6), we find that it was 1,656 years from Adam to the flood.

Then, in Genesis 11:1-25 we find the genealogy from the flood to Terah, the father of Abraham, totaled 322 years, adding the two years after the flood when Arphaxad was born. Then Terah had children when he was 70 years old (Gen. 11:26), Abraham the most important, named first, but when you compare Genesis 11:32 and learn that Terah died at 205 years, with Acts 7:4 and Genesis 12:4 and 5 we learn that Abraham was 75 years old when his father died at 205. So, Abraham was born when his father was 130 years old.

Now, add that 130 years to the list in the genealogy from Shem down to the birth of Abraham and we find it was 452 years until Abraham was born, then 75 years more when he went to Canaan and 25 more till Isaac was born.

Are these genealogies reliable? Yes, they are. Some good, fundamental men like Morris and Whitcomb think that the genealogies are not primarily intended to give a chronology and they see a case in a Bible chronology where at least one name was omitted. We do not know all the answers, but if God was primarily talking about something else in these genealogies still they are literally true and trustworthy. God cannot lie even in an illustration or a casual statement. Note: months and fractions of years are not given but the figures are exact to the year. If I should say my first child was born when I was 26 years old, I would not pretend to say that my child was born on my birthday, but if that statement were inaccurate by 10 or 20 years it would be an inexcusable lie—whatever the motive.

Even so, the Ussher chronology may not be accurate within a year because many extra months are not counted up. But the Bible itself, properly translated, properly understood is exactly accurate. That means that within a few years at most we can count how far back it was to the flood and how old the world was before the flood.

Radiocarbon Dating Indicates Earth Only About Age Scriptures Indicate

The radiocarbon dating method was first developed by W. F. Libby in 1946. But of the surprising results of the investigation, Dr. Libby himself writes in the *American Scientist* of January, 1956, page 107,

> The first shock Dr. Arnold and I had was that our advisors informed us that history extended back only 5,000 years. We had thought initially that we would be able to get samples all along the curve back to 30,000

years, put the points in, and then our work would be finished. You read books and find statements that such and such a society or archaeological site is 20,000 years old. We learned rather abruptly that these numbers, these ancient ages, are not known; in fact, it is at about the time of the first dynasty in Egypt that the last historical date of any real certainty has been established.

Even the dates of the first dynasty in Egypt have been greatly stretched by the assumption that the dynasties were followed consecutively instead of some of them being parallel. But, put it down, any dates beyond that time are purely estimations and guesswork and not reliable.

VERSES 31,32:

31 And Terah took Abram his son, and Lot the son of Haran his son's son, and Sâr-́ā-ī his daughter in law, his son Abram's wife; and they went forth with them from Ur of the Chäl-́déeŝ, to go into the land of Cā- nă-ăn; and they came unto Haran, and dwelt there.

32 And the days of Terah were two hundred and five years: and Terah died in Haran.

Abram Stops in Haran

Note that Terah died at the age of 205. Acts 7:4 tells us, of Abraham, "Then came he out of the land of the Chaldeans, and dwelt in Charran: and from thence, when his father was dead, he removed him into this land, wherein ye now dwell." So Abram left Haran or Charran after his father died, and at that time he was "seventy and five years old when he departed out of Haran" (Gen. 12:4). But Genesis 12:4 says Abram was then 75. That would mean that Abram must have been born when Terah was 130 years old.

Fausset, in his *Bible Encyclopaedia and Dictionary,* says:

The statement in Gen. xi. 26, that Terah *was* 70 when he begat Abram, Nahor, and Haran, must apply only to the oldest, Haran. His being *oldest* appears from the fact that his brothers married his daughters, and that

Sarai was only ten years younger than A. (Gen. xvii. 17); the two younger were born subsequently, Abram, the youngest, when Terah was 130, as appears from comparing xi. 31 with Gen. xii. 4, Acts vii. 3, 4: "before he dwelt in Charran (Haran), while he was in Mesopotamia," in his 60th year, at Ur he received his *first* call: "Depart from thy land, to a land which I will show thee" (as yet *the exact* land was not defined).

Matthew Henry concurs with that explanation:

Though it is said (v. 26) that when Terah was seventy years old he begat Abram, Nahor, and Haran (which seems to tell us that Abram was the eldest son of Terah, and was born in his seventieth year), yet, by comparing v. 32, which makes Terah to die in his 205th year, with Acts vii. 4 (where it is said that Abram removed from Haran when his father was dead), and with ch. xii. 4 (where it is said that he was but seventy-five years old when he removed from Haran), it appears that he was born in the 130th year of Terah, and probably was his youngest son; for, in God's choices, the last are often first and the first last.

GENESIS 12

VERSES 1-3:

NOW the LORD had said unto Abram, Get thee out of thy country, and from thy kindred, and from thy father's house, unto a land that I will shew thee:

2 And I will make of thee a great nation, and I will bless thee, and make thy name great; and thou shalt be a blessing:

3 And I will bless them that bless thee, and curse him that curseth thee: and in thee shall all families of the earth be blessed.

Call of Abram

"Now the Lord *had* said. . . ." In the preceding chapter evidently when Abram was at Ur of the Chaldees, he had had the call of God. And he and his father Terah and Lot and their entourage evidently intended to come to Canaan. But Hebrews 11:8,9 says:

"By faith Abraham, when he was called to go out into a place which he should after receive for an inheritance, obeyed; and he went out, not knowing whither he went. By faith he sojourned in the land of promise, as in a strange country, dwelling in tabernacles with Isaac and Jacob, the heirs with him of the same promise."

At least Abram did not know where in all Palestine he would live.

But Terah was old. I can imagine that he was displeased with the travel. He wanted to settle down in Haran and there he stayed and eventually died there.

Was Abram wrong in taking along his father? Clearly he was. The Lord had said, "Get thee out of thy country, and from thy kindred, and from thy father's house." Abram did not leave his father nor his kinfolks; he took Lot, and he did not go on to Canaan for a time.

Abram was to leave Ur of the Chaldees, the country. Why? It was largely given over to idolatry. He must leave his father's house. Why? Because Terah, Abraham's father, and Nahor, his grandfather, were idolaters.

Joshua 24:1,2 says, "And Joshua gathered all the tribes of Israel to Shechem, and called for the elders of Israel, and for their heads, and for their judges, and for their officers; and they presented themselves before God. And Joshua said unto all the people, Thus saith the Lord God of Israel, Your fathers dwelt on the other side of the flood in old time, even Terah, the father of Abraham, and the father of Nachor: and they served other gods."

Terah was reluctant to go on to Canaan; wanted to stop and did stop in Haran. His influence was bad. Abram ought to have followed God's command and left his father's house and people entirely.

It is the price of discipleship that, "If any man come to me, and hate not his father, and mother, and wife, and children, and brethren, and sisters, yea, and his own life also, he cannot be my disciple" (Luke 14:26). One man had said to Jesus that when his father was buried he would come and follow Jesus and Jesus said, "Follow me; and let the dead bury their dead" (Matt. 8:22).

After the father died, Abram still took his nephew Lot. Abram's brother, Lot's father, Haran, died (Gen. 11:28). Lot was younger, and Abram felt responsible for him, so took him along. But Lot will prove to be trouble. At last Abram will find he must separate from Lot, told in the 13th chapter, and Lot will move into Sodom and there will lose his wife and married children in the destruction of that city. Abram ought to have left his father's house completely, but he did not.

Abram is to be the father of a great nation. God promises to bless those that bless Abram and to curse those that curse him.

That would be true about Abram. In a general sense, surely it would be true about the nation Israel, but not necessarily true about wicked and ungodly Jews who did not follow the faith of their father Abram. So Galatians 3:8,9 reminds us of this blessing: "And the scripture, foreseeing that God would justify the heathen through faith, preached before the gospel unto Abraham, saying, In thee shall all nations be blessed. So then they which be of faith are blessed with faithful Abraham." Galatians 3:14 says, "That the blessing of Abraham might come on the Gentiles through Jesus Christ; that we might receive the promise of the Spirit through faith." Again Galatians 3:29 says, "And if ye be Christ's, then are ye Abraham's seed, and heirs according to the promise." Romans 2:28,29 tells us, "For he is not a Jew, which is one outwardly; neither is that circumcision, which is outward in the flesh: But he is a Jew, which is one inwardly; and circumcision is that of the heart, in the spirit, and not in the letter; whose praise is not of men, but of God."

So the blessing on godly Abram is for him and those who follow in his faith, not necessarily for every unrepentant, rebellious, unbelieving Jew.

VERSES 4-9:

4 So Abram departed, as the LORD had spoken unto him; and Lot went with him: and Abram *was* seventy and five years old when he departed out of Haran.

5 And Abram took Sâr'-ā-ī his wife, and Lot his brother's son, and all their substance that they had gathered, and the souls that they had gotten in Haran; and they went forth to go into the land of Cā'-nă-ăn; and into the land of Cā'-nă-ăn they came.

6 ¶ And Abram passed through the land unto the place of Sī'-chĕm, unto the plain of Moreh. And the Cā'-nă-ăn-īte *was* then in the land.

7 And the LORD appeared unto Abram, and said, Unto thy seed will I give this land: and there builded he an altar unto the LORD, who appeared unto him.

8 And he removed from thence unto a mountain on the east of Beth–el, and pitched his tent, *having* Beth–el on the west, and Hā'-ī on the east: and there he builded an altar unto the LORD, and called upon the name of the LORD.

9 And Abram journeyed, going on still toward the south.

Abram in Land of Canaan

God had blessed Abram and Lot and they had gotten great flocks and herds. They left Haran and came down to the land of Canaan. Abram was 75 years old. He came to Sichem (probably Shechem), and the plain of Moreh. There the Lord gave one of the many promises: "Unto thy seed will I give this land." There Abram built an altar. Then he moved to a mountain east of Bethel, which was not far away. Again he built an altar to the Lord. Then Abram moved on south. Later he made his home near what is now Hebron, south and a little west of Jerusalem.

One might preach a sermon on Abram's seed! 1. The seed as the dust of the earth, meaning literal Israel, the race, and promise to inherit the land of Israel. Through this people came prophets, the Bible, the Saviour (Gen. 13:16). 2. The seed "as the stars for multitude," all the spiritual seed, all of the faith of Abram, like him saved by believing, spiritually circumcised (Gen. 15:5). 3. The great Seed, which is Christ, in whom all the world was to be blessed (Gen. 13:15; Gal. 3:16).

VERSES 10-20:

10 ¶ And there was a famine in the land: and Abram went down into Egypt to sojourn there; for the famine *was* grievous in the land.

11 And it came to pass, when he was come near to enter into Egypt, that he said unto Sâr-́ā-ī his wife, Behold now, I know that thou *art* a fair woman to look upon:

12 Therefore it shall come to pass, when the Egyptians shall see thee, that they shall say, This *is* his wife: and they will kill me, but they will save thee alive.

13 Say, I pray thee, thou *art* my sister: that it may be well with me for thy sake; and my soul shall live because of thee.

14 ¶ And it came to pass, that, when Abram was come into Egypt, the Egyptians beheld the woman that she *was* very fair.

15 The princes also of Phâr-́āōh saw her, and commended her before Phâr-́āōh: and the woman was taken into Phâr-́āōh's house.

16 And he entreated Abram well for her sake: and he had sheep, and oxen, and he asses, and menservants, and maidservants, and she asses, and camels.

17 And the Lᴏʀᴅ plagued Phâr-́āōh and his house with great plagues because of Sâr-́ā-ī Abram's wife.

18 And Phâr-́āōh called Abram, and said, What *is* this *that* thou hast done unto me? why didst thou not tell me that she *was* thy wife?

19 Why saidst thou, She *is* my sister? so I might have taken her to me to wife: now therefore behold thy wife, take *her*, and go thy way.

20 And Phâr-́āōh commanded *his* men concerning him: and they sent him away, and his wife, and all that he had.

Abram Down in Egypt

There was a famine in the land. It was hard for Abram to

follow explicitly the command of the Lord. It was hard for him to leave his father. Later it was hard to separate from Lot. And in this land that God has promised there came a famine. So, discouraged, he thinks, "I will go down temporarily to Egypt until the famine is over."

But trouble awaits him in Egypt. Sarai must have been a beautiful woman. And Abram, thinking the famous Egyptian king will want her for his wife, planned with Sarai to say, "I am your sister." She was in truth his half-sister, but in this case a half truth is only a lie. So sure enough—the princes of Pharaoh saw Sarai and thinking she was single recommended her to Pharaoh, so Pharaoh had the woman taken to his house, and he gave Abram, the supposed brother, many gifts for her sake.

But God would not let His servant come to disaster in this matter. So plagues came on Pharaoh's house until he came to see that he had been deceived and that Sarai was a wife. So he rebuked Abram and Sarai; and so he and his princes sent Abram and his wife away and they left Egypt. Surely Abram would have been better to have stayed in the Land of Promise and have God's care there, than down to Egypt in bad company.

It was lack of faith that led Abram to flee away from the place that God had sent him. Dr. C. I. Scofield says:

> A famine was often a disciplinary testing of God's people in the land. (Cf. Gen. 26.1; 42.5; Ruth 1.1; 2 Sam. 24.13; Psa. 105.16.) The resort to Egypt (the world) is typical of the tendency to substitute for lost spiritual power the fleshly resources of the world, instead of seeking, through confession and amendment, the restoration of God's presence and favour.

Could not God help His own who was in a famine-stricken land where God had led him? And Abram had not depended on God to deliver him from Pharaoh but had schemed to have Sarai say half a lie—that she was his sister. He would not have assurance of God's care in Egypt, perhaps, in his disobedience.

In Canaan, obeying, he could trust. In Egypt, fleeing the famine without God's instruction, he could not.

GENESIS 13

AND Abram went up out of Egypt, he, and his wife, and all that he had, and Lot with him, into the south.

2 And Abram *was* very rich in cattle, in silver, and in gold.

3 And he went on his journeys from the south even to Beth–el, unto the place where his tent had been at the beginning, between Beth–el and Hā̄-ī;

4 Unto the place of the altar, which he had made there at the first: and there Abram called on the name of the LORD.

Back From Egypt to Altar and Promised Land

Abram went "into the south," that is, into the south part of the land of Canaan, then on north, near Bethel. Bethel is north of Jerusalem. Remember Jerusalem did not become a Jewish city until the time of King David but was a city of the Jebusites and not mentioned in these times of Abram.

But there, between Bethel and Hai, "unto the place of the altar, which he had made there at the first . . . Abram called on the name of the Lord." Oh, he had not called on the Lord, he had had no altar in Egypt as far as the record shows. But now, back in the Land of Promise, back to his altar, Abram could offer a sacrifice and feel free to call upon God. God had cared for him in Egypt, as God cares for His own now, unworthy as we are. God cared for Jonah and had a whale to rescue him from the deep, then vomit him out onto dry land, although Jonah had been fleeing from God. But God has made His promise to Abram and God has His plans! He cares for His own.

Lot was with Abram. Abram has not obeyed in every detail the command of God of Genesis 12:1, "Get thee out of thy country, and from thy kindred, and from thy father's house." He had started with his old father Terah, intending to go to Canaan (Gen. 11:31), but doubtless at the old father's insistence, had stopped some years in

Haran until Terah died. Now, he still has with him Lot, his brother's son, one of his kindred, one of his father's house. Now, both Abram and Lot are rich. God has been with them, has increased their flocks and herds, even in Egypt.

VERSES 5-9:

5 ¶ And Lot also, which went with Abram, had flocks, and herds, and tents.

6 And the land was not able to bear them, that they might dwell together: for their substance was great, so that they could not dwell together.

7 And there was a strife between the herdmen of Abram's cattle and the herdmen of Lot's cattle: and the Că-nă-ăn-īte and the Pĕ-rĭz-zīte dwelled then in the land.

8 And Abram said unto Lot, Let there be no strife, I pray thee, between me and thee, and between my herdmen and thy herdmen; for we *be* brethren.

9 *Is* not the whole land before thee? separate thyself, I pray thee, from me: if *thou wilt take* the left hand, then I will go to the right; or if *thou depart* to the right hand, then I will go to the left.

At Last He Must Separate From Lot

How patiently God dealt with Abram! Do not judge him harshly. Have you really experienced what it means to obey Luke 14:26? "If any man come to me, and hate not his father, and mother, and wife, and children, and brethren, and sisters, yea, and his own life also, he cannot be my disciple"? Has that ever been real to you? Have you had to walk off and leave loved ones or be separated not only in distance but in principles and fellowship from those you love? Do you know what Jesus really demands in Luke 14:33, "So likewise, whosoever he be of you that forsaketh not all that he hath, he cannot be my disciple"? Who is ever a proven, mature Christian until he goes through the fire and is tried of God?

Remember that even Saul had gone back to Tarsus, temporarily leaving the ministry, after his life was threatened again and again (Acts 9:29,30). We know that Eli, Samuel, and David loved their children too well and did not discipline them enough. Adam fell, God said, "because thou hast hearkened unto the voice of thy wife. . ." (Gen. 3:17).

In jail, Paul writes, "All they which are in Asia be turned away from me; of whom are Phygellus and Hermogenes" (II Tim. 1:15). He wrote later and said, "Demas hath forsaken me, having loved this present world. . .Only Luke is with me" (II Tim. 4:10,11).

Who reaches full stature of dependence on God alone and leaves all, until they leave him? Wesley tried hard to stay in the Anglican church even when they would not allow him to preach in their churches, and outside the church at Epworth he preached on his father's tombstone. He did not intend the Methodist movement to be a separate denomination. But God intended it.

So God has serious things to teach Abram and it is not easy. Abram is willing to give any part of the land to Lot. Circumstances mean they must separate. Thus God at last brings Abram to the separation that he ought to have made gladly on principle years before.

VERSES 10-13:

10 And Lot lifted up his eyes, and beheld all the plain of Jordan, that it *was* well watered every where, before the LORD destroyed Sodom and Gō-mŏr-́răh, *even* as the garden of the LORD, like the land of Egypt, as thou comest unto Zoar.
11 Then Lot chose him all the plain of Jordan; and Lot journeyed east: and they separated themselves the one from the other.
12 Abram dwelled in the land of Cā-́nă-ăn, and Lot dwelled in the cities of the plain, and pitched *his* tent toward Sodom.
13 But the men of Sodom *were* wicked and sinners before the LORD exceedingly.

Lot Chooses to Move Toward Sodom

Lot was to make the choice, then Abraham would take whatever was left. If Lot chose to go to the right, Abraham would go to the left. Lot looked down in the Jordan Valley. It seems certain that what is now the lower half of the Dead Sea was once a garden spot, a lush land, with fine grass for the flocks and herds of Lot. Down there also are five little cities, Sodom, Gomorrah, Admah, Zeboiim and Zoar. I think Lot was intrigued with the thought of prosperity. Perhaps he thought, "Uncle Abe doesn't mind staying out in those barren hills. I'll get mine while I can." Yes, and, oh, too bad, he did not fear and did not shrink from the wickedness of the cities, so wicked, so lewd, that God must eventually destroy them. So Lot pitched his tent toward Sodom.

The Dead Sea has filled up until it covers now what was once the cities that were destroyed. An expedition led by Dr. Melvin Grove Kyle, then from Xenia Theological Seminary, found graveyards of the wicked cities, cities now covered in the waters of the Dead Sea. They found lewd inscriptions, they found evidence of the fire and brimstone from Heaven that destroyed them (*Explorations of Sodom*, by Kyle).

Did Lot hunger for the cities, the society, the settled civilization of Ur of the Chaldees from which he came? At any rate, he was greatly attracted toward these wicked cities. He who "pitched his tent toward Sodom," alas, soon moved into the city.

There is a fateful progress in sin, a way of degeneration. Note this progress in Psalm 1:1, "Blessed is the man that walketh not in the counsel of the ungodly, nor standeth in the way of sinners, nor sitteth in the seat of the scornful." First, one walks in the counsel of unsaved people. Second, he stops and stands in the way of outbroken sinners and keeps company with them. Third, he sits down in the seat of the scornful, the scoffer. So Lot first pitched toward Sodom and then moved into Sodom, then his wife and children absorbed the wicked viewpoint of Sodom.

Pope says:

> Vice is a monster of so frightful mien,
> As to be hated needs but to be seen;
> Yet seen too oft, familiar with her face,
> We first endure, then pity, then embrace.

David looked on Bathsheba bathing, then sent for her,

then seduced her, then murdered her husband (II Sam. 11).

The young man who at first drinks soft drinks at the bar will later drink alcoholic drinks there. The girl who dates unsaved men will likely love and marry an unsaved man. Young people who neck and pet then will commit adultery. Those who tolerate sin later choose it and then embrace it. Lot now is in the great place of wickedness.

As the person who at first is a moderate drinker gets to be a drunkard, so the one who pitches his tent toward Sodom then lands in Sodom. At least, so it was with Lot.

Lot did not know it, but moving in toward Sodom meant the loss, not only of his wealth but of his family—yea, even the loss of their souls. And later, with his wife turned to a pillar of salt, with married daughters and grandchildren burned up in the fiery holocaust from Heaven, and the two single daughters with illegitimate children, Lot will rue that choice that moved him toward Sodom.

VERSES 14-18:

14 ¶ And the LORD said unto Abram, after that Lot was separated from him, Lift up now thine eyes, and look from the place where thou art northward, and southward, and eastward, and westward:

15 For all the land which thou seest, to thee will I give it, and to thy seed for ever.

16 And I will make thy seed as the dust of the earth: so that if a man can number the dust of the earth, *then* shall thy seed also be numbered.

17 Arise, walk through the land in the length of it and in the breadth of it; for I will give it unto thee.

18 Then Abram removed *his* tent, and came and dwelt in the plain of Mamre, which *is* in Hebron, and built there an altar unto the LORD.

God's Covenant With Abram Restated

It is significant that after the close ties with Lot are broken, God can reveal Himself more plainly to Abram.

Note the threefold nature of the promise to Abram here.

1. All the land was given to him, the literal land of Canaan where he was then. He was to walk through the

land, north and south and east and west, and God would give it to him.

2. God would give him a great posterity, seed "as the dust of the earth" for multitude. That is a promise of the nation Israel to come.

3. Moreover, this land was to be given to Abram and to his seed "for ever." Galatians 3:16 reminds us, "Now to Abraham and his seed were the promises made. He saith not, And to seeds, as of many; but as of one, And to thy seed, which is Christ." So really, the promise is to Christ, the Seed of Abram, and here the reign of Jesus Christ on earth is promised.

In my novel story of the life of Abraham, *Seeking a City*, I call attention to the fact that Abraham has for himself and for Jesus Christ a title deed to the land of Canaan. And whatever else may come, and even if God burns over this whole earth by fire and destroys what fire will destroy, yet He has promised to make a new land of Eden on earth, and Christ is then to reign as Abraham's Seed over the whole earth.

Abram must have understood that it was a certain single Seed, particularly, that this promise involves, and so it was part of his understanding about the coming Messiah, the Saviour, whom he came to know and trust.

Now, Abram moved from his place near Bethel, north of Jerusalem, down to the plain of Mamre near Hebron, south of Jerusalem and south of Bethlehem. This will be the principal center of Abram's life; and here at the Cave of Machpelah in Hebron will he and Sarah be buried.

GENESIS 14

VERSES 1-12:

AND it came to pass in the days of Ăm-ră-́phĕl king of Shī-́när, r-́ĭ-ŏch king of Ĕl-lā-́sär, Chĕd-ôr-.-ō-́mĕr king of Elam and Tidal ing of nations;

2 That these made war with Bera ing of Sodom, and with Birsha king f Gō-mŏr-́räh, Shinab king of Ad-ah, and Shĕm-ē-́bĕr king of Zĕ-ō̂î-́ĭm, and the king of Bela, which Zoar.

3 All these were joined together in the ale of Siddim, which is the salt sea.

4 Twelve years they served Chĕd-r-lā-ō-́mĕr, and in the thirteenth ear they rebelled.

5 And in the fourteenth year came hĕd-ôr-lā-ō-́mĕr, and the kings that ere with him, and smote the Rĕph-́ĭms in Ăsh-́tĕ-rŏth Kär-nā-́ĭm, and ne Zuzims in Ham, and the Ē-́mĭms Shā-́vēh Kĭr-ĭ-ă-thā-́ĭm,

6 And the Horites in their mount eir, unto Ĕl-pâr-́ăn, which is by the vilderness.

7 And they returned, and came to En–mishpat, which is Kadesh, and smote all the country of the Ă-mălĕk-ītes, and also the Amorites, that dwelt in Hăz-́ĕ-zŏn–tā-́mär.

8 And there went out the king of Sodom, and the king of Gō-mŏr-́räh, and the king of Admah, and the king of Zĕ-bô̂î-́ĭm, and the king of Bela (the same is Zoar;) and they joined battle with them in the vale of Siddim;

9 With Chĕd-ôr-lā-ō-́mĕr the king of Elam, and with Tidal king of nations, and Ăm-ră-́phĕl king of Shī-́när, and Ăr-́ĭ-ŏch king of Ĕl-lā-́sär; four kings with five.

10 And the vale of Siddim was full of slimepits; and the kings of Sodom and Gō-mŏr-́räh fled, and fell there; and they that remained fled to the mountain.

11 And they took all the goods of Sodom and Gō-mŏr-́räh, and all their victuals, and went their way.

12 And they took Lot, Abram's brother's son, who dwelt in Sodom, and his goods, and departed.

Lot Taken Captive in War

Lot was now in Sodom (vs. 12).

Now, a war came into the vale of Siddim to devastate the five cities, Sodom, Gomorrah, Admah, Zeboiim, and Zoar. At first there were four kings sweeping the south country—Kadesh, the country of the Amalekites and the Amorites; Mount Seir, the country of the Edomites; Esau's people at Petra and around that rock city. The four kings included Amraphel, king of Shinar, which is Babylon. Note the vengeance on "the Rephaims in Ashteroth Karnaim, and the Zuzims in Ham, and the Emmims in Shaveh Kiriathaim, And the Horites in their mount Seir, unto El-paran" (Gen. 14:5,6). Here, giants and all in that country are overcome in a great punitive crusade through the south, clearing, no doubt, the trails of the traffic down to Egypt.

In the vale of Siddim were these five cities, Sodom, Gomorrah, Admah, Zeboiim, and Zoar (or Bela). They had been in subjection to Chedorlaomer for fourteen years and then rebelled. Perhaps they refused to pay tribute and cast out his officers. So the armies that have swept through Moab, Amalek, and Edomite country came against these five cities and conquered them speedily. Sodom and Gomorrah are looted of riches and food. And Lot, being a very rich man, was taken along with his riches. Very probably he was kept as a hostage. Lot's flocks and herds are taken, too. And these kings go on north with their booty, little thinking there can be any retribution after they have conquered city after city after city.

Amraphel, king of Shinar, is identified as Hammurabi of Babylon, says *Encyclopedia Britannica.* So these kings of strong nations had strong, victorious armies.

VERSES 13-16:

13 ¶ And there came one that had escaped, and told Abram the Hebrew; for he dwelt in the plain of Mamre the Amorite, brother of Eshcol, and brother of Ā-nĕr: and these *were* confederate with Abram.

14 And when Abram heard that his brother was taken captive, he armed his trained *servants,* born in his own house, three hundred and eighteen, and pursued *them* unto Dan.

15 And he divided himself against them, he and his servants, by night, and smote them, and pursued them unto Hobah, which *is* on the left hand of Damascus.

16 And he brought back all the goods, and also brought again his brother Lot, and his goods, and the women also, and the people.

Abram, Man of God, Man of War

Godly Abram—is he too nice and kind to fight? No. See the courage, the decision, the energy, the determination of this good man. God is with him. Lot, with great riches but with little touch with God and little of the courage and the decision which Abram has, could not defend himself. And even the five kings and their armies were helpless before this marauding host.

But Abram had 318 trained servants, born in his own house. Oh, no doubt he had taught them the use of the bow and the spear. And had drilled them in obedience and courage. In that frontier region, with every small city having its own king and with no strong central government, people took what they wanted if they could, and men must defend themselves, their families and herds.

But Abram had allies. He had made a confederation with Aner, Eshcol and Mamre, neighboring stockmen, each with his own servants and families. They joined in with Abram in the pursuit of these kings. Far into the north they rode with their camels. They struck the camp of these four kings at night and then followed them, harassed them and slaughtered them all the way to Dan in the northern part of Israel and just a little way from Damascus. The kings themselves were slaughtered (vs. 17). All the booty was taken and the captives released to come back with Abram.

Good Christians ought to have courage. They must often stand alone against sin. Sometimes they must fight for what is right. The government stands for God. But in this case Abram was not under the government of any other king, so he must be responsible for his people. He had trained his servants and soldiers, so they went out to fight and deliver the innocent from their captivity and to punish the murdering, slaughtering hosts of the kings who came against them. Abram came to deliver Lot and he did.

Those liberals who discourage people from fighting for their country and so then make heroes of the draft-evaders and the rebels do not honor God. Remember that "the powers that be are ordained of God." The ruler is "the minister of God to thee for good." "He beareth not the sword in vain" but is the avenger to punish sin (Rom. 13). Godliness means patriotism. It means the support of the weak, the care of our country and the care of our families, too.

We must remember that God was with Abram, and so Melchizedek could bless "the most high God, which hath delivered thine enemies into thy hand," he said to Abram (vs. 20).

How often God has delivered His own in times of deadly combat! He gave victory to the lad David against the giant Goliath (I Sam. 17:42-51); to Jonathan and his armorbearer (I Sam. 14:4-16); to King Asa in victory over the million-man army of the Ethiopians (II Chron. 14:9-15) and many others.

VERSES 17-24:

17 ¶ And the king of Sodom went out to meet him after his return from the slaughter of Chĕd-ôr-lā-ō-́mĕr, and of the kings that *were* with him, at the valley of Shā-́vēh, which *is* the king's dale.

18 And Mĕl-chĭz-́ĕd-ĕk king of Salem brought forth bread and wine: and he *was* the priest of the most high God.

19 And he blessed him, and said, Blessed *be* Abram of the most high God, possessor of heaven and earth:

20 And blessed be the most high God, which hath delivered thine enemies into thy hand. And he gave him tithes of all.

21 And the king of Sodom said unto Abram, Give me the persons, and take the goods to thyself.

22 And Abram said to the king of Sodom, I have lift up mine hand unto the LORD, the most high God, the possessor of heaven and earth,

23 That I will not *take* from a thread even to a shoelatchet, and that I will not take any thing that *is* thine, lest thou shouldest say, I have made Abram rich:

24 Save only that which the young men have eaten, and the portion of the men which went with me, Ā-́nĕr, Eshcol, and Mamre; let them take their portion.

Triumphant Return With Captives

The king of Sodom went out to meet Abram after his return, "And Melchizedek king of Salem brought forth bread and wine: and he was the priest of the most high God." We do not know much about Melchizedek. He is mentioned in Psalm 110:4, and again in Hebrews 5,6 and 10. And Hebrews 7:1-3 tells us:

"For this Melchisedec, king of Salem, priest of the most high God, who met Abraham returning from the slaughter

of the kings, and blessed him; To whom also Abraham gave a tenth part of all; first being by interpretation King of righteousness, and after that also King of Salem, which is, King of peace; Without father, without mother, without descent, having neither beginning of days, nor end of life; but made like unto the Son of God; abideth a priest continually."

Who Was Melchizedek?

In his book, *Through the Pentateuch, Chapter by Chapter,* W. H. Griffith Thomas says about Melchizedek, "He was one of the line of Shem that still worshiped the true God." *Halley's Bible Handbook* says,

> Priest-King of Salem (Jerusalem). Hebrew tradition says that he was Shem, survivor of the Flood, who was still alive, earth's oldest living man, priest, in the patriarchal age, of the whole race. If so, it is a hint that, thus early, right after the Flood, God chose Jerusalem to be the scene of Human Redemption. Whoever he was, he was a picture and type of Christ (Ps. 110; Heb. 5:6,7).

Some people think that he was Christ in pre-incarnate form. I hardly think so. He was called a man. Jesus is to be "after the order of Melchizedek"; so evidently Melchizedek was supposed to be a likeness of Christ, not Christ Himself. He is listed as "without father, without mother, without descent"; so we would think the Bible simply means that God left off the record of father and mother and descent and pedigree so Melchizedek would properly represent and picture the Lord Jesus.

Shem himself was still alive in Abram's day. He lived 502 years after the flood (Gen. 11:10,11). In my novel, *Seeking a City,* on the life of Abraham, I, too, suggest that possibly Shem himself was Melchizedek, now become king of a little town, Salem or Peace, and the priest of God. That would be suitable, but that is only conjecture.

Abram gave tithes to Melchizedek, thus picturing that the Levitical priesthood would come from Abram's grandson not yet born, and was subject to Christ, pictured here by Melchizedek. Christ is a greater Priest than Aaron.

His sacrifice is greater than that of any Levitical offerings. Incidentally, it is certainly indicated that before any Mosaic law, people felt it normal and right to show their faith and dependence on God by bringing in tithes. That was proper and right then, as it is now. Not just as a matter of law, but because when we rent God's house (our home) we should pay rent. When we borrow God's money (our money is really His), we should pay interest. When all we have belongs to God, we should see He gets some income from it.

The king of Sodom suggested to Abram, "Give me the persons and take the goods to thyself," but Abram refused to take a thing for himself. He asked that the young men who went with him should take their portions of the spoil and the rest was returned. Lot went back to his city and the others had their goods restored.

This little story reveals some things about the character of this great man Abram that delight our heart.

GENESIS 15

AFTER these things the word of the LORD came unto Abram in a vision, saying, Fear not, Abram: I *am* thy shield, *and* thy exceeding great reward.

God's Protection and Reward for His Own

God said to Abram, "I am thy shield." Had He not just proved it? Abram had gone out against four kings and their armies, who were triumphant after destroying cities, and looting city after city. Yet Abram, with his 318 servants and possibly a few hundred allies, had not only routed these kings but had slaughtered them and their armies, had released every captive and taken back all the booty! And he had done it without harm to himself. God had been with him. God was his shield! Abram was learning to trust the Lord.

It is true that God was a shield to Abram, but is He not a shield to all who trust in Him? Psalms 33:20 and 59:11 call Him "our shield." The Psalmist cried out in Psalm 84:9, "Behold, O God our shield," and verse 11 says, "For the Lord God is a sun and shield: the Lord will give grace and glory: no good thing will he withhold from them that walk uprightly." O thou Shield of Abraham and of all who trust in Thee!

Abram found what many another trusting Christian has found, that "the angel of the Lord encampeth round about them that fear him, and delivereth them" (Ps. 34:7). Abram is learning the sweet promise that later will be written down in Hebrews 13:5 and 6, "I will never leave thee, nor forsake thee. So that we may boldly say, The Lord is my helper, and I will not fear what man shall do unto me."

But God said to Abram also, "I am. . .thy exceeding great reward." Abram had given to Lot his choice of all the richest land which God had promised Abram. He had refused to profit from the spoil taken at great exertion and great risk. Lot, on the other hand, seeking riches, could not hold his possessions against the invaders, nor have God's assurance. But Lot is a friend of the wicked, and soon he is to lose wife, family and riches, and live in a cave.

Abram had given tithes to Melchizedek, the priest of God, and he will learn that by sowing bountifully, he reaps bountifully. Proverbs 3:9,10 tells us, "Honour the Lord with thy substance, and with the firstfruits of all thine increase: So shall thy barns be filled with plenty, and thy presses shall burst out with new wine." Abram has learned to give and it will be given to him.

What will one get for serving God? Peter asked that question of Jesus, saying:

"Behold, we have forsaken all, and followed thee; what shall we have therefore? And Jesus said unto them, Verily I say unto you, That ye which have followed me, in the regeneration when the Son of man shall sit in the throne of his glory, ye also shall sit upon twelve thrones, judging the twelve tribes of Israel. And every one that hath forsaken houses, or brethren, or sisters, or father, or mother, or wife, or children, or lands, for my name's sake, shall receive an hundredfold, and shall inherit everlasting life."—Matt. 19:27-29.

Oh, the Lord is our "exceeding great reward." I have had great joy out of the command of God that the Levites were not to be provided an inheritance with the other tribes of Israel because "the Lord God of Israel was their inheritance" (Josh. 13:33).

So the Lord is the exceeding great reward of Abram and of all of us who trust Him.

VERSES 2-11:

2 And Abram said, Lord GOD, what wilt thou give me, seeing I go childless, and the steward of my house *is* this Ĕl-ĭ-ē-́zĕr of Damascus?

3 And Abram said, Behold, to me thou hast given no seed: and, lo, one born in my house is mine heir.

4 And, behold, the word of the LORD *came* unto him, saying, This shall not be thine heir; but he that shall come forth out of thine own bowels shall be thine heir.

5 And he brought him forth abroad, and said, Look now toward heaven, and tell the stars, if thou be able to number them: and he said unto him, So shall thy seed be.

6 And he believed in the LORD; and he counted it to him for righteousness.

7 And he said unto him, I *am* the LORD that brought thee out of Ur of the Chăl-́dēĕs̀, to give thee this land to inherit it.

8 And he said, Lord GOD, whereby shall I know that I shall inherit it?

9 And he said unto him, Take me an heifer of three years old, and a she goat of three years old, and a ram of three years old, and a turtledove, and a young pigeon.

10 And he took unto him all these, and divided them in the midst, and laid each piece one against another: but the birds divided he not.

11 And when the fowls came down upon the carcases, Abram drove them away.

Abram Wants a Son

Look at verses 2, 3, and 8. Abram was a man of like passions as we are, and his faith wavered often. Besides here, it wavered in Genesis 12:10-13, in 16:1-3, in 17:17 and 18, and again in chapter 20. The doubter Abram, who again and again lost hope and wanted a sign, or wanted to get a child another way besides the way God had promised, finally became "faithful Abraham" (Gal. 3:9); the man who believed that God would raise up Isaac even from the dead, and was willing to sacrifice him (Gen. 22; Heb. 11:17-19). There is hope for us. We, too, may grow in faith if we try God. Remember that there were about forty years between the first promise and the sacrifice of Isaac.

Abram wanted a son. That great desire in his heart was stirred up more and more by the promises of God about his seed, his descendants. He had a greatly loved and trusted servant Eliezer. Is that the only heir that he could have? "Hope deferred maketh the heart sick"! No, the Lord told him, "This shall not be thine heir; but he that shall come forth out of thine own bowels shall be thine heir." A long delayed promise is still a promise. He will have a son.

How many descendants will Abram have? Abram, look at all the stars in the heavens: can you count them? "So shall thy seed be," God said. How many descendants? "As the dust of the earth" is the promise of Genesis 13:16. Here it is as the stars in Heaven.

That must mean that not only will Abraham have an earthly seed—literal descendants of his body—but he will have spiritual seed also. All the born-again of the faith of Abraham are in that sense Abraham's, for Galatians 3:29 says, "And if ye be Christ's, then are ye Abraham's seed, and heirs according to the promise." Oh, the starry heavens that Abram saw that night picture all the hosts that would trust in Abram's Saviour and in Abram's greater Seed, Jesus Christ. Galatians 3:14 tells us ". . .that the blessing of Abraham might come on the Gentiles through Jesus Christ. . . ."

How much did Abram understand about this? Far more than appears on the surface, I am sure, because there is a Gospel in this, a Gospel which Abram understood, at least faintly. His great Seed would be a Saviour and Abram trusted in that Saviour not yet clearly revealed.

We know that Abram understood about Christ because Jesus said, "Abraham rejoiced to see my day: and he saw it, and was glad" (John 8:56). And when he would offer Isaac as a sacrifice, he said, "My son, God will provide himself a lamb for a burnt-offering."

So, on this great promise, kept in Abram's mind and over which he had meditated and dreamed, no doubt—that promise of a coming seed and of a great multitude of others who would be saved through this same faith—"Abraham believed God, and it was counted unto him for righteousness."

You must remember that Abram had long been offering bloody sacrifices. Did he not know that they pictured the Lamb of God that would take away the sin of the world? Did he not understand the substitutionary atonement which God someway had promised to make? Surely he did.

Remember, this is not some other strange plan of salvation. This is the same salvation offered in John 3:16, the same Gospel described in I Corinthians 15:3,4. That Gospel saved Abram. Peter said in Acts 10:43, "To him give all the prophets witness, that through his name whosoever believeth in him shall receive remission of sins." So every prophet in the Old Testament, including Abram, preached the same Gospel of salvation through the coming Messiah and trusting in Him.

In Romans, chapter 4, we are told Abraham is now our example in this matter of salvation. Verses 1 to 4 tell us:

"What shall we say then that Abraham our father, as pertaining to the flesh, hath found? For if Abraham were justified by works, he hath whereof to glory; but not before God. For what saith the scripture? Abraham believed God, and it was counted unto him for righteousness. Now to him that worketh is the reward not reckoned of grace, but of debt."

The rest of Romans 4 reminds us that Abraham was not yet circumcised and this is not a matter of ceremonial law, but that Abraham, thus trusting the coming Saviour, was a good example for both Jews and Gentiles, "For the promise, that he should be the heir of the world, was not to Abraham, or to his seed, through the law, but through the righteousness of faith" (Rom. 4:13). Oh, Abraham is saved, is now a child of God!

The Sacrifices

Note the sacrifices in verse 9: "an heifer of three years old, and a she goat of three years old, and a ram of three years old, and a turtledove, and a young pigeon."

In the first place, there is great variety in the sacrifices. Surely God is trying to remind Abraham of the great multitude of all nations and tribes which will trust in the coming Saviour. The females, the heifer and the she goat, mean someway a sacrifice taking the place of the weak and needy.

Once when Israel was in great distress and was about to

be destroyed by the Philistines, Samuel offered a suckling lamb (I Sam. 7:9). Surely that pictured a helpless people calling on the Lord for mercy, as those without defense. More often it was a male lamb that was offered, or a bullock, but now it is a heifer and a she goat. All the weak, the sinful, the downtrodden of the world are invited to come to be spiritually Abraham's seed.

The sacrifice of the pigeon and the turtledove were for those who were too poor to bring any other. It may be that the she goat some way represented Gentiles as well as Jews. Jesus used the picture of goats to picture the lost (Matt. 25:31-46). At any rate, we understand that God is by these sacrifices picturing that the blood of Jesus Christ is for all the sinful world.

The sacrifices were divided in two parts except the two birds. There is some indication that that had reference to the fact that it takes two people to enter into a treaty or covenant and in this case God and Abraham. Lange's commentary says,

> The animals named here, are the sacrificial animals of the Levitical cultus. The future possession of Canaan was represented beforehand in the sacrifices of Canaan. The sacrificial animals were all divided. . . .

Again Lange says, "The individual specimens of the collective sacrificial animals, designate, in Calvin's view, all Israel in all its parts, as one sacrifice. In the three years age, Theodoret finds an intimation of the three generations of bondage in Egypt; which Keil approves, with a reference to Judg. vi.25 (seven years' bondage, a seven-year-old bullock)."

VERSES 12-17:

12 And when the sun was going down, a deep sleep fell upon Abram; and, lo, an horror of great darkness fell upon him.

13 And he said unto Abram, Know of a surety that thy seed shall be a stranger in a land *that is* not their's, and shall serve them; and they shall

afflict them four hundred years;

14 And also that nation, whom they shall serve, will I judge: and afterward shall they come out with great substance.

15 And thou shalt go to thy fathers in peace; thou shalt be buried in a good old age.

16 But in the fourth generation they shall come hither again: for the iniquity of the Amorites *is* not yet full.

17 And it came to pass, that, when the sun went down, and it was dark, behold a smoking furnace, and a burning lamp that passed between those pieces.

Israel to Be in Bondage in Egypt

"An horror of great darkness" on Abram, indicating hard things for Abram and his descendants. Abram spent lonely years in tents as a sojourner, a stranger, in the land of promise. In Acts 7:5 we read that "he gave him none inheritance in it, no, not so much as to set his foot on." He and Sarai waited, praying impatiently for a son. Then there would be a troubled nation, and long years in Egypt.

Israel shall serve them four hundred years: "And they shall afflict them four hundred years." It is clear that this prophecy involves the land of Egypt. But it involves more than Egypt.

But when does the four hundred years begin? It is repeated in Acts 7:6,7, "And God spake on this wise, That his seed should sojourn in a strange land; and that they should bring them into bondage, and entreat them evil four hundred years. And the nation to whom they shall be in bondage will I judge, said God: and after that shall they come forth, and serve me in this place." But Exodus 12:41 names "four hundred and thirty years."

400 Years of Sojourning Ahead

Note carefully verse 13. It involves the 400 years from Abraham on to the exodus, no doubt.

Martin Luther says:

With regard to the four hundred years, of which the text speaks, there has been much discussion. I believe that we must reckon them from the time when the call came to Abraham in Ur of the Chaldees. From that time until the children of Israel went down into Egypt there were 215 years. Likewise, the Israelites spent 215 years in Egypt. So we get a total of 430 years, and this agrees with both Exodus 12:40 and Galatians 3:17.

We think that the 430 years began when God first made the promises and covenant with Abraham and called him to leave Ur of the Chaldees. Now, some 30 years later, we suppose, 400 years yet remain of the 430 years.

Exodus 12:40,41 says:

"Now the sojourning of the children of Israel, who dwelt in Egypt, was four hundred and thirty years. And it came to pass at the end of the four hundred and thirty years, even the selfsame day it came to pass, that all the hosts of the Lord went out from the land of Egypt."

Galatians 3:17 says:

"And this I say, that the covenant, that was confirmed before of God in Christ, the law, which was four hundred and thirty years after, cannot disannul, that it should make the promise of none effect."

In Stephen's inspired sermon in Acts 7:6 he referred to this promise in Genesis 15: "And God spake on this wise, That his seed should sojourn in a strange land; and that they should bring them into bondage, and entreat them evil four hundred years."

The Ussher chronology is evidently in error in supposing that the Israelites spent 430 years in Egypt itself. The Septuagint reading of Exodus 12:40 (the Old Testament translated by seventy Jewish scholars into Greek) says, "The sojourning of the children and of their fathers, which they sojourned in the land of Canaan and in the land of Egypt. . . ."

Josephus, as a great Hebrew scholar of ancient times, understood the verse so. He said, "They left Egypt in the month Xanthicus, on the fifteenth day of the lunar month; four hundred and thirty years after our forefather Abraham came into Canaan, but two hundred and fifteen years only after Jacob removed into Egypt" (*Antiquities of the Jews*, Book II, chapter 15, paragraph 2).

We need to remember what God will be emphasizing chapter after chapter in the life of Abraham, Isaac, and Jacob. All this period from the time Abraham left Ur of the

Chaldees until the exodus of the children of Israel from Egypt, is a period of "sojourning." That term is used again and again about Abraham and about Isaac and about Jacob. All these years they sojourned in a land which was not their own.

Matthew Henry says:

> The continuance of their sufferings—*four hundred years.* This persecution began with mocking, when Ishmael, the son of an Egyptian, persecuted Isaac, who was *born after the Spirit,* ch. xxi. 9; Ga. iv. 29. It continued in loathing; for it was an abomination to the Egyptians to eat bread with the Hebrews, ch. xliii. 32; and it came at last to murder, the basest of murders, that of their new-born children; so that, more or less, it continued 400 years, though, in extremity, not so many. This was a long time, but a limited time.

On this matter Martin Luther says:

> Already then *(in Ur)* Abraham, by the divine promise, was the father of the Israelites, though as yet he had no heir. Similarly, we read in Hebrews 7:9,10 that Levi, who received tithes according to the Mosaic Law, paid tithes in Abraham, while he was yet in the loins of his father, when Melchizedek met him. As Abraham was troubled *(all his life),* so *(in him)* all his descendants were troubled. Likewise, when his descendants were troubled, he himself *(as their father)* was troubled. How precious therefore is Holy Scripture! There is nothing like this in the histories of the heathen. Not a single ancestor could foretell what was to happen to his descendants after four hundred years, in particular, how they were to be greatly afflicted and yet finally be gloriously delivered. It is only the true God who calls those things which are not as though they were (Rom. 4:17). In His sight there is neither a past nor a future, but all things are ever present before Him that are to happen to His saints. This chapter therefore is one of the most important in the whole Bible, and out of it, by inspiration of the Holy Spirit, the prophets have drawn many lessons of great comfort. But the sweetest consolation is this that God's truth never fails, neither in the past nor in the future.

A burning lamp passed between the pieces of the sacrifice Abram had made. Oh, God sees the lonely years, and He

sees all the people who are oppressed and troubled, and He
knows and cares for all the multitudes who will be the
spiritual descendants of Abram, as well as the nation
Israel.

Lange says, "The smoking furnace is analogous to the
burning bush, and pillar of fire of Moses."

Verse 16 says, "But in the fourth generation they shall
come hither again. . . ." Compare this with the genealogy
in I Chronicles 6:1-3, Levi, Kohath, Amram, Moses.

However, we find that Kohath, son of Levi, came with
him and Jacob into Egypt, as you see in Genesis 46:11,27, so
you might count from Kohath, Amram, Moses and Moses'
sons already living when the exodus occurred.

VERSES 18-21:

18 In the same day the LORD made
a covenant with Abram, saying, Unto
thy seed have I given ⁶this land, from
the river of Egypt unto the great
river, the river Eu̇-phrā́-tēṡ:
19 The Kḗ-nītes, and the Kĕ-nĭź-
zītes, and the Kadmonites,
20 And the Hittites, and the Pĕ-
rĭź-zītes, and the Rĕph́-ā-ĭms,
21 And the Amorites, and the Cā́-
nă-ăn-ītes, and the Gĭŕ-gă-shītes, and
the Jĕb́-ū-ṡītes.

Land Again Promised to Abram and His Seed

Already the Lord had promised Abram all he could see of
the land of Canaan (Gen. 13:14-17). And in Genesis 12:7
God had said, "Unto thy seed will I give this land." But
now some explicit limits are given. The land all the way
from the Nile River to the Euphrates is to be given to
Abram's seed and the land of the people named here—
Kenites, Kenizzites, Kadmonites, Hittites, Perizzites,
Rephaims, Amorites, Canaanites, Girgashites and
the Jebusites. Second Samuel, chapter 8, tells how King
David recovered his border at the river Euphrates, how he
had garrisons in Damascus, though the Philistines still
resisted down toward Egypt.

Solomon reached the same   proportions in his kingdom.
"And Solomon reigned over all kingdoms from the river

unto the land of the Philistines, and unto the border of Egypt: they brought presents, and served Solomon all the days of his life" (I Kings 4:21). Again we are told in verse 24, "For he had dominion over all the region on this side the river, from Tiphsah even to Azzah, over all the kings on this side the river: and he had peace on all sides round about him." We suppose the complete and perfect control of all the territory God planned for Israel will not take place until Christ returns to restore the kingdom of Israel and sit on the throne. When Christ returns to sit on "the throne of his father David" (Luke 1:32), then Abram's greater Seed will inherit the land of Palestine (Isa. 11; Jer. 23:1-8; Deut. 30:1-6; Ezek. 37:24; Dan. 2:44,45; Zech. 14:9).

GENESIS 16

VERSES 1-4:

NOW Sâr-ā-ī Abram's wife bare him no children: and she had an handmaid, an Egyptian, whose name was Hagar.

2 And Sâr-ā-ī said unto Abram, Behold now, the LORD hath restrained me from bearing: I pray thee, go in unto ⁷my maid; it may be that I may obtain children by her. And Abram hearkened to the voice of Sâr-ā-ī.

3 And Sâr-ā-ī Abram's wife too Hagar her maid the Egyptian, afte Abram had dwelt ten years in th land of Cā-nă-ăn, and gave her t her husband Abram to be his wife.

4 ¶ And he went in unto Hagar and she conceived: and when sh saw that she had conceived, her mis tress was despised in her eyes.

In Unbelief, Abram Takes Hagar to Wife

God had made rich promises to Abram. He partly believed and partly doubted. He was old. Sarai had more doubts still. She was long past childbearing age—about seventy-five now, ten years younger than Abram. How could God give her the son they had prayed for so long? She persuaded Abram to take her Egyptian maid Hagar as a wife, hoping thus to help God fulfill His promise and someway give Abram a son!

"And Abram hearkened to the voice of Sarai," we are told. The curse had fallen on Adam "because thou hast hearkened unto the voice of thy wife" (Gen. 3:17). There is some disappointment and trouble by this mistake, but no curse was upon Abram and Sarai.

Hagar was taken as a second wife. There was no law of God against two wives. The ceremonial law provided that if two brothers lived together and the wife of one died, the other was to take his brother's wife to raise up seed to the dead brother (Deut. 25:5). If a man had two wives, the firstborn son must be given his proper inheritance as the firstborn, even if he were not the son of the best loved wife. If one wife was not as well loved as the second wife, the husband must still fulfill his "duty of marriage" to the unloved wife (Exod. 21:10). Kings were commanded not to multiply wives to themselves (Deut. 17:17). But it was not forbidden to have more than one wife. However, here Abram and Sarai acted in unbelief, so trouble came—jealousy and envy between the two wives. That seems always inevitable with two wives. It was so with Hannah and the other wife, "her adversary" (I Sam. 1). So it was between Rachel and Leah later.

Hagar was a wife but not counted as a social equal, not counted a wife in the fuller sense. She was still a servant, perhaps a slave. She was still subject to Sarai's beck and call. She was called a concubine, not a wife, even as the later wife Keturah (Gen. 25:1-6). The record does not indicate that after the conception of Ishmael, Abram ever used Hagar as a wife again.

Dr. Joseph Free in his book, *Archaeology and Bible History*, says, "Nowhere do we read that God instructed Sarah to give Hagar to Abraham as a secondary wife. It was quite evidently her own idea. Archaeological discoveries show us the probable source of the idea. The Code of Hammurabi indicates that in Babylonia a wife might give a servant as a secondary wife to her husband, in order to have children by the servant girl. Thus Abraham and Sarah were not following the directive will of God, but rather the laws and customs of the old land out of which they had come."

VERSES 5-16:

5 And Sâr-ā-ī said unto Abram, My wrong *be* upon thee: I have given my maid into thy bosom; and when she saw that she had conceived, I was despised in her eyes: the LORD judge between me and thee.

6 But Abram said unto Sâr-ā-ī, Behold, thy maid *is* in thine hand; do to her as it pleaseth thee. And when Sâr-ā-ī dealt hardly with her, she fled from her face.

7 ¶ And the angel of the LORD found her by a fountain of water in the wilderness, by the fountain in the way to Shur.

8 And he said, Hagar, Sâr-ā-ī's maid, whence camest thou? and whither wilt thou go? And she said, I flee from the face of my mistress Sâr-ā-ī.

9 And the angel of the LORD said unto her, Return to thy mistress,

and submit thyself under her hands.

10 And the angel of the LORD said unto her, I will multiply thy seed exceedingly, that it shall not be numbered for multitude.

11 And the angel of the LORD said unto her, Behold, thou *art* with child, and shalt bear a son, and shalt call his name Ishmael; because the LORD hath heard thy affliction.

12 And he will be a wild man; his hand *will be* against every man, and every man's hand against him; and he shall dwell in the presence of all his brethren.

Ishmael Born—Beloved but Not the Promised Son

"For three things the earth is disquieted, and for four which it cannot bear . . . an handmaid that is heir to her mistress" (Prov. 30:21-23). Now the slave girl has been taken to the bosom of her lord and master; she is to have a child and poor old Sarai has none! So Hagar takes on airs and despises her older and barren mistress! Abram is in trouble between the two, and he instructs Sarai to carry on as she wills. Hagar runs away in rebellion.

The angel addressed Hagar, "Hagar, Sarai's maid, whence camest thou?" She is still regarded as subject to Sarai and the angel puts her in a proper place. She is not a wife equal to Sarai. She is still, we suppose, a slave girl, and although she is allowed to bear a son to Abram, the angel regards her as "Sarai's maid." She is instructed, "Return to thy mistress, and submit thyself under her hands."

When one is blessed of God in great spiritual matters, that does not necessarily change human relationships and responsibilities. A child who has great blessing from God and loves the Lord is still to be obedient to his parents. A wife may be a better Christian than her husband, but she is still to love, honor and obey him as she vowed to do and as the Bible commands, "And thy desire shall be to thy husband, and he shall rule over thee" (Gen. 3:16). Even if the husband is unsaved she is still to obey her husband: "Likewise, ye wives, be in subjection to your own husbands; that, if any obey not the word, they also may without the word be won by the conversation of the wives; While they behold your chaste conversation coupled with fear" (I Pet. 3:1,2). One who is a good Christian is still to obey the authority of the government God puts over him: "The powers that be are ordained of God. Whosoever therefore resisteth the power, resisteth the ordinance of God" (Rom. 13:1,2). The ruler is still God's minister for good and Christians are subject to their civil rulers.

So Hagar still is "Sarai's maid," she is to return to be an obedient servant to Sarai.

Oh, but God loves poor people. He loves the servant as well as the mistress. He loves the despised wife as well as the loved one. So the angel of the Lord met Hagar and instructed her. She is to return to Sarai. She is to submit herself as a servant. Oh, but Ishmael shall have a multitude of descendants. He will be a wild man, a lone wolf, but Hagar can be proud of him. She is not to bear the promised son to Abraham through whom all the earth is to be blessed, but she is to have a son.

Hagar knew about God. How often she had seen the sacrifices! No doubt she heard the prayers of Abram and she looked up in belief and said, "Thou God seest me." No doubt Hagar told Abram the name assigned to the unborn child, so Abram called him Ishmael. Abram was eighty-six years old; he must wait fourteen years more before the birth of the promised son through old Sarai.

The great Arab nation, with its Moslem religion, is the enemy of Israel, even as Ishmael and Isaac were in some sense opposing.

GENESIS 17

AND when Abram was ninety years old and nine, the LORD appeared to Abram, and said unto him, I *am* the ʾAlmighty God; walk before me, and be thou ʾperfect.

Almighty God, El Shaddai

Long, long waiting for a promise gives great need for continued reassurance. "Hope deferred maketh the heart sick" (Prov. 13:12). So God in lovingkindness appears to Abram again and here reveals Himself as El Shaddai. Dr. Scofield's note here says:

> The etymological signification of Almighty God (*El Shaddai*) is both interesting and touching. God (*El*) signifies the "Strong One" (Gen. 1.1, note). The qualifying word *Shaddai* is formed from the Hebrew word "*shad,*" the breast, invariably used in Scripture for a woman's breast; e.g. Gen. 49.25; Job 3.12; Psa. 22.9; Song 1.13; 4.5; 7.3,7,8; 8.1,8,10; Isa. 28.9; Ezk. 16.7. *Shaddai* therefore means primarily "the breasted." God is "*Shaddai,*" because He is the Nourisher, the Strength-giver, and so, in a secondary sense, the Satisfier, who pours Himself into believing lives. As a fretful, unsatisfied babe is not only strengthened and nourished from the mother's breast, but also is quieted, rested, satisfied, so *El Shaddai* is that name of God which sets Him forth as the Strength-giver and Satisfier of His people. It is on every account to be regretted that "*Shaddai*" was translated "Almighty." The primary name *El* or *Elohim* sufficiently signifies almightiness. "All-sufficient" would far better express both the Hebrew meaning and the characteristic use of the name in Scripture.

Oh, Abram, God is able! He who is the Sustainer of all life, the All-sufficient and Almighty One, can give the promised son to an old man and woman where men would think it impossible!

———

VERSES 2-6:

2 And I will make my covenant between me and thee, and will multiply thee exceedingly.

3 And Abram fell on his face: and God talked with him, saying,

4 As for me, behold, my covenant *is* with thee, and thou shalt be a father of many nations.

5 Neither shall thy name any more be called Abram, but thy name shall be Abraham; for a father of many nations have I made thee.

6 And I will make thee exceeding fruitful, and I will make nations of thee, and kings shall come out of thee.

Abram Becomes Abraham, Father of Many Nations

The term Abram means "high father." But Abraham means "father of many nations." Abraham is not only to have a son Isaac, but from him is to come the Davidic line of kings ruling in Israel, and this race of Jews will scatter in all the world to take their important part in the nations of the world. And Abraham is to be father not only of literal, physical Israel but, in a spiritual sense, of all those who trust in Christ and believe in Abraham's God and Saviour, his greater Son.

VERSES 7,8:

7 And I will establish my covenant between me and thee and thy seed after thee in their generations for an everlasting covenant, to be a God unto thee, and to thy seed after thee.

8 And I will give unto thee, and to thy seed after thee, the land wherein thou art a stranger, all the land of Că-nă-ăn, for an everlasting possession; and I will be their God.

God's Covenant Restated

God is stating again the wonderful promise. He is to be God to Abraham and to Abraham's seed. And then to him and to his seed after him, all the land of Canaan is to be given for a possession and it is to be "an everlasting possession."

Oh, there is much involved here. Jacob and his sons are down in Egypt, but the land of Canaan is promised them. Later, Israel will be carried captive into Babylon, but God has promised the land of Canaan for an everlasting possession. Titus may destroy Jerusalem in A. D. 70 and the Jews may be scattered to all the world, but God has promised the land of Canaan as an everlasting possession.

One day this old world will be wrapped in flame, and everything that fire will burn will be destroyed. But God still has promised an everlasting possession of the land of Canaan. So, in Revelation we see the heavenly Jerusalem coming down from God out of Heaven, coming to the land of Canaan, we believe, on a new earth, the Garden of Eden restored, and the Son will turn over the kingdom to His Father. Then God the Father and God the Son will live and reign on earth with glorified saints.

In the millennial age, when the "lame man leap as an hart, and the tongue of the dumb sing" and the time that "the desert shall rejoice, and blossom as the rose"—that involves the desert places of Israel now. Then in the ages ahead, when God makes the earth into a new Garden of Eden and the heavenly Jerusalem rests upon it, He will still keep His promise to Abraham. It is an "everlasting covenant" about an everlasting possession. It will be fulfilled in Christ.

But notice that Abraham is here still a stranger in the land of Canaan. He has not entered into the inheritance as promised. He is a foreigner, a sojourner, dwelling in tents.

VERSES 9-14:

9 ¶ And God said unto Abraham, Thou shalt keep my covenant therefore, thou, and thy seed after thee in their generations.

10 This *is* my covenant, which ye shall keep, between me and you and thy seed after thee; Every man child among you shall be ¹circumcised.

11 And ye shall circumcise the flesh of your foreskin; and it shall be a token of the covenant betwixt me and you.

12 And he that is eight days old shall be circumcised among you, every man child in your generations, he that is born in the house, or bought with money of any stranger, which *is* not of thy seed.

13 He that is born in thy house, and he that is bought with thy money, must needs be circumcised: and my covenant shall be in your flesh for an everlasting covenant.

14 And the uncircumcised man

child whose flesh of his foreskin is not circumcised, that soul shall be cut off from his people; he hath broken my covenant.

Circumcision, a Sign of God's Covenant With Abraham

Here is established circumcision as a sign of the Abrahamic or Jewish covenant. Circumcision was never established with any people but the Jews and their slaves. It was not of law alone, for both Ishmael and Isaac were circumcised, as well as Abraham himself. It was a sign of the covenant between God and Abraham, that Abraham's seed was to remain a separate, chosen people, and God would give them the land of Canaan forever, etc. It does not represent conversion, nor baptism, nor church membership, nor anything of the kind, since it was only for males, was to be observed when each boy was only eight days old, and was never for the Gentile nations. The only thing of the kind we have is circumcision of the heart (Rom. 2:29).

Circumcision was a sign of Abraham's faith in God, and faith was before circumcision. Abraham was saved by faith. The command to circumcise was later included in the law, in Leviticus 12:3, (see also Exod. 4:24-26; 12:48; Josh. 5:2-9). John the Baptist was circumcised (Luke 1:59), as was Jesus (Luke 2:21) and Paul (Phil. 3:5). All these were Jews and the new covenant had not been given at their birth, or was not announced.

But neither circumcision nor uncircumcision availeth anything (Gal. 5:2,6; I Cor. 7:18,19). In the New Testament, the words "the circumcision" refer usually to the Jews as a whole, and "the uncircumcision" are the Gentiles (Gal. 2:7). We now have a new circumcision made without hands (Col. 2:11), and a new covenant (Heb. 8:8-13).

This sign of circumcision is to set the Israelites apart all through the centuries. Every male child eight days old was to be circumcised. However, this rite was often neglected for a period. After Israel was let out of Egypt, all the males were circumcised. Then none were circumcised during the forty years in the wilderness. But after they came into the

land of Canaan, across the River Jordan, then Joshua had
all the males circumcised (Josh. 5:4,5).

Circumcision was a mark of separation. And it has
special significance for Christians. The Jew who was
circumcised ought to have turned his heart to the Lord and
become a child of God. And it is promised in that distant
day, when the Lord Jesus Himself shall return and when
all Israel shall turn to obey the Lord God with all their
heart and all their soul, that then the Lord will turn the
captivity of Israel. Deuteronomy 30:6 says, "The Lord thy
God will circumcise thine heart, and the heart of thy seed,
to love the Lord thy God with all thine heart, and with all
thy soul, that thou mayest live."

You may be sure that the return of Jews in unbelief to
Palestine now is not the fulfillment of this promise.
Zionism is Jewish nationalism, not Christianity.
Circumcision of the flesh only does not satisfy God. In
Colossians 2:11 we are told, "In whom also ye are
circumcised with the circumcision made without hands, in
putting off the body of the sins of the flesh by the circumcision of Christ." Then circumcision in the flesh alone
avails nothing (Gal. 5:6). He is not a Jew who is only a Jew
outwardly, and that is not circumcision which is only of the
flesh in God's sight and in spiritual meaning.

In the nation Israel no man would be recognized as an
Israelite except he be circumcised. So surely God intends a
Christian to be openly marked and branded by the way he
lives. People should claim Christ openly and live Christ
before others. There should be a clear demarcation between
saved and lost, between Bible believers and infidels.

VERSES 15-19:

15 ¶ And God said unto Abraham,
As for Sâr-́ā-ī thy wife, thou shalt
not call her name ⸵Sâr-́ā-ī, but Sarah
shall her name *be*.

16 And I will bless her, and give
thee a son also of her: yea, I will bless
her, and she shall be *a mother* of nations; kings of people shall be of her.

17 Then Abraham fell upon his face, and laughed, and said in his heart, Shall *a child* be born unto him that is an hundred years old? and shall Sarah, that is ninety years old, bear?

18 And Abraham said unto God, O that Ishmael might live before thee!

19 And God said, Sarah thy wife shall bear thee a son indeed; and thou shalt call his name Isaac: and I will establish my covenant with him for an everlasting covenant, *and* with his seed after him.

Isaac Promised and Named

Now Sarai becomes Sarah, which means *princess* because "she shall be a mother of nations; kings of people shall be of her."

That was almost too good to be true. Abraham laughed in his heart at such a wild promise! Should a child be born to a man one hundred years old? And Sarah, a withered old woman of ninety—could she conceive and bear a child? Oh, if God would only bless Ishmael and fulfill His promises in him! No, "Sarah thy wife shall bear thee a son indeed." His name shall be Isaac. Does Abraham laugh when he hears the promise? Sarah will laugh, too, when she hears it (Gen. 18:12). All right, God says, "We will call the child *Isaac*" (meaning laughter). And all their lives they will remember that instead of the laughter of unbelief, they can have the joy of fulfilled promise. And the promise God has given Abraham, He will repeat to Isaac and to his seed after him.

VERSES 20-27:

20 And as for Ishmael, I have heard thee: Behold, I have blessed him, and will make him fruitful, and will multiply him exceedingly; twelve princes shall he beget, and I will make him a great nation.

21 But my covenant will I establish with Isaac, which Sarah shall bear unto thee at this set time in the next year.

22 And he left off talking with him, and God went up from Abraham.

23 ¶ And Abraham took Ishmael his son, and all that were born in his house, and all that were bought with his money, every male among the men of Abraham's house; and circumcised the flesh of their foreskin in the selfsame day, as God had said unto him.

24 And Abraham *was* ninety years old and nine, when he was circumcised in the flesh of his foreskin.

25 And Ishmael his son *was* thirteen years old, when he was circumcised in the flesh of his foreskin.

26 In the selfsame day was Abraham circumcised, and Ishmael his son.

27 And all the men of his house, born in the house, and bought with money of the stranger, were circumcised with him.

Ishmael and Abraham Circumcised

Abraham is now ninety-nine years old (vs. 1), Ishmael is thirteen. God repeats to Abraham the promise He made to Hagar. God will bless Ishmael, "will make him fruitful, and will multiply him exceedingly; twelve princes shall he beget." But, God reminds Abraham His covenant is with Isaac, and Isaac will be born "at this set time in the next year"!

Now it is time for the act of faith. Abraham gathered his workers and servants, every male among them, and circumcised them that same day. At ninety-nine years old Abraham was circumcised; Ishmael, thirteen, was circumcised. Thus, Abraham accepts and professes his faith in the coming son and the coming Saviour and openly acknowledges to his family and thus, to the whole outside world, that he is chosen and set apart for God and from him will come the great nation that is promised and the Messiah, the promised Seed, in whom all the earth will be blessed.

GENESIS 18

AND the LORD appeared unto him in the plains of Mamre: and he sat in the tent door in the heat of the day;

2 And he lift up his eyes and looked, and, lo, three men stood by him: and when he saw *them*, he ran to meet them from the tent door, and bowed himself toward the ground,

3 And said, My Lord, if now I have found favour in thy sight, pass not away, I pray thee, from thy servant:

4 Let a little water, I pray you, be fetched, and ¹wash your feet, and rest yourselves under the tree:

5 And I will fetch a morsel of bread, and comfort ye your hearts; after that ye shall pass on: for therefore are ye come to your servant. And they said, So do, as thou hast said.

6 And Abraham hastened into the tent unto Sarah, and said, Make ready quickly three measures of fine meal, knead *it*, and make cakes upon the hearth.

7 And Abraham ran unto the herd, and fetcht a calf tender and good, and gave *it* unto a young man; and he hasted to dress it.

8 And he took butter, and milk, and the calf which he had dressed, and set *it* before them; and he stood by them under the tree, and they did eat.

The Lord and Angels Visit Abraham

"And the *LORD* appeared unto him."

God, in visible form, met and talked with Abraham. We think this a pre-incarnation appearance of Christ. All through the New Testament Christ is called "the Lord." We think it was Christ in pre-incarnation form, that angel who wrestled with Jacob, for Jacob said, "I have seen God face to face, and my life is preserved" (Gen. 32:30). Jesus is called "the Angel which redeemed me from all evil" by old Jacob as he blessed his grandsons (Gen. 48:16). Abraham seems to have recognized that it was the Lord (see vs. 3). We would suppose that Abraham did not at first recognize God and the angels. Hebrews 13:2 may refer to this incident when it says, "Be not forgetful to entertain strangers: for thereby some have entertained angels unawares." No doubt also the Scripture refers to Lot in chapter 19, who was visited by two angels.

Before this, there was awe and majesty when the Lord appeared to Abraham. It was then in a dream, a vision; but

now the Lord came and talked with Abraham face to face.
What a simple, wonderful setting! It reminds us that the
Lord Jesus Himself will come to earth to buy back for God a
race of sinners. He was born of a humble village virgin. He
grew up in poverty in the little country province of Galilee.
He worked in a carpenter shop. Oh, He is sweetly described:
". . . for I am meek and lowly in heart: and ye shall find
rest unto your souls. For my yoke is easy, and my burden is
light." God is an approachable God. Those who seek Him
find Him.

It seems that from the very first God has longed to have
intimate fellowship with men. He came and walked and
talked with Adam in the Garden of Eden (Gen. 3:8). God
sent His Son to be born of man, and to be tempted in all
points like as we are. Then one day when the wicked are all
destroyed and sent to Hell, the Lord Himself will come
down to earth and will reign on this world (Luke 1:32,33).
And next to the last chapter in the Bible tells about the
heavenly Jerusalem coming down from God out of Heaven,
and then there will be no need for the sun, for the Lord God
will be the light of it and God will then make His dwelling
again with men.

When the Lord came to Abraham before Abraham's tent,
and was served a simple meal by him under a tree and had
intimate discourse and friendly talk with Abraham, it is a
sweet reminder of an approachable God who loves us, who
wants fellowship with us.

Abraham Was Hospitable

Abraham would offer water to wash the feet of these
angels and the Lord, all in human form. Then a proper part
of Oriental hospitality is discussed in the next chapter
where Lot also offers to have these same angels wash their
feet. And Abraham hastened to offer food, as did Lot in
Sodom in chapter 19. Hospitality is a virtue required of
Christians. Remember the New Testament injunction to
offer hospitality to strangers, "for thereby some have
entertained angels unawares" (Heb. 13:2). That must refer
to these two instances.

Being a Christian ought to make one eager to serve others, to entertain others. One of the requirements of a spiritual pastor is that he should be "given to hospitality" (I Tim. 3:2).

The story Jesus told of the good Samaritan is an indication that Christians ought to have an out-going heart of love toward those about us. And Jesus who washed the disciples' feet taught us that with loving forgiveness and humility we should wash one another's feet. Good Christian character is not austere, not selfish, not retired, not reserved from those who need our love and help. The unselfish heart of Abraham, who was willing to give Lot the choice of all the land which really had been promised to Abraham, is illustrated in the way he cared for strangers.

We must remember that though rich in flocks and herds and servants and in money, yet Abraham "by faith. . .sojourned in the land of promise, as in a strange country, dwelling in tabernacles [tents] with Isaac and Jacob, the heirs with him of the same promise: For he looked for a city which hath foundations, whose builder and maker is God" (Heb. 11:9,10). So Abraham sat in the door of his tent as Sarah cooked over a campfire. And Abraham himself ran to catch a calf and had the veal dressed so some could be broiled quickly over the coals. And Sarah herself, though she had many servants, prepared the three measures of meal and made three cakes and cooked them on the hearth.

In pioneer days in America, people made johnnycakes of cornmeal, cooked on the hot stone hearth by the fireplace. Possibly Sarah had a flat tile over a fire, supported by stones. At any rate, it was simple camp accommodations. Simple virtues, simple food, simple enjoyments well fit Christians.

A Feast of Unleavened Bread

It was doubtless unleavened bread. There was no time for the dough to rise, and that is suitable. Lot also fed the two angels unleavened bread (Gen. 19:3). Jesus said leaven pictured the false doctrine of the Pharisees and Sadducees (Matt. 16:6,12). Concerning fellowship with men living in outbroken sin, Paul wrote the Corinthians:

"Your glorying is not good. Know ye not that a little leaven leaveneth the whole lump? Purge out therefore the old leaven, that ye may be a new lump, as ye are unleavened. For even Christ our passover is sacrificed for us: Therefore let us keep the feast, not with old leaven, neither with the leaven of malice and wickedness; but with the unleavened bread of sincerity and truth."—I Cor. 5:6-8.

And in the feast of unleavened bread (Exod. 12:15) following the passover, the bread pictured Christ, so it must have no leaven. And it is very suitable that the bread prepared for the Lord and His angels was unleavened.

God and the angels rested "under the tree" (vs. 4). They did not come into the tent. While God is approachable and loving and wants fellowship with men, He wants a man to pull himself away from the ordinary affairs of life to meet God. Jacob, alone, wrestled with the angel of God in Genesis 32. Jesus went apart forty days and was tempted of Satan. Abraham went three days' journey to offer Isaac on Mount Moriah. Moses went up into Mount Sinai and stayed forty days communing with God and receiving the Ten Commandments on tables of stone.

In the area of Mamre, near Hebron, is a very ancient oak tree which is called "Abraham's Oak." I do not suppose that it is really 3,600 years old, but it is reverenced by Moslems, and at least it represents the tree near Abraham's tent. It is now propped up with steel beams and fenced in for protection.

It is still remembered that Abraham made his home most of the time near Mamre. He and Sarah, Isaac and Rebekah, Jacob and Leah are buried in Hebron in the Cave of Machpelah over which is built a great mosque.

Notice the simple meal: veal steaks (we suppose broiled over the open fire), hot cakes of fine meal or flour (wheat or barley?), milk and butter.

VERSES 9-15:

9 ¶ And they said unto him, Where Sarah thy wife? And he said, Behold, in the tent.

10 And he said, I will certainly return unto thee according to the time of life; and, lo, Sarah thy wife shall have a son. And Sarah heard *it* in the tent door, which *was* behind him.

11 Now Abraham and Sarah *were* old *and* well stricken in age; *and* it ceased to be with Sarah after the manner of women.

12 Therefore Sarah laughed within herself, saying, After I am waxed old shall I have pleasure, my lord being old also?

13 And the LORD said unto Abraham, Wherefore did Sarah laugh, saying, Shall I of a surety bear a child, which am old?

14 Is any thing too hard for the LORD? At the time appointed I will return unto thee, according to the time of life, and Sarah shall have a son.

15 Then Sarah denied, saying, I laughed not; for she was afraid. And he said, Nay; but thou didst laugh.

Old Sarah, Laughing in Unbelief, Assured She Will Have a Son

It is always profitable to meet God on His own terms with loving attention and service. Now Abraham receives good news from God. The covenant is repeated. Sarah will have a son.

Where is Sarah, the wife? In the tent. God's prophet must often meet God alone. We suppose Sarah was out of sight. She may have brought out the cakes, but probably Abraham did since he served the veal, the butter, the milk, to God and the angels who ate under the tree as he stood by.

In spiritual matters God deals with men before their wives. Joshua decided for his wife, children and servants and all. "As for me and my house, we will serve the Lord" (Josh. 24:15). God is dealing primarily with Abraham. "The husband is the head of the wife, even as Christ is the head of the church" (Eph. 5:23). If a woman wants to know spiritual things, she should ask her husband (I Cor. 14:34,35). Abraham went wrong when he listened to Sarah's plea that he take Hagar as a wife. Sarah has not as much faith as Abraham. He doubted and laughed (Gen. 17:17), but dealing with God and being reassured, he believed.

Now Sarah laughs. She is ninety years old. "After I am waxed old. . . ." Would she have pleasure, conceive a child and bear a son? She might have believed it when she was young and of normal child-bearing age, with the customary periods that might indicate fertility month after month—but now! A ninety-year-old withered woman!

And "my lord being old also," she said. Could old Abraham beget a child? The implication is that Abraham at this time was impotent and not fertile. Hebrews 11:12 speaks of Abraham, ". . .and him as good as dead." So the miracle is alike for both Abraham and Sarah.

Sarah laughed! Laughed in unbelief. But quickly she denied it. Perhaps she laughed secretly, not intending it to be known, but the Lord knew. Ah, merciful, forbearing God! Instead of punishment, He will give Sarah a laughing heart for her old age! The boy will be called Isaac, "laughter."

Sarah had laughed in unbelief, but now she did believe! For Hebrews 11:11 says, "Through faith also Sara herself received strength to conceive seed, and was delivered of a child when she was past age, because she judged him faithful who had promised." Now Abraham and Sarah joined in believing God's sweet promise.

Sarah an Example for Wives

Note Sarah called Abraham "my lord." That is intended to be very significant. First Peter 3:1-3 says:

"Likewise, ye wives, be in subjection to your own husbands; that, if any obey not the word, they also may without the word be won by the conversation of the wives; While they behold your chaste conversation coupled with fear. Whose adorning let it not be that outward adorning of plaiting the hair, and of wearing of gold, or of putting on of apparel."

So Sarah, calling Abraham "lord," meant that she had given herself to him, to obey him "until death do us part." She evidently meant the kind of obedience and submission which is commanded in Ephesians 5:24, "As the church is subject unto Christ, so let the wives be to their own husbands in every thing."

Women everywhere are commanded to follow the good example of Sarah, who loved Abraham, called him "lord," set out to make him happy, to be wholly his. Does anyone think that Sarah was downtrodden and abused because of her loyalty as a good wife?

"Is any thing too hard for the Lord?" the Lord asked Sarah. Oh, how often God tries to make us believe that He can do anything He wants to do! Jeremiah asked himself that question and God asked Jeremiah the question (Jer. 32:17,27). In Psalm 81:10 the Lord reminded of His marvelous works with the children of Israel: "I am the Lord thy God, which brought thee out of the land of Egypt: open thy mouth wide, and I will fill it."

Now the time is set: "At the time appointed I will return unto thee, according to the time of life, and Sarah shall have a son."

The miracle is not just in the birth of Isaac. The miracle is that both Sarah and Abraham were somewhat restored to youth so the child would be conceived. Then we may look to see results of this youthful vigor in Abraham and Sarah. In this chapter, verse 7 says, "And Abraham ran unto the herd, and fetcht a calf tender and good, and gave it unto a young man; and he hasted to dress it." Do you see this old man ninety-nine years old running to the herd, seizing a calf and either carrying or dragging it to one of his servants to dress it? Remember that Hebrews 11:12 speaks of him as one "as good as dead." Already the miracle has begun, we believe, in the life of Abraham.

I discuss this in my novel, *Seeking a City*, on the life of Abraham and suggested this truth. You may expect to see Sarah young and beautiful again and admired of men and wanted by King Abimelech in chapter 20.

VERSES 16-22:

16 ¶ And the men rose up from thence, and looked toward Sodom: and Abraham went with them to bring them on the way.

17 And the LORD said, Shall I hide from Abraham that thing which I do;

18 Seeing that Abraham shall surely become a great and mighty nation, and all the nations of the earth shall be blessed in him?

19 For I know him, that he will command his children and his household after him, and they shall keep the way of the LORD, to do justice and judgment; that the LORD may bring upon Abraham that which he hath spoken of him.

20 And the LORD said, Because the cry of Sodom and Gō-mŏr-́răh is great, and because their sin is very grievous;

21 I will go down now, and see whether they have done altogether according to the cry of it, which is come unto me; and if not, I will know.

22 And the men turned their faces from thence, and went toward Sodom: but Abraham stood yet before the LORD.

Sins of Sodom Cry for Judgment

"And the men rose up from thence. . . ." These are angels who look like men, like the two angels in Genesis 19:1 who are called men (Gen. 19:5,10). They were entertained as strangers but were angels unawares, we judge from Hebrews 13:2.

". . . and Abraham went with them to bring them on the way." It is wonderfully sweet that Abraham and God have gotten very close. God wants friendship and His heart is hungry for His people. That is part of the sadness of John 1:11, "He came unto his own, and his own received him not." That is part of the sadness of Jesus weeping over Jerusalem, "O Jerusalem, Jerusalem, which killest the prophets, and stonest them that are sent unto thee; how often would I have gathered thy children together, as a hen doth gather her brood under her wings, and ye would not" (Luke 13:34).

God delighted in the fellowship of Abraham. He grieved over the wickedness of Sodom. Remember how He had sought the children of Israel in their backsliding: "And the Lord God of their fathers sent to them by his messengers, rising up betimes, and sending; because he had compassion on his people, and on his dwelling place: But they mocked the messengers of God, and despised his words, and misused his prophets, until the wrath of the Lord arose against his people, till there was no remedy" (II Chron. 36:15,16).

God Loves to Tell His Secrets to Those Who Seek Him

We believe that the Lord delights to tell His secrets to those who love Him. Psalm 25:14 says, "The secret of the Lord is with them that fear him." Proverbs 3:32 says, ". . . but his secret is with the righteous." Amos 3:7 says, "Surely the Lord God will do nothing, but he revealeth his secret unto his servants the prophets." The Lord God is a lonely God. He wants people to share His thoughts, share His love, share even His sorrow over people in sin.

So, long ahead of time God revealed to faithful open hearts about the promised Messiah and the wonderful things that would happen to Him. Prophets wrote them down. So the course of this age is charted again and again in the New Testament for spiritual people to see it.

God revealed to Paul that the time of his departure was at hand and he was about to be beheaded (II Tim. 4:6). He revealed to Peter, "Knowing that shortly I must put off this my tabernacle, even as our Lord Jesus Christ hath shewed me" (II Pet. 1:14). So now God feels He must tell Abraham about His sad duty to destroy Sodom.

This author preached to a great crowd in a revival campaign in Waxahachie, Texas, in 1932, where hundreds were saved. There had been several very remarkable instances of people who had heard the Gospel and rebelled against it dying suddenly. In the midst of a sermon I suddenly said, "Some man hears me tonight who in twenty-four hours will be dead and in Hell." I stopped and stammered. I had hardly intended to say it that way. I explained, "I intended to say that I feared such is the case, but I will leave it as a prophecy of God. I believe it is true."

The next afternoon at 5:45 a wicked man who had heard me preach that night was found shot through the heart at the city waterworks. His loving family insisted that I must preach the funeral sermon, since I had given him God's last warning!

God says, "Shall I hide from Abraham that thing which I do; Seeing that Abraham shall surely become a great and mighty nation, and all the nations of the earth shall be blessed in him? For I know him, that he will command his children and his household after him, and they shall keep the way of the Lord, to do justice and judgment. . . ."

"The cry of Sodom and Gomorrah is great, and because their sin is very grievous," the Lord said. The other cities which have joined in their wickedness and will be like them in destruction are Admah and Zeboiim. But Sodom is mentioned particularly, we suppose because Lot is there and it is to Sodom where the two angels will go.

Must God check on Sodom again to see their wickedness and review again whether he can have mercy? Oh, God seeks every occasion He can find for mercy. He wants Abraham to know, and I suppose Lot also, to know and He wants us to know that if He could have found ten righteous men in Sodom, He would have spared the city yet for further opportunity for repentance!

The two angels go on their way to Sodom: ". . . but Abraham stood yet before the Lord."

God Told Abraham, Not Worldly Lot

It ought to be a suggestion to all of us that many a time God shuts up His communication to men who do not rear their children with godly instruction and discipline. Old Eli the high priest must have been a godly man, but "his sons made themselves vile, and he restrained them not" (I Sam. 3:13). So when God had something to tell Eli, He called the little boy Samuel and revealed it to him instead of to Eli!

Here God tells Abraham what He did not tell Lot. Lot had put his family in the midst of vilest wickedness and had not taught any of them to know the Lord. How different from Abraham! He would rear Isaac to fear and serve the Lord. His old servant Eliezer was a godly man who prayed and got the answer (Gen. 24:12-23). Even Hagar knew to look for God and trust in Him. And those 318 servants, who went with Abraham on his daring foray after the kings who had conquered Sodom and taken Lot captive, had the blessing of God upon them, no doubt, for Abraham commands his whole household after God! Therefore, he is worthy of God's confidences and revelation.

VERSES 23-33:

23 ¶ And Abraham drew near, and said, Wilt thou also destroy the righteous with the wicked?

24 Peradventure there be fifty righteous within the city: wilt thou also destroy and not spare the place for the fifty righteous that *are* therein?

25 That be far from thee to do after this manner, to slay the righteous with the wicked: and that the righteous should be as the wicked, that be far from thee: Shall not the Judge of all the earth do right?

26 And the LORD said, If I find in Sodom fifty righteous within the city, then I will spare all the place for their sakes.

27 And Abraham answered and said, Behold now, I have taken upon me to speak unto the Lord, which *am but* dust and ashes:

28 Peradventure there shall lack five of the fifty righteous: wilt thou destroy all the city for *lack of* five? And he said, If I find there forty and five, I will not destroy *it*.

29 And he spake unto him yet again, and said, Peradventure there shall be forty found there. And he said, I will not do *it* for forty's sake.

30 And he said *unto him*, Oh let not the Lord be angry, and I will speak: Peradventure there shall thirty be found there. And he said, I will not do *it*, if I find thirty there.

31 And he said, Behold now, I have taken upon me to speak unto the Lord: Peradventure there shall twenty found there. And he said, I will not destroy *it* for twenty's sake.

32 And he said, Oh let not the Lord be angry, and I will speak yet but this once: Peradventure ten shall be found there. And he said, I will not destroy *it* for ten's sake.

33 And the LORD went his way, as soon as he had left communing with Abraham: and Abraham returned unto his place.

Abraham Intercedes and Argues With God

See how familiar and unrestrained was the conversation between Abraham and the Lord! Abraham asked, "Wilt thou also destroy the righteous with the wicked?" Was Lot righteous? Yes, "For that righteous man dwelling among them, in seeing and hearing, vexed his righteous soul from day to day with their unlawful deeds" (II Pet. 2:8). And in II Peter 2 Lot is called "just Lot, vexed with the filthy conversation of the wicked." He is called a "righteous man"; he had a "righteous soul." The 9th verse says, "The Lord knoweth how to deliver the godly out of temptations." Here was a just man, a righteous man, with a righteous soul. So he is saved and is a godly man.

Lot Was a Righteous Man

Oh, but Lot is in the wrong place. He did not live effectively. He did not influence his family for God, but he had learned to know the God of Abraham and had learned to trust in Him. He had been saved and his soul was vexed day by day with the wickedness in Sodom.

Let that remind us that "man looketh on the outward appearance, but the Lord looketh on the heart" (I Sam. 16:7). You do not know the heart by the outward appearance. If one had seen David, first looking with lustful eyes on Bathsheba at her bath, then sending for her, seducing her and leading her into adultery; then finally to hide his sin, having Uriah killed—oh, one might think that David was a wicked man, that the praises in the Psalms were hypocritical. But David had the same fight every good man has: "For the flesh lusteth against the Spirit." Like Paul, he would have had to say, "When I would do good, evil is present with me" (Rom. 7:21). Or one hearing Simon Peter cursing and swearing, denying that he ever knew Jesus, then quitting the ministry and going back to his fishing, might well think that Peter had never been converted, that he was not a good man. But, oh, what a mistake that would be! For righteous men still have the flesh to deal with, and good men are not wholly good. Meek Moses will lose his temper and flail at the rock when he should have spoken to it. Jonah the prophet will disobey God and run from duty. Oh, how much in the heart of everyone of us ought to convince us that though we love the Lord Jesus, we want to please Him, we long for righteousness, yet it is not always apparent to those who see our daily walk. Lot was a righteous man and inwardly his soul was vexed and burdened day by day with the wickedness of Sodom.

Abraham surely knew that Lot was a believer in the Lord, one who had trusted in the Messiah to come, though he had never been active in his sacrifices as had Abraham.

God's Tender Compassion Shows Here

In verses 20 and 21 we read, "And the Lord said, Because the cry of Sodom and Gomorrah is great, and because their sin is very grievous; I will go down now, and see whether they have done altogether according to the cry of it, which is come unto me; and if not, I will know."

Did God really not know how wicked were Sodom and Gomorrah? He had heard "the cry of it." Angels had reported every detail. He knew the heart of every person there. Why, then, do we read that He would go down to see for Himself "whether they have done altogether according to the cry of it"? Oh, even when God knows He must punish, He prolongs His compassion. The Lord is "slow to anger, and plenteous in mercy" (Ps. 103:8). So it is here in the Bible so we would know that in His heart He longed for a way to show mercy, even when He knew the wickedness of the cities.

Abraham pleaded and evidently with a good deal of trepidation. When he thought that perhaps Lot would not have won his herdsmen, not all the fifty that Abraham had suggested might be righteous, then he spoke humbly, "I have taken upon me to speak unto the Lord, which am but dust and ashes." Abraham, do not fear! God listens more willingly than you ask Him.

In verse 30 Abraham said, "Oh let not the Lord be angry, and I will speak." Go ahead, Abraham, God delights to hear one pleading for the sinner, pleading for mercy. Your heart is not as tender as the heart of God!

And again in verse 32, Abraham, with deep humility and fearfulness, says, "Oh let not the Lord be angry, and I will speak yet but this once. . . ." I am saying that God delights to have one plead for sinners.

Do we not read in Ezekiel 22:30, "And I sought for a man among them, that should make up the hedge, and stand in the gap before me for the land, that I should not destroy it:

but I found none"? Oh, God sought for someone to stand in the gap, to intercede for Israel before He must cast that nation into captivity.

And in Exodus 32, when God had threatened to put aside the wicked, stiffnecked Israel that Moses had found drunken and naked dancing around the golden calf, God was pleased at the intercession of Moses that God would spare them and God did.

Oh, let anyone who feels a burden to plead for the forgiveness and salvation of any wicked sinner and for God's mercy on those who have sinned, be bold about it. God's heart is more tender than yours; His compassion is beyond measurement.

God must sometimes punish sin drastically, but you may be sure He always does it after love and mercy have gone to their utter limits! You do not displease God when you plead for the wicked.

The Christian Should Be Persistent in Prayer

It is interesting that Abraham felt free to argue with God, and more interesting still that the Lord was not displeased with him.

Of the Lord Jesus it is said, "And he spake a parable unto them to this end, that men ought always to pray, and not to faint" (Luke 18:1), and He told of a poor widow who besought a wicked judge until he was distraught and gave her vengeance. And the sweet promise of Isaiah 40:31 is, "They that wait upon the Lord shall renew their strength." The Christian who is to put on the whole armor of God is commanded, "Praying always with all prayer and supplication in the Spirit, and watching thereunto with all perseverance and supplication for all saints" (Eph. 6:18). That importunate friend pleading for bread for another friend (we believe it means the Bread of Life) would not be heard because he was a friend, "yet because of his importunity he will rise and give him as many as he needeth" (Luke 11:8). In that connection we are commanded, "Ask, and it shall be given you; seek, and ye shall find; knock, and it shall be opened unto you." And the verb of the command in each case is continued action, continued asking, seeking, knocking!

Oh, let us be like the Psalmist who said, "When thou saidst, Seek ye my face; my heart said unto thee, Thy face, Lord, will I seek." God gets too little of our attention until we are in trouble. Oh, then, Christian, seek the Lord. Seeking the Lord is in God's plan for revival, as He said in II Chronicles 7:14.

So Abraham argued with God. And he had a good argument, too. He knew the heart of God. He knew the power of intercessory prayer. If there were fifty righteous, would God spare the city and give others a chance to repent? Or if there were only forty-five? or forty? or thirty? or twenty? or ten?

Here we have two great principles weighed one against the other. First, there is the principle that sin must be punished. "He, that being often reproved hardeneth his neck, shall suddenly be destroyed, and that without remedy" (Prov. 29:1). "But if ye will not do so, behold, ye have sinned against the Lord: and be sure your sin will find you out" (Num. 32:23). "Be not deceived; God is not mocked: for whatsoever a man soweth, that shall he also reap. For he that soweth to his flesh shall of the flesh reap corruption; but he that soweth to the Spirit shall of the Spirit reap life everlasting" (Gal. 6:7,8). There is a rule that "the wages of sin is death" (Rom. 6:23). Ah, there is a sad, sad truth that "the way of transgressors is hard" (Prov. 13:15). Sin must be punished.

But there is another weighty truth here. A good man may intercede for a wicked man. Ezekiel 22:30 tells us that when the wickedness of the nation Israel was out of all bounds and they were about to be subdued and carried into captivity, God says, "I sought for a man among them, that should make up the hedge, and stand in the gap before me for the land, that I should not destroy it: but I found none." There is a sense in which one may bear the grief which belongs to another, and one may so intercede with God sometimes as to hold off the judgment of God.

A mother suffers when the child is born and the child does not. The care and expense and the burden of rearing children falls on the father, not on the sons or daughters. Moses could plead for Israel and so plead that God repented that He had thought to destroy the nation, and He gave them another chance (Exod. 32:7-14).

Four Cities Gone to Hell for Lack of a Soul Winner!

Now, if Lot had won only nine other people to know and serve the true God, nine righteous in soul trusting in the coming Messiah, however little they might know about Him, God would have spared the city.

Abraham started with suggesting there might be fifty righteous. Would that include all of Lot's family and perhaps his herdmen and servants and a few others? Ah, but Lot is so busy making money, maybe there will be only forty-five, or forty; and with some restraint and much pleading Abraham came down to ten. If Lot had won his wife, the two single daughters, three married daughters and three sons-in-law, that would have made the ten and God would have spared the city. Oh, if Lot had even won all of his own family, there would be a chance for him to win others, a chance for wicked Sodom to be spared. But he had not won one! So the city is to be destroyed.

God Sometimes Puts Limit on What We Should Ask

It must be a mark of Abraham's spiritual understanding that he did not plead for the city to be spared if Lot had not won his family. Persistence in prayer is good, but sometimes the sin crying for judgment overweighs the arguments we could bring for forgiveness of others.

An example is that of the nation Israel. In Ezekiel 14:13,14 God says:

"Son of man, when the land sinneth against me by trespassing grievously, then will I stretch out mine hand upon it, and will break the staff of the bread thereof, and will send famine upon it, and will cut off man and beast from it: Though these three men, Noah, Daniel, and Job,

were in it, they should deliver but their own souls by their righteousness, saith the Lord God."

Again in verse 20 He says:

"Though Noah, Daniel, and Job, were in it, as I live, saith the Lord God, they shall deliver neither son nor daughter; they shall but deliver their own souls by their righteousness."

Sometimes even persistence in prayer must not go against the will of God. When Moses had dishonored God and the type of salvation by smiting the rock the second time instead of speaking to it as commanded, then later he besought the Lord that the sentence that he could not enter Canaan might be revoked and he might be allowed to go into the land of promise. In Deuteronomy 3:25,26 we read Moses reported that he prayed:

"I pray thee, let me go over, and see the good land that is beyond Jordan, that goodly mountain, and Lebanon. But the Lord was wroth with me for your sakes, and would not hear me: and the Lord said unto me, Let it suffice thee; speak no more unto me of this matter."

When Paul besought the Lord three times about his thorn in the flesh, the Lord did not change His plan but explained that it would be better for Paul to be weak and God strong. Paul must not be exalted above measure by being free from this encumbrance but God would give him special grace. And in that Paul rejoiced. (See II Cor. 12:1-9.)

Oh, God would have delighted to withdraw judgment for the time if there had been any chance that the Sodomites would turn to the Lord, but there was no such probability.

"The Lord went his way, as soon as he had left communing with Abraham: and Abraham returned unto his place." So Abraham is content. God will do right. Oh, yes, and for Abraham's sake, no doubt Lot will be spared.

But is there not here a little window into the heart of God, seeing how He loves the wicked world and how He will give His Son to die for the sins of the world?

It is true the Sodomites deserve destruction, but so does every person in the world. "There is none righteous, no, not one," and, "There is no difference: For all have sinned, and come short of the glory of God" (Rom. 3:10,22,23).

God is willing for the innocent to suffer for the guilty. And in temporarily redeeming people from the wrath of God to keep them from sudden destruction, a Christian may sometimes intervene. But for the redeeming of souls from Hell, only Christ Himself, the pure Lamb of God, is a fit Sacrifice to pay that debt, a fit Intercessor to appeal to God for sinners. But even the sacrifice of Christ will not save an impenitent sinner who seeks no forgiveness.

GENESIS 19

AND there came two angels to Sodom at even; and Lot sat in the gate of Sodom: and Lot seeing *them* rose up to meet them; and he bowed himself with his face toward the ground;

2 And he said, Behold now, my lords, turn in, I pray you, into your servant's house, and tarry all night, and wash your feet, and ye shall rise up early, and go on your ways. And they said, Nay; but we will abide in the street all night

3 And he pressed upon them greatly; and they turned in unto him, and entered into his house; and he made them a feast, and did bake unleavened bread, and they did eat.

Angels Visit Sodom

We understand the same two angels who were with the Lord near Abraham's tent have now come to Sodom.

"Lot sat in the gate of Sodom." That was a public meeting place in the cities. At the gate of the city of the people of the sons of Heth, Abraham inquired of and bought the Cave of Machpelah for the burial of Sarah (Gen. 23:10). When King Hamor and his son Shechem agreed for all the males to be circumcised so they might have Jacob's family among them, they met at the city gate (Gen. 34:20). When Moses would call together all who were on the Lord's side to help him clean out the idolaters, after the golden calf, he stood in the gate of the camp (Exod. 32:26).

Dr. Joseph Free in *Archaeology and Bible History* says:

Lot was sitting at the gate of Sodom when the angels came to the city (Gen. 19:1). Archaeological excavations show that the gates of Palestinian cities often had stone benches or seats as a built-in part of the structure, so that people might sit there and wait for their friends, or engage in conversation with those whom they had agreed to meet at the gate. The excavation by the Pacific School of Religion at Tell en-Nasbeh (1926-1935), believed by the excavators to be the site of the Biblical Mizpah, revealed a gate which was lined with stone benches (MLPP, 211).

At the gate people would sit in order to meet their associates, hear the news, and engage in trade. Here it was that legal transactions were carried on, as exemplified in the making of the marriage contract between Ruth and Boaz, which was arranged at the gate of the town (Ruth 4:1,2). The gate was the place of public proclamation; it was here that David waited to hear the news of Absalom, and then went to the chamber over the gate to weep for him (II Sam. 18:24,33). Likely it was the place where the prophets made their proclamations.

The significance of the gate becomes evident if one notes how often it is mentioned in the Old Testament. Archaeological discoveries have given us further light on the size and arrangement of the gates of Biblical times and illuminate the importance of this structure in Near Eastern life.

But there is probably more meaning here. Lot sat at the gate of Sodom very possibly as an influential man, honest and greatly respected, perhaps to settle disputes among the people, because in verse 9 they say, "This one fellow came in to sojourn, and he will needs be a judge." Lot was so well known, so respected and so rich and influential, that he had been the one taken away as hostage by the kings who had conquered and looted the city. Now he had returned as a great man in the city.

Lot's Hospitality

Lot saw the angels and "rose up to meet them." Did he recognize them as angels? Probably not at first. But they were strangers, visitors. They evidently appeared to be serious, important men. As a prominent citizen and principal businessman, Lot would meet them. But knowing the wickedness of the city, he doubtless felt they would be molested and injured, so they dare not sleep outside. In verse 8, when the perverts beat at the door to molest these men, he said, ". . . for therefore came they under the shadow of my roof."

Note the hospitality of Lot. They must stay at his house. They will be received graciously. They can wash their feet.

After walking in sandals, with no pavement and without socks, the first thing people did after a journey was to take off their sandals and wash their tired feet. Even now in

Eastern countries—India, China, Japan, Korea—it is customary to take off one's shoes upon entering the house. In Bible times hospitality would ordinarily provide water to wash their feet.

So Jesus complained to the Pharisee in whose house He was a guest, "I entered into thine house, thou gavest me no water for my feet: but she hath washed my feet with tears, and wiped them with the hairs of her head" (Luke 7:44). And the widow, if she is to be supported by the church, must have proved herself to be hospitable and kindly, with a heart of love toward God's people. Only a widow sixty years old, "having been the wife of one man, Well reported of for good works; if she have brought up children, if she have lodged strangers, if she have washed the saints' feet, if she have relieved the afflicted, if she have diligently followed every good work" (I Tim. 5:9,10), was to be cared for by the church. She should have received visitors and strangers; she should have washed the saints' feet. No doubt Lot, like Abraham, was one who, careful to entertain strangers, had thus "entertained angels unawares" (Heb. 13:2).

So Jesus, showing the love that we should have one for another, washed the disciples' feet, as recorded in John 13:14, and He said, "If I then, your Lord and Master, have washed your feet; ye also ought to wash one another's feet." He meant, of course, in a spiritual way that Christians should help restore Christians. We walk in a dirty world. We need daily cleansing and help. If anyone be overtaken in a fault, we should "restore such an one in the spirit of meekness." But surely He meant also that Christians ought to be hospitable, ought to receive one another kindly. In this matter, Lot and Abraham were blessed examples. We should follow their example.

Unleavened Bread for Angels

Lot "made them a feast, and did bake unleavened bread" for the angels. So did Abraham, with these angels and the Lord, in a quickly prepared meal. Now Lot also furnished unleavened bread. Leaven, a type of evil, was not in it. Did

Lot know that these men were angels? Possibly not. It may be that since they needed to have fresh, hot bread, there was no dough rising and ready to fix a meal quickly, but God arranged it so His angels would have unleavened bread, quickly made without yeast.

VERSES 4-11:

4 ¶ But before they lay down, the men of the city, *even* the men of Sodom, compassed the house round, both old and young, all the people from every quarter:

5 And they called unto Lot, and said unto him, Where *are* the men which came in to thee this night? bring them out unto us, that we may know them.

6 And Lot went out at the door unto them, and shut the door after him,

7 And said, I pray you, brethren, do not so wickedly.

8 Behold now, I have two daughters which have not known man; let me, I pray you, bring them out unto you, and do ye to them as *is* good in your eyes: only unto these men do nothing; for therefore came they under the shadow of my roof.

9 And they said, Stand back. And they said *again*, This one *fellow* came in to sojourn, and he will needs be a judge: now will we deal worse with thee, than with them. And they pressed sore upon the man, *even* Lot, and came near to break the door.

10 But the men put forth their hand, and pulled Lot into the house to them, and shut to the door.

11 And they smote the men that *were* at the door of the house with blindness, both small and great: so that they wearied themselves to find the door.

City of Sodomites

Verse 4 tells us that the men of Sodom, "both old and young, all the people from every quarter," came seeking to debase these angels! They had seen these angels. Supposing they were men, they were determined to force and rape these angels!

Remember, there was not one righteous person in the city besides Lot. The whole city—all the men, old and young—are here for this lewdness and perversion.

When sin goes on unrestrained, judgment must come. Jude, verse 7, says, "Even as Sodom and Gomorrah, and the cities about them in like manner, giving themselves over to fornication, and going after strange flesh, are set forth for an example, suffering the vengeance of eternal fire."

Isaiah 1:4-7 likens Israel to Sodom:

"Ah sinful nation, a people laden with iniquity, a seed of evildoers, children that are corrupters: they have forsaken the Lord, they have provoked the Holy One of Israel unto anger, they are gone away backward. Why should ye be stricken any more? ye will revolt more and more: the whole head is sick, and the whole heart faint. From the sole of the foot even unto the head there is no soundness in it; but wounds, and bruises, and putrifying sores: they have not been closed, neither bound up, neither mollified with ointment. Your country is desolate, your cities are burned with fire: your land, strangers devour it in your presence, and it is desolate, as overthrown by strangers."

But there was a remnant, thank God. So Israel had a few years before the captivity. Nineveh would have been destroyed like Sodom and Gomorrah, Admah and Zeboiim, but for the repentance of many under Jonah.

Sodomy Hated of God, a Sure Sign of Judgment

This vile, homosexual act is still called sodomy everywhere in memorial of this wicked city. Remember that after the flood wicked people turned to being Lesbians and homosexuals. Romans 1:26-28 says:

"For this cause God gave them up unto vile affections: for even their women did change the natural use into that which is against nature: And likewise also the men, leaving the natural use of the woman, burned in their lust one toward another; men with men working that which is unseemly, and receiving in themselves that recompence of their error which was meet. And even as they did not like to retain God in their knowledge, God gave them over to a reprobate mind, to do those things which are not convenient."

The passage says that God "gave them up to uncleanness," that He "gave them up unto vile affections"

and that He "gave them over to a reprobate mind." That is
how the world became heathen after the flood. The people
went away from the civilization of Noah and his sons and
became the debased heathens of the world.

In Leviticus 20:10,13,15, adultery with another man's
wife, sodomy with a man, or intercourse with a beast, are
all listed alike as deserving the death penalty. Thus in the
Scriptures before the ceremonial law, then in the
ceremonial law, then again in the New Testament, sodomy
is marked as a vile sin worthy of death. Sodomites go to
Hell. The homosexual is not sick; he is perverted and
intentionally wicked, and his sin is no more excusable than
adultery or murder.

Lot Calls These Evil Men "Brethren"

What an awful compromise had slipped into the life of
Lot! He had not been enough appalled at the sin of Sodom;
he moved into it with all his family. Now he calls the
wicked "brethren." Now he is willing, if need be, for his
virgin daughters to be raped in order to save his guests.
How Lot sought the friendship of these wicked men! His
attitude should have been like Ephesians 5:11, "And have
no fellowship with the unfruitful works of darkness, but
rather reprove them."

Do you wonder that these two daughters later schemed
to commit incest with their father? They had absorbed too
much of the spirit of Sodom!

Lot himself is about to be abused by all this crowd, but
the angels pull him within the door and smite with
blindness those who fumble to find the door.

Doubtless this scene is pictured in the Scriptures to show
that the judgment of God on Sodom was justly deserved
and that such sin must be punished.

Matthew Henry says here:

> Abuses offered to God's messengers and to faithful
> reprovers soon fill the measure of a people's wickedness,
> and bring destruction without remedy. See Prov. xxix. 1,
> and 2 Chron. xxxvi. 16. If reproofs remedy not, there is no
> remedy. See 2 Chron. xxv. 16.

Angels Defend God's People

The angels defended Lot. He was God's man. He was in the wrong place, had the wrong company but was still a godly man. "The angel of the Lord encampeth round about them that fear him, and delivereth them" (Ps. 34:7). Is not that the main business of angels? "Are they not all ministering spirits, sent forth to minister for them who shall be heirs of salvation?" (Heb. 1:14). We remember that an angel was sent to get Peter out of prison in Acts 12. An angel who was captain of the Lord's host met Gideon to assure him of victory. In Acts 5:19 we find that when Peter and John were in prison for preaching, "the angel of the Lord by night opened the prison doors, and brought them forth."

An angel of God came to Paul on shipboard to assure him of his safety en route to Rome (Acts 27:23). And these same angels would lead Lot and his two daughters to safety the next morning.

VERSES 12-14:

12 ¶ And the men said unto Lot, Hast thou here any besides? son in law, and thy sons, and thy daughters, and whatsoever thou hast in the city, bring *them* out of this place:

13 For we will destroy this place, because the cry of them is waxen great before the face of the LORD; and the LORD hath sent us to destroy it.

14 And Lot went out, and spake unto his sons in law, which married his daughters, and said, Up, get you out of this place; for the LORD will destroy this city. But he seemed as one that mocked unto his sons in law.

Can Lot Save His Loved Ones?

Now the angels show their true character. They are not only men, they are angels of God who say plainly, "We will destroy this place, because the cry of them is waxen great before the face of the Lord; and the Lord hath sent us to destroy it."

There is an urgency now; Lot must leave. He had not been told that before. He is urged to get daughters and sons and sons-in-law out of this place. We are not told that he had sons. He had sons-in-law. It is possible that, since Abraham had suggested that for ten righteous people the Lord might spare the city, that there were ten in Lot's family. That would include three married daughters and three sons-in-law. There were more than one; how many, we are not told.

Urgently Lot said to his sons-in-law, "Up, get you out of this place: for the Lord will destroy this city." But Lot is too late. He has put his approval on Sodom, moving near it, then into it, then calling the wicked men there his brethren. These sons-in-law are doubtless of the same wicked people. His married daughters no doubt had absorbed the philosophy and moral standards of the city.

These sons-in-law are not acquainted with angels. They do not take Lot seriously. He is like one who mocks or jokes! It is a sad, sad thing when parents so live that their children are not impressed by their warnings! If Lot had been in outright opposition to sin, if he had avoided the company of the wicked, if he had not been so busy making money, it is probable that these sons-in-law would have respected and been greatly impressed with the warning. They were not. They must be left behind! The married daughters, the sons-in-law, are really a part of the wicked Sodom which the angels are sent to destroy.

VERSES 15-23:

15 ¶ And when the morning arose, then the angels hastened Lot, saying, Arise, take thy wife, and thy two daughters, which are here; lest thou be consumed in the iniquity of the city.

16 And while he lingered, the men laid hold upon his hand, and upon the hand of his wife, and upon the hand of his two daughters; the LORD being merciful unto him: and they brought him forth, and set him without the city.

17 ¶ And it came to pass, when they had brought them forth abroad, that he said, Escape for thy life; look not behind thee, neither stay thou in all the plain; escape to the mountain, lest thou be consumed.

18 And Lot said unto them, Oh, not so, my Lord:

19 Behold now, thy servant hath

found grace in thy sight, and thou hast magnified thy mercy, which thou hast shewed unto me in saving my life; and I cannot escape to the mountain, lest some evil take me, and I die:

20 Behold now, this city *is* near to flee unto, and it *is* a little one: Oh, let me escape thither, (*is* it not a little one?) and my soul shall live.

21 And he said unto him, See, I have accepted thee concerning this thing also, that I will not overthrow this city, for the which thou hast spoken.

22 Haste thee, escape thither; for I cannot do any thing till thou be come thither. Therefore the name of the city was called Zoar.

23 ¶ The sun was risen upon the earth when Lot entered into Zoar.

Lot Brought Out of Sodom

Lot himself still lingered. The angel must hasten him out! What about all his wealth? Must it be left here? What about his unsaved married daughters? Must they remain here? What about his friends?

Lot must not wait for the others. One angel takes him and his wife by the hand and the other angel takes the hand of his two daughters, we suppose, and thus they are urged and led precipitately out of wicked Sodom. They must get out or "be consumed in the iniquity of the city."

We believe that the deliverance of Lot from Sodom, with his wife and two daughters, is in answer to the prayer of Abraham. Verse 29 says, "God remembered Abraham and sent Lot out of the midst of the overthrow."

Abraham had appealed to the Lord, "Wilt thou also destroy the righteous with the wicked?" and again, "That be far from thee to do after this manner, to slay the righteous with the wicked: and that the righteous should be as the wicked, that be far from thee" (Gen. 18:23,25). That is true as a general principle. But I Corinthians 5:5 tells how a saved man, living in open sin, should be delivered "unto Satan for the destruction of the flesh, that the spirit may be saved in the day of the Lord Jesus."

And Jesus said in Matthew 18:15-17 that if a brother in the church, when entreated by the offended one and visited by others and then dealt with by the church, will not hear, then "let him be unto thee as an heathen man and a publican."

Righteousness is a relative matter. A Christian may live

an unrighteous life, as Lot did, although he is called a righteous man with a righteous soul. But godly Jonathan died with his father King Saul (I Sam. 31:2). And Balaam was a prophet of God and spoke sometimes with the power of God upon him. We would suppose that he was a believer and thus a child of God. But he lived among the wicked Midianites, and he had helped tempt the children of Israel to sin. His prophecies came true but his counsel was wicked (Num. 31:16). He was destroyed with the Midianites (Num. 31:8).

The prophet of God who went to cry against the false altar of Jeroboam was sent of God and God worked a miracle to indicate it. The altar was rent and Jeroboam was made powerless. But contrary to the plain command of God, he was invited to stay and he stayed for a meal and a lion came and killed him (I Kings 13:24).

Saved people are not guaranteed to be always protected when they live in sin or when they disobey God. But God heard the cry of Abraham, surely, and delivered Lot. He might have done so anyway, because Lot was a saved man. But He did it, remembering Abraham.

Judgment Cannot Come Until Lot Is Delivered

It is wonderfully sweet and suggestive that in verse 22 the angel said, "Haste thee, escape thither; for I cannot do any thing till thou be come thither." The fire could not fall on wicked Sodom until Lot was gone!

Lot makes a plea. Of the five cities in the valley of Siddim which is now the bed of the southern part of the Dead Sea, the small one was Zoar. Lot pleads he cannot go out into the mountains. Why not? Would not God who was sparing his life and rescuing him take care of him in the mountains? In the mountains in the will of God is far better than a wicked city. Zoar was wicked, but not perhaps with as much wickedness as the larger city. But the angel answered the prayer. How merciful God is to His people!

But Lot's conscience did not allow him to stay in Zoar. He later moved out to a cave into the hills.

Lot was accustomed to riches, comforts, and luxuries. He was not willing to live in the mountains. He will come to more despair in his own sinful way.

VERSES 24,25:

24 Then the LORD rained upon Sodom and upon Gō-mŏr-răh brimstone and fire from the LORD out of heaven;

25 And he overthrew those cities, and all the plain, and all the inhabitants of the cities, and that which grew upon the ground.

Four Cities Destroyed

Five cities are named in this valley: Sodom, Gomorrah, Admah, Zeboiim, and Bela or Zoar (Gen. 14:2). Zoar, we suppose, is saved as a mercy to Lot.

We were told that "the sun was risen upon the earth when Lot entered into Zoar" (vs. 23), so this destruction was not brought by an ordinary storm. No, "the Lord rained upon Sodom and upon Gomorrah brimstone and fire from the Lord out of heaven." It meant a total destruction of "those cities, and all the plain, and all the inhabitants of the cities, and that which grew upon the ground." This is not a destruction brought by normal natural causes. It is supernatural—a rain of fire and brimstone from God out of Heaven.

Sodom and Gomorrah "are set forth for an example, suffering the vengeance of eternal fire" (Jude 7). Eternal fire? Then evidently like the fire in Hell, a symbol of that fire. Second Peter 2:6 tells us that Sodom and Gomorrah were turned into ashes "making them an ensample unto those that after should live ungodly." This is a reminder and a picture of eternal destruction in Hell. Nothing in time can adequately picture eternity, and nothing within known limits can adequately portray the infinite. But the awfulness of an eternal Hell is here held up as a warning, and we are reminded of that by the destruction of Sodom and Gomorrah and their nearby cities by the wrath of God.

"Fire and brimstone." We are told that in this area there is a good deal of evidence of fire and brimstone among the stones and land nearby.

We take the Bible at literal face value: there was a rain of fire and brimstone from the Lord out of Heaven. Some think it was a rain of meteors from the sky that exploded when they got into the atmosphere. However, there were slime pits, or asphalt; they had the valley full of them (Gen. 14:10).

Archaeological Exploration Proves Literal Cities Destroyed as Bible Says

A detailed archaeological exploration of Sodom and Gomorrah and the whole area was made from 1926 to 1928 by an expedition headed by Dr. Melvin Grove Kyle, president of Xenia Theological Seminary, St. Louis, and by Dr. W. F. Albright, director of the American School of Oriental Research at Jerusalem, assisted by other well-known scholars. This was reported in the book, *Explorations at Sodom,* by Dr. Kyle. The conclusion of these scientists was:

1. The civilization of the days of Abraham which the Bible represents to have been on the Plain at that time is found to have been actually there and the absence of any trace of civilization of any kind from that time down to A.D. 600, is in exact accord with the silence of biblical history concerning this Plain from the destruction of the city to the end of the history.

2. The natural conditions of life on the Plain also as described in the account in Genesis are exactly confirmed today; "like the garden of the Lord, before the Lord destroyed Sodom and Gomorrah."

3. The great catastrophe described in the Bible did actually take place.

4. The cities are clearly shown to have stood in front of Jebel Usdum where they lie under the waters today. The High Place of the Plain, clearly a place of great importance, as shown by the fortifications, is now well known.

5. And last of all, the evidence makes it quite possible that Lot should be the progenitor of Moabite civilization,

which certainly had attained considerable importance by the time Moses passed by the old Kir of Moab.

They found that the salt waters in the lower half of the Dead Sea covered forests of trees, which can still be seen as far as a mile from the shore; that the waters of the Dead Sea are rising and that the cities destroyed were in this vale of Siddim, and their ruins are under these waters. The conclusion of these Christian scientists is that the destruction came about possibly by a giant explosion of accumulated gas and oil and asphalt which became some way ignited, and this fiery, burning mixture flew into the air and then down on these cities. On pages 128-130 Dr. Kyle says:

> This region was found by the geologists to be a burned-out region of oil and asphalt, of which material, indeed, there is again an accumulation that will soon be exploited; even now, as I write, such exploitation is being reported. Now wherever these conditions exist there is an accumulation of gases, and the geologists tell us that here, at some time which they cannot exactly fix, these gases were ignited by some means, also to them unknown, and there was a great explosion, with first an upheaval, and then a subsidence of the strata.
>
> The character of the ruptured strata has also been determined, with most interesting conclusions. There is along the lower part of this Plain a great stratum of rock salt, which on the western side of the Plain shows itself in that great salt mountain, now known as Jebel Usdum. At its base is a stratum of rock salt about one hundred and fifty feet thick. It is almost pure salt, but lies in layers of varying thickness. Mixed with the layers of salt, and falling down over them also, is a marl in which is much free sulphur, lumps of which we picked up along the sea.
>
> When the explosion of the gases took place, this stratum of salt mixed with sulphur was ruptured with the other strata, and the salt and sulphur carried up into the heavens red-hot, and so rained down upon Sodom and Gomorrah and over the whole region, exactly as the Scripture describes the rain of fire and brimstone from Heaven. Mixed with the salt and sulphur was also the asphalt, heated to a high degree.
>
> Now, what makes a greater smoke than a vat of boiling asphalt at work on the street? Thus we have an exact

accounting for the smoke up to heaven, "as the smoke of a furnace." A low place in the hills toward Hebron opened the way for Abraham to see this distinctly from that distant point.

VERSE 26:

26 ¶ But his wife looked back from behind him, and she became a pillar of salt.

"Remember Lot's Wife" (Luke 17:32)

She looked back and thus disobeyed the express command of the angels. Possibly she doubted whether Sodom would really be destroyed.

She looked back on the neighbors and friends, looked back toward her married daughters and perhaps grandchildren, all left behind. Perhaps she, who was accustomed to luxury, looked back with great distress about the loss of house and furniture and possessions.

And she was struck dead and became a pillar of salt.

Matthew Henry interprets this as follows:

> She was struck dead in the place; yet her body did not fall down, but stood fixed and erect like a pillar, or monument, not liable to waste nor decay, as human bodies exposed to the air are, but metamorphosed into a metallic substance which would last perpetually.

Salt was everywhere in that country, and even today there are great layers of rock salt in the base of the hills. Perhaps the Lord piled falling hot salt around her and the body was covered, and perhaps was the core of a pillar of salt, or God could have miraculously turned that frail human body into a pillar of salt.

How wrong to hesitate when God says go! How sad to look back at the past which is forbidden!

We remember when a man said he would follow Jesus, but, said he, "Suffer me first to go and bury my father." When the aged father died and had been buried and the matter settled, then he would follow Jesus. But Jesus said, "Let the dead bury their dead. . . . No man, having put his hand to the plough, and looking back, is fit for the kingdom of God" (Luke 9:60,62).

It is always wrong to contemplate sin, to consider sin, to cherish thoughts of sin. It is always wrong to play with sin. With his head in the lap of Delilah, Samson dallied until his resistance was overcome and he betrayed his calling, lost his hair and his power.

Oh, we are reminded of the Lord, "Remember Lot's wife."

VERSES 27-29:

27 ¶ And Abraham gat up early in the morning to the place where he stood before the LORD:

28 And he looked toward Sodom and Gō-mŏr-´räh, and toward all the land of the plain, and beheld, and, lo, the smoke of the country went up as the smoke of a furnace.

29 ¶ And it came to pass, when God destroyed the cities of the plain, that God remembered Abraham, and sent Lot out of the midst of the overthrow, when he overthrew the cities in the which Lot dwelt.

Lot Spared for Abraham's Sake

Abraham, in the plain of Mamre near Hebron, thirty-five miles away, looked down toward Sodom and Gomorrah: "Lo, the smoke of the country went up as the smoke of a furnace." So the burning asphalt (slime or coal tar) created a giant pillar of smoke. Or, if God chose simply to create and rain down fire from Heaven without using any natural sources, the smoke of burning cities would still go up high in the air. Abraham had great concern. He had done all he could. Oh, was Lot saved? But "God remembered Abraham, and sent Lot out of the midst of the overthrow." It was principally for Abraham's sake that God delivered Lot. Oh, how we ought to pray for our friends, for "the effectual fervent prayer of a righteous man availeth much" (Jas. 5:16).

VERSES 30-38:

30 ¶ And Lot went up out of Zoar, and dwelt in the mountain, and his two daughters with him; for he feared to dwell in Zoar: and he dwelt in a cave, he and his two daughters.

31 And the firstborn said unto the younger, Our father *is* old, and *there is* not a man in the earth to come in unto us after the manner of all the earth:

32 Come, let us make our father drink wine, and we will lie with him, that we may preserve seed of our father.

33 And they made their father drink wine that night: and the firstborn went in, and lay with her father; and he perceived not when she lay down, nor when she arose.

34 And it came to pass on the morrow, that the firstborn said unto the younger, Behold, I lay yesternight with my father: let us make him drink wine this night also; and go thou in, *and* lie with him, that we may preserve seed of our father.

35 And they made their father drink wine that night also: and the younger arose, and lay with him; and he perceived not when she lay down, nor when she arose.

36 Thus were both the daughters of Lot with child by their father.

37 And the firstborn bare a son, and called his name ¹Moab: the same *is* the father of the Moabites unto this day.

38 And the younger, she also bare a son, and called his name Bĕn–ăm´-mī: the same *is* the father of the children of Ammon unto this day.

Lot's Poverty, Ruined Daughters, Illegitimate Children

Here is an outline for a sermon on Lot: "The Ruin of a Christian," using passages from Genesis and II Peter 2:6-8. For Lot was a righteous man, a godly man, a just man, he had a righteous soul.

I. Lot's worldliness.

    1. He put money, prosperity first. So chose the fruitful valley and proximity of wicked cities. "And Lot . . .pitched his tent toward Sodom" (Gen. 13:12).

    2. He called the wicked brethren (Gen. 19:7).

    3. He took up the habits of Sodom. If he was a habitual drinker, now he is a drunken man.

II. His spiritual ruin.

    1. His religion was a joke to his in-laws (Gen. 19:14).

    2. He could not even win his wife to the Lord. She was sold on Sodom (Gen. 19:26).

    3. He took the two unmarried daughters out of Sodom, but he couldn't get Sodom out of the girls. They were already sold to evil.

    4. Lot let his whole city go to Hell. If he had won nine other people, with those ten the city would have been spared (Gen. 18:32).

CONCLUSION: Now in poverty, in disgrace, his only descendants were these two illegitimate children of his incest.

Lot went up out of Zoar. The awful destruction on the other four cities frightened him. He lived in a cave. There are many caves along the shores of the Dead Sea even now, including those in which were found the Dead Sea Scrolls.

The daughters may have thought that all civilization was wiped out. They thought, "There is not a man in the earth to come in unto us." They thought they might never have husbands and children, that their father was the only man left alive. And so, with a Sodom morality, they planned to make their father drunken and lie with him, and so it worked out.

The two children born are Moab and Ben-ammi, the latter being the father of the children of Ammon. Later the Moabites will fill the area south and east of the Dead Sea and the Ammonites north of there in what is now the Hashemite Kingdom of Jordan. Amman, the capital city, is named for Ammon. It was Rabbah in the time of David.

Let every reader take a lesson from the avarice and worldliness of Lot! He was a righteous man but "the care of this world, and the deceitfulness of riches, choke the word, and he becometh unfruitful" (Matt. 13:22). And remember, there are great temptations that go with riches, and Jesus said, "How hardly shall they that have riches enter into the kingdom of God!" (Mark 10:23). Yes, it is possible but riches greatly hinder a man from putting Christ first. We must remember: Beware of "covetousness, which is idolatry" (Col. 3:5).

Proverbs 23:4 says, "Labour not to be rich. . . ." The rich man whose barns were filled with plenty but was not rich toward God is called a fool by the Saviour in Luke 12. First Timothy 6:9 admonishes us, "They that will be rich fall into temptation and a snare, and into many foolish and hurtful lusts, which drown men in destruction and perdition." And Psalm 62:10 tells us, ". . . if riches increase, set not your heart upon them."

It is not wrong to be thrifty, to work hard, and Abraham was as rich as Lot, but he did not love his riches. Oh, that God would give us each a heart to be content with such as we have and thank God and serve Him!

GENESIS 20

VERSES 1,2:

AND Abraham journeyed from thence toward the south country, and dwelled between Kadesh and Shur, and sojourned in Gerar.

2 And Abraham said of Sarah his wife, She is my sister: and Ā-bĭm´-ĕ-lĕch king of Gerar sent, and took Sarah.

Abraham's Deception Again Leads to Trouble

Abraham "sojourned in Gerar." He had "dwelt in the plain of Mamre," near Hebron, ever since before he delivered Lot after the kings looted Sodom and took Lot captive. But the "plain of Mamre the Amorite" really belonged, at least in possession, to the man Mamre and his brothers Eschol and Aner who had helped Abraham (Gen. 14:13). Now after fifteen or twenty years he goes away south "between Kadesh and Shur," the very southern part of occupied Canaan.

We must remember that Abraham was a stranger, living in tents. He owned no property in the land of Canaan, "no, not so much as to set his foot on" (Acts 7:5). He built no houses, but lived in tents as do the Bedouins now, and moved with his flocks and herds when it became necessary.

Why did he leave the area of Mamre? Possibly his old friends there and confederates had died and the next generation may have been fearful or suspicious of him. Such a mighty warrior, with his own little private army! Or Abraham may have been so greatly distressed by the destruction of Sodom, Gomorrah, Admah, and Zeboiim, by the ruin that came to Lot and by his drunken incest, that he felt a need for change. But wherever Abraham dwelt in the land he was more or less a "sojourner." The land was promised to him but he had not yet possession of any of it as his own.

But camping in a new area meant new associations and new dangers. Before, when he "sojourned" in Egypt, he had been fearful about his beautiful wife, and he and Sarah both said that she was his sister, and Pharaoh took her and God had to deliver him there.

Now again, in the country of a king he did not know or trust, he felt desperately fearful about his wife. Remember that Sarah has now a second youth; she is young and beautiful, and with the face and form of a young woman.

Charles R. Erdman says:

> That at her age she could have been attractive to the king seems incredible, yet it must be remembered that her physical vigor had been so preserved or restored that within a year she bore a child, and further that Abimelech may have wished merely to form an alliance with such a rich and powerful chieftain as Abraham seemed to be.

Abraham knows she would be attractive to any lustful king. He fears for his life. Before he had told a half lie, "She is my sister"; now he tells it again and instructs Sarah to say the same!

A second lie comes easier after a first. The second drink comes easier after the first drink. A man who had cursed and sworn before he was saved, in great temptation may fall to cursing again as did Peter at the campfire of the soldiers who crucified Jesus (Matt. 26:74,75). So fearful Abraham takes up the same scheme he had used before.

We do not read that Abraham made an altar at Gerar or gave any witness. He seems to have thought that King Abimelech was a heathen and his people were heathen, wicked and dangerous. We are reminded that we ought to take a plain stand anywhere we go so that people may know the Lord, know that we are Christians, know that we have strict standards of godliness. No doubt Abraham would have had more confidence and would have been less fearful had he boldly said that the beautiful woman was his wife. There ought to have been a proud and joyful faith in Abraham. Sarah had already conceived, or would soon conceive, the child for whom he had prayed these many, many years! But doubting and fearing and without a clear witness, we suppose, Abraham told the half-truth, half-lie;

and Sarah was taken to the king's palace.

In this world Christians have to face contact with the ungodly about us. So we are commanded to "be ready always to give an answer to every man that asketh you a reason of the hope that is in you" (I Pet. 3:15).

VERSES 3-7:

3 But God came to Ă-bĭm-́ĕ-lĕch in a dream by night, and said to him, Behold, thou *art but* a dead man, for the woman which thou hast taken; for she *is* a man's wife.

4 But Ă-bĭm-́ĕ-lĕch had not come near her: and he said, Lord, wilt thou slay also a righteous nation?

5 Said he not unto me, She *is* my sister? and she, even she herself said, He *is* my brother: in the integrity of my heart and innocency of my hands have I done this.

6 And God said unto him in a dream, Yea, I know that thou didst this in the integrity of thy heart; for I also withheld thee from sinning against me: therefore suffered I thee not to touch her.

7 Now therefore restore the man *his* wife; for he *is* a prophet, and he shall pray for thee, and thou shalt live: and if thou restore *her* not, know thou that thou shalt surely die, thou, and all that *are* thine.

"God Came to Abimelech in a Dream"

Was Abimelech a godly man? Perhaps, or at least a God-fearing man. The indication is that God knew he would listen, and he appeals to God: "Lord, wilt thou slay also a righteous nation?" So he meant to be a righteous man and have his people righteous. He said, "In the integrity of my heart and innocency of my hands have I done this." God knew that was true. Abimelech shows well in this.

He had sent to take Sarah, supposing that this beautiful young woman was single, and would doubtless, as would other young women, be greatly honored to become the bride of a king. We suppose that Abraham, fearful and already having disclaimed Sarah, made no protest and did not defend her nor resist. Sarah is now in the palace but unharmed.

There are people, unknown to us, who have a heart turned toward God. Sometimes they are those whom we would not suspect as knowing or loving God. Cornelius, a Roman centurion in Acts, chapter 10, was a God-fearing, praying man who sought the Lord with all his heart.

In the midst of the storm with Jonah aboard, the sailors prayed to God for deliverance and were heard, though we do not suppose they were godly men. God had an angel visit the wife of Manoah to tell her she would be the mother of Judge Samson. God revealed much in dreams to the world ruler Nebuchadnezzar.

I talked to a Catholic bishop on a plane. He had such a tender heart, such an earnest desire to please God. He earnestly asked me to pray for him that he, old and sick, might be able to go back to his charge in the Solomon Islands. I felt surely, despite the trappings of Romanism and the false doctrine, he must know the Lord whom he loved.

On Mount Tabor in the Holy Land, a monk sang for our group some old hymns. After I had preached to our crowd, he earnestly asked me to pray for him. Oh, God deals with many a heart we might not suspect had sought the Lord. So God in great kindness talked to Abimelech and admitted the king's good intentions.

Let No Man Presume He Knows How Long He Will Live

"Thou art but a dead man," God said to Abimelech. God does kill people for some sins. He holds the key of death for every man. The Lord Jesus keeps every heart beating until His time comes for it to stop. But He sometimes kills people suddenly by a direct act of God, as He did the armies of Sennacherib, when the 185,000 died (Isa. 37:36); as He did Ananias and Sapphira (Acts 5:5,10); and as the Lord destroyed Korah, Dathan, and Abiram and those about them when the earth swallowed them and fire destroyed the 250 men who offered sacrifice (Num. 16:28-35).

But let every man take heed. Your very breath is in the hand of the Lord. You live not a heartbeat but at His permission. The sick may die and the well may die. Old people die and young people die. Your life is in the hands of the Lord. What a foolish and wicked thing it is to ignore the God whose hand holds our breath!

It is to Abimelech's credit that he believed the Word of God in a dream, and seemed to want to do right.

Again God Takes Care of His Own

But here is sweet comfort for every one of us who are "sojourners," who live in some touch with the outside wicked world. We can remember that among the blessings of the Lord promised in Psalm 103 is, "The Lord executeth righteousness and judgment for all that are oppressed." Again, the sweet promise of Hebrews 13:5,6 is, "Let your conversation be without covetousness; and be content with such things as ye have: for he hath said, I will never leave thee, nor forsake thee. So that we may boldly say, The Lord is my helper, and I will not fear what man shall do unto me."

Does God care for His own only when they are in His perfect will? No, God had protected Abraham and Sarah down in Egypt when their folly put them in danger. Here again they are not praiseworthy in their actions, yet God delivers them. If God cared for us only when we are perfect, there would be little occasion for His mercy.

God did not give up Peter when he cursed and swore and denied the Saviour, but met him and called him back to service and anointed him for it. God called Jonah the second time when, after disaster, God had delivered him from the storm and the whale's belly. We must remember,

"The Lord is merciful and gracious, slow to anger, and plenteous in mercy. He will not always chide: neither will he keep his anger for ever. He hath not dealt with us after our sins; nor rewarded us according to our iniquities. For as the heaven is high above the earth, so great is his mercy toward them that fear him. As far as the east is from the west, so far hath he removed our transgressions from us. Like as a father pitieth his children, so the Lord pitieth them that fear him. For he knoweth our frame; he remem-

bereth that we are dust. As for man, his days are as grass: as a flower of the field, so he flourisheth. For the wind passeth over it, and it is gone; and the place thereof shall know it no more. But the mercy of the Lord is from everlasting to everlasting upon them that fear him, and his righteousness unto children's children; To such as keep his covenant, and to those that remember his commandments to do them."—Ps. 103:8-18.

Salvation is by grace, not of our works, not of our deservings. So also are all the mercies poured upon us daily. We are heirs of God and joint heirs with Christ. God has committed Himself to us as our Father and Christ as our Saviour forever, when we have trusted in Him. Thank God, He often delivers the unworthy as well as the worthy.

". . .he is a prophet, and he shall pray for thee." To be a prophet is to speak in the power and wisdom of the Spirit of God. Joel 2:28-32 tells how at Pentecost and beyond the Holy Spirit would come upon "all flesh" (literally all kinds of people), and they would prophecy. A prophet is one who has a revelation from God, has special touch with God. Abraham was such an one. Abel also was a prophet (Luke 11:50,51), although he is not given that name in Genesis.

So Abraham will pray for Abimelech and his family. They will be forgiven and healed. Although Abraham is not perfect, he is God's man and must be treated as such. Oh, how much responsibility is put upon all of us who presume to speak for God in the ministry—preachers and teachers!

VERSES 8-13:

8 Therefore Ă-bĭm-́ĕ-lĕch rose early in the morning, and called all his servants, and told all these things in their ears: and the men were sore afraid.

9 Then Ă-bĭm-́ĕ-lĕch called Abraham, and said unto him, What hast thou done unto us? and what have I offended thee, that thou hast brought on me and on my kingdom a great sin? thou hast done deeds unto me that ought not to be done.

10 And Ă-bĭm-́ĕ-lĕch said unto Abraham, What sawest thou, that thou hast done this thing?

11 And Abraham said, Because I

thought, Surely the fear of God *is* not in this place; and they will slay me for my wife's sake.

12 And yet indeed *she is* my sister; she *is* the daughter of my father, but not the daughter of my mother; and she became my wife.

13 And it came to pass, when God caused me to wander from my father's house, that I said unto her, This *is* thy kindness which thou shalt shew unto me; at every place whither we shall come, say of me, He *is* my brother.

Abimelech Faces Abraham With His Fault

Abraham is charged, "Thou hast brought on me and on my kingdom a great sin." Abimelech said, "Thou hast done deeds unto me that ought not to be done." Abraham should explain why.

In the early morning Abimelech "called all his servants" and told them of the solemn warning of God. Fear fell upon them all. Had they had some contact with God before? Possibly. It is to the credit of Abimelech and his people that they listened to the warning of God, that they feared God. And the punishment would not have been on Abimelech alone but on his kingdom! We suppose that his servants had taken part in taking Sarah to the palace. Loyal to the king, they were accountable with him.

Abraham had thought, "Surely the fear of God is not in this place." But he was wrong. There was the fear of God in the king and his servants. They may have been wicked people, but they did not intentionally sin in this matter. They listened quickly to the Word of God by a dream.

Verse 13 gives us a little of Abraham's attitude: "God caused me to *wander* from my father's house." That is, all his life Abraham was a sojourner, a dweller in tents. He looked into the next world, to the kingdom age, when he "looked for a city which hath foundations, whose builder and maker is God" (Heb. 11:10).

Christians should take notice that a weak Christian may lead others to sin. How many lost men, even wicked men, would be deterred from sin with the proper Christian influence or the proper warning?

Once in Fort Worth, Texas, in a great conference I sent some young Christians and a minister to do personal work and to witness for Christ. They went into a bar on the north side and perhaps not very wisely they insisted that everybody stop drinking while they preached the Word of God. They were not tactful, possibly not kind, and the owner of the tavern insisted that they leave and they did.

But he learned later that I had sent these young people. Although he had never seen me, he had heard me many times on a daily radio broadcast. He wrote me a most earnest and apologetic letter. If he had known that I had sent them, he would have gladly listened to them. He respected my ministry and would listen to what I had to say. Would I come to preach the Gospel in his bar?

In a large restaurant in Delaware some of us sat at a table and more than once heard men at the table near us take God's name in vain. My beloved companion, Rev. Bill Harvey, stepped over to the table and very kindly asked them not to use that kind of language. "I am a Christian. I love the Saviour. It grieves me to have anyone take His name in vain," he said. The men were very respectful and quiet.

O God, help Christians to let their lights shine and not be a cause of stumbling either by our sin or by our neglect.

Abraham would have caused Abimelech to sin.

Evidently Abimelech properly felt that to take Sarah, if she were Abraham's wife, would be adultery, a shameful thing. He admits it would be a sin and would deserve the judgment of God. Oh, that Christian people everywhere would be bold in condemning such sin and build sentiment everywhere that would demand morality.

Matthew Henry suggests:

> Those that travel abroad, and converse much with strangers, as they have need of the wisdom of the serpent, so it is requisite that that wisdom be ever tempered with the innocence of the dove. It may, for aught I know, be suggested that God denied to Abraham and Sarah the blessing of children so long to punish them for this sinful compact which they had made to deny one another; if they will not own their marriage, why should God own it? But we may suppose that, after this reproof which Abimelech gave them, they agreed never to do so again, and then presently we read (ch. xxi. 1,2) that *Sarah conceived.*

VERSES 14-18:

14 And Ă-bĭm-́ĕ-lĕch took sheep, and oxen, and menservants, and womenservants, and gave *them* unto Abraham, and restored him Sarah his wife.

15 And Ă-bĭm-́ĕ-lĕch said, Behold, my land *is* before thee: dwell where it pleaseth thee.

16 And unto Sarah he said, Behold, I have given thy brother a thousand *pieces* of silver: behold, he *is* to thee a covering of the eyes, unto all that *are* with thee, and with all *other:* thus she was reproved.

17 ¶ So Abraham prayed unto God: and God healed Ă-bĭm-́ĕ-lĕch, and his wife, and his maidservants; and they bare *children.*

18 For the LORD had fast closed up all the wombs of the house of Ă-bĭm-́ĕ-lĕch, because of Sarah Abraham's wife.

Abraham and Sarah Rebuked Kindly by Abimelech

So Abraham is a prophet? Then Abimelech will treat him as a prophet, with great gifts of "sheep, and oxen, and menservants, and womenservants," and "a thousand pieces of silver." Abraham will pray for him and his nation, and they will be healed.

We remember that Pharaoh had "entreated Abram well for her sake: and he had sheep, and oxen, and he asses, and menservants, and maidservants, and she asses, and camels" (Gen. 12:16). That was when he first took Sarah, thinking he was rewarding the brother for the beautiful sister Pharaoh had taken. But here Abimelech gives these gifts when he restores Sarah. They are a token of Abimelech's penitence, of his respect for Abraham as a prophet of God and trying honestly to some way atone for the mistake he had made. Abimelech told Abraham, "Behold, my land is before thee: dwell where it pleaseth thee." He would not offend Abraham. Doubtless he was glad to have a prophet, a man of God, nearby.

There is a rebuke for Sarah, too. "Behold, I have given thy brother a thousand pieces of silver: behold, he is to thee a covering of the eyes, unto all that are with thee, and with all other." Sarah was reproved. The word *"pieces"* is in italics. It may have been a thousand shekels or a certain small weight. In Genesis 23 Abraham paid for the cave of Machpelah with four hundred shekels of silver, weighed out (Gen. 23:15,16). We do not know that coins were minted at this time and silver was weighed, as gold dust was in the mining areas of the West in pioneer times.

Abimelech said to Sarah, ". . .thy brother." It is a mocking reference to her lie. He is to be to her "a covering of the eyes." She was married and not free to look with desire on other men, as he was not free to desire other women. Matthew Henry calls attention: "The marriage-covenant is a covenant with the eyes, like Job's, ch. xxxi. 1."

Now Abraham prayed "and God healed Abimelech, and his wife, and his maidservants; and they bare children. For the Lord had fast closed up all the wombs of the house of Abimelech."

Had the matter continued some time? Were the household conscious that God's curse was upon them? Had it become obvious that now these women could not bear children until the curse was removed? That seems possible. But now Abraham prayed for Abimelech and the curse is removed and the king's wives and maidservants bare children.

We remember that Moses prayed for Miriam when she had opposed him and become a leper (Num. 12:13). Job's friends grieved him and charged him and God had Job pray for them, too (Job 42:8-10). Oh, how serious and important are the prayers of godly men for those who sin!

GENESIS 21

AND the LORD visited Sarah as he had said, and the LORD did unto Sarah as he had spoken.

2 For Sarah conceived, and bare Abraham a son in his old age, at the set time of which God had spoken to him.

3 And Abraham called the name of his son that was born unto him, whom Sarah bare to him, Isaac.

4 And Abraham circumcised his son Isaac being eight days old, as God had commanded him.

5 And Abraham was an hundred years old, when his son Isaac was born unto him.

6 ¶ And Sarah said, God hath made me to laugh, *so that* all that hear will laugh with me.

7 And she said, Who would have said unto Abraham, that Sarah should have given children suck? for I have born *him* a son in his old age.

8 And the child grew, and was weaned: and Abraham made a great feast the *same* day that Isaac was weaned.

Isaac Born According to Promise

Yes, the Lord visited Sarah and "as he had said."

At least thirteen times God had promised Abraham a son or his seed.

Genesis 12:3 says, ". . .in thee shall all families of the earth be blessed" through the Greater Seed, the Lord Jesus.

Genesis 13:15: ". . .thy seed."

Genesis 13:16: ". . .seed as the dust of the earth."

Genesis 15:4: One "that shall come forth out of thine own bowels shall be thine heir."

Genesis 15:18: "Unto thy seed have I given. . . ."

Genesis 17:2: ". . .and will multiply thee exceedingly."

Genesis 17:4,5: ". . .thou shalt be a father of many nations."

Genesis 17:6: "I will make thee exceeding fruitful."

Genesis 17:9: ". . .thou, and thy seed after thee."

Genesis 17:15,16: "Sarai. . .And I will bless her, and give thee a son also of her."

Genesis 17:19: "Sarah thy wife shall bear thee a son indeed."

Genesis 18:10: "I will certainly return unto thee

according to the time of life, and, lo, Sarah thy wife shall have a son."

Genesis 18:14: "At the time appointed I will return unto thee, according to the time of life, and Sarah shall have a son."

There was no promise when Abraham was down in Egypt in chapter 12. No promise is recorded in chapter 20 while Abraham is in Gerar, where in both cases he claimed that Sarah was his sister.

The birth of Isaac was "at the set time." So it was "according to the time of life"—that is, we think, after a menstrual period, then the regular nine months of gestation.

The Lord visited Sarah and she conceived. First the visitation, youth restored, then conception. When? In this short passage we have listed God's visit, conception, birth, circumcision of the child and a feast. We suppose that Sarah was already visited with youth and beauty of form and face when she attracted the attention of King Abimelech in chapter 20, and perhaps had already conceived. Now the promises are fulfilled, and Isaac is born. "Call his name Isaac," God said (Gen. 17:19). So it is Isaac (laughter).

Isaac, a Type or Illustration of Christ

I think that Abraham understood that Isaac was to be the ancestor and the type of Christ. Hebrews 11:17-19 says:

"By faith Abraham, when he was tried, offered up Isaac: and he that had received the promises offered up his only begotten son. Of whom it was said, That in Isaac shall thy seed be called: Accounting that God was able to raise him up, even from the dead; from whence also he received him in a figure."

Sometimes in those promises to Abraham the "seed" mentioned refers to Christ (Gen. 13:15; Gal. 3:16). Sometimes the son promised had to be exactly Isaac (as in Gen. 17:16,19; Gen. 18:10). But every time "seed" was mentioned—whether it was the nation Israel as the dust for multitude or even if it was Christ—it meant that they must come through Isaac. So Isaac is the type of Christ.

We remember that Jesus said to the Jews, "Your father Abraham rejoiced to see my day: and he saw it, and was glad" (John 8:56). When Abraham was about to offer Isaac he said, "My son, God will provide himself a lamb for a burnt-offering" (Gen. 22:8). Abraham knew that Isaac some way typified the coming Messiah, and he expected that God would raise Isaac from the dead, as Christ would be raised up.

It is not surprising that Isaac is like Christ in another way. He was born miraculously, as Jesus was born miraculously. He was not born of a virgin, and was not the "only begotten Son of God" as Jesus was, but it was a miracle that made the birth of Isaac possible and it was a superior, unique miracle when Jesus was conceived in the womb of a virgin.

Isaac was like Christ in another way, no doubt. Through the long ages, spiritually-minded people had longed for the coming of the Saviour. Ever since God had promised that the "Seed" of the woman should bruise the serpent's head (Gen. 2:15), so Moses had promised "a prophet. . .like unto me; him shall ye hear" (Acts 3:22), so Isaiah had promised a great Suffering Servant in Isaiah 53, so Micah foretold His birth in Bethlehem (Micah 5:2). Many, many prophets had foretold His coming kingdom and reign.

How many heart-cries must have gone up to God, waiting for the Messiah promised! Old Simeon was "waiting for the consolation of Israel" (Luke 2:25). Anna, the prophetess, seeing the Baby Jesus, "spake of him to all them that looked for redemption in Jerusalem" (Luke 2:38). The rejoicing of Zacharias over the birth of John the Baptist, foretelling the coming of the Saviour, must have been the rejoicing of thousands who had been longing for Jesus to come. So Isaac came after long waiting and expectation and after many promises.

How long had Abraham and Sarah prayed for a son? No doubt they had earnestly longed for a child even from their marriage, but Sarah was barren. And even after they had gone into the land of promise, the twenty-five years of earnest prayer went up before Isaac was born!

We remember that many times in the Bible godly women prayed earnestly and long for a son. Genesis 25:21 says about Rebekah, "And Isaac intreated the Lord for his wife, because she was barren: and the Lord was intreated of him, and Rebekah his wife conceived." After that definite answer to prayer, Rebekah had no more children.

Rachel was married to Jacob many years before God gave the son Joseph and eventually Benjamin (Gen. 30:1,22).

Hannah wept and prayed before God long before God answered her prayer and helped the barren woman conceive and bear the Prophet Samuel (I Sam. 1).

Zacharias and Elisabeth "had no child, because that Elisabeth was barren, and they both were now well stricken in years." Ah, but the angel of the Lord appeared to Zacharias and said:

"Fear not, Zacharias: for thy prayer is heard; and thy wife Elisabeth shall bear thee a son, and thou shalt call his name John. And thou shalt have joy and gladness; and many shall rejoice at his birth. For he shall be great in the sight of the Lord, and shall drink neither wine nor strong drink; and he shall be filled with the Holy Ghost, even from his mother's womb. And many of the children of Israel shall he turn to the Lord their God. And he shall go before him in the spirit and power of Elias, to turn the hearts of the fathers to the children, and the disobedient to the wisdom of the just; to make ready a people prepared for the Lord."—Luke 1:13-17.

So John the Baptist was born in answer to long and fervent prayers. Again it may be that as in the case of Sarah and Abraham, but for special, miraculous help from God, they could not have borne a child.

We should note that in each of these cases—Isaac, Joseph, Samuel, John the Baptist—these children born of prayer turned out to be great and godly men. Oh, then, godly parents ought to pray much about children.

This writer has, in eight or ten cases, prayed for women long barren and God has given children in answer to prayer. Such prayers must often please the Lord greatly.

Now Isaac was circumcised when eight days old, the beginning of a pattern set for all the males of Israel. This is a child of covenant and promise, the ancestor of a race set apart through whom the Scriptures and the Messiah would come.

Sarah rejoiced. When she had thought and doubted about the promised child, in Genesis 18:12, Sarah was thinking about the pleasure and comfort of wifehood and said, "After I am waxed old shall I have pleasure, my lord being old also?" But now that the baby is in arms, she rejoices in the joy of motherhood and says, "Who would have said unto Abraham, that Sarah should have given children suck?" Now the barren has become fruitful; the withered breast now full to feed the son God has given.

Matthew Henry says here,

> What it was she thought so wonderful: That *Sarah should give children suck,* that she should not only bear a child, but be so strong and hearty at that age as to give it suck. Note, mothers, if they be able, ought to be nurses to their own children. Sarah was a person of quality, was aged; nursing might be thought prejudicial to herself, or to the child, or to both; she had choice of nurses, no doubt, in her own family: and yet she would do her duty in this matter; and her daughters the good wives are while they thus *do well,* 1 Pet. iii. 5,6. See Lam. iv. 3.

———————

VERSE 9:

9 ¶ And Sarah saw the son of Hagar the Egyptian, which she had born | unto Abraham, mocking.

Isaac Mocked by Ishmael

Again we quote Matthew Henry:

> Ishmael himself gave the occasion by some affronts he

gave to Isaac his little brother, some think on the day that
Abraham made the feast for joy that Isaac was safely
weaned, which the Jews say was not till he was three
years old, others say five. Sarah herself was an eye-
witness of the abuse: she *saw the son of the Egyptian
mocking* (v. 9), mocking Isaac, no doubt, for it is said,
with reference to this (Gal. iv. 29), that *he that was born
after the flesh persecuted him that was born after the
Spirit*. Ishmael is here called the *son of the Egyptian*,
because, as some think, the 400 years' affliction of the
seed of Abraham by the Egyptians began now, and was to
be dated hence, ch. xv. 13.

Little Isaac is three years old or more and the tormenting
older brother, seventeen or more, is probably more severe
and more hateful than at first might appear. The older boy
"persecuted" the little fellow (Gal. 4:29). Since this is held
up as a type of the conflict between the flesh and the Spirit,
it may have been a sacrilegious sneering at the promise of
great blessing to all nations through Isaac.

Children's attitudes reflect those of their parents. In a
home not long ago a little girl, five or six, ran to put her
arms around my neck. She had not met me before but had
heard me preach, and in that home my name was often
called and the father and mother prayed for me. Their love
and confidence had begotten her love and confidence. So
Ishmael has a jealous and spiteful attitude toward little
Isaac which he absorbed from his mother's attitude.

When Hagar had conceived a child by Abraham, then
she despised her barren mistress (Gen. 16:4). So when
Sarah dealt hardly with her, she ran away. But God sent
her back to serve Sarah. Now that she had borne a child to
Abraham, she felt superior to Sarah. The years had not
taken away her jealousy and rebellion, we suppose, and it
was not simply a boy's exuberance laughing at her baby; it
was active, long-felt bitterness and animosity toward the
child that supplanted Ishmael as the promised seed of
Abraham.

10 Wherefore she said unto Abraham, Cast out this bondwoman and er son: for the son of this bondwoman shall not be heir with my son, *ven* with Isaac.

11 And the thing was very grievous a Abraham's sight because of his son.

12 ¶ And God said unto Abraham, et it not be grievous in thy sight because of the lad, and because of thy bondwoman; in all that Sarah hath said unto thee, hearken unto her voice; for in Isaac shall thy seed be called.

13 And also of the son of the bondwoman will I make a nation, because he *is* thy seed.

Hagar and Ishmael Cast Out

Sarah said, "Cast out this bondwoman and her son: for the son of this bondwoman shall not be heir with my son, even with Isaac" (vs. 10). That seemed cruel. Abraham was greatly grieved. Would the woman and the son starve in the wilderness? Sarah was right—the promise was through Isaac. Ishmael could not inherit on the same basis as Isaac. But Hagar and her boy Ishmael will not go unprotected. God had promised Hagar, "I will multiply thy seed exceedingly," and although he would be a lonely man, a wild man, "he shall dwell in the presence of all his brethren" (Gen. 16:10,12). Yes, and God had promised Abraham also, "Behold, I have blessed him, and will make him fruitful, and will multiply him exceedingly; twelve princes shall he beget, and I will make him a great nation" (Gen. 17:20).

God told Abraham that Sarah was right: "In Isaac shall thy seed be called." God would take care of Hagar. He had met her in the wilderness before and she had called Him, "Thou God seest me" (Gen. 16:13), and He will provide water in the wilderness and other things for this poor, rebellious, hard-treated servant woman and her son.

Abraham loved the boy Ishmael, of course. He grieved to part with the young fellow. Ah, but God would make the whole Arab race descendants of Ishmael and that is indeed a great nation. But the nation Israel, the Bible, the Messiah, would come through Isaac's seed. So God comforts Abraham again with the promise of verse 13:

"And also of the son of the bondwoman will I make a nation, because he is thy seed."

VERSES 14-21:

14 And Abraham rose up early in the morning, and took bread, and a bottle of water, and gave *it* unto Hagar, putting *it* on her shoulder, and the child, and sent her away: and she departed, and wandered in the wilderness of Beer–sheba.

15 And the water was spent in the bottle, and she cast the child under one of the shrubs.

16 And she went, and sat her down over against *him* a good way off, as it were a bowshot: for she said, Let me not see the death of the child. And she sat over against *him*, and lift up her voice, and wept.

17 And God heard the voice of the lad; and the angel of God called to Hagar out of heaven, and said unto her, What aileth thee, Hagar? fear not; for God hath heard the voice of the lad where he *is*.

18 Arise, lift up the lad, and hold him in thine hand; for I will make him a great nation.

19 And God opened her eyes, and she saw a well of water; and she went, and filled the bottle with water, and gave the lad drink.

20 And God was with the lad; and he grew, and dwelt in the wilderness, and became an archer.

21 And he dwelt in the wilderness of Paran: and his mother took him a wife out of the land of Egypt.

Ishmael and Hagar Preserved in Wilderness

As would be expected, the bottle of water, probably made of a goatskin, was after awhile gone and Hagar thought the boy would die. Probably being very active and young, he needed the water more than his mother and soon he appeared to be near death. But God keeps His promises to Abraham and to Hagar. And God cares for people in trouble. He who notes the fall of every sparrow, He who counts all the hairs of every person's head, He who paints the wild flowers and perfumes each one, oh, He knows how to care for the poor and needy. And in this case verse 13 indicates that he is cared for as God told Abraham, ". . .because he is thy seed." God, who brought Lot out of Sodom because He remembered Abraham, cares for Ishmael because of Abraham.

"And God heard the voice of the lad." Angels, unseen,

were around those two desolate ones in the wilderness! And the angel spoke to Hagar and showed her a well of water.

We remember it is said about the children of Israel, "Yea, they spake against God; they said, Can God furnish a table in the wilderness?" (Ps. 78:19). The God who brought a river of water from the rock smitten by Moses to care for some three million people and their livestock, the God who brought the manna from Heaven every day for forty years to feed this multitude—that God can furnish a table in the wilderness for Hagar and Ishmael!

Psalm 65:2 says, "O thou that hearest prayer, unto thee shall all flesh come." Oh, yes, the good and the bad, all flesh can call on God. When God has a king make a wedding feast for his son, he sends his servants to gather all, "both bad and good," and the wedding was furnished with guests (Matt. 22:10). Again, Psalm 72:12,13 says, "For he shall deliver the needy when he crieth, the poor also, and him that hath no helper. He shall spare the poor and needy, and shall save the souls of the needy."

Ishmael cannot be the chosen seed of the promise, but he can be blessed and protected of God.

Ishmael grew up in the plain of Paran. *Oxford Bible Atlas* says it was "south of Canaan, north of Sinai." He was an archer. His mother brought him a wife out of Egypt, which was not far away. So Ishmael and his Arab descendants turned out to be largely desert people, even as they are today.

Ishmael, cast out of the household of Abraham, is symbolic of all those who were from Abraham after the flesh, but not believing as Abraham did and not the spiritual seed of Abraham and so cast out as far as Christ and Heaven are concerned.

Romans 11:7 says, "What then? Israel hath not obtained that which he seeketh for; but the election hath obtained it, and the rest were blinded." An Israelite is not a true son of Abraham until he is born again and thus spiritually follows the faith of Abraham.

———————

22 ¶ And it came to pass at that time, that Ă-bĭm-´ĕ-lĕch and Phī-´chŏl the chief captain of his host spake unto Abraham, saying, God *is* with thee in all that thou doest:

23 Now therefore swear unto me here by God that thou wilt not deal falsely with me, nor with my son, nor with my son's son: *but* according to the kindness that I have done unto thee, thou shalt do unto me, and to the land wherein thou hast sojourned.

24 And Abraham said, I will swear.

25 And Abraham reproved Ă-bĭm-´ĕ-lĕch because of a well of water, which Ă-bĭm-´ĕ-lĕch's servants had violently taken away.

26 And Ă-bĭm-´ĕ-lĕch said, I wot not who hath done this thing: neither didst thou tell me, neither yet heard I *of it*, but to day.

27 And Abraham took sheep and oxen, and gave them unto Ă-bĭm-´ĕ-lĕch; and both of them made a covenant.

28 And Abraham set seven ewe lambs of the flock by themselves.

29 And Ă-bĭm-´ĕ-lĕch said unto Abraham, What *mean* these seven ewe lambs which thou hast set by themselves?

30 And he said, For *these* seven ewe lambs shalt thou take of my hand, that they may be a witness unto me, that I have digged this well.

31 Wherefore he called that place Beer–sheba; because there they sware both of them.

32 Thus they made a covenant at Beer–sheba: then Ă-bĭm-´ĕ-lĕch rose up, and Phī-´chŏl the chief captain of his host, and they returned into the land of the Philistines.

33 ¶ And *Abraham* planted a grove in Beer–sheba, and called there on the name of the LORD, the everlasting God.

34 And Abraham sojourned in the Philistines' land many days.

Abraham Makes Covenant With King Abimelech

A few years before this, when Isaac had been promised but not yet born, Abraham had been in Gerar, the country of King Abimelech (chap. 20). There Abimelech had said to Abraham, "Behold, my land is before thee: dwell where it pleaseth thee." Abraham then stayed nearby at Beer-sheba and there we understand Isaac was born. There the bondwoman Hagar and Ishmael were sent out into the desert.

Now Abimelech and his chief captain, and prime minister, Phichol, came to Abraham wanting a covenant. They said, "God is with thee in all that thou doest." It was later so with Joseph in Egypt, "And the Lord was with Joseph, and he was a prosperous man; and he was in the house of his master the Egyptian" (Gen. 39:2), and again: "But the Lord was with Joseph, and shewed him mercy, and gave him favour in the sight of the keeper of the prison. And the keeper of the prison committed to Joseph's hand all the prisoners that were in the prison; and whatsoever they did there, he was the doer of it. The keeper of the prison looked not to any thing that was under his hand; because the Lord was with him, and that which he did, the Lord made it to prosper" (Gen. 39:21-23).

When Samuel anointed David to be a future king of Israel, we read, ". . .and the Spirit of the Lord came upon David from that day forward" (I Sam. 16:13).

Abraham did not have a Bible, except as the Word of God came to him personally from the Lord. But he evidently met the conditions of Psalm 1:1-3 in the promise, ". . .whatsoever he doeth shall prosper." So was the promise to Joshua:

"Only be thou strong and very courageous, that thou mayest observe to do according to all the law, which Moses my servant commanded thee: turn not from it to the right hand or to the left, that thou mayest prosper whithersoever thou goest. This book of the law shall not depart out of thy mouth; but thou shalt meditate therein day and night, that thou mayest observe to do according to all that is written therein: for then thou shalt make thy way prosperous, and then thou shalt have good success. Have not I commanded thee? Be strong and of a good courage; be not afraid, neither be thou dismayed: for the Lord thy God is with thee whithersoever thou goest."—Josh. 1:7-9.

Abimelech greatly respected Abraham because he was a prophet of God, and Abraham had prayed for his family that the curse might be removed when Abimelech had been misinformed and had taken Abraham's wife. He had given great gifts to Abraham and invited him to dwell in the land. But along with this respect there was also some fear. This man Abraham was mighty and influential, and God was with him.

With a man so certain of God's blessing, a man of such strength, Abimelech felt he must make some covenant. We are reminded in Scripture about King Saul, "And Saul was afraid of David, because the Lord was with him, and was departed from Saul" (I Sam. 18:12). Abraham would be a good friend but a dangerous enemy. Had he not, with 318 servants and some neighbors to help, defeated the four great kings and slaughtered them after their enormous raids through Moab and Petra and the vale of Siddim? So Abimelech and the chief of his armies asked Abraham for a covenant of peace.

There is no doubt that King Abimelech takes very seriously Abraham's God. He sees God is with Abraham; he wants Abraham to swear by God. He does not speak of Abraham's God as one of many gods, but rather as the Lord God.

He reminds Abraham ". . .according to the kindness that I have done unto thee." He had restored Abraham's wife when he came to know she was his wife. He had given Abraham "sheep, and oxen, and menservants, and womenservants" and "a thousand pieces of silver" (Gen. 20:14,16).

Abraham set aside seven ewe lambs which he gave to Abimelech to be a constant reminder that the well which Abimelech's servants had seized was really Abraham's. Abraham was a man of peace. He sought no controversy with Abimelech. He most generously made sure that Abimelech and his workers had a reminder that the well was Abraham's. How careful Christians ought to be to avoid controversies!

Jesus commanded, "Agree with thine adversary quickly" (Matt. 5:25), as the 34th Psalm says one should "seek peace, and pursue it."

The name was called Beer-sheba. There is a well there now which is called Abraham's well, though there is no evidence to prove it is the one he dug.

Again, Abraham "sojourned" in the land of the Philistines. He claimed a well which he had dug, but not the land. All his days Abraham, Isaac, and Jacob will dwell in tents as pilgrims, due to receive a great inheritance but not yet owning it.

"The land of the Philistines." Abimelech went back to the land of the Philistines. But in the 20th chapter Gerar is mentioned as a separate city-state and nothing is said about it being the land of the Philistines. It is possible the Philistines came from Philistim, son of Mizraim, thought to be Menes, the first recorded king of Egypt, son of Ham. Tradition, language, religion, and customs, as indicated by archaeological study, indicates that the Philistines may have been from Phoenicia or the Aegean Islands or the Island of Crete particularly. But they had made efforts to settle in Egypt and perhaps did for a time. It is thought now, at the time of Abraham, they may have been settling in the Gaza Strip and otherwise along the southern part of the East Mediterranean Coast and south. Gerar may have been an independent city-state, not Philistines, but the land might now have begun to be known as the land of the Philistines. Or it may be that by the time of Moses, who was inspired to write this down, it had begun to be called the land of the Philistines. These Philistines would be of great importance as the enemies of Israel for many years in the days of the judges, King Saul, David, and others. Here we read that Abraham dwelt in this land for some time.

He has had three particular centers for his camps in the land of Canaan: near Bethel, ten or twelve miles north of Jerusalem; at the plain of Mamre down at Hebron, some more than twenty miles south of Jerusalem; and now at Beer-sheba, which is down in the Negev toward the Sinai Peninsula.

Now Abraham set this up as a regular place of sacrifice and worship and "called there on the name of the Lord, the everlasting God."

GENESIS 22

AND it came to pass after these things, that God did tempt Abraham, and said unto him, Abraham: and he said, Behold, *here* I *am*.

Abraham's Faith Must Be Tested

We are told that God tempted Abraham. Tempt means to try or to prove. God's dealing with Abraham these long years has been preparing him. God is planning a nation, a race of Israelites, to be set apart, so stubbornly and eternally separate from the rest of the world that it will never get away from God's dealing with Abraham and his seed. Jews will backslide, will lose their spiritual significance of circumcision but not the circumcision. They may lose some of the spiritual riches of the ceremonies but not the format nor the offerings, the events, the days. They will never lose Abraham, Isaac, and Jacob. They will be driven out of Palestine for their sins, but will never lose the promises, the history, the yearning of the homeland.

So God continued His training, His maturing of Abraham by this trial of his faith.

Let us remember it takes a lot of Christian trials, proving, chastening, a lot of leaving things dear, of praying long and getting answers, to make a good Christian. We have said that one may trust Christ and in a moment become a Christian, but it takes long rearing to make a lady or a gentleman.

So being saved is a miraculous transformation in the heart that God does for one when he, repenting, turns in faith to Christ. But it takes a lot of growing in grace to grow within a carnal Christian a babe in Christ. So God proved Abraham with this test.

———

VERSES 2-5:

2 And he said, Take now thy son, thine only *son* Isaac, whom thou lovest, and get thee into the land of Mō-rī́-ăh; and offer him there for a burnt offering upon one of the mountains which I will tell thee of.

3 ¶ And Abraham rose up early in the morning, and saddled his ass, and took two of his young men with him, and Isaac his son, and clave the wood for the burnt offering, and rose up, and went unto the place of which God had told him.

4 Then on the third day Abraham lifted up his eyes, and saw the place afar off.

5 And Abraham said unto his young men, Abide ye here with the ass; and I and the lad will go yonder and worship, and come again to you.

Isaac on Way to Calvary

We have said that Isaac prefigured Christ in some ways. Now he is to be offered in "the land of Moriah." But II Chronicles 3:1 says, "Then Solomon began to build the house of the Lord at Jerusalem in mount Moriah, where the Lord appeared unto David his father, in the place that David had prepared in the threshingfloor of Ornan the Jebusite." The mount is identified. It is that ridge that goes through Jerusalem. On one end was built Solomon's Temple, in the southeast corner of Jerusalem. On the other end a great gash was cut through the ridge long before Christ, to make a moat outside the city wall. Then looking down on the city is the cut face of this part of Mount Moriah like the face of a skull—Calvary, where the Lord Jesus was crucified outside the gate (Heb. 13:12) and "nigh to the city" (John 19:20).

God had Calvary in mind centuries ahead. If the proposed interrupted sacrifice of Isaac was a picture of the death of Christ, let it be on the same hill! So God instructed David to buy the threshingfloor belonging to the Jebusite in Jerusalem later (II Sam. 24:18-24). God is heading toward Calvary and pictures it so.

That may be why also they went "three days' journey"—from Beer-sheba to Jerusalem. But the three days' journey may also picture the three days that a passover lamb was kept up before the sacrifice (Exod. 12:3,6). The lamb was kept up for three days to prove it was in perfect health and suitable, we suppose, and so Isaac makes a three days' journey to his place of sacrifice.

Thus Abraham had three tragic days to consider: will he
back down? The awful suspense gave Abraham time to
figure: If I kill Isaac, God must then raise him from the
dead (Heb. 11:19).

God said, "Thine only son Isaac." That is, the only one
through whom the promise can be fulfilled. He is the son of
promise. Ishmael, whom Sarah schemed to be a substitute,
is not counted here, and Abraham understood. Isaac was
the only one in the plans for the nation Israel through
whom will come the Scriptures and the Saviour.

". . .whom thou lovest." Oh, Abraham loved Isaac. If
you do not offer to God the very person and the things you
love best, your love is not enough. Three days they
journeyed and two nights they camped en route. Let's
imagine Isaac, the healthy boy, still asleep and the servants
who were along. But Abraham, on his goatskin pallet, may
have reached out and let a handful of sand run through his
fingers: ". . .seed as the dust of the earth!" He thought,
What about this promise if Isaac is dead?

Another night, we suppose, the uncounted stars looked
down on Abraham's sleepless eyes and he may have
thought, How, then, will the heavenly seed be as the stars
innumerable if Isaac dies?

But faith, leaping up, had the answer, "Then God must
raise him from the dead!" And so Abraham believed (Heb.
11:19)

Abraham "clave the wood for the burnt-offering" (vs. 3).

How strange! Why pack the wood on a donkey or two to
carry three long days? There will be wood enough there at
Mount Moriah. But that wood pictures the "dead works"
which will come into judgment, the "wood, hay, stubble" of
I Corinthians 3:12, the unworthy building material that
will be burned up at the judgment of Christians. Oh, Christ
is to be crucified and offered for our sins. The wood must
picture all the wicked sins that make the fire of God's
judgment.

But why cut the wood and start with it so far away from

the sacrifice and from Mount Moriah? Well, the Lord Jesus is "the Lamb slain from the foundation of the world" (Rev. 13:8). Our sins have broken God's heart all the centuries before Calvary. And Christ was in His grieving, suffering heart bearing our sins all the years. So we will see that wood long prepared, strapped on Isaac's back a little later as he goes up the mountain to the altar.

VERSES 6-9:

6 And Abraham took the wood of the burnt offering, and laid *it* upon Isaac his son; and he took the fire in his hand, and a knife; and they went both of them together.

7 And Isaac spake unto Abraham his father, and said, My father: and he said, Here *am* I, my son. And he said, Behold the fire and the wood: but where *is* the lamb for a burnt offering?

8 And Abraham said, My son, God will provide himself a lamb for a burnt offering: so they went both of them together.

9 And they came to the place which God had told him of; and Abraham built an altar there, and laid the wood in order, and bound Isaac his son, and laid him on the altar upon the wood.

Isaac on Altar

Dr. Scofield says,

> The typical lessons here are: (1) Isaac, type of Christ "obedient unto death" (Phil. 2. 5-8); (2) Abraham, type of the Father, who "spared not His own son, but delivered Him up for us all" (John 3.16; Rom. 8. 32); (3) the ram, type of substitution—Christ offered as a burnt-offering in our stead (Heb. 10. 5-10); (4) cf. resurrection (Heb. 11. 17-19). See also Jas. 2. 21-23.

Isaac did not struggle. He did not rebel. Just so the Lord Jesus faced His suffering eagerly: "But I have a baptism to be baptized with; and how am I straightened till it be accomplished!" He said (Luke 12:50). We are told that He went like a lamb to the slaughter and like a sheep before her shearers is dumb so opened He not His mouth (Isa. 53:7).

Some expositors have understood that in Gethsemane when Jesus prayed, "O my Father, if it be possible, let this cup pass from me" (Matt. 26:39), that He was shrinking from the cross and urged to be excused from it. Oh, no! The Lord Jesus knew, had known before the world began, that He would die. Why, I can read the Old Testament and know there was no way for sin ever to be paid for without the death of the Saviour. He knew that, too, so well.

No, He prayed that He would not die in the garden that night when He said, "My soul is exceeding sorrowful, even unto death" (Matt. 26:38). He prayed *in the will of God*, not against the will of God, that He might die tomorrow at the time appointed when passover lambs are slain, on the cross when the curse of hanging on a tree would be His. He must die between two thieves. He must be mocked on the cross and God must turn His face away (Ps. 22). Oh, Jesus knew He must die: ". . .according to the scriptures" (I Cor. 15:3,4), if there was ever to be a saving Gospel.

So Jesus prayed and was delivered: "Who in the days of his flesh, when he had offered up prayers and supplications with strong crying and tears unto him that was able to save him from death, and was heard in that he feared" (Heb. 5:7).

Jesus settled the matter of the crucifixion and all its shame before the world began! He would not pray against it but prayed for it!

How Pilate and Herod were astonished that Jesus made no answer to the charges, no plea for delivery from crucifixion (Matt. 27:14; Luke 23:9; Mark 15:4,5). So we think Isaac made no resistance. He was laid tenderly on the wood and bound.

What was Sarah's opinion of this? Most likely she was not consulted. It must have been part of Abraham's burden that he must face Sarah if Isaac should die!

Isaac was accustomed to seeing sacrifices. Here was wood and here was fire, probably kept burning in a copper pot. "But where is the lamb for a burnt-offering?" he asks.

With trembling lips, perhaps with a tear and some agitation, Abraham answered, "My son, God will provide himself a lamb for a burnt-offering." Oh, surely, Abraham meant the Lamb of God who would come. "Your father Abraham rejoiced to see my day: and he saw it, and was glad," Jesus said (John 8:56). It may be that here Abraham saw it better than ever before! Then these animal sacrifices could never pay for man's sin. Every sacrifice offered just reminds us that sin had not yet been paid for; it will take another sacrifice. God's Lamb will pay the debt forever by one offering (Heb. 10:14).

VERSES 10-14

10 And Abraham stretched forth his hand, and took the knife to slay his son.

11 And the angel of the LORD called unto him out of heaven, and said, Abraham, Abraham: and he said, Here *am* I.

12 And he said, Lay not thine hand upon the lad, neither do thou any thing unto him: for now I know that thou fearest God, seeing thou hast not withheld thy son, thine only *son* from me.

13 And Abraham lifted up his eyes, and looked, and behold behind *him* a ram caught in a thicket by his horns: and Abraham went and took the ram, and offered him up for a burnt offering in the stead of his son.

14 And Abraham called the name of that place Jĕ-hŏ-́văh-jī-́rĕh: as it is said *to* this day, In the mount of the LORD it shall be seen.

Isaac Spared—a Substitute Provided

Stop, Abraham! The angel of God held back the gleaming knife that would have been struck to the heart of Isaac on the altar. But God might say, "Abraham, when your heart gave Isaac, that was all I wanted. Now the test is over." Abraham was willing to give his dearest and best and let God work out whatever it took to fulfill the promises. Now God is satisfied and Abraham has proved his faithfulness and his love.

Many young people surrender to go to Africa as a missionary, but not half of them go. And it was not meant for many of them to go. God did not want all of them in Africa, but He wanted all to be willing to go, willing to give up plans of money, of comfort, of career, to live in a mud hut perhaps, and never to see some of their loved ones again. So the heart of Abraham giving his son satisfied God.

We had a gifted, cultured daughter, a college graduate, who planned to go to Tibet as a missionary with her young husband. She was accepted by the China Inland Mission. I at first said, "Lord, I will grieve and will weep, but I will be reconciled to it." Then when shame flooded my heart I said with tears, "Lord, I will not just be reconciled; I will praise You and rejoice. And I will pay the whole expense and the salary. Lord, all six of mine may go to Tibet or Africa or anywhere You wish. All are Yours if I never see them again."

As the young couple prepared, the communists overran Tibet where there are more graves of missionaries than there are of converts! And the field was closed. The son-in-law went into the pastorate, but many times since I have joyfully reminded the Lord, "I gave them to Thee! Lord; they are Thine."

Substitute Was at Hand

God had a substitute ready for the burnt-offering. A ram was caught by his horns in the bushes. Isaac's bonds were cut and the ram was slain and put on the prepared wood on the altar.

Now we have the same picture again. It is a substitution. First, Isaac pictured Christ bearing our sins and dying in our stead. Now Isaac pictures all of us poor sinners and the ram prefigures Jesus, our Substitute. How eternally faithful is God! The substitute was provided there in plain sight; so Abraham called the place Jehovah-jireh, "the Lord will provide."

VERSES 15-19:

15 ¶ And the angel of the LORD called unto Abraham out of heaven the second time,

16 And said, By myself have I sworn, saith the LORD, for because thou hast done this thing, and hast not withheld thy son, thine only *son*:

17 That in blessing I will bless thee,

and in multiplying I will multiply thy seed as the stars of the heaven, and as the sand which *is* upon the sea shore; and thy seed shall possess the gate of his enemies;

18 And in thy seed shall all the na-tions of the earth be blessed; because thou hast obeyed my voice.

19 So Abraham returned unto his young men, and they rose up and went together to Beer-sheba; and Abraham dwelt at Beer-sheba.

The Covenant With Abraham Repeated

Before the covenant, God said one time, "I will make thy seed as the dust of the earth" (Gen. 13:16). Another time Abraham was commanded, "Tell the stars, if thou be able to number them: and he said unto him, So shall thy seed be" (Gen. 15:5). But this time God repeats both illustrations, picturing, we think, the earthly seed and the heavenly seed, the literal Israel and the spiritual Israel. He said, "I will multiply thy seed as the stars of the heaven, and as the sand which is upon the sea shore." God added to the blessing, "And in thy seed shall all the nations of the earth be blessed," this additional blessing, "...and thy seed shall possess the gate of his enemies."

That surely is a promise of the triumph of Jesus Christ to reign forever: "And he shall reign over the house of Jacob for ever; and of his kingdom there shall be no end" (Luke 1:33). "Of the increase of his government and peace there shall be no end, upon the throne of David, and upon his kingdom, to order it, and to establish it with judgment and with justice from henceforth even for ever" (Isa. 9:7).

Isaiah 53 tells of the sufferings of the Saviour in the first ten verses. Ah, but verses 11 and 12 tell of the wonderful triumph of the Saviour:

"He shall see of the travail of his soul, and shall be satisfied: by his knowledge shall my righteous servant justify many; for he shall bear their iniquities. Therefore will I divide him a portion with the great, and he shall divide the spoil with the strong; because he hath poured out his soul unto death: and he was numbered with the transgressors; and he bare the sin of many, and made intercession for the transgressors."

The inspired Psalmist in Psalm 22 pictured the broken

heart of the Lord Jesus on the cross. He is to be despised and mocked by the people. They were to challenge Him to come down from the cross. His bones were out of joint. They will have pierced His hands and His feet.

Oh, but the Psalmist cannot stop there; he breaks into wonderful prophecy of all the blessings when "the kingdom is the Lord's: and he is the governor among the nations" (vs. 28).

Now a little party goes gladly, joyfully home! Isaac is as one raised from the dead, reprieved from death because of a substitute.

VERSES 20-24:

20 ¶ And it came to pass after these things, that it was told Abraham, saying, Behold, Milcah, she hath also born children unto thy brother Nā-hôr;

21 Huz his firstborn, and Buz his brother, and Kĕ-mū-ĕl the father of Aram,

22 And Chĕs-ĕd, and Hazo, and Pildash, and Jidlaph, and Bĕ-thū-ĕl.

23 And Bĕ-thū-ĕl begat Rebekah: these eight Milcah did bear to Nā-hôr, Abraham's brother.

24 And his concubine, whose name was Rēu-mäh, she bare also Tebah, and Gaham, and Thā-hăsh, and Mā-ă-chäh.

Abraham's Kindred

Since Rebekah is soon to marry Isaac and be an ancestress of the nation and of the Saviour, her genealogy is briefly given here.

GENESIS 23

VERSES 1,2:

AND Sarah was an hundred and seven and twenty years old: *these were* the years of the life of Sarah.

2 And Sarah died in Kĭr-jăth-är-bǎ; the same *is* Hebron in the land of Cā-nă-ăn: and Abraham came to mourn for Sarah, and to weep for her.

Death of Sarah

She was first named Sarai, then her name was changed in Genesis 17:15. Sarai, according to *Young's Analytical Concordance*, means "Jah is prince." Some have thought it means "contentious." But her name was changed to Sarah, princess.

Sarah died at 127 years of age. That was thirty-seven years after the birth of Isaac. Before then, Sarah had already said, "I am waxed old" (Gen. 18:12). But Sarah, who seems to have been made young again thirty-seven years ago, now has grown old and she dies.

When Abraham "came to mourn for Sarah, and to weep for her," he may have sat in the tent by the body for some time and then he "stood up from before his dead. . . ."

The tie between Abraham and Sarah was very sweet and strong. It was probably all the stronger because for many, many years they prayed together for the child not yet given. Often when a woman has a number of children, she becomes so occupied with them that though she may love her husband, yet he is not the principal object of her attention and ministrations. But with Sarah, Abraham was first.

"Sara obeyed Abraham, calling him lord," (I Pet. 3:6), and "my lord being old also" (Gen. 18:12). It may be that Sarah was slower to trust the Lord than was Abraham. That is not surprising. God would intend that the head of the home should be the first in trusting and serving God. But her unselfishness, her anxiety that Abraham should have the son he wanted, made her willing even to give the servant girl Hagar to Abraham's bosom that he might have that son.

The grief of Abraham is very genuine, not just a formal, an official mourning. Abraham came there to weep over the form of his beloved wife.

Oh, some women may foolishly long for careers before the public and in competition with men, but Proverbs 31:10-12 says, "Who can find a virtuous woman? for her price is far above rubies. The heart of her husband doth safely trust in her, so that he shall have no need of spoil. She will do him good and not evil all the days of her life."

Oh, Sarah was such a wife. The heart of her husband safely trusted in her and she did him good and not evil all the days of her life. There can be no greater career, we think, for a woman than to be a wife of a good man, to help him, to make him happy, to be true to him, and be wrapped up in husband and children. Then "her children arise up, and call her blessed; her husband also, and he praiseth her" (Prov. 31:28).

A wonderful thing said about Sarah was that she "received strength to conceive seed, and was delivered of a child when she was past age, because she judged him faithful who had promised" (Heb. 11:12). But her serving God was principally as she served her husband and with her husband.

Isaac now was thirty-seven years old. It was three more years before he took Rebekah as his wife, but they must have been lonely years because Isaac had been very close to his mother. And when God sent him Rebekah, we read, "And Isaac brought her into his mother Sarah's tent, and took Rebekah, and she became his wife; and he loved her: and Isaac was comforted after his mother's death" (Gen. 24:67). Abraham and Isaac had preserved the tent, Sarah's tent, and no doubt the little intimate things that a woman would collect around her. Now the lonely heart of Isaac is comforted when Rebekah comes to his arms and home and fills the empty place left by his greatly loved mother, Sarah.

VERSES 3-15:

3 ¶ And Abraham stood up from before his dead, and spake unto the sons of Heth, saying,

4 I *am* a stranger and a sojourner with you: give me a possession of a buryingplace with you, that I may bury my dead out of my sight.

5 And the children of Heth answered Abraham, saying unto him,

6 Hear us, my lord: thou *art* a mighty prince among us: in the choice of our sepulchres bury thy dead; none of us shall withhold from thee his sepulchre, but that thou mayest bury thy dead.

7 And Abraham stood up, and bowed himself to the people of the land, *even* to the children of Heth.

8 And he communed with them, saying, If it be your mind that I should bury my dead out of my sight; hear me, and intreat for me to Ephron the son of Zohar,

9 That he may give me the cave of Măch-pē′-läh, which he hath, which *is* in the end of his field; for as much money as it is worth he shall give it me for a possession of a buryingplace amongst you.

10 And Ephron dwelt among the children of Heth: and Ephron the Hittite answered Abraham in the audience of the children of Heth, *even* of all that went in at the gate of his city, saying,

11 Nay, my lord, hear me: the field give I thee, and the cave that *is* therein, I give it thee; in the presence of the sons of my people give I it thee: bury thy dead.

12 And Abraham bowed down himself before the people of the land.

13 And he spake unto Ephron in the audience of the people of the land, saying, But if thou *wilt give it*, I pray thee, hear me: I will give thee money for the field; take *it* of me, and I will bury my dead there.

14 And Ephron answered Abraham, saying unto him,

15 My lord, hearken unto me: the land *is worth* four hundred shē′-kĕls of silver; what *is* that betwixt me and thee? bury therefore thy dead.

Godly Abraham Seeks Burying Place of His Friends

Abraham owned no property, and to bury Sarah he must first purchase a burying place. He reminds these heathen friends, "I am a stranger and a sojourner with you." He was a foreigner. He was only a temporary dweller in this land which God had promised his seed forever. He did not own a foot of ground that he might claim as his own.

He was thus somewhat a type of all Christians. Our citizenship is in Heaven, not in this world. It is said about Abraham, "By faith he sojourned in the land of promise, as in a strange country, dwelling in tabernacles with Isaac and Jacob, the heirs with him of the same promise: For he looked for a city which hath foundations, whose builder and maker is God" (Heb. 11:9,10).

Abraham's mind was set on Heaven. I'm sure the city he looked for that has foundations was that heavenly city that will come down from God out of Heaven to be "the new Jerusalem" in that land which God has promised to Abraham and his seed (Rev. 21:1-10).

Oh, Abraham never forgot that he was only a temporary dweller, a sojourner, a stranger and foreigner in this earth, and that he is a pattern for Christians as he was in the matter of salvation by faith. So the Christian can sing:

> I am a stranger here,
> Within a foreign land;
> My home is far away,
> Upon a golden strand.

Yes, and in the words of another song, we can say,

> I'm a pilgrim, and I'm a stranger,
> I can tarry, I can tarry but a night!

And we can say,

> Of that city, to which I journey;
> My Redeemer, my Redeemer is the light.

And again some sing gladly,

> This world is not my home,
> I'm just a passing thru.

Oh, then, may our minds be set on heavenly things, and let us make sure we are not hindered by the cares of this world, and the deceitfulness of riches, and the lusts of other things entering in, and so choking the Word of God in our lives.

Note the respect that these heathen neighbors had for Abraham: "Thou art a mighty prince among us: in the choice of our sepulchres bury thy dead; none of us shall withhold from thee his sepulchre." King Abimelech and Phichol the chief captain had said to Abraham, "God is with thee in all that thou doest" (Gen. 21:22). They knew he was successful, brave, and good and they were confident that his success would continue.

Abraham was freely offered a burying place but he would not take it without paying for it. He was an honest, good man. He believed that God's people should pay their way, that one should earn what he gets.

That principle is taught in II Thessalonians, chapter 3. Paul reminds them how earnestly he worked among them.

"For yourselves know how ye ought to follow us: for we behaved not ourselves disorderly among you; Neither did we eat any man's bread for nought; but wrought with labour and travail night and day, that we might not be chargeable to any of you."—Vss. 7,8.

Then he commanded ". . .that if any would not work, neither should he eat."

Busybodies, Christians who did not do their part, should not eat with the rest at the expense of the church. And a widow was not to be taken into the support of the church unless she was sixty years old, "having been the wife of one man, well reported of for good works, if she have brought up children, if she have lodged strangers, if she have washed the saints' feet, if she have relieved the afflicted, if she have diligently followed every good work" (I Tim. 5:9,10). Christians ought to pay their way.

It is sometimes said and usually it is untrue, that some ministers preach for money. It is true that sometimes unconverted modernists and liberals want the prestige, salary, and security that comes from claiming to be ministers of Christ when they are really false prophets. Second Peter 2:1-3 tells about these false prophets, false teachers "who privily shall bring in damnable heresies, even denying the Lord that bought them. . . . And through covetousness shall they with feigned words make merchandise of you. . . ." But let every true minister of God make sure that he obeys the command, meets the condition, "not greedy of filthy lucre" (I Tim. 3:3).

Christians are to "provide things honest in the sight of all men" (Rom. 12:17). If a Christian be persecuted for righteousness' sake, well and good, but no Christian ought to suffer as an evil doer. No Christian ought to so live, no

Christian ought to be so careless in his personal life, in the rearing of his family, in the payment of honest debts, in doing honest work, that he will bring disgrace on the cause of Christ.

The people knew Abraham, evidently as God did, "For I know him, that he will command his children and his household after him, and they shall keep the way of the Lord, to do justice and judgment. . ." (Gen. 18:19). The whole household of Abraham was honest and greatly respected, and even heathen men could see that Abraham was different from others. They respected him.

It may be that you cannot have the love or even the understanding of the lost world about you, but you can compel respect by the way you live. Certainly Abraham had done so.

Abraham will pay for the Cave of Machpelah where he wants to bury Sarah. Not every Christian will have the wealth of Abraham, but every Christian can claim the blessing and profusion of God. And he ought to be able to say with Paul, "But my God shall supply all your need according to his riches in glory by Christ Jesus" (Phil. 4:19).

VERSES 16-20:

16 And Abraham hearkened unto Ephron; and Abraham weighed to Ephron the silver, which he had named in the audience of the sons of Heth, four hundred shĕ́-kĕls of silver, current *money* with the merchant.

17 ¶ And the field of Ephron, which *was* in Măch-pḗ-läh, which *was* before Mamre, the field, and the cave which *was* therein, and all the trees that *were* in the field, that *were* in all the borders round about, were made sure

18 Unto Abraham for a possession in the presence of the children of Heth, before all that went in at the gate of his city.

19 And after this, Abraham buried Sarah his wife in the cave of the field of Măch-pḗ-läh before Mamre: the same *is* Hebron in the land of Cắ-nă-ăn.

20 And the field, and the cave that *is* therein, were made sure unto Abraham for a possession of a buryingplace by the sons of Heth.

Abraham Buys Cave of Machpelah

Abraham paid four hundred shekels of silver. It was weighed. It may have been in pieces but probably not in uniformly minted coins. Four hundred shekels of silver would mean that Abraham paid perhaps $275.00 or $280.00, since a shekel is worth sixty-five cents according to Scofield's notes. But that included the cave, the field, the trees.

It was all done officially, before witnesses, and all those who were present would know in the future that the cave belonged to Abraham and his seed.

The Cave of Machpelah, where Sarah was buried, is at Hebron. There later Abraham will be buried, then Isaac and Rebekah, Jacob and Leah (Gen. 49:29-32). Over it now is a great Moslem mosque. During the time of the Crusades, we think Crusaders turned it for a time into a church. The burial place is in the cave where people are not allowed to go, but cenotaphs above give honor to those buried below.

We think it much more suitable for a Christian's body to be buried with proper honors instead of cremation. It is true that at the resurrection God can regather the materials and make new and change that body into a resurrection body, but cremation does little to show respect for that body which was the temple of the Holy Spirit and which will rise again at the call of Christ and the trumpet sound.

GENESIS 24

AND Abraham was old, *and* well stricken in age: and the LORD had blessed Abraham in all things.

2 And Abraham said unto his eldest servant of his house, that ruled over all that he had, Put, I pray thee, thy hand under my thigh:

3 And I will make thee swear by the LORD, the God of heaven, and the God of the earth, that thou shalt not take a wife unto my son of the daughters of the Că-nă-ăn-ītes, among whom I dwell:

4 But thou shalt go unto my country, and to my kindred, and take a wife unto my son Isaac.

5 And the servant said unto him, Peradventure the woman will not be willing to follow me unto this land: must I needs bring thy son again unto the land from whence thou camest?

6 And Abraham said unto him, Beware thou that thou bring not my son thither again.

7 ¶ The LORD God of heaven, which took me from my father's house, and from the land of my kindred, and which spake unto me, and that sware unto me, saying, Unto thy seed will I give this land; he shall send his angel before thee, and thou shalt take a wife unto my son from thence.

8 And if the woman will not be willing to follow thee, then thou shalt be clear from this my oath: only bring not my son thither again.

9 And the servant put his hand under the thigh of Abraham his master, and sware to him concerning that matter.

Eliezer Sworn to Get Proper Bride for Isaac

Abraham called "his eldest servant of his house, that ruled over all that he had." This surely was Eliezer, mentioned in Genesis 15:2. He was from Damascus and was intended to be the heir of Abraham if God gave no children. He managed all of Abraham's business, and was a greatly loved and trusted servant.

His "eldest *servant*"—the Hebrew word is *ebed* which means "servant, doer, tiller, slave" (*Young's Concordance*). It is the same word for the slave "bought with money" in Exodus 12:44; Exodus 21:2,5,26; the same word used in Deuteronomy 15:17 and 23:15.

So this man was probably a slave but loved as a son and manager of all of Abraham's business. Abraham required Eliezer to swear "by the Lord, the God of heaven, and the God of the earth." Now, it is not simply Abraham's God, but the one and only true God whom certainly Eliezer would know and love. Eliezer was one of that household of whom God said in Genesis 18:19, "For I know him, that he will command his children and his household after him, and they shall keep the way of the Lord, to do justice and judgment; that the Lord may bring upon Abraham that which he hath spoken of him."

It is unthinkable that one as intimately close to Abraham for a lifetime as was this servant, would not know and love Abraham's God. We find that he was a praying man (see vss. 12-14). It seems clear that Abraham has put this in God's hands.

Isaac must not marry a woman of the Canaanites! He must not even go back to visit in that country lest he be tempted or someway tainted with the awful wickedness of the inhabitants from which God had commanded Abraham to depart and leave his kindred and his father's house. God has selected some descendants of Shem, and from a very narrow group. Abraham married his own half sister. Isaac will marry his own cousin, his mother's brother's daughter, Rebekah. Jacob will marry his cousins, Rachel and Leah. We do not suppose that these kinspeople were ardent and devoted servants of God as was Abraham, but at least they knew Abraham and knew his stand and knew what was expected if one was to marry into his family.

How carefully fathers and mothers ought to go into the matter of the company their sons and daughters keep, their dating and those with whom they may fall in love.

Isaac is forty years old (Gen. 25:20). But a wife selected for him by the Lord from the best family possible and with close ties of interest and character, is far safer than a wife selected for her beauty or by her sex attraction. Godly married love is better than youthful and perhaps temporary infatuation with an unworthy person.

Why is the servant's name never used? In this chapter alone he is called twelve times "the servant" or "Abraham's servant." He is called "the man" seven times.

But he is never called Eliezer, though we feel sure that was his name. But here, it seems likely that he is meant to typify the Holy Spirit. And as Isaac pictures an illustration of Christ, the Holy Spirit helps to get a bride for Christ as this servant got a bride for Isaac. And we may be sure that only with Holy Spirit power can we assemble that blessed group that will be the heavenly bride of Jesus. Later, we find that Isaac and Rebekah will grieve that Esau married a Hittite woman (Gen. 26:35). And then "Isaac called Jacob, and blessed him, and charged him, and said unto him, Thou shalt not take a wife of the daughters of Canaan. Arise, go to Padan-aram, to the house of Bethuel thy mother's father; and take thee a wife from thence of the daughters of Laban thy mother's brother" (Gen. 28:1,2).

Abraham made Eliezer to swear and so he did (vs. 3). A good many times in the Old Testament an oath is mentioned as permitted and favorable. And it is said that God swore by Himself and God made a covenant with an oath. (See Deut. 29:12; Ezek. 17:13-19; Exod. 22:11; I Chron. 16:16; Heb. 7:21-28.) However, so frivolous and irresponsible is the human heart that man is likely to swear so lightly or even profanely; so Jesus commanded in Matthew 5:34, "But I say unto you, Swear not at all; neither by heaven; for it is God's throne," and James 5:12 also commands, "Above all things, my brethren, swear not, neither by heaven, neither by the earth, neither by any other oath: but let your yea be yea; and your nay, nay; lest ye fall into condemnation."

In government, one is required to swear, or to solemnly promise, but he may use "I solemnly affirm" if he prefers; that is held just as binding as an oath. It is not wrong to promise solemnly and with all of our hearts. It is wrong to be frivolous about it or to be profane and use God's name in any wise.

There is the sweet promise that God "shall send his angel before thee." So Abraham is depending on God to bring success in this matter and if the servant cannot complete the assignment exactly as given, then he is to return empty-handed. Isaac must not go back to the heathen country!

VERSES 10-28:

10 ¶ And the servant took ten camels of the camels of his master, and departed; for all the goods of his master *were* in his hand: and he arose, and went to Mĕs-ŏ-pŏ-tā-́mĭ-ă, unto the city of Nā-́hôr.

11 And he made his camels to kneel down without the city by a well of water at the time of the evening, *even* the time that women go out to draw *water*.

12 And he said, O Lord God of my master Abraham, I pray thee, send me good speed this day, and shew kindness unto my master Abraham.

13 Behold, I stand *here* by the well of water; and the daughters of the men of the city come out to draw water:

14 And let it come to pass, that the damsel to whom I shall say, Let down thy pitcher, I pray thee, that I may drink; and she shall say, Drink, and I will give thy camels drink also: *let the same be* she *that* thou hast appointed for thy servant Isaac; and thereby shall I know that thou hast shewed kindness unto my master.

15 ¶ And it came to pass, before he had done speaking, that, behold, Rebekah came out, who was born to Bĕ-thū-́ĕl, son of Milcah, the wife of Nā-́hôr, Abraham's brother, with her pitcher upon her shoulder.

16 And the damsel *was* very fair to look upon, a virgin, neither had any man known her: and she went down to the well, and filled her pitcher, and came up.

17 And the servant ran to meet her, and said, Let me, I pray thee, drink a little water of thy pitcher.

18 And she said, Drink, my lord: and she hasted, and let down her pitcher upon her hand, and gave him drink.

19 And when she had done giving him drink, she said, I will draw *water* for thy camels also, until they have done drinking.

20 And she hasted, and emptied her pitcher into the trough, and ran again unto the well to draw *water*, and drew for all his camels.

21 And the man wondering at her held his peace, to wit whether the Lord had made his journey prosperous or not.

22 And it came to pass, as the camels had done drinking, that the man took a golden earring of half a shĕ-́kĕl weight, and two bracelets for her hands of ten *shĕ-́kĕls* weight of gold;

23 And said, Whose daughter *art* thou? tell me, I pray thee: is there room *in* thy father's house for us to lodge in?

24 And she said unto him, I *am* the daughter of Bĕ-thū-́ĕl the son of Milcah, which she bare unto Nā-́hôr.

25 She said moreover unto him, We have both straw and provender enough, and room to lodge in.

26 And the man bowed down his head, and worshipped the Lord.

27 And he said, Blessed *be* the Lord God of my master Abraham, who hath not left destitute my master of his mercy and his truth: I *being* in the way, the Lord led me to the house of my master's brethren.

28 And the damsel ran, and told *them of* her mother's house these things.

God Led to Right Young Woman

Here is a beautiful story of God's leading. Abraham and
Eliezer are agreed that God Himself must provide the right
young woman, and it turns out so. The servant went to the
right place, he expectantly called upon the Lord to give him
wisdom, God controlled the circumstances, and so here is a
beautiful young woman, a virgin, daughter of Bethuel, the
son of Nahor, Abraham's brother! Actually, Isaac is
Abraham's son while Rebekah is his brother's
granddaughter, although called his daughter or descendant
in verse 48.

How is Eliezer to know the right girl that God has
selected? He makes a severe test. He will ask the girl for a
drink of water and she then must voluntarily offer to draw
water for all of his ten camels. They had been on a long
journey across desert country. They would be thirsty. A
camel will drink nearly half of a barrel of water.

Rebekah offered to take her pitcher, go down the steps
into the well, fill her pitcher, bring it to pour into the
trough for the camels again and again and again, until ten
camels have drunk their fill! Old Eliezer must feel that if
she is going to be God's woman to rear a nation of godly
people, she must have a heart to bear her end of the load, to
be helpful, to be hospitable. She is that kind of a woman
and, by the leading of God, she fulfills the proposed
conditions exactly. Oh, praise the Lord! God has been with
the old servant! God has heard his prayer!

And when he learned that she was indeed a
granddaughter of Nahor, Abraham's brother, then he felt
all the more assured that God has been with him.

Notice that it is in "Mesopotamia, unto the city of
Nahor" (vs. 10). We are not told the name of that city, just
as the name of Eliezer is not mentioned here. In the parable
of the prodigal son there is a far country, but it is not
named. Neither is the prodigal boy named nor the elder
brother, nor the man who "sent him into his fields to feed
swine," for that had great universal significance to every
prodigal and every far country where a man might run

away from God and righteousness. So, here, this story takes
on some of the elements of type and parable. The blessed
Holy Spirit may lead us to every city, to knock on every
door to win souls and help get a bride for the Lord Jesus.

It is wonderfully sweet that one who walks in the way of
the Lord may find that God guides all his steps. God
arranges the incidents and the people and the weather so
things turn out just right for the person who is in His will.

We are reminded of the sweet promise, "If any of you
lack wisdom, let him ask of God, that giveth to all men
liberally, and upbraideth not; and it shall be given him"
(Jas. 1:5). If God would guide old Eliezer, He will guide any
of His children who rely upon Him and walk in His way.

It is very sweet that the servant, telling about God's
leadership, said, "I being in the way, the Lord led me to the
house of my master's brethren" (vs. 27). Oh, that we may
always be "in the way" so it is easy for God to lead us!

To add to the assurance that God is leading, he has a
most hospitable reception. In verse 25 she said, "We have
both straw and provender enough, and room to lodge in."
And then "the damsel ran, and told them of her mother's
house these things" (vs. 28).

Eliezer Gave Rebekah Earring and Bracelets

He has indicated that his master Abraham is rich. So it
is only fair and proper that he should give to the intended
bride of Isaac these jewels.

A preacher friend who uses this chapter as an
illustration of the Holy Spirit going out to get sinners saved
says we must keep in mind this one thing: He is to bring
back a bride. So here Eliezer is to bring back a bride for
Isaac. He did not come to pass out jewels; the jewels are
only part of his work in showing the bounty and the blessed
prosperity of his master and of Isaac and of winning the
admiration and the love of this girl for her unseen
bridegroom-to-be.

Some good people suppose that jewelry is forbidden for a
Christian, but I think they misunderstand I Peter 3:3-6:

"Whose adorning let it not be that outward adorning of plaiting the hair, and of wearing of gold, or of putting on of apparel; But let it be the hidden man of the heart, in that which is not corruptible, even the ornament of a meek and quiet spirit, which is in the sight of God of great price. For after this manner in the old time the holy women also, who trusted in God, adorned themselves, being in subjection unto their own husbands: Even as Sara obeyed Abraham, calling him lord: whose daughters ye are, as long as ye do well, and are not afraid with any amazement."

The Scripture does not forbid the "plaiting of hair, and of the wearing of gold, or putting on of apparel." What is forbidden is that that should not be the adornment, or the beauty, or the pride of a woman. The real beauty and attraction of a godly woman is that of a heart not corruptible, the ornament of a meek and quiet spirit. Sarah is an example of this. She obeyed Abraham, calling him lord, and other women are to be like that.

It is probable that these very jewels brought for Rebekah are jewels that once belonged to Sarah. Abraham and Isaac had sacredly kept her tent and it was there that Isaac took Rebekah as his wife. We suppose that the earring and bracelets and the "jewels of silver, and jewels of gold, and raiment" of verse 53 were brought also.

Beautiful things for adornment are not necessarily wrong. Just so, the plaiting of the hair mentioned in I Peter 3:3 is not forbidden. It is only forbidden that it should be a matter for pride and that a woman should think of the adornment of her hair of her jewels or her face and clothes as if they made her beautiful. Real beauty must be of character, and a godly woman's character is beautiful in the sight of God and others.

Again this teaching is given in I Timothy 2:9,10, "In like manner also, that women adorn themselves in modest apparel, with shamefacedness and sobriety; not with broided hair, or gold, or pearls, or costly array; But (which becometh women professing godliness) with good works."

So it is not the braided hair or gold or pearls or costly

array that is to be counted as a woman's real adornment, but good works.

Note those verses again carefully. If the Lord meant that gold or pearls were wrong for a woman, then the same verse is saying that to braid the hair is a sin. It is significant that that Scripture says that women should "adorn themselves." It is not wrong for a woman to be beautiful, to be neat, to dress with harmony, simplicity, and to be attractive. What is wrong is if the heart is set on that.

Similarly, it is not wrong to make money, but it is wrong to love riches and to be too much occupied with them. The love of riches was a curse to Lot. It was not a curse to Abraham. Abraham, we suppose, did not have that same temptation or did not succumb to it.

If a man becomes vain and proud and arrogant about an education, that would be a cause for sin, just as would wealth or just as would jewelry or degrees or honors among men. The important thing is, "Whether therefore ye eat, or drink, or whatsoever ye do, do all to the glory of God" (I Cor. 10:31).

The dear Lord Jesus was pleased when a penitent woman brought that most expensive thing she could bring—an alabaster box of precious perfume—and poured it on His head and feet. So perfume could be used to the glory of God. And some woman, in love for the Lord Jesus, had a garment woven without a seam, in one piece. It must have been a beautifully fashioned thing.

So, it is not wrong for a woman to adorn herself or for a man to dress sensibly and attractively. It is a sin to be too much concerned about dress or ornament. Our real concern ought to be that we be beautiful in character, pleasing to God, the wife subject to her husband, the man putting Christ first.

The servant offered praise and worship to God because of answered prayer and because the angel of the Lord had directed him clearly in his way. He said, "Blessed be the Lord God of my master Abraham, who hath not left destitute my master of his mercy and his truth" (vs. 27).

Matthew Henry well says, "What we win by prayer we must bear with praise; for mercies in answer to prayer lay us under particular obligation."

VERSES 29-48:

29 ¶ And Rebekah had a brother, and his name *was* Laban: and Laban ran out unto the man, unto the well.

30 And it came to pass, when he saw the earring and bracelets upon his sister's hands, and when he heard the words of Rebekah his sister, saying, Thus spake the man unto me; that he came unto the man; and, behold, he stood by the camels at the well.

31 And he said, Come in, thou blessed of the LORD; wherefore standest thou without? for I have prepared the house, and room for the camels.

32 ¶ And the man came into the house: and he ungirded his camels, and gave straw and provender for the camels, and water to wash his feet, and the men's feet that *were* with him.

33 And there was set *meat* before him to eat: but he said, I will not eat, until I have told mine errand. And he said, Speak on.

34 And he said, I *am* Abraham's servant.

35 And the LORD hath blessed my master greatly; and he is become great: and he hath given him flocks, and herds, and silver, and gold, and menservants, and maidservants, and camels, and asses.

36 And Sarah my master's wife bare a son to my master when she was old: and unto him hath he given all that he hath.

37 And my master made me swear, saying, Thou shalt not take a wife to my son of the daughters of the Cā-nä-ăn-ites, in whose land I dwell:

38 But thou shalt go unto my father's house, and to my kindred, and take a wife unto my son.

39 And I said unto my master, Peradventure the woman will not follow me.

40 And he said unto me, The LORD, before whom I walk, will send his angel with thee, and prosper thy way; and thou shalt take a wife for my son of my kindred, and of my father's house:

41 Then shalt thou be clear from *this* my oath, when thou comest to my kindred; and if they give not thee *one*, thou shalt be clear from my oath.

42 And I came this day unto the well, and said, O LORD God of my master Abraham, if now thou do prosper my way which I go:

43 Behold, I stand by the well of water; and it shall come to pass, that when the virgin cometh forth to draw *water*, and I say to her, Give me, I pray thee, a little water of thy pitcher to drink;

44 And she say to me, Both drink thou, and I will also draw for thy camels: *let* the same *be* the woman whom the LORD hath appointed out for my master's son.

45 And before I had done speaking in mine heart, behold, Rebekah came forth with her pitcher on her shoulder; and she went down unto the well, and drew *water*: and I said unto her, Let me drink, I pray thee.

46 And she made haste, and let down her pitcher from her *shoulder*, and said, Drink, and I will give thy camels drink also: so I drank, and she

made the camels drink also.

47 And I asked her, and said, Whose daughter *art* thou? And she said, The daughter of Bĕ-thū-ĕl, Nā-hôr's son, whom Milcah bare unto him: and I put the earring upon her face, and the bracelets upon her hands.

48 And I bowed down my head, and worshipped the LORD, and blessed the LORD God of my master Abraham, which had led me in the right way to take my master's brother's daughter unto his son.

Eliezer Meets the Family, Tells His Story

Eliezer was received with gracious hospitality. Laban, Rebekah's brother, "ran out unto the man, unto the well." How cordial was his invitation: "Come in, thou blessed of the Lord; wherefore standest thou without? for I have prepared the house, and room for the camels" (vs. 31).

First, old Eliezer cared for the camels. They were ungirded, unloaded, and fed with grain and straw. They have already been watered. "A righteous man regardeth the life of his beast," says Proverbs 12:10. Matthew Henry says, "If the ox knows his owner to serve him, the owner should know his ox to provide that which is fitting for him."

Laban provided water and told Eliezer and the men with him to wash their feet. It is not only a comfort to be graciously received, but a real comfort, after the heat and dust of long travel, to wash the feet. We remember that Abraham invited the Lord and the two angels to wash their feet and be fed (Gen. 18:4). Lot invited the two angels when they came to Sodom to wash their feet (Gen. 19:2). The Pharisee missed that kindly hospitality with Jesus in Luke 7:44, but how sweet it was to the heart of Jesus to feel on His feet the kisses of a poor, forgiven woman and have His feet washed with her tears and anointed with a sweet perfume! Oh, hospitality is a great virtue and those whom God blesses, we should receive.

Now, Eliezer and his fellow servants are urged to eat. The table is set, but Eliezer will not eat. First, he must tell his lord's business (vs. 33); so with painstaking care and a heart full of praise, he recounted the oath that he had given to Abraham. The son must not come back to the land from whence Abraham was led out. He must not marry one of the Canaanite women. The angel of the Lord had led old Eliezer. He had made an earnest, definite prayer and it had been answered to the letter. The young woman he sought was not only beautiful and a virgin, but kindly and eager to serve, of good family and good breeding. God had answered his prayer. Now the old servant has praised the Lord. They must come to a decision.

VERSES 49-53:

49 And now if ye will deal kindly and truly with my master, tell me: and if not, tell me; that I may turn to the right hand, or to the left.

50 Then Laban and Bĕ-thŭ-ĕl answered and said, The thing proceedeth from the LORD: we cannot speak unto thee bad or good.

51 Behold, Rebekah *is* before thee, take *her*, and go, and let her be thy master's son's wife, as the LORD hath spoken.

52 And it came to pass, that, when Abraham's servant heard their words, he worshipped the LORD, *bowing himself* to the earth.

53 And the servant brought forth jewels of silver, and jewels of gold, and raiment, and gave *them* to Rebekah: he gave also to her brother and to her mother precious things.

The Family Consents, Rebekah Given to Be Isaac's Bride

Remember that Eliezer has not yet eaten after his long journey. First, he must get settled the business so dear to his heart. Oh, that all of us might be so concerned about the Lord's business that it would come before eating or drinking or sleeping or the ordinary affairs of life! Sometimes we should fast as we pray before the Lord and delay our eating, and sometimes we should keep the night watches in prayer and postpone the necessary sleep. Oh, and the ordinary affairs of business and school and family and pleasure ought to take second place to the Lord's business.

Now the question is bluntly put, "If ye will deal kindly and truly with my master, tell me: if not, tell me; that I may turn to the right hand, or to the left" (vs. 49). Laban, the brother, and Bethuel, the father, acknowledge that "the thing proceedeth from the Lord: we cannot speak unto thee bad or good. Behold, Rebekah is before thee, take her, and go, and let her be thy master's son's wife, as the Lord hath spoken" (vss. 50,51). Oh, we see Eliezer again bow to the ground in worship and praise to God.

Now, quickly in his packs he searches: "jewels of silver, and jewels of gold, and raiment," for Rebekah, and also "to her brother and to her mother precious things."

They have been impressed with the jewels. It must be true that Abraham is greatly blessed with riches and they are going to his son Isaac. They were greatly impressed with this godly man: how sincere, how business-like, how obviously trustworthy he is! But, more than that, they are impressed that this is the hand of God. They dare not oppose God!

How wonderful it is when we know we are in the will of God! We can step out into the dark if we know He is leading.

VERSES 54-61:

54 And they did eat and drink, he and the men that *were* with him, and tarried all night; and they rose up in the morning, and he said, Send me away unto my master.

55 And her brother and her mother said, Let the damsel abide with us *a few* days, at the least ten; after that she shall go.

56 And he said unto them, Hinder me not, seeing the LORD hath prospered my way; send me away that I may go to my master.

57 And they said, We will call the damsel, and enquire at her mouth.

58 And they called Rebekah, and said unto her, Wilt thou go with this man? And she said, I will go.

59 And they sent away Rebekah their sister, and her nurse, and Abraham's servant, and his men.

60 And they blessed Rebekah, and said unto her, Thou *art* our sister, be thou *the mother* of thousands of millions, and let thy seed possess the gate of those which hate them.

61 ¶ And Rebekah arose, and her damsels, and they rode upon the camels, and followed the man: and the servant took Rebekah, and went his way.

Urgent Need to Finish Job Now

He said, "Hinder me not, seeing the Lord hath prospered

my way; send me away that I may go to my master." So they asked Rebekah, and she, by faith and already beginning to love the man she had never seen, said, "I will go."

Did they know a little of the covenant God had made with Abraham and Isaac and later with Isaac and Jacob? Perhaps they had sensed a little of it. They sent her away with a blessing: ". . .be thou the mother of thousands of millions, and let thy seed possess the gate of those which hate them" (vs. 60).

Eliezer brought along ten camels. No doubt there were extra ones provided for Rebekah and the damsel who would wait on her and serve her. We are reminded that we also have surrendered ourselves to Him "whom having not seen, ye love" (I Pet. 1:8). He is richer than Isaac who pictured Him, and at the end of our journey, we will see His precious face.

VERSES 62-67:

62 And Isaac came from the way of the well Lā-ĥaî-rôî; for he dwelt in the south country.

63 And Isaac went out to meditate in the field at the eventide: and he lifted up his eyes, and saw, and, behold, the camels *were* coming.

64 And Rebekah lifted up her eyes, and when she saw Isaac, she lighted off the camel.

65 For she *had* said unto the servant, What man *is* this that walketh in the field to meet us? And the servant *had* said, It *is* my master: therefore she took a vail, and covered herself.

66 And the servant told Isaac all things that he had done.

67 And Isaac brought her into his mother Sarah's tent, and took Rebekah, and she became his wife; and he loved her: and Isaac was comforted after his mother's *death*.

The Meeting, the Wedding

Isaac went out to meditate. What about the bride coming whom he never saw? Will she be beautiful? Will he really love her? Will she some way fill the void after these three lonely years following the death of his mother Sarah? I wonder, was he thinking of the Messiah promised and pictured in his intended sacrifice on Mount Moriah? Was he thinking about the multitude of descendants as the dust of the earth and as the stars of the sky which should come from him and through this woman coming to be his bride? "And he lifted up his eyes, and saw, and, behold, the camels were coming" (vs. 63).

No doubt Rebekah had been as much concerned, as deeply in thought, as Isaac. Through the long journey she had pictured the man she had never seen. Would he be kind? Would he be good to her? Would she find him as lovely as old Eliezer had pictured him? So, when she saw a man walking and meditating, she asked who it was. Eliezer told her, "It is my master"—Isaac.

Rebekah took a veil and covered herself. It was a proper modesty. She must not be bold. Isaac must ask to see her face. He must seek her love.

They stopped for a time of counseling. "And the servant told Isaac all things that he had done" (vs. 66). We are not told how Rebekah was taken before Abraham, though doubtless she was. But Isaac is joyful. He took her into that sacred tent kept these three years since his mother's death and, no doubt, there he showed her the beautiful hangings of silk, the cushions and the jewels and such other furnishings and beauties that would have pleased the godly old woman who had lived there with plenty, but in a tent.

Note the order then. Rebekah is taken to Sarah's tent and she became his wife. They were married and then "he loved her." Oh, what a comfort and joy to the hungry heart of this forty-year-old man! Now he has a wife to love him, to comfort him, to bear his children.

Let us all learn from Isaac.

> Take time to be holy, Speak oft with Thy Lord;
> Abide in Him always, And feed on His Word:
> Make friends of God's children, Help those who are weak;
> Forgetting in nothing His blessing to seek.

I have sometimes said that the secret of preaching, after one knows the Scripture, after one has a fervent and burning message on his heart—is meditation, meditating until the heart burns and until the dark things are made clear, until holy zeal and holy indignation mount high. Wait upon the Lord! Seek His face!

We should note here that men need the fellowship of good women. In the Garden of Eden, God had said, "It is not good that man should be alone; I will make him an help meet for him."

If men are to be strong, they need the tenderness of good women. It is foolish to talk too much about equality between men and women. Men and women are different. A man ought to be a good man and a woman ought to be a good woman. Each has his place, and each needs the other.

GENESIS 25

THEN again Abraham took a wife, and her name was Keturah.

2 And she bare him Zimran, and Jokshan, and Medan, and Midian, and Ishbak, and Shuah.

3 And Jokshan begat Sheba, and Dedan. And the sons of Dedan were Assh-ŭ-́rĭm, and Lĕ-tû-́shĭm, and Lĕ-ŭm-́mĭm.

4 And the sons of Midian; Ephah, and Epher, and Hā-́nŏch, and Ă-bĭ-́däh, and Ĕl-dā-́äh. All these *were* the children of Keturah.

5 ¶ And Abraham gave all that he had unto Isaac.

6 But unto the sons of the concubines, which Abraham had, Abraham gave gifts, and sent them away from Isaac his son, while he yet lived, eastward, unto the east country.

7 And these *are* the days of the years of Abraham's life which he lived, an hundred threescore and fifteen years.

8 Then Abraham gave up the ghost, and died in a good old age, an old man, and full *of years;* and was gathered to his people.

9 And his sons Isaac and Ishmael buried him in the cave of Măch-pē-́läh, in the field of Ephron the son of Zohar the Hittite, which *is* before Mamre;

10 The field which Abraham purchased of the sons of Heth: there was Abraham buried, and Sarah his wife.

Abraham's Last Years and Death

Abraham married again. Forty years before, Sarah had thought that both she and Abraham were too old to have a child. "After I am waxed old shall I have pleasure, my lord being old also?" (Gen. 18:12). Even then, Hebrews 11:12 said that God gave a child to "him as good as dead." But Abraham's youthful strength is renewed and now, forty years later, he marries again and has from Keturah six sons.

Abraham would have been lonely. Sarah is dead. Isaac is married. With the great establishment and many servants, it was not good for Abraham to have no nurse, no comforter, no companionship. Matthew Henry supposes that Keturah was **"probably the chiefest maidservant born in his house or bought with money."** She was called a concubine (vs. 6) along with Hagar. That means she was a legally married wife but a social inferior and did not rate with the principal wife, Sarah. So these sons are sent away to the East. One of the sons of Keturah was Midian, father of the great host of Midianites and other men of the East later.

"And Abraham gave all that he had unto Isaac" (vs. 5). Matthew Henry well says:

> He made Isaac his heir as he was bound to do in justice to Sarah, the first and principal wife and to Rebekah who married Isaac on the assurance of it (Gen. 24:36). In this *all* which he settled upon Isaac perhaps included the promise of the land of Canaan and the entail of the covenant. For God having already made him the heir of the promise, Abraham therefore made him heir of his estate.

The other children were not sent away empty. "Unto the sons of the concubines, [Hagar's son, Ishmael, and the sons of Keturah] which Abraham had, Abraham gave gifts, and sent them away from Isaac his son, while he yet lived, eastward, unto the east country" (vs. 6). Now there would be no question of quarreling over the inheritance. No one will have a claim on the land or the promises that through Isaac will come the great Seed of Abraham, through whom all the world will be blessed. Through Isaac and "in Isaac shall thy seed be called" (Gen. 21:12; Heb. 11:18).

But Abraham died. He lived thirty-five years after Isaac was married, dying at the age of 175 years. He was "gathered to his people," I think to the heavenly hosts of the saved gone on before, as well as to his believing ancestors.

Isaac and Ishmael together buried him in the cave of Machpelah where Sarah had been buried and where later Isaac, Rebekah, Jacob, and Leah will be buried. It is fitting that Ishmael, not the favored son but a son greatly beloved, had part in the burial of his father, along with Isaac.

VERSES 11-18:

11 ¶ And it came to pass after the death of Abraham, that God blessed his son Isaac; and Isaac dwelt by the well Lā-hăi-rôi.

12 ¶ Now these *are* the generations of Ishmael, Abraham's son, whom Hagar the Egyptian, Sarah's handmaid, bare unto Abraham:

13 And these *are* the names of the sons of Ishmael, by their names, according to their generations: the firstborn of Ishmael, Nĕ-bā-jŏth; and Kedar, and Adbeel, and Mibsam,

14 And Mishma, and Dumah, and Massa,

15 Hadar, and Tema, Jetur, Nā-phĭsh, and Kĕ-dĕ-mäh:

16 These *are* the sons of Ishmael, and these *are* their names, by their towns, and by their castles; twelve princes according to their nations.

17 And these *are* the years of the life of Ishmael, an hundred and thirty and seven years: and he gave up the ghost and died; and was gathered unto his people.

18 And they dwelt from Hăv-ĭ-läh unto Shur, that *is* before Egypt, as thou goest toward Assyria: *and* he died in the presence of all his brethren.

Isaac and Ishmael After Abraham's Death

The great blessing of God on Abraham continued on his son Isaac. The promises are all in effect still, and now that Abraham is dead we are reminded of the two sons, Isaac and Ishmael. Note the twelve princes from Ishmael. It was promised him that he would have a great people, and Ishmael lived 137 years.

––––––––

VERSES 19-21:

19 ¶ And these *are* the generations of Isaac, Abraham's son: Abraham begat Isaac:

20 And Isaac was forty years old when he took Rebekah to wife, the daughter of Bĕ-thū-ĕl the Syrian of Pā-dăn–aram, the sister to Laban the Syrian.

21 And Isaac intreated the LORD for his wife, because she *was* barren: and the LORD was intreated of him, and Rebekah his wife conceived.

Barren Rebekah Conceives in Answer to Prayer

We do not know how old was Rebekah when she married, I suppose forty. But after waiting twenty years, barren Rebekah, in answer to prayer, conceived. How often we are reminded that "Lo, children are an heritage of the Lord: and the fruit of the womb is his reward. As arrows are in the hand of a mighty man; so are children of the youth. Happy is the man that hath his quiver full of them. . ." (Ps. 127:3-5).

How blessed it was in the Bible when godly women prayed and others prayed for them and the barren woman became the happy mother of children. It was so in the case of Hannah who, after brokenhearted prayer, received strength to conceive the child Samuel. It was so with Sarah and Abraham who prayed so many years before God miraculously gave the conception and birth of Isaac. It was so about Zacharias and Elisabeth who prayed long. Both were well stricken in years before the angel announced that Elisabeth would conceive and bear the son John who became John the Baptist, filled with the Holy Ghost even from his mother's womb, forerunner of the Lord Jesus. How blessed are these children which are born of prayer! And how we ought to make sure that every child is born well, that it is surrounded with fervent prayers and the trust of a father and mother who plead with God to be with the child mightily.

VERSES 22-28:

22 And the children struggled together within her; and she said, If *it be* so, why *am* I thus? And she went to enquire of the LORD.

23 And the LORD said unto her, Two nations *are* in thy womb, and two manner of people shall be separated from thy bowels; and *the one* people shall be stronger than *the other* people; and the elder shall serve the younger.

24 ¶ And when her days to be delivered were fulfilled, behold, *there were* twins in her womb.

25 And the first came out red, all over like an hairy garment; and they called his name Esau.

26 And after that came his brother out, and his hand took hold on Esau's heel; and his name was called Jacob: and Isaac *was* threescore years old when she bare them.

27 And the boys grew: and Esau was a cunning hunter, a man of the field; and Jacob *was* a plain man, dwelling in tents.

28 And Isaac loved Esau, because he did eat of *his* venison: but Rebekah loved Jacob.

Jacob and Esau—Twins

The twins struggled in the womb of Rebekah. She inquired of the Lord. He told her, "Two nations are in thy womb." We should not be surprised that God's plan was already made for these two boys.

God had called Isaiah from the womb and named him (Isa. 49:1).

And to Jeremiah He said, "Before I formed thee in the belly I knew thee; and before thou camest forth out of the womb I sanctified thee, and I ordained thee a prophet unto the nations" (Jer. 1:5).

The wonderful career of John the Baptist was outlined and announced before he was born. "For he shall be great in the sight of the Lord, and shall drink neither wine nor strong drink; and he shall be filled with the Holy Ghost, even from his mother's womb. And many of the children of Israel shall he turn to the Lord their God" (Luke 1:15,16).

It was foretold that Cyrus would decree the rebuilding of the Temple in Jerusalem (Isa. 44:28; 45:1) and that was foretold before Cyrus was born.

First Kings 13:2 names King Josiah three hundred years before his birth.

So here, God tells Rebekah that "the elder shall serve the younger." We will not be surprised, then, to find her working hard to bring it about, that Jacob the younger gets the birthright. There is a great difference in them—Esau, strong, manly, with a hairy body, a cunning hunter, man of the field; Jacob, a plain man, dwelling in tents. Isaac favored Esau, but Rebekah favored Jacob.

We think that Rebekah may have been more discerning, although we do not excuse her deceit of Isaac later.

Why must Isaac wait twenty years for the birth of his sons? I suppose that God must train him as He needed to train Abraham, to wait patiently, to believe the promises long before they were fulfilled. When it seems that God's promises fail, God wants us to believe anyway and hold on to the promises. So Isaac and Rebekah waited these twenty years, then in answer to prayer the two sons were conceived and born. The promises are to be fulfilled through Jacob. The covenant will be repeated to him at Bethel and elsewhere. Esau will become the father of the Edomites.

VERSES 29-34:

29 ¶ And Jacob sod pottage: and Esau came from the field, and he *was* faint:

30 And Esau said to Jacob, Feed me, I pray thee, with that same red *pottage*; for I *am* faint: therefore was his name called Edom.

31 And Jacob said, Sell me this day thy birthright.

32 And Esau said, Behold, I *am* at the point to die: and what profit shall this birthright do to me?

33 And Jacob said, Swear to me this day; and he sware unto him: and he sold his birthright unto Jacob.

34 Then Jacob gave Esau bread and pottage of lentiles; and he did eat and drink, and rose up, and went his way: thus Esau despised *his* birthright.

Esau Despised His Birthright

Esau, the active, bold extrovert, the outdoorsman, the hunter, came in from the field faint with hunger. Jacob had cooked "a red pottage," perhaps layered with tomatoes and thus red. Esau was not of strong character. He said, "Behold, I am at the point to die: and what profit shall this birthright do to me?" So Esau despised his birthright and later, when he would have changed his mind, "found no place of repentance, though he sought it carefully with tears" (Heb. 12:17). Jacob had probably been taught by his mother what God had told her before the children were born. The elder should serve the younger. Jacob should have the birthright. So now he made his bargains.

The name Jacob means "supplanter." I wonder if Rebekah did not intentionally name him so, looking for the elder to serve the younger. One day his name will be changed to Israel, "a prince." But now, he supplants and enters into the succession of Abraham and Isaac, as the father of the nation Israel. Through him will come the Scriptures and the Lord Jesus according to the flesh.

It is supposed that because Esau said, "Give me some of

that red" (that red, as it is in the original) "pottage," in reproach to him for this, he was ever after called Edom, "red." Later, Jacob will get a special blessing also, which God intended for him, all that the fond father intended for his favored Esau. The story from now on will center on Jacob and his descendants, not Esau.

GENESIS 26

AND there was a famine in the land, beside the first famine that was in the days of Abraham. And Isaac went unto Ă-bǐm-́ĕ-lĕch king of the Philistines unto Gerar.

2 And the LORD appeared unto him, and said, Go not down into Egypt; dwell in the land which I shall tell thee of:

Isaac in Philistine Country

"There was a famine in the land." Famines came quite often to the land of Palestine. So it was in Genesis 12:10 when Abraham went down to Egypt to sojourn there. Now, another famine and Isaac sojourns in the country of the Philistines, forbidden to go to Egypt. In the days of Joseph there was a famine in the land and Joseph's brethren came down to Egypt for food. In the days of Judges the book of Ruth tells how Naomi, her husband Elimelech, and the two sons went to the land of the Moabites because of a famine in Israel. In the days of Elijah and Ahab, because of the sins of Israel Elijah declared, "As the Lord God of Israel liveth, before whom I stand, there shall not be dew nor rain these years, but according to my word" (I Kings 17:1). In II Kings 8:1, Elisha said, "The Lord hath called for a famine; and it shall also come upon the land seven years."

We know that often a famine, plagues of locusts, or war, came because of the sins of the people. Deuteronomy 28:23,24 warned that if the people forsook the Lord God, then, "Thy heaven that is over thy head shall be brass, and the earth that is under thee shall be iron. The Lord shall make the rain of thy land powder and dust: from heaven shall it come down upon thee, until thou be destroyed."

Haggai 1:10,11 tells of God's punishment for Israel's sin: "Therefore the heaven over you is stayed from dew, and the earth is stayed from her fruit. And I called for a drought upon the land, and upon the mountains, and upon the corn, and upon the new wine, and upon the oil, and upon that which the ground bringeth forth, and upon men, and upon cattle, and upon all the labour of the hands."

Amos 4:6-8 tells us also: "And I also have given you cleanness of teeth in all your cities, and want of bread in all your places: yet have ye not returned unto me, saith the Lord. And also I have withholden the rain from you, when there were yet three months to the harvest: and I caused it to rain upon one city, and caused it not to rain upon another city: one piece was rained upon, and the piece whereupon it rained not withered. So two or three cities wandered unto one city, to drink water; but they were not satisfied: yet have ye not returned unto me, saith the Lord."

However, we do not know that the famine in Isaac's time was punishment for any sin of Isaac. It may have been God's dealing with the wicked heathen around who lived in the land. And it may have been for Isaac's sake, too, a testing, as was the case of Abraham. "The trial of your faith worketh patience," says the Scripture. Paul had a thorn in the flesh "lest I should be exhalted above measure" (II Cor. 12:7) but not as punishment for sin.

Isaac went to Abimelech, king of the Philistines. Is this the same Abimelech whom Abraham knew more than forty years before, before Isaac was born? It may have been his son, of the same name, but there had been other developments. When Abraham was there long ago it was "Abimelech, king of Gerar." He was king of a city. The Philistines were not mentioned. Somewhere about that time the Philistine people had begun to come into Palestine, possibly from Crete or Aegean countries, but were not prominent enough to be mentioned then.

After Isaac is weaned and Hagar and Ishmael were cast out, we are told in Genesis 21, "Then Abimelech rose up, and Phichol the chief captain of his host, and they returned into the land of the Philistines" (vs. 32), "And

Abraham sojourned in the Philistines' land many days" (vs. 34).

But now in verse 26 Abimelech is king of the Philistines. After Joshua has led in the conquest of the land of Canaan some hundreds of years later, the Philistines would be the strongest and most aggressive enemy that Israel will have most of the time.

VERSES 3-5:

3 Sojourn in this land, and I will be with thee, and will bless thee; for unto thee, and unto thy seed, I will give all these countries, and I will perform the oath which I sware unto Abraham thy father;

4 And I will make thy seed to multiply as the stars of heaven, and will give unto thy seed all these countries; and in thy seed shall all the nations of the earth be blessed;

5 Because that Abraham obeyed my voice, and kept my charge, my commandments, my statutes, and my laws.

God's Covenant Now Repeated With Isaac

God said, "Sojourn in this land." He was not to go down to Egypt, possibly lest he should be tempted to their ways, probably for the same reason that Abraham would not allow him to go back to the land of Mesopotamia for a bride. He is to sojourn in the land.

God said to Abraham in Genesis 15:16, "The iniquity of the Amorites is not yet full." So Isaac, like Abraham and Jacob later, will be a sojourner, a tent-dweller, not owning the land. Only two spots in the whole land of Canaan actually came to ownership by these patriarchs. Abraham bought the Cave of Machpelah for a burying place. Jacob "bought a parcel of a field, where he had spread his tent, at the hand of the children of Hamor, Shechem's father. . . ." (Gen. 33:19). And Hebrews 11:9,10 makes much of this fact that Abraham, Isaac, and Jacob lived in tents, heirs of a promise which had not yet been fulfilled, and thus they are patterns for Christians in a world which is not really our home.

But what God promised to Abraham, He promises now to Isaac. He will "perform the oath which I sware." He promises that Isaac's seed will "multiply as the stars of heaven, and will give unto thy seed all these countries." Here is a promise of the Scriptures and in this Messiah, "thy seed shall all the nations of the earth be blessed."

Isaac is here blessed "because that Abraham obeyed my voice." How the sons do inherit the blessings of God because of godly fathers! And how many times did God help kings of Judah for David's sake!

VERSES 6-11:

6 ¶ And Isaac dwelt in Gerar:

7 And the men of the place asked *him* of his wife; and he said, She *is* my sister: for he feared to say, *She is* my wife; lest, *said he*, the men of the place should kill me for Rebekah; because she *was* fair to look upon.

8 And it came to pass, when he had been there a long time, that Ă-bĭm´-ĕ-lĕch king of the Philistines looked out at a window, and saw, and, behold, Isaac *was* sporting with Rebekah his wife.

9 And Ă-bĭm´-ĕ-lĕch called Isaac, and said, Behold, of a surety she *is* thy wife: and how saidst thou, She *is* my sister? And Isaac said unto him, Because I said, Lest I die for her.

10 And Ă-bĭm´-ĕ-lĕch said, What *is* this thou hast done unto us? one of the people might lightly have lien with thy wife, and thou shouldest have brought guiltiness upon us.

11 And Ă-bĭm´-ĕ-lĕch charged all *his* people, saying, He that toucheth this man or his wife shall surely be put to death.

Son Follows Sin of Father

Isaac had been greatly blessed because of Abraham (vs. 5), but here Isaac was led into sin very possibly by the example of his father. Abraham had told the lie, a half truth, that Sarah was his sister and she was taken by Pharaoh and then he had lied again at Gerar with Abimelech before Isaac was born. Now we are shocked to find that Isaac did the same thing when he said of Rebekah, "She is my sister," without the excuse that she was half-sister as Sarah was to Abraham. Rebekah was beautiful as Sarah had been. He feared he would be killed for her! It is blessedly true that ". . .the mercy of the Lord is from everlasting to everlasting upon them that fear him, and his righteousness unto children's children; To such as keep his covenant. . . ." (Ps. 103:17,18). But it is also true that God visits "the iniquity of the fathers upon the children. . . ." (Exod. 20:5). It is not that God visits the punishment of the father's sins on the children but the sins themselves. The father sins, then the child follows the father's footsteps in sin. The father eats sour grapes, and the children's teeth are set on edge.

David committed adultery with Bath-sheba and had her husband murdered. I have no doubt that Amnon who raped his half-sister Tamar knew about the sin of his father David and did not think it so bad. Absalom knew of the innocent blood David had shed, and his own sin murdering his rapist brother was not so bad as David's sin.

We find that good king Asa took silver and gold out of the treasures of the Lord's house to hire Ben-hadad of Syria to be an ally against the Northern Kingdom. God rebuked his compromise with the heathen by Hanani in II Chronicles 16:7. But the next chapter tells us how Asa's son Jehoshaphat, also a good man but following his father, "joined affinity with Ahab," the wicked idolater of the Northern Kingdom. The son followed the pattern of the father. And it is also blessed that he was rebuked by Jehu, the son of Hanani who had rebuked Jehoshaphat's father (II Chron. 19:1-3). The sin went on to the third generation. When Jehoshaphat was in close affinity with wicked Ahab, his son Jehoram fell in love with and married the daughter of Ahab, "And he walked in the way of the kings of Israel, like as did the house of Ahab: for he had the daughter of Ahab to wife: and he wrought that which was evil in the eyes of the Lord" (II Chron. 21:6).

So Isaac, a good man, followed the bad pattern that Abraham had set in lying about his wife. No one seized Rebekah and no one attempted to kill Isaac over her, but his subterfuge was discovered and Abimelech rebuked him.

Isaac did not know that Abimelech was desperately afraid of the God of Isaac and would not have taken the man's wife nor allowed his people to do so. It is wonderful that God preserves his people, erring and frail as we are.

---

12 Then Isaac sowed in that land, and received in the same year an hundredfold: and the LORD blessed him.

13 And the man waxed great, and went forward, and grew until he became very great:

14 For he had possession of flocks, and possession of herds, and great store of servants: and the Philistines envied him.

15 For all the wells which his father's servants had digged in the days of Abraham his father, the Philistines had stopped them, and filled them with earth.

16 And Ă-bĭm-'ĕ-lĕch said unto Isaac, Go from us; for thou art much mightier than we.

Riches of Isaac

We know that Isaac got great riches from Abraham, although some gifts were given to other of Abraham's sons—the sons of Keturah, and to Ishmael. But now Isaac was prospered. In one year he sowed and received an hundredfold, and so flocks and herds and wealth increased. "The Philistines envied him." They had stopped up the wells that Abraham had dug before. The Philistines evidently were not now strong enough to be a great menace to Isaac, but they would grow stronger.

Abimelech and the Philistines wanted Isaac out of the country. As Abimelech and Phichol wanted a sworn covenant with Abraham, now they fear Isaac and perhaps, too, partly disgusted by his lie, they want him to leave, and he does.

---

17 ¶ And Isaac departed thence, and pitched his tent in the valley of Gerar, and dwelt there.

18 And Isaac digged again the wells of water, which they had digged in the days of Abraham his father; for the Philistines had stopped them after the death of Abraham: and he

called their names after the names by which his father had called them.

19 And Isaac's servants digged in the valley, and found there a well of springing water.

20 And the herdmen of Gerar did strive with Isaac's herdmen, saying, The water *is* our's: and he called the name of the well Esek; because they strove with him.

21 And they digged another well, and strove for that also: and he called the name of it Sitnah.

22 And he removed from thence, and digged another well; and for that they strove not: and he called the name of it Rē-hŏ-bōth; and he said, For now the LORD hath made room for us, and we shall be fruitful in the land.

23 And he went up from thence to Beer–sheba.

Isaac Digging Wells

Isaac had left the presence of Abimelech but still was in the valley of Gerar. We do not believe it was an accident that Abraham and then Isaac were wealthy. They were thrifty, hard-working, strong characters. Abraham would not live in a country without improving it; so he dug wells for his flocks and herds. A well near Hebron is still called Abraham's well. A well at Beer-sheba is still called Abraham's well. The Philistines filled the wells and Isaac dug them again. Over one well the herdmen of Gerar fought with Isaac's men, and he called it Esek. There was a fight also at the next well he called Sitnah. The third well he dug, he called Rehoboth because God had made room and there was no fighting over that well. Now he moved somewhat away from the valley of Gerar down to Beer-sheba.

VERSES 24,25:

24 And the LORD appeared unto him the same night, and said, I *am* the God of Abraham thy father: fear not, for I *am* with thee, and will bless thee, and multiply thy seed for my servant Abraham's sake.

25 And he builded an altar there, and called upon the name of the LORD, and pitched his tent there: and there Isaac's servants digged a well.

Isaac at Beer-sheba

Here Isaac made an altar "and called upon the name of the Lord." God repeated to Isaac the covenant He had made with Abraham, the covenant mentioned to Isaac in Genesis 26:3,4. We are not told at that time that Isaac had built an altar, but here he did. "And he builded an altar there, and called upon the name of the Lord."

How Abraham and Isaac Worshiped God

We are apt to think of the worship of Abraham, Isaac, and Jacob in the light of the ceremonial law and the sacrifices that were required among Israel, as given by the inspired Moses. Oh, but that would be a mistake.

God had repeated His blessed covenant and promise to Isaac in the Philistine land (a part of the Promised Land), and again in verse 24 He appeared to Isaac. Notice that Isaac pitched his tent and built an altar and called on the Lord. This is the first and only time we are told Isaac "builded an altar." Abraham had built an altar at Sichem (Gen. 12:6) when first coming into the land of promise. After the unhappy episode in Egypt when Abraham built no altar, he returned to the altar at Sichem (Gen. 13:4). Thus, when Abraham moved his tent to the plain of Mamre near Hebron, he built an altar there (Gen. 13:18). Abraham dwelt for a time at Beer-sheba (Gen. 22:19). We are not told that he built an altar there.

God appeared directly to these godly patriarchs again and again. They prayed as Abraham did, who was "a prophet" (Gen. 18:22-33; Gen. 20:7; for example). Eliezer, the long-time trusted servant and agent of Abraham, prayed (Gen. 24:12,13). Rebekah prayed (Gen. 25:22,23). So Isaac here "called upon the name of the Lord" (vs. 25). There is much evidence that Isaac meditated often on spiritual truth (Gen. 24:63). He relied on the Lord and praised Him (vs. 22).

Did the patriarchs Abraham, Isaac, and Jacob regularly offer animal sacrifices? No, they had no command to do so as a regular matter and there is no record that they had sacrifices daily. Once God instructed Abraham to offer certain sacrifices (Gen. 15:9-17), and God instructed Abraham to offer Isaac. But Abraham had sacrificed

before, for the lad Isaac said, "Where is the lamb for a
burnt-offering?" (Gen. 22:7). Then Abraham offered the
ram which was caught in the bushes. We know that Abel
"by faith" had offered an acceptable sacrifice. We are not
told that the sacrifice was commanded. More likely he, by
faith and from promises that God had made, knew that
there would be a Saviour, "the Lamb of God, which taketh
away the sin of the world," and the sacrifice was his
testimony, his confession of faith. Even so Cain's offering
was his insistence on his self-sufficiency but admitting his
obligation to God for God's provision.

Abraham and Isaac certainly knew the sacrifices
pictured the atoning death of the Saviour who was to come.

Note that the altar seemed to be a part of establishing a
home, as Christian people who live in a city want a church
home where they can regularly attend. The offerings were
occasional. Such an altar was somewhat of a holy place, a
reminder, not only or always for sacrifice. The altar of
Reuben and Gad on the east side of Jordan in Joshua
22:10-27 had no sacrifices or burnt offerings. Jacob set up
and anointed a stone at Bethel and said, "This . . . shall
be God's house" (Gen. 28:22).

Later in the ceremonial law Moses would be inspired to
command certain sacrifices. But aside from some few
special cases, there are no recorded commands for regular,
scheduled sacrifices before the ceremonial law. I think that
when Jacob said, "I will surely give the tenth unto thee,"
He meant sacrifices, but no details of Jacob's sacrifices are
ever revealed to us.

VERSES 26-33:

26 ¶ Then Ă-bĭm-́ĕ-lĕch went to
him from Gerar, and Ă-hŭz-́zăth one
of his friends, and Phī-́chŏl the chief
captain of his army.

27 And Isaac said unto them,
Wherefore come ye to me, seeing ye
hate me, and have sent me away from
you?

28 And they said, We saw certainly
that the LORD was with thee: and we
said, Let there be now an oath betwixt us, even betwixt us and thee,

and let us make a covenant with thee;

29 That thou wilt do us no hurt, as we have not touched thee, and as we have done unto thee nothing but good, and have sent thee away in peace: thou *art* now the blessed of the LORD.

30 And he made them a feast, and they did eat and drink.

31 And they rose up betimes in the morning, and sware one to another:

and Isaac sent them away, and they departed from him in peace.

32 And it came to pass the same day, that Isaac's servants came, and told him concerning the well which they had digged, and said unto him, We have found water.

33 And he called it Shebah: therefore the name of the city *is* Beersheba unto this day.

Abimelech and Phichol Come to Isaac, as They Came to Jacob, for a Treaty

In Genesis 21:22-31 we find that King Abimelech and Phichol, the chief captain of his hosts, came to plead with Abraham that he should swear to a treaty with them that he would not deal falsely with them. Now King Abimelech, Phichol and another friend have come to Isaac with the same plea. They recognize that Isaac is a mighty man of wealth and that God is with him. Before Abimelech had asked Isaac to leave his immediate territory, and Isaac had done so. But now, he wants a treaty for he said, "We saw certainly that the Lord was with thee." So the treaty is made solemnly: They are not to do harm one to the other.

Although the herdmen of King Abimelech had quarreled with Isaac's herdmen, all recognized that he was a mighty man of God and that God was with him.

Abraham had made a similar covenant with Abimelech (Gen. 21:31).

---

34 ¶ And Esau was forty years old when he took to wife Judith the daughter of Bĕẽr-́ī the Hittite, and Băsh-́ĕ-măth the daughter of Elon the Hittite:

35 Which were a grief of mind unto Isaac and to Rebekah.

Esau Marries Heathen Women

The Hittites were a great race. Unbelieving scholars for

many years said that there had been no such race of people or that they were of no importance and that the Bible estimate of their power and influence was inaccurate.

However, they are wrong. Inscriptions have been found indicating that the Hittites were a great nation of people and that they were part of the time competitive with Egypt and Babylon in power and influence. But the Hittites were heathen people. Now Esau, who had despised his birthright, marries two women from these heathen families causing great grief to Isaac and Rebekah. That is indicated further in verse 46 of the next chapter, and in Genesis 28 where Isaac sends Jacob away to get a wife from among his own people.

GENESIS 27

AND it came to pass, that when Isaac was old, and his eyes were dim, so that he could not see, he called Esau his eldest son, and said unto him, My son: and he said unto him, Behold, *here am* I.

2 And he said, Behold now, I am old, I know not the day of my death:

3 Now therefore take, I pray thee, thy weapons, thy quiver and thy bow, and go out to the field, and take me *some* venison;

4 And make me savoury meat, such as I love, and bring *it* to me, that I may eat; that my soul may bless thee before I die.

5 And Rebekah heard when Isaac spake to Esau his son. And Esau went to the field to hunt *for* venison, *and* to bring *it*.

6 ¶ And Rebekah spake unto Jacob her son, saying, Behold, I heard thy father speak unto Esau thy brother, saying,

7 Bring me venison, and make me savoury meat, that I may eat, and bless thee before the LORD before my death.

8 Now therefore, my son, obey my voice according to that which I command thee.

9 Go now to the flock, and fetch me from thence two good kids of the goats; and I will make them savoury meat for thy father, such as he loveth:

10 And thou shalt bring *it* to thy father, that he may eat, and that he may bless thee before his death.

11 And Jacob said to Rebekah his mother, Behold, Esau my brother *is* a hairy man, and I *am* a smooth man:

12 My father peradventure will feel me, and I shall seem to him as a deceiver; and I shall bring a curse upon me, and not a blessing.

13 And his mother said unto him, Upon me *be* thy curse, my son: only obey my voice, and go fetch me *them*.

14 And he went, and fetched, and brought *them* to his mother: and his mother made savoury meat, such as his father loved.

15 And Rebekah took goodly raiment of her eldest son Esau, which *were* with her in the house, and put them upon Jacob her younger son:

16 And she put the skins of the kids of the goats upon his hands, and upon the smooth of his neck:

17 And she gave the savoury meat and the bread, which she had prepared, into the hand of her son Jacob.

Rebekah and Jacob Deceive Isaac

Isaac urged his son Esau to bring venison and prepare a savory meal so he could eat because Isaac is old and he said, ". . .that my soul may bless thee before I die." Isaac knew that he had a gift of prophecy in this matter and would speak for God.

The announcement that old Isaac, inspired of God, would announce a blessing from God is striking. In this case it turned out contrary to his own plan. Later Jacob will bless his sons prophetically before his death (Gen. 49).

We are reminded of Balaam whose greedy heart would have cursed Israel for money but was compelled instead to bless them repeatedly (Num. chapters 22-24). And it was from God. Caiaphas, the wicked high priest who wanted to kill the Lord Jesus, prophesied: "And one of them, named Caiaphas, being the high priest that same year, said unto them, Ye know nothing at all, Nor consider that it is expedient for us, that one man should die for the people, and that the whole nation perish not. And this spake he not of himself: but being high priest that year, he prophesied that Jesus should die for that nation" (John 11:49-51).

Here is an interesting sidelight on the doctrine of inspiration. Jesus said, "It is written, Man shall not live by bread alone, but by every word that proceedeth out of the mouth of God" (Matt. 4:4). Paul said that his inspired message was "not in the words which man's wisdom teacheth, but which the Holy Ghost teacheth; comparing spiritual things with spiritual" (I Cor. 2:13), that is, with spiritual matter and Spirit-given words. Those who wrote the Scriptures did not necessarily have a mind any keener than usual, nor a clear understanding of what they wrote. What they said was not the result of their planning nor of their wisdom but words direct from God.

So prophets of old "inquired and searched diligently . . . Searching what, or what manner of time the Spirit of Christ which was in them did signify, when it testified beforehand the sufferings of Christ, and the glory that should follow." It was revealed to them "that not unto themselves, but unto us they did minister. . ." (I Pet. 1:10-12). They set down and studied, seeking to understand what they themselves, moved by the Spirit of God, had written!

Balaam's donkey could speak (though donkeys cannot speak)! And unconverted Caiaphas could be made to prophesy the atonement which he did not understand or want! Thus Isaac, deceived by Rebekah and Jacob, will bless Jacob as God wanted him blessed, thinking all the time it was Esau of whom he prophesied!

Was Rebekah justified in deceit? Or Jacob? No. God does not need men's lies to work out His will. We think that if Isaac had known he was blessing Jacob, God would have put the same words in his mouth. God can control a prophet who knows what he does, as well as He controlled old Isaac who did not know he was putting the younger above the elder.

No doubt the bitterness and hatred of Esau would have been largely avoided if the blessing had come by legitimate means so he could see it was from God. As it was, unspiritual Esau blamed Jacob for the blessing God would have given without Jacob's deceit and the harm that followed.

God Brings Good Out of Evil

We see also that God, who makes the wrath of men to praise Him, can overrule and use even the maneuvering of men. "And we know that all things work together for good to them that love God, to them who are the called according to his purpose" (Rom. 8:28). When wicked brothers sold young Joseph as a slave in Egypt they meant it for evil, "but God meant it unto good" (Gen. 45:5,8; Gen. 50:20).

The Apostle Paul, in jail and persecuted, rejoiced and said that all "have fallen out rather unto the furtherance of the gospel" (Phil. 1:12). Thus when the Gospel is preached he would rejoice, whether it was preached in envy or sincerely.

Spiritual Discernment of Rebekah

We must say a word for Rebekah. She had prayed when the twins struggled in her womb and God had revealed to her, "Two nations are in thy womb, and two manner of people shall be separated from thy bowels; and the one people shall be stronger than the other people; and the elder shall serve the younger" (Gen. 25:23). So she remembered that Jacob was to be head and Esau was to serve him. She surely knew also that the blessed Seed through whom all nations were to be blessed would come from Jacob, the nation Israel, the Scriptures, the Saviour. Surely she understood that the covenant will be fulfilled through Jacob. She knew he had the birthright. She was right to favor him over the unspiritual and carnal Esau, but she was wrong to deceive Isaac. She saw the end that God had planned, but she foolishly thought her deceiving would help bring about what God wanted.

In this matter she reminds us of Sarah who, not believing that God would give her a son, urged Abraham to take Hagar, hoping that Hagar might bear the son who was promised and through whom the great blessing of the world was to come. Rebekah was wrong to deceive, but she was evidently more spiritually-minded in some ways than Isaac, or perhaps she was not blinded by personal preference as Isaac was for Esau who was a good outdoor man, a hunter and favored of his father.

Jacob and his mother Rebekah were wrong to deceive and lie to old Isaac. And I think sorrow will come from their deceit. Christians may sin and may be punished for their sin, but God never casts away His own and He will not break His covenant with Jacob.

VERSES 18-25:

18 ¶ And he came unto his father, and said, My father: and he said, Here *am* I; who *art* thou, my son?

19 And Jacob said unto his father, I *am* Esau thy firstborn; I have done according as thou badest me: arise, I pray thee, sit and eat of my venison, that thy soul may bless me.

20 And Isaac said unto his son, How *is* it that thou hast found *it* so quickly, my son? And he said, Because the LORD thy God brought *it* to me.

21 And Isaac said unto Jacob, Come near, I pray thee, that I may feel thee, my son, whether thou *be* my very son Esau or not.

22 And Jacob went near unto Isaac his father; and he felt him, and said, The voice *is* Jacob's voice, but the hands *are* the hands of Esau.

23 And he discerned him not, because his hands were hairy, as his brother Esau's hands: so he blessed him.

24 And he said, *Art* thou my very

son Esau? And he said, I *am*.

25 And he said, Bring *it* near to me, and I will eat of my son's venison, that my soul may bless thee. And he brought *it* near to him, and he did eat: and he brought him wine, and he drank.

The Deceit Successful

Rebekah planned carefully. Kids made savory meat as good as a deer. The fond father fancied that the meat brought by his favorite Esau would be better, but it was not. The clothes of Esau smelled "as the smell of a field" (vs. 27). The goatskins allowed the blind old man to think that the hands, arms and neck were of hairy Esau!

We think Isaac does not appear too well here. Perhaps he was growing senile, although he lived many more years after this. At any rate, he gave the blessing of the firstborn to Jacob, the younger.

Although Isaac had said, "Behold now, I am old, I know not the day of my death" (vs. 2), he did not die until more than twenty years later (Gen. 35).

VERSES 26-29:

26 And his father Isaac said unto him, Come near now, and kiss me, my son.

27 And he came near, and kissed him: and he smelled the smell of his raiment, and blessed him, and said, See, the smell of my son *is* as the smell of a field which the LORD hath blessed:

28 Therefore God give thee of the dew of heaven, and the fatness of the earth, and plenty of corn and wine:

29 Let people serve thee, and nations bow down to thee: be lord over thy brethren, and let thy mother's sons bow down to thee: cursed *be* every one that curseth thee, and blessed *be* he that blesseth thee.

Blessing of Jacob

Consider the blessing Isaac prophetically declared on Jacob. He promised (1) physical prosperity: ". . .the fatness of the earth, and plenty of corn and wine." Then we need not be surprised that Jacob will prosper when he runs away to Laban.

Surely this means that Jacob's descendants, the nation

Israel, are to inherit the land of Canaan "flowing with milk and honey." And does not this hint also of the thrift, the hard work, the honest character, loyalty, and faithfulness that would prosper Jacob through his lifetime, and perhaps the thrift that would follow many Jews around the world?

Jacob was promised (2) rule in Palestine. "Let people serve thee. . .thy mother's sons bow down to thee." That means not only Esau, the immediate brother, but evidently the descendants of Esau would bow down to the Jews. For instance, David and Solomon would rule over the Edomites. And many, many other nations must bow to these descendants of Jacob, as they come in to conquer the land of Palestine later and through the reign of David and Solomon particularly. Yes, and eventually in the reign of Jesus Christ Himself the great Seed of Jacob.

VERSES 30-33:

30 ¶ And it came to pass, as soon as Isaac had made an end of blessing Jacob, and Jacob was yet scarce gone out from the presence of Isaac his father, that Esau his brother came in from his hunting.

31 And he also had made savoury meat, and brought it unto his father, and said unto his father, Let my father arise, and eat of his son's venison, that thy soul may bless me.

32 And Isaac his father said unto him, Who *art* thou? And he said, I *am* thy son, thy firstborn Esau.

33 And Isaac trembled very exceedingly, and said, Who? where *is* he that hath taken venison, and brought *it* me, and I have eaten of all before thou camest, and have blessed him? yea, *and* he shall be blessed.

"Yea, and He Shall Be Blessed"

Esau came in. He had killed the game, cooked the venison and he brought it to Isaac his father. Note that Esau would like to have claimed the blessing of the firstborn, although he had already sold that birthright to Jacob. He said, "I am thy son, thy firstborn Esau."

Old Isaac trembled in astonishment. But he knew that the blessing he had given was prophetic, was given from God. So, although he himself had been mistaken in thinking he blessed Esau, he realized the truth and he said

about Jacob, "Yea, and he shall be blessed"! The blessing
God intended for Jacob had come to Jacob.

VERSES 34-38:

34 And when Esau heard the words of his father, he cried with a great and exceeding bitter cry, and said unto his father, Bless me, *even* me also, O my father.

35 And he said, Thy brother came with subtilty, and hath taken away thy blessing.

36 And he said, Is not he rightly named Jacob? for he hath supplanted me these two times: he took away my birthright; and, behold, now he hath taken away my blessing. And he said, Hast thou not reserved a blessing for me?

37 And Isaac answered and said unto Esau, Behold, I have made him thy lord, and all his brethren have I given to him for servants; and with corn and wine have I sustained him: and what shall I do now unto thee, my son?

38 And Esau said unto his father, Hast thou but one blessing, my father? bless me, *even* me also, O my father. And Esau lifted up his voice, and wept.

How Esau Wanted That Blessing!

No doubt his desire was sincere. But he was a double-minded man, more concerned with the ordinary comforts and pleasures of the flesh than with the great spiritual blessing and to be used of God. So he sold his birthright for a mess of red pottage. Hebrews 12:15-17 tells us how God saw Esau.

Christians are all exhorted:

"Looking diligently lest any man fail of the grace of God; lest any root of bitterness springing up trouble you, and thereby many be defiled; Lest there be any fornicator, or profane person, as Esau, who for one morsel of meat sold his birthright. For ye know how that afterward, when he would have inherited the blessing, he was rejected: for he found no place of repentance, though he sought it carefully with tears."

So in God's sight Esau was a "profane person," a man who would rather have a satisfactory meal than to inherit the great blessing God had promised to the seed of Abraham.

We are reminded of James 4:4, "Ye adulterers and adulteresses, know ye not that the friendship of the world is enmity with God? whosoever therefore will be a friend of the world is the enemy of God." So one who puts worldly things ahead of God, in that sense is guilty of spiritual adultery. Then let us beware not to be double-minded and not only to lay aside the open sin but the weights that may hinder our race. Esau lost out. He wept bitterly. But there was no change of mind and plan. Jacob had been given the blessing of God and it would not be taken away.

It was partly because of the carnal nature of Esau that he did not see that this was the hand of God. He thought that Jacob's scheming had gotten him the blessing.

Isaac was troubled. He wanted to bless Esau but he could not undo the blessing on Jacob. So he must give a secondary and lesser blessing to Esau.

VERSES 39-46:

39 And Isaac his father answered and said unto him, Behold, thy dwelling shall be the fatness of the earth, and of the dew of heaven from above;

40 And by thy sword shalt thou live, and shalt serve thy brother; and it shall come to pass when thou shalt have the dominion, that thou shalt break his yoke from off thy neck.

41 ¶ And Esau hated Jacob because of the blessing wherewith his father blessed him: and Esau said in his heart, The days of mourning for my father are at hand; then will I slay my brother Jacob.

42 And these words of Esau her elder son were told to Rebekah: and she sent and called Jacob her younger son, and said unto him, Behold, thy brother Esau, as touching thee, doth comfort himself, *purposing* to kill thee.

43 Now therefore, my son, obey my voice; and arise, flee thou to Laban my brother to Haran;

44 And tarry with him a few days, until thy brother's fury turn away;

45 Until thy brother's anger turn away from thee, and he forget *that* which thou hast done to him: then I will send, and fetch thee from thence: why should I be deprived also of you both in one day?

46 And Rebekah said to Isaac, I am weary of my life because of the daughters of Heth: if Jacob take a wife of the daughters of Heth, such as these *which are* of the daughters of the land, what good shall my life do me?

Jacob Must Flee From Murderous Anger of Esau

Note the blessing on Esau. He should have material blessings: ". . . the fatness of the earth, and of the dew of heaven from above." Esau's people would live by the sword. He would have to serve his brother. The Edomites would serve Israel, but the Edomites would throw off their dominion. Even today, we suppose, the animosity between Moslem Arabs and the Jews is partly foretold in this word about the sword.

"Esau hated Jacob." It is a sad thing that those who get God's best blessings are sometimes hated and blamed by those who are profane, double-minded, unspiritual, and do not get the same blessings God would like to give them.

Esau thought his father would soon die, and then he planned to kill Jacob, but he was mistaken. Isaac would not die soon.

Now Rebekah was greatly troubled. Jacob must leave and go to her brother Laban up in the country of Haran, and she thought that Jacob need "tarry with him a few days." Oh, but it will be many long years and he may never see his mother again. Esau did not so soon forget. Later, when Jacob came back from Padan-aram, Esau went to meet him with four hundred men. I am sure that originally he intended harm to Jacob; but now the boy must leave home.

God has a plan in this also. Isaac and Rebekah have been greatly grieved at Esau who took heathen wives (Gen. 26:34,35). Rebekah and Isaac were both troubled about that. That would be a good excuse; so she put the matter up to Isaac. Jacob must not marry one of these heathen women; he must go, as Abraham's servant went for a bride for Isaac, back to the land of his people.

GENESIS 28

AND Isaac called Jacob, and blessed him, and charged him, and said unto him, Thou shalt not take a wife of the daughters of Cā-nă-ăn.

2 Arise, go to Pā-dăn–aram, to the house of Bĕ-thū-ĕl thy mother's father; and take thee a wife from thence of the daughters of Laban thy mother's brother.

3 And God Almighty bless thee, and make thee fruitful, and multiply thee, that thou mayest be a multitude of people;

4 And give thee the blessing of Abraham, to thee, and to thy seed with thee; that thou mayest inherit the land wherein thou art a stranger, which God gave unto Abraham.

5 And Isaac sent away Jacob: and he went to Pā-dăn–aram unto Laban, son of Bĕ-thū-ĕl the Syrian, the brother of Rebekah, Jacob's and Esau's mother.

Jacob Must Flee From Esau to Haran

Isaac commanded Jacob, "Thou shalt not take a wife of the daughters of Canaan." Now convinced that God has selected Jacob to inherit the covenant, Isaac insists, as Abraham had insisted about Isaac, that Jacob must not marry a heathen woman. We think he had been fretted, as Rebekah had been, by the heathen wives of Esau. Now on the prodding of his wife, Isaac sends Jacob back to Rebekah's brother Laban to get a wife of Laban's daughters. Isaac, in ignorance but under divine inspiration, had given Jacob a blessing. He is now convinced that through him will come the blessing of the covenant, and he prophesies that the promise will be fulfilled in Jacob. In fact, as soon as Isaac knew he had inadvertently pronounced God's blessing on Jacob instead of Esau as he had supposed, he saw it was the hand of God and said, "Yea, and he shall be blessed" (Gen. 27:33). So the blessing of Abraham was now to be his, as Isaac prophesied.

"Arise, go to *Padan-aram*." The term means between the rivers. It is perhaps synonymous with Mesopotamia. It refers to the general area of the Euphrates and Tigris

Rivers. Most specifically here it refers to Haran (Gen. 27:43; 28:10; 29:4). That is where Abraham first went when he started from Ur of the Chaldees to Canaan. At Haran he stayed until his father Terah died (Gen. 11:31,32; Acts 7:4), then on to Canaan.

We suppose from Genesis 11:23-31, that the family had all been at Ur of the Chaldees; that is, Abraham and his three brothers, sons of Terah. When Abraham, Terah and Lot left, Nahor and his family are not mentioned as going with them to Haran. But we find now that Laban is in Haran. He is called "son of Nahor" (Gen. 29:5), but is probably a son of Bethuel, Reuben's father, and thus a grandson (a descendant was called a son) of Nahor. Eliezer did not deal with Bethuel but with Laban about Rebekah as a bride for Isaac, and the old servant of Abraham gave gifts to Rebekah's brother and mother; so we judge that Nahor and Bethuel were both dead. Laban lived at Haran or near there, not in the country of Ur of the Chaldees. To him Jacob goes.

Jacob must leave his mother whom he loved so well, and his aged father. Deceit has caused the hate of Esau; so sin has its wages. And though Jacob was his mother's favorite, we doubt he ever saw her again.

VERSES 6-9:

6 ¶ When Esau saw that Isaac had blessed Jacob, and sent him away to Pă-dăn-aram, to take him a wife from thence; and that as he blessed him he gave him a charge, saying, Thou shalt not take a wife of the daughters of Că-nă-ăn;

7 And that Jacob obeyed his father and his mother, and was gone to Pă-dăn-aram;

8 And Esau seeing that the daughters of Că-nă-ăn pleased not Isaac his father;

9 Then went Esau unto Ishmael, and took unto the wives which he had Mă-hă-lăth the daughter of Ishmael Abraham's son, the sister of Nĕ-bă-jŏth, to be his wife.

Esau Marries Third Wife

Esau now is impressed that his heathen wives grieve

Isaac and Rebekah. Why not before? Those heathen wives "were a grief of mind unto Isaac and to Rebekah" (Gen. 26:35). But the sending away of Jacob to avoid his having heathen wives greatly impresses Esau, so he gets the daughter of Ishmael for a third wife. She is Mahalath (called Bashemath in Gen. 36:10), a sister of Nebajoth, the firstborn son of Ishmael (Gen. 25:13). Although Jacob is now the son of the promise, yet Esau and Ishmael were of the family and some record is kept of them. Later the Edomites, descended from Esau, will be neighbors to Israel and the Midianites and other descendants from Ishmael will plague Israel.

VERSES 10-15:

10 ¶ And Jacob went out from Beer-sheba, and went toward Haran.

11 And he lighted upon a certain place, and tarried there all night, because the sun was set; and he took of the stones of that place, and put *them for* his pillows, and lay down in that place to sleep.

12 And he dreamed, and behold a ladder set up on the earth, and the top of it reached to heaven: and behold the angels of God ascending and descending on it.

13 And, behold, the LORD stood above it, and said, I *am* the LORD God of Abraham thy father, and the God of Isaac: the land whereon thou liest, to thee will I give it, and to thy seed;

14 And thy seed shall be as the dust of the earth, and thou shalt spread abroad to the west, and to the east, and to the north, and to the south: and in thee and in thy seed shall all the families of the earth be blessed.

15 And, behold, I *am* with thee, and will keep thee in all *places* whither thou goest, and will bring thee again into this land; for I will not leave thee, until I have done *that* which I have spoken to thee of.

God Reveals Himself in a Dream

Before the Bible (already settled forever in Heaven—Ps. 119:89) was written down for men, God spoke often to men in dreams. Here Jacob's dream is of a ladder up to Heaven. Joseph dreamed dreams of his coming great eminence which he told to the anger of his brothers. The butler and baker of Pharaoh dreamed dreams, and in prison Joseph interpreted them. Pharaoh had dreams that foretold seven years of plenty and seven years of famine, and Joseph gave

God's interpretation of that. In Judges 7:13-15 God gave a Midianite a dream and let Gideon hear it in order to be encouraged. God appeared to Solomon in a dream (I Kings 3:5-15). In Daniel 2, Nebuchadnezzar had a dream of the four great world empires, and in Daniel 4 he had a dream of the disaster that would come to him because of his pride.

An angel appeared to Joseph in a dream to tell him that Mary was a virgin. In Matthew 2:12 the Wise Men were warned of God in a dream. In Matthew 2:13 and 19 God instructed Joseph to go to Egypt, then to return to Nazareth. It is possible that the vision of Paul in Acts 16:9 was a dream. It was in the night. The angel that appeared to him also in Acts 27:23,24 may have been in a dream—we do not know.

That means that God can use dreams to warn and teach people. But there is less occasion of that now—first, because of the written Word of God; second, because a Christian may have the leadership of the Holy Spirit. Beware of anyone who tells a dream to teach a doctrine, without clear statements of Scripture.

"The ladder to Heaven" pictured Christ. This is a marvelous dream. A ladder reaching from earth to Heaven no doubt is a reminder of the sweet truth that God will become Man, that Christ will lay aside the garments of glory and be born of a virgin, will live among men and make a way to Heaven.

Jesus is the Door to Heaven. He is the Gate to the sheepfold. He is the link between earth and Heaven!

"Behold the angels of God ascending and descending on it." The work of angels seems to be primarily on earth. "Are they not all ministering spirits, sent forth to minister for them who shall be heirs of salvation?" (Heb. 1:14). So angels ascend to Heaven to report (see Job 1:6; 2:1; II Chron. 18:19-22), and then they return to minister to men, protect people on earth. "The angel of the Lord encampeth round about them that fear him, and delivereth them" (Ps. 34:7; see also Ps. 91:11,12).

Notice the many promises made to Jacob.

1. His seed shall be as the dust of the earth and spread west, east, north and south.

2. In his seed shall all the families of the earth be blessed. That surely is a promise of Christ and perhaps also of the Scriptures and the prophets that will come through Israel (See Rom. 3:1,2).

3. The Lord will protect and keep Jacob in all his ways. The scheming of Laban cannot defeat him. The heathen who may hate him will not destroy him. In famine he will be led down to Egypt where there is plenty.

4. God will bring him again into this land of Cannan, though he will go to Haran and Mesopotamia and be gone more than twenty years.

VERSES 16-22:

16 ¶ And Jacob awaked out of his sleep, and he said, Surely the LORD is in this place; and I knew it not.

17 And he was afraid, and said, How dreadful is this place! this is none other but the house of God, and this is the gate of heaven.

18 And Jacob rose up early in the morning, and took the stone that he had put for his pillows, and set it up for a pillar, and poured oil upon the top of it.

19 And he called the name of that place Beth–el: but the name of that city was called Luz at the first.

20 And Jacob vowed a vow, saying, If God will be with me, and will keep me in this way that I go, and will give me bread to eat, and raiment to put on,

21 So that I come again to my father's house in peace; then shall the LORD be my God:

22 And this stone, which I have set for a pillar, shall be God's house: and of all that thou shalt give me I will surely give the tenth unto thee.

Jacob's Vow: the Place Becomes Bethel, "House of God"

Jacob was afraid and said, "How dreadful is this place!" It is a remarkable thing that always when angels appear to men they must first say, "Fear not." God's angels always mean well to God's children, yet there is a proper, holy awe, a proper humility, a proper fear of God. Conscious of our own weakness and frailty, it is not surprising that men stand abashed when they are conscious of the very presence of God.

Jacob said, "Surely the Lord is in this place; and I knew it not." We may think that God is far off, but He never is. Jeremiah 23:23,24 says, "Am I a God at hand, saith the Lord, and not a God afar off? Can any hide himself in secret places that I shall not see him? saith the Lord. Do not I fill heaven and earth? saith the Lord."

God was with Hagar, the bondwoman cast out in the desert, and her starving boy, and the angel showed her a well and saved them. He was with Joseph, sold by his jealous brothers into Egypt as a slave. He was with David fleeing from King Saul.

In Psalm 139:7-12 we read this wonderful truth:

"Whither shall I go from thy spirit? or whither shall I flee from thy presence? If I ascend up into heaven, thou art there: if I make my bed in hell, behold, thou art there. If I take the wings of the morning, and dwell in the uttermost parts of the sea; Even there shall thy hand lead me, and thy right hand shall hold me. If I say, Surely the darkness shall cover me; even the night shall be light about me. Yea, the darkness hideth not from thee; but the night shineth as the day: the darkness and the light are both alike to thee."

Christians have a right to claim the wonderful promises in Isaiah 41:8-14. The marvelous song, "How Firm a Foundation," was inspired somewhat by this passage and Isaiah 43:1,2:

"But now thus saith the Lord that created thee, O Jacob, and he that formed thee, O Israel, Fear not: for I have redeemed thee, I have called thee by thy name; thou art mine. When thou passest through the waters, I will be with thee; and through the rivers, they shall not overflow thee: when thou walkest through the fire, thou shalt not be burned; neither shall the flame kindle upon thee."

And we remember Galatians 3:29, "And if ye be Christ's, then are ye Abraham's seed, and heirs according to the promise."

So we may boldly claim the promises in Hebrews 13:5,6: "Let your conversation be without covetousness; and be content with such things as ye have: for he hath said, I will never leave thee, nor forsake thee. So that we may boldly say, The Lord is my helper, and I will not fear what man shall do unto me."

Now Luz becomes Bethel, the house of God. Jacob took the stone he had put for his pillow and set it up for a pillar and poured oil on top. Now this is a marker in Jacob's memory, even more than of the place, that this is set apart for the house of God.

Note Jacob's vow, based on God's promises. When he said, "If God will be with me. . . ," I think he did not mean to doubt it but simply meant, "Since God will be with me. . . ."

1. "Then shall the Lord be my God."

2. This stone is to be God's house to him.

3. "Of all that thou shalt give me I will surely give the tenth unto thee."

I doubt if Jacob kept these vows very carefully. We think he did not come back to this house of God until after more than twenty years (chap. 35). He may have regularly offered sacrifices to God and thus fulfilled his vow about the tithe, but we have no record of it. But whether Jacob is faithful or not, God is faithful. He has chosen Jacob and promised him, and Jacob will be the father of a great nation.

GENESIS 29

THEN Jacob went on his journey, and came into the land of the people of the east.

2 And he looked, and behold a well in the field, and, lo, there *were* three flocks of sheep lying by it; for out of that well they watered the flocks: and a great stone was upon the well's mouth.

3 And thither were all the flocks gathered: and they rolled the stone from the well's mouth, and watered the sheep, and put the stone again upon the well's mouth in his place.

4 And Jacob said unto them, My brethren, whence *be* ye? And they said, Of Haran *are* we.

5 And he said unto them, Know ye Laban the son of Nā-hôr? And they said, We know *him*.

6 And he said unto them, *Is* he well? And they said, *He is* well: and,
behold, Rachel his daughter cometh with the sheep.

7 And he said, Lo, *it is* yet high day, neither *is it* time that the cattle should be gathered together: water ye the sheep, and go *and* feed *them*.

8 And they said, We cannot, until all the flocks be gathered together, and *till* they roll the stone from the well's mouth; then we water the sheep.

9 ¶ And while he yet spake with them, Rachel came with her father's sheep: for she kept them.

10 And it came to pass, when Jacob saw Rachel the daughter of Laban his mother's brother, and the sheep of Laban his mother's brother, that Jacob went near, and rolled the stone from the well's mouth, and watered the flock of Laban his mother's brother.

Jacob Comes to Haran

All the way from Beer-sheba, at the southern borders of the land of Canaan, up to Haran, beyond the northern boundaries of Palestine proper, Jacob has come "into the land of the people of the east." The "people of the east" evidently include the descendants of Abraham through Hagar and Keturah. Genesis 25:6 says, "But unto the sons of the concubines, which Abraham had, Abraham gave gifts, and sent them away from Isaac his son, while he yet lived, eastward, unto the east country." Judges 6:3 mentions the Midianites, Amalekites "and the children of the east" against Israel. Verse 33 again mentions them: ". . . the children of the east." Judges 7:12 says, "And the Midianites and the Amalekites and all the children of the east lay along in the valley like grasshoppers for multitude. . . ." Judges 8:10 mentions them again.

The Edomites are descended from Esau and they were south of the Dead Sea, not here. The Amalekites were descended from Lot, and along with the "children of the east" the Midianites were descended from Midian, son of Abraham and Keturah.

It is interesting that Job is called "the greatest of all the men of the east" (Job 1:3). And he may have been living at this time. The Sabeans who raided Job's workers and herds in Job 1:15 were descended from Sheba, son of Jokshan or Yokshan, son of Keturah and Abraham. The Chaldeans who attacked Job's property were of the country from which Abraham left to go to the land of Canaan. We suppose, then, the Sabeans would come a little after Abraham's time.

But the book of Job was written before the Pentateuch because there is no mention of the ceremonial law, of the Sabbath, of Israel, or Moses, or of the Israelite captivity; so the book of Job was evidently the first book written in the Bible. But Job may have lived in the time of Jacob. Scofield says that the land of Uz in which Job lived was "a region at the south of Edom, and west of the Arabian desert, extending to Chaldea." But Jacob was far north, at Haran. Jacob inquired of Laban, "son of Nahor," that is, descendant of Nahor. They did not know Nahor but they knew Laban.

Note the thrift of this man Jacob. What a waste to have flocks of sheep lying about in thirst, waiting for the stone to be moved from the well so they could drink. The purposeful energy of this man and his thrift will make him rich!

Laban must have been an old man. He was a young man, evidently the nominal head of the family, when Rebekah was sent to be a bride to Isaac in chapter 24. After that, Rebekah had been barren twenty years, then she bore Jacob and Esau: now Esau is thrice married and Jacob is mature. Ussher's chronology indicates ninety-seven years may have gone by. At any rate, Laban now has a family with two grown daughters. Rachel, the younger and more beautiful, tends the flocks of sheep as they graze over the countryside.

One who sees vigorous Jacob insisting that the sheep be watered at once so they can get back to grazing, and arbitrarily rolling away the stone from the well, not waiting for others, indicates how he will be greatly prospered, and Laban will want him to manage his flocks and herds.

VERSES 11-14:

11 And Jacob kissed Rachel, and lifted up his voice, and wept.

12 And Jacob told Rachel that he *was* her father's brother, and that he *was* Rebekah's son: and she ran and told her father.

13 And it came to pass, when Laban heard the tidings of Jacob his sister's son, that he ran to meet him, and embraced him, and kissed him, and brought him to his house. And he told Laban all these things.

14 And Laban said to him, Surely thou *art* my bone and my flesh. And he abode with him the space of a month.

Jacob Meets Rachel

One can sense the loneliness in Jacob, compelled to leave mother and father because of the fear of an angry brother. How glad he was to greet kinspeople and dear ones! He kissed Rachel and "lifted up his voice and wept." Here was intense emotion and, we think, the birth of love. Rachel ran at once to tell her father Laban. Laban, who perhaps had not seen his sister since she went away long years before and had never seen his nephews, gladly welcomed Jacob. He "ran to meet him, and embraced him, and kissed him." Without any pay, Jacob steadfastly sets out to work for Laban.

VERSES 15-30:

15 ¶ And Laban said unto Jacob, Because thou *art* my brother, shouldest thou therefore serve me for nought? tell me, what *shall* thy wages *be?*

16 And Laban had two daughters:

the name of the elder *was* Leah, and the name of the younger *was* Rachel.

17 Leah *was* tender eyed; but Rachel was beautiful and well favoured.

18 And Jacob loved Rachel; and said, I will serve thee seven years for Rachel thy younger daughter.

19 And Laban said, *It is* better that I give her to thee, than that I should give her to another man: abide with me.

20 And Jacob served seven years for Rachel; and they seemed unto him *but* a few days, for the love he had to her.

21 ¶ And Jacob said unto Laban, Give *me* my wife, for my days are fulfilled, that I may go in unto her.

22 And Laban gathered together all the men of the place, and made a feast.

23 And it came to pass in the evening, that he took Leah his daughter, and brought her to him; and he went in unto her.

24 And Laban gave unto his daughter Leah Zilpah his maid *for* an handmaid.

25 And it came to pass, that in the morning, behold, it *was* Leah: and he said to Laban, What *is* this thou hast done unto me? did not I serve with thee for Rachel? wherefore then hast thou beguiled me?

26 And Laban said, It must not be so done in our country, to give the younger before the firstborn.

27 Fulfil her week, and we will give thee this also for the service which thou shalt serve with me yet seven other years.

28 And Jacob did so, and fulfilled her week: and he gave him Rachel his daughter to wife also.

29 And Laban gave to Rachel his daughter Bilhah his handmaid to be her maid.

30 And he went in also unto Rachel, and he loved also Rachel more than Leah, and served with him yet seven other years.

Deceiver Himself Deceived

As Jacob deceived his father Isaac, now Laban deceives him. Seven long years he will labor for Rachel, the beautiful girl he loves. Then on the wedding night he meets his bride in the darkened tent and does not know until the next day that it is Leah in his arms!

Laban is a schemer. We are not surprised to find Jacob later reporting to his wives, "Your father hath deceived me, and changed my wages ten times" (Gen. 31:7).

But now, what about the beloved Rachel? Scheming Laban demands seven more years of labor for this bride. So after being married a week to Leah, he is given Rachel also but he must stay the long years to pay for her, and did.

The love story of Jacob and Rachel is one of the sweetest in the Bible. It seemed to have been love at first sight. It never wavered. The long years of labor for her seemed not too much to pay for such a beautiful one and so greatly loved. Later, Jacob's passionate love for Joseph and for

Benjamin, the two sons of this wife Rachel, indicate that Jacob's love for Rachel never wavered.

---

31 ¶ And when the LORD saw that Leah *was* hated, he opened her womb: but Rachel *was* barren.

32 And Leah conceived, and bare a son, and she called his name Reuben: for she said, Surely the LORD hath looked upon my affliction; now therefore my husband will love me.

33 And she conceived again, and bare a son; and said, Because the LORD hath heard that I *was* hated, he hath therefore given me this *son* also: and she called his name Simeon.

34 And she conceived again, and bare a son; and said, Now this time will my husband be joined unto me, because I have born him three sons: therefore was his name called Levi.

35 And she conceived again, and bare a son: and she said, Now will I praise the LORD: therefore she called his name Judah; and left bearing.

Leah, Hated, Was Blessed of God

We have genuine sympathy for Jacob, married to a woman he did not at first love and did not want. He loved Rachel more. However, a good man is commanded to love his wife and, no doubt, the faithfulness of Leah won the sincere respect and eventually the love, if not the favored place, of Jacob.

He wanted to be buried in the Cave of Machpelah, saying, "There they buried Abraham and Sarah his wife; there they buried Isaac and Rebekah his wife; and there I buried Leah" (Gen. 49:31). Instead of being buried by Rachel, Jacob wanted to be buried with Abraham and Isaac and his wife Leah.

A Loving God Looked on Leah's Lonely Heart

Leah was not to blame that she was "tender-eyed" and not as beautiful nor as attractive as Rachel. We believe she was not much to blame in the fact that she was wed to Jacob without his consent. She would do what her father said. Naturally she hoped to have a home, with a husband and children.

And although she did not have the place she coveted as the first love of Jacob, God remembered her and He paid her back. When the Lord saw that Leah was hated, He gave her children for the time Rachel was barren! It is wonderful how God evens up things for those who trust Him.

One multimillionaire had such ill health that he lived mainly on crackers and milk. One young man I knew was very poor and worked very, very hard. He had a wife who was beautiful, young, healthy, loving and devoted to her husband. And he had two beautiful children. All were very happy in poverty. One who is first in one matter may be second in another. So Rachel had first place in Jacob's heart and Leah had the children she wanted. It is interesting that one of Leah's sons was Judah through whom will come the Saviour, the promised blessing through Abraham's seed!

And let us remember that those about us who seem prosperous may have secret pain and sorrow. Those who seem to have money and honor may have a lonely, hungry heart. Above all, let us remember that a loving God looks down and sees the need of the heart, as He did with Leah and Hagar.

GENESIS 30

AND when Rachel saw that she bare Jacob no children, Rachel envied her sister; and said unto Jacob, Give me children, or else I die.

2 And Jacob's anger was kindled against Rachel: and he said, *Am* I in God's stead, who hath withheld from thee the fruit of the womb?

3 And she said, Behold my maid Bilhah, go in unto her; and she shall bear upon my knees, that I may also have children by her.

4 And she gave him Bilhah her handmaid to wife: and Jacob went in unto her.

5 And Bilhah conceived, and bare Jacob a son.

6 And Rachel said, God hath judged me, and hath also heard my voice, and hath given me a son: therefore called she his name Dan.

7 And Bilhah Rachel's maid conceived again, and bare Jacob a second son.

8 And Rachel said, With great wrestlings have I wrestled with my sister, and I have prevailed: and she called his name Năph-ta-li.

9 When Leah saw that she had left bearing, she took Zilpah her maid, and gave her Jacob to wife.

God Give Us Children!

We can see that the dearest thing to the heart of a godly wife is children. Rachel felt she would die if she could not have children. She had the first place in the heart of her husband, but that was not enough. Barren Hannah was the most beloved wife of Elkanah who thought his love should be better to her than ten sons, but she was in bitterness of soul and wept sore (I Sam. 1:8,10).

The eagerness and heart hunger of the great woman of Shunem for the son she had never had is revealed in II Kings 4:16, "And he said, About this season, according to the time of life, thou shalt embrace a son. And she said, Nay, my lord, thou man of God, do not lie unto thine handmaid."

God gave the child, and she could hardly believe that the blessing was hers! And when he died, she came to Elisha brokenhearted. "Then she said, Did I desire a son of my lord? did I not say, Do not deceive me?" What joy when the boy was restored! Godly Bible women longed for children.

Now when godly Rachel found herself barren for years, and Leah, less loved, had four, she thought she must some way mend this disgrace! She would give her slave girl Bilhah as a concubine and the child would really belong to her and she could count it hers! How glad she was when Bilhah bore Jacob a child! "Rachel said, God hath judged me, and hath also heard my voice, and hath given me a son: therefore called she his name Dan." Oh, how she wrestled in prayer; and now she had a second son by Bilhah.

Leah for a season was barren; so she took her maid Zilpah and gave her to Jacob to wife. Oh, they must have sons in some way!

We remember that Sarah had given her maid Hagar to Abraham to bear her a child. That was not needed then. Abraham and Sarah were the models; so Isaac had lied about his wife saying she was his sister, following the pattern of Abraham. Now Jacob's two wives pattern after Sarah and offer their maids to bear children for Jacob and for them! Oh, traditions of a family go down through the long years! Asa compromised by joining with Ben-hadad, then his son Jehoshaphat compromised by joining with wicked Ahab (II Chron. 16:7-9; 18:1).

God had not then forbidden that a man should have more than one wife. Some provision was made for that in the Mosaic law. But that is not the ideal way. And just as there was jealousy and strife between Sarah and Hagar, so now there is jealousy and strife between Rachel and Leah.

By giving such detail in these passages, surely God intends to show that He wants big families. Married couples should desire children. Psalm 127:3-5 says, "Lo, children are an heritage of the Lord: and the fruit of the womb is his reward. As arrows are in the hand of a mighty man; so are children of the youth. Happy is the man that hath his quiver full of them: they shall not be ashamed, but they shall speak with the enemies in the gate."

God gives children. Not to want them, not to prize them, not to want many of them, is a dishonor to God and disregarding His holy heritage and reward. Happy or fortunate is the man who has many children, is the plain meaning of verse 5.

Again in Psalm 128 we are told that the man who fears the Lord and walks in His way will be especially blessed with a lovely, big family:

"Blessed is every one that feareth the Lord; that walketh in his ways. For thou shalt eat the labour of thine hands: happy shalt thou be, and it shall be well with thee. Thy wife shall be as a fruitful vine by the sides of thine house: thy children like olive plants round about thy table. Behold, that thus shall the man be blessed that feareth the Lord."—Vss. 1-4.

When Jephthah's daughter was to be offered as a burnt offering in gratitude to God for the victory He gave Israel, she agreed to that but with this condition: Give her two months to mourn over her virginity and then she could die (Judg. 11:37,38). Onan married his dead brother's wife Tamar but because he refused to have children, God killed him (Gen. 38:9,10).

Let us consider some conclusions on this matter.

1. People who marry and do not want children do not have a scriptural attitude toward marriage and home and are unworthy. They ought not marry. Like a whoremonger and harlot, they want the pleasures and comforts of marriage without the responsibility and the holy fruit which God plans to give for marriage.

2. Birth control, used to prevent having any children, is sinful and wicked. It may be that Christians might properly take care to space the coming of children, but to refuse to take what God wants to give would be wicked rebellion against God.

3. Abortion, the murder of the unborn baby, means a deliberate refusal of what God has given. It is not only murder; it is heart rebellion against God and the privileges and God-ordained duty of parents.

VERSES 10-21:

10 And Zilpah Leah's maid bare Jacob a son.

11 And Leah said, A troop cometh: and she called his name Gad.

12 And Zilpah Leah's maid bare Jacob a second son.

13 And Leah said, Happy am I, for the daughters will call me blessed: and she called his name Asher.

14 ¶ And Reuben went in the days of wheat harvest, and found mandrakes in the field, and brought them unto his mother Leah. Then Rachel said to Leah, Give me, I pray thee, of thy son's mandrakes.

15 And she said unto her, *Is it* a small matter that thou hast taken my husband? and wouldest thou take away my son's mandrakes also? And Rachel said, Therefore he shall lie with thee to night for thy son's mandrakes.

16 And Jacob came out of the field in the evening, and Leah went out to meet him, and said, Thou must come in unto me; for surely I have hired thee with my son's mandrakes. And he lay with her that night.

17 And God hearkened unto Leah, and she conceived, and bare Jacob the fifth son.

18 And Leah said, God hath given me my hire, because I have given my maiden to my husband: and she called his name Ĭs-̕să-̲chär.

19 And Leah conceived again, and bare Jacob the sixth son.

20 And Leah said, God hath endued me *with* a good dowry; now will my husband dwell with me, because I have born him six sons: and she called his name Zĕ-bū-̕lŭn.

21 And afterwards she bare a daughter, and called her name Dinah.

Leah Has Sixth Son and a Daughter

The twelve sons of Jacob came thus: Leah bore him four sons, then Bilhah, Rachel's maid, bore him two. Then Zilpah, Leah's maid, bore him two sons. Then God gave Leah two more sons. And at last God gave Rachel two sons, Joseph and Benjamin.

Leah's boy Reuben found mandrakes in the field, sometimes called "love apples." There was a tradition in the east that they increased fertility. They probably did not but both Rachel and Leah desired them and at least God allowed Leah to conceive again. She had the fifth, then the sixth son.

Verse 18 shows that Leah felt she had made a real sacrifice in giving her slave girl to her husband; now she felt God had paid her back. Verse 20 shows that she felt assured that she had a permanent place in the affections and attention of her husband, now that she had borne him six sons. After the sixth son she had a daughter, Dinah.

VERSES 22-24:

22 ¶ And God remembered Rachel, and God hearkened to her, and opened her womb.

23 And she conceived, and bare a son; and said, God hath taken away my reproach:

24 And she called his name Joseph; and said, The LORD shall add to me another son.

Rachel at Last Has a Son, Joseph

"And God remembered Rachel." Oh, how many times she must have felt that God had forgotten her! But we may be sure that all the heartbroken pleas of this woman who wanted children were kept safely before God and never forgotten. The tears of her lonely heart God put in His bottle. So God remembered her. How often this comes up in the Bible:

"And God remembered Noah" (Gen. 8:1).

"God remembered Abraham" (Gen. 19:29).

"And God remembered Rachel" (Gen. 30:22).

Of Hannah it is said, "And the Lord remembered her" (I Sam. 1:19).

Oh, yes, and God remembers His covenant, His mercy, His promises. He remembers that we are dust. But there is the sweet promise about us that "their sins and iniquities will I remember no more," when they are confessed and put under the blood and all forgiven.

God heard the groaning of the children of Israel in slavery in Egypt and "God remembered his covenant."

It is easy to think that God has forgotten us, has forgotten His promises, has forgotten our sorrows, our needs. But He never does.

So God remembered Rachel and gave her the blessed child Joseph. Now she had faith and she knew "the Lord shall add to me another son." The reproach on Rachel is taken away. She is a mother, barren no longer!

VERSES 25-30:

25 ¶ And it came to pass, when Rachel had born Joseph, that Jacob said unto Laban, Send me away, that I may go unto mine own place, and to my country.

26 Give *me* my wives and my children, for whom I have served thee, and let me go: for thou knowest my service which I have done thee.

27 And Laban said unto him, I pray thee, if I have found favour in thine eyes, *tarry: for* I have learned by experience that the LORD hath blessed me for thy sake.

28 And he said, Appoint me thy wages, and I will give *it.*

29 And he said unto him, Thou knowest how I have served thee, and how thy cattle was with me.

30 For *it was* little which thou hadst before I *came,* and it is *now* increased unto a multitude; and the LORD hath blessed thee since my coming: and now when shall I provide for mine own house also?

Jacob Hungers to See Father and Mother in Blessed Land

Long years Jacob has served. He has had, we suppose, only a meager living, with ordinary provisions for his wives and children. Now he wants to go away. He must accumulate for himself and his family.

But Laban felt he must not lose Jacob! Just as Joseph down in Egypt "was a prosperous man"; just as Potiphar, his owner, found that all of his affairs prospered in Joseph's hand (Gen. 39:2-5); just as the jailer found about Joseph, "And the keeper of the prison committed to Joseph's hand all the prisoners that were in the prison; and whatsoever they did there, he was the doer of it. The keeper of the prison looked not to any thing that was under his hand; because the Lord was with him, and that which he did, the Lord made it to prosper" (Gen. 39:22,23)—just so it was with Jacob working under Laban. God was with him. Whatever he put his hand to prospered. Hard work, sincere interest, loyalty and faithfulness bring such results everywhere. Under compulsion, Laban would pay Jacob better wages. What does he ask?

VERSES 31-43:

31 And he said, What shall I give thee? And Jacob said, Thou shalt not give me any thing: if thou wilt do this thing for me, I will again feed *and* keep thy flock.

32 I will pass through all thy flock to day, removing from thence all the speckled and spotted cattle, and all the brown cattle among the sheep, and the spotted and speckled among the goats: and *of such* shall be my hire.

33 So shall my righteousness answer for me in time to come, when it shall come for my hire before thy face: every one that *is* not speckled and spotted among the goats, and brown among the sheep, that shall be counted stolen with me.

34 And Laban said, Behold, I would it might be according to thy word.

35 And he removed that day the he goats that were ringstraked and spotted, and all the she goats that were speckled and spotted, *and* every one that had *some* white in it, and all the brown among the sheep, and gave *them* into the hand of his sons.

36 And he set three days' journey betwixt himself and Jacob: and Jacob fed the rest of Laban's flocks.

37 ¶ And Jacob took him rods of green poplar, and of the hazel and chesnut tree; and pilled white strakes in them, and made the white appear which *was* in the rods.

38 And he set the rods which he had pilled before the flocks in the gutters in the watering troughs when the flocks came to drink, that they should conceive when they came to drink.

39 And the flocks conceived before the rods, and brought forth cattle ringstraked, speckled, and spotted.

40 And Jacob did separate the lambs, and set the faces of the flocks toward the ringstraked, and all the brown in the flock of Laban; and he put his own flocks by themselves, and put them not unto Laban's cattle.

41 And it came to pass, whensoever the stronger cattle did conceive, that Jacob laid the rods before the eyes of the cattle in the gutters, that they might conceive among the rods.

42 But when the cattle were feeble, he put *them* not in: so the feebler were Laban's, and the stronger Jacob's.

43 And the man increased exceedingly, and had much cattle, and maidservants, and menservants, and camels, and asses.

God Prospers Jacob's Flocks

I think the only way to approach this passage is to understand that Jacob depended on God. He selected a device so there would be no room for argument. He would take the brown among the sheep and the spotted and speckled among the goats, and that would be his hire!

Do you think that the white pealed rods which appeared in stripes had anything to do with the conception of animals "ringstraked, speckled, and spotted"? No, this was evidently a token between Jacob and God. It was God who did it, not the pealed rods!

We baptize converts not to save them but to witness to salvation. Men lay hands on a preacher to ordain him, but the hands themselves do not make a preacher. It is the Holy Spirit power for which we pray. Elders of the church are invited to anoint with oil and pray over the sick, but the olive oil on the forehead does not make the sick man well. It is a symbol of the Holy Spirit of God living within who can heal and often does.

So Jacob depended on God, and God continued to bless him. Now after long years of serving Laban unselfishly, at last we find that Jacob "increased exceedingly, and had much cattle, and maidservants, and menservants, and camels, and asses."

GENESIS 31

A^ND he heard the words of La-ban's sons, saying, Jacob hath taken away all that *was* our father's; and of *that* which *was* our father's hath he gotten all this glory.

2 And Jacob beheld the countenance of Laban, and, behold, it *was* not toward him as before.

3 And the LORD said unto Jacob, Return unto the land of thy fathers, and to thy kindred; and I will be with thee.

4 And Jacob sent and called Rachel and Leah to the field unto his flock,

5 And said unto them, I see your father's countenance, that it *is* not toward me as before; but the God of my father hath been with me.

6 And ye know that with all my power I have served your father.

7 And your father hath deceived me, and changed my wages ten times; but God suffered him not to hurt me.

8 If he said thus, The speckled shall be thy wages; then all the cattle bare speckled: and if he said thus, The ringstraked shall be thy hire; then bare all the cattle ringstraked.

9 Thus God hath taken away the cattle of your father, and given *them* to me.

10 And it came to pass at the time that the cattle conceived, that I lifted up mine eyes, and saw in a dream, and, behold, the rams which leaped upon the cattle *were* ringstraked, speckled, and grisled.

11 And the angel of God spake unto me in a dream, *saying*, Jacob: And I said, Here *am* I.

12 And he said, Lift up now thine eyes, and see, all the rams which leap upon the cattle *are* ringstraked, speckled, and grisled: for I have seen all that Laban doeth unto thee.

13 I *am* the God of Beth–el, where thou anointedst the pillar, *and* where thou vowedst a vow unto me: now arise, get thee out from this land, and return unto the land of thy kindred.

Laban's Sons Displeased With Jacob's Prosperity

The sons have not been mentioned before. Evidently the great work of caring for Laban's flocks and herds has fallen on Jacob, not on Laban's sons. Jacob is a hired man. When Jacob had first come, Rachel had been caring for the sheep. Now we suppose for these twenty years Jacob has taken the main burden of caring for all Laban's property.

But the sons and even Laban are jealous and envious of Jacob's prosperity. Laban had deceived Jacob "and changed my wages ten times," Jacob said, but God had not suffered him to lose. Whatever deal Laban agreed to from time to time to profit from Jacob's labor and to keep Jacob in poverty was overcome by the special blessing of God.

But the time has come for Jacob to go back to the land of Canaan, back to the Promised Land. The Lord has said to him, "Return unto the land of thy fathers, and to thy kindred." Until this time he had not had that instruction and that assurance that he would be safe to go back and face Esau.

The "Have Nots" Blame the "Haves"

The envy of Laban and his sons is part of the curse on the human race. The man who works harder and earns more is envied by the lazy, the improvident, the ignorant who do not prosper as well. The man who runs for office, in order to get the votes of the crowd, suggests more taxes on the rich and on the big corporations! The poor man, who pays only 20% on income tax, is envious of the man who has to pay 80% or 90% of his total income in taxes to help support the poor man. The poor man wants him taxed more and restrained more! When a man by ceaseless toil and planning and saving and thrift has built a great business and while he has made riches for himself has given work for thousands more, he is envied and hated for his prosperity!

The successful man will have enemies simply because he is successful. And the improvident, lazy and jealous people will think the rich man got rich by oppressing them or by some crookedness! So Laban's sons hate Jacob and Laban is displeased with him.

They do not consider the loyalty that Jacob has shown (vs. 6) and the serving as Jacob said, "with all my power," the meticulous care that he mentions in verse 40. His honest accounting, his honest taking of responsibility (vs. 39) is ignored. Laban had left all the work to Jacob and now frets that God has blessed him.

In America where about half the population is either employed by the government (city, county, state or national) or are on relief or getting food stamps or farm subsidies or free school lunches or disaster relief—that nation will be a nation of complainers at the success of those who, by free enterprise and hard work, have prospered greatly. It is sad for the nation, and prophesies disaster in the future, when most people want to live partly on the labors and taxes of other men.

Laban does not look well compared to Jacob. He cheated Jacob and lied, giving Leah to Jacob by deceit instead of Rachel for whom he had bargained. Seven years' labor for the wife he didn't want, then seven years more for Rachel whom he loved! He had changed Jacob's wages ten times, always seeking to get some advantage of the man who did the work there. He claimed the right to control his daughters, married thirteen years, and the grandchildren, when they are all bought and paid for. He acted as though he believed God when Eliezer had come many years ago to seek Rebekah as a wife for Isaac; but now he has idols. He is not a godly man.

Now God has commanded Jacob, "Return unto the land of thy fathers, and to thy kindred; and I will be with thee." Ah, the God who met him at Bethel twenty years before still loves him, still promises him the blessings He had promised before to Abraham and Isaac. Jacob was conscious that all these years God had protected him from the scheming Laban and had provided wonderfully for him.

Jacob's Symbol: That God Would Give Him the Increase

When Jacob had taken the bark from rods and left stripes before the sheep and goats when they came to breed, did that mean that the rods themselves influenced the kind of offspring? Of course not, and Jacob did not think so. Those "pilled" rods were simply a symbol between Jacob and God. He knew in a dream from God that God would fulfill what was to him a token and increase the flocks of the speckled and spotted and grizzled cattle and sheep.

When the nation Israel marched six days around the city of Jericho, that did not make the walls of Jericho fall. That was simply a token as they obeyed God that He would tear the walls down, and He did on the seventh day.

When Naaman the Syrian dipped in the waters of Jordan seven times, it was not the waters of Jordan nor the dipping that cleansed Naaman's leprosy. It was the hand of God. The dipping was simply a required act of faith.

So here Jacob used those rods before the sheep as a symbol between him and God.

One little grandson of mine was born prematurely and for weeks the tiny body could not retain food. He weighed only four pounds. I got in my car and drove around and around the block where he lay in the hospital and called upon God until I had assurance He would raise the child up. That day they found a formula that would suit the baby's stomach, he gained an ounce and mended and was soon growing well and strong. It was not the driving around the hospital that healed the lad. That was only a gesture of faith on my part.

So it was, we are sure, with Jacob and the "pilled" rods.

When D. L. Moody, inspired by the promise to Joshua in Joshua 1:3, "Every place that the sole of your foot shall tread upon, that have I given unto you," knelt down on a certain lot in Chicago and claimed it for the first great building of Moody Bible Institute, his prayer was answered. Kneeling on that particular lot was simply a token between Moody and God.

Now the God of Bethel has spoken to Jacob. God reminds him of that time twenty years before when he anointed the pillar and said, "This shall be to me the house of God." There Jacob made vows unto God. God commanded Jacob, "Now arise, get thee out from this land, and return unto the land of thy kindred." Oh, twenty long years out of the land of promise, away from the hatred of his brother Esau, out of touch with father and mother and the Promised Land! But God has not forgotten Jacob! The promise still holds. He must go back home.

VERSES 14-18:

14 And Rachel and Leah answered and said unto him, *Is there* yet any portion or inheritance for us in our father's house?

15 Are we not counted of him strangers? for he hath sold us, and hath quite devoured also our money.

16 For all the riches which God hath taken from our father, that *is* our's, and our children's: now then, whatsoever God hath said unto thee, do.

17 ¶ Then Jacob rose up, and set his sons and his wives upon camels;

18 And he carried away all his cattle, and all his goods which he had gotten, the cattle of his getting, which he had gotten in Pā-dăn-aram, for to go to Isaac his father in the land of Cā-nă-ăn.

Jacob Leaves Padan-aram

The two wives knew well about the unfairness of their father, his deceit, his greedy heart, his continually trying to get the best of Jacob and make more by Jacob's loss. But God had cared for them. Now these wives say, "For all the riches which God hath taken from our father, that is our's, and our children's: now then, whatsoever God hath said unto thee, do." Jacob put wives and children on camels. He had many flocks and herds. God had prospered him. With all these, he leaves for the land of Canaan where God had promised him great blessings and where his heart had been for years.

VERSES 19-29:

19 And Laban went to shear his heep: and Rachel had stolen the mages that *were* her father's.

20 And Jacob stole away unawares o Laban the Syrian, in that he told im not that he fled.

21 So he fled with all that he had; nd he rose up, and passed over the iver, and set his face *toward* the nount Gil-ĕ-ăd.

22 And it was told Laban on the hird day that Jacob was fled.

23 And he took his brethren with im, and pursued after him seven ays' journey; and they overtook him in the mount Gil-ĕ-ăd.

24 And God came to Laban the Syrian in a dream by night, and said unto him, Take heed that thou speak not to Jacob either good or bad.

25 ¶ Then Laban overtook Jacob. Now Jacob had pitched his tent in the mount: and Laban with his brethren pitched in the mount of Gil-ĕ-ăd.

26 And Laban said to Jacob, What hast thou done, that thou hast stolen away unawares to me, and carried away my daughters, as captives *taken* with the sword?

27 Wherefore didst thou flee away secretly, and steal away from me; and didst not tell me, that I might have sent thee away with mirth, and with songs, with tabret, and with harp?

28 And hast not suffered me to kiss my sons and my daughters? thou hast now done foolishly in *so* doing.

29 It is in the power of my hand to do you hurt: but the God of your father spake unto me yesternight, saying, Take thou heed that thou speak not to Jacob either good or bad.

Laban Pursues Jacob

Laban was away from his tents to shear the sheep, and during that time Rachel had stolen her father's images. Will you note that in all the Scriptures they are simply called images (vss. 19,34), but Laban called them "my gods" (vs. 30). Perhaps they were gold or ceramic figurines. Rachel may have coveted them because they were beautiful; perhaps she had played with them as a child. At any rate, Laban regarded them as gods.

Later, in Genesis 35:2, Jacob commanded his family, "Put away the strange gods that are among you." Verse 4 says, "And they gave unto Jacob all the strange gods which were in their hand, and all their earrings. . . ." Whether Rachel worshiped these images as gods, we do not know, but they were a snare and were wrong and God had them put away before they came to worship Him at Bethel. Perhaps the earrings were a sign of worldliness. At any rate, some things are not necessarily sin but they are "weights" according to Hebrews 12:1. And we remember that even the brazen serpent that Moses made in the wilderness to represent Christ on the cross and the way of salvation had become an idol and people burned incense to it; so King Hezekiah had it destroyed (II Kings 18:4). But even covetousness is idolatry. How careful Christians ought to be to "flee idolatry," that is, any overweening love or deference to things that might come between us and God.

Jacob set his face toward Mount Gilead. That is in the land of Canaan but east of the Jordan River. Ah, that will be in his own country again!

But Laban gathered his "brethren," evidently kinsmen,

probably not blood brothers, and they chased hard after Jacob and in seven days they caught him. Jacob would have had to travel slowly with the flocks and herds, and speedy camels could cover in four days the ground they had covered in seven. And at Mount Gilead they caught up with him and overtook him.

What was Laban's intention? It may well have been to kill Jacob, or he may have intended to take back his daughters and the grandchildren with him and seize the flocks and herds. Jacob had feared that, as verse 31 tells us.

But God had met Laban in a dream and warned him strictly he is to leave Jacob alone: "Take heed that thou speak not to Jacob either good or bad."

Note the arrogance of Laban. A man goes away quietly with his own wives and children. Laban is angry they did not report and ask permission! He would make Jacob feel like a criminal for going away with his own family! It is doubtful that with Laban and his sons and others feeling as they did about Jacob that he would really have sent them "with songs, with tabret, and with harp," as he says. But now that he has come so far, he must say goodby and excuse himself the best he can.

He was warned in a dream (vs. 24), as Pilate's wife had been warned in a dream about the Lord Jesus. The truth is that God's angels are about the children of God to protect and care for them. An angel brought Peter and John out of the prison when they were arrested and told them to speak boldly in Jerusalem (Acts 5:17-20).

VERSES 30-35:

30 And now, *though* thou wouldest needs be gone, because thou sore longedst after thy father's house, *yet* wherefore hast thou stolen my gods? 31 And Jacob answered and said to Laban, Because I was afraid: for I said, Peradventure thou wouldest take by force thy daughters from me.

32 With whomsoever thou findest thy gods, let him not live: before our brethren discern thou what *is* thine with me, and take *it* to thee. For Jacob knew not that Rachel had

stolen them.

33 And Laban went into Jacob's tent, and into Leah's tent, and into the two maidservants' tents; but he found *them* not. Then went he out of Leah's tent, and entered into Rachel's tent.

34 Now Rachel had taken the images, and put them in the camel's furniture, and sat upon them. And Laban searched all the tent, but found *them* not.

35 And she said to her father, Let it not displease my lord that I cannot rise up before thee; for the custom of women *is* upon me. And he searched, but found not the images.

Laban's Idols Hidden

Not knowing that Rachel had stolen her father's idols, Jacob openly demanded a search. They are to go through all his tents and baggage and find anything they can. His conscience is clear. Rachel, who for some reason wanted those images, hid them in the camel furniture and sat upon it and excused herself, so they were not found. All the while Jacob's anger mounted all the more at the high-handed way of Laban.

VERSES 36-43:

36 ¶ And Jacob was wroth, and chode with Laban: and Jacob answered and said to Laban, What *is* my trespass? what *is* my sin, that thou hast so hotly pursued after me?

37 Whereas thou hast searched all my stuff, what hast thou found of all thy household stuff? set *it* here before my brethren and thy brethren, that they may judge betwixt us both.

38 This twenty years *have* I *been* with thee; thy ewes and thy she goats have not cast their young, and the rams of thy flock have I not eaten.

39 That which was torn *of beasts* I brought not unto thee; I bare the loss of it; of my hand didst thou require it, *whether* stolen by day, or stolen by night.

40 *Thus* I was; in the day the drought consumed me, and the frost by night; and my sleep departed from mine eyes.

41 Thus have I been twenty years in thy house; I served thee fourteen years for thy two daughters, and six years for thy cattle: and thou hast changed my wages ten times.

42 Except the God of my father, the God of Abraham, and the fear of Isaac, had been with me, surely thou hadst sent me away now empty. God hath seen mine affliction and the labour of my hands, and rebuked *thee* yesternight.

43 ¶ And Laban answered and said unto Jacob, *These* daughters *are* my daughters, and *these* children *are* my children, and *these* cattle *are* my cattle, and all that thou seest *is* mine: and what can I do this day unto these my daughters, or unto their children which they have born?

Jacob's Strong Defense

For twenty years Jacob had put up with the deceit, the cheating methods of Laban. Now God has released him from his duty with Laban; he is to go back to his land. The angel of God has openly spoken in his defense. He has afresh the promise of God to care for him. So he speaks boldly. He reminds Laban that he served fourteen years for two daughters, one of whom he did not want He served six years for cattle, and Laban had changed his wages ten times, trying to cheat and keep Jacob from acquiring property. Jacob is quite conscious that the God of his father and the God of Abraham has been with him all the time to protect him. Yes and "the fear of Isaac"—without that "surely thou hadst sent me away now empty."

Isaac was a great man, great enough that King Abimelech wanted a treaty with him that there be no strife. His fame had gone far, and ever since Laban had heard of Isaac's riches and property some sixty or seventy years before, he had great regard for that strong and mighty man. We did not have occasion to see it, but he may have thought and it may have been true that Isaac would have been as energetic in protecting Jacob as Abraham had been to rescue Lot.

Note the arrogance of Laban: "These daughters are my daughters, and these children are my children, and these cattle are my cattle, and all that thou seest is mine." That was not true. All of these are bought and paid for with labor and service beyond computation. Laban only tries to excuse himself for wanting all Jacob had and wanting to control them.

The truth is, the allegiance of a daughter to her father is cancelled by her subjection to her husband. A married daughter or a son is still commanded to "honour thy father and thy mother." And it is still required, "But if any widow have children or nephews, let them learn first to shew piety at home, and to requite their parents: for that is good and acceptable before God" (I Tim. 5:4). Married men and women are still "to requite their parents," and one is to "provide. . .for those of his own house" (I Tim. 5:8). But the wife's desire is to be to her own husband and he shall rule over her (Gen. 3:16). She is to submit herself to her husband "as unto the Lord" (Eph. 5:22). Laban should have, of course, the respect of these daughters, but he was to have no control over them.

VERSES 44-55:

44 Now therefore come thou, let us make a covenant, I and thou; and let it be for a witness between me and thee.

45 And Jacob took a stone, and set it up *for* a pillar.

46 And Jacob said unto his brethren, Gather stones; and they took stones, and made an heap: and they did eat there upon the heap.

47 And Laban called it Jĕ́-gär-sā-hă-dŭ́-thă: but Jacob called it Gā́-lĕ̄ed.

48 And Laban said, This heap *is* a witness between me and thee this day. Therefore was the name of it called Gā́-lĕ̄ed;

49 And Mizpah; for he said, The LORD watch between me and thee, when we are absent one from another.

50 If thou shalt afflict my daughters, or if thou shalt take *other* wives beside my daughters, no man *is* with us; see, God *is* witness betwixt me and thee.

51 And Laban said to Jacob, Behold this heap, and behold *this* pillar which I have cast betwixt me and thee;

52 This heap *be* witness, and *this* pillar *be* witness, that I will not pass over this heap to thee, and that thou shalt not pass over this heap and this pillar unto me, for harm.

53 The God of Abraham, and the God of Nā́-hôr, the God of their father, judge betwixt us. And Jacob sware by the fear of his father Isaac.

54 Then Jacob offered sacrifice upon the mount, and called his brethren to eat bread: and they did eat bread, and tarried all night in the mount.

55 And early in the morning Laban rose up, and kissed his sons and his daughters, and blessed them: and Laban departed, and returned unto his place.

Covenant of Peace by Jacob and Laban

Now Laban wants a treaty, a covenant with Jacob. He recognizes that God is with Jacob and it may well be that Jacob is now the stronger of the two. At any rate, he is greatly blessed of God.

Abraham made a treaty with Abimelech, then Isaac made a treaty with Abimelech, king of the Philistines. Heathen men recognized these men as godly men who would keep a covenant, and it was not wise to oppose them.

Laban recognizes the same thing about Jacob. As Potiphar in Egypt, then the jailer, then Pharaoh recognized that God was with Joseph, and as Nebuchadnezzar saw beyond a doubt that God was with Daniel, so here Laban recognizes the strength and the certain future blessings of Jacob. They must have a treaty.

So Jacob took a stone and set it up for a pillar and all gathered stones and made a heap. They stopped and had a meal of fellowship and friendship there upon that heap. Laban called it *Jegarsahadutha*, the Chaldean word for witness. Jacob called it *Galeed*, the Hebrew word for witness. But it was also called "Mizpah," in the sense of a watch, that is, "beacon in the sense of a watchtower." Jacob is trusting the God who has preserved in the past, to watch between him and this avaricious, ill-tempered father-in-law. They mutually pledge that neither will pass that heap to do the other wrong.

Note that Laban, trying, we suppose, to follow the pattern of Jacob, calls on "the God of Abraham, and the God of Nahor, the God of their father" to judge betwixt them. He does not note the distinction which Jacob knew. God had plainly commanded Abraham to leave his country, his kindred and his father's house (Gen. 12:2) because they were largely heathen. Laban though is as heathen as these others are, and he does not speak of God as his God but simply as God in general. And "Jacob sware by the fear of his father Isaac." He wants Laban to remember his father is mighty and that God has proved to be with Isaac.

"Then Jacob offered sacrifice upon the mount"—Mount Gilead, in the land of Canaan. Now Jacob builds an altar and offers a sacrifice. We are not told that he offered sacrifices these twenty years past in the heathen country near Haran. He may have done so, but it is not recorded. In some way sacrifices and altars do not seem fitting to Abraham, Isaac and Jacob outside the land of promise. Abraham had no altar in Egypt and Jacob had no altar in Haran, as far as the record shows.

Oh, Jacob has had a great reviving of heart. God has made promises anew. He is to go back to the land of his father and God has promised protection, and we believe that in that sacrifice Jacob had some understanding of the meaning, that it pictured the coming Saviour, the Messiah.

They all had a feast together, and early in the morning Laban kissed the daughters and grandchildren and departed.

GENESIS 32

VERSES 1,2:

AND Jacob went on his way, and the angels of God met him.

2 And when Jacob saw them, he said, This *is* God's host: and he called the name of that place Mā-hă-nā-ĭm.

Met by God's Angels

Jacob has offered a sacrifice. He has openly acknowledged that God blessed and protected him. He has accepted his right and his part in the family from which the Messiah is to come and bless all the world. So now, "the angel of God met him."

Already God has been reviving the heart of Jacob. After twenty, long, tedious, lonely years, Jacob is back in the land and is evidently revived in heart and seeking the face of God. How glad he was to see the host of God and to call the name of the place "Mahanaim." The Scofield Bible says the name means "*two hosts, or two bands*—the visible band, Jacob and his servants; the invisible band, God's angels. Cf. 2 Ki. 6. 13-17."

VERSES 3-8:

3 And Jacob sent messengers before him to Esau his brother unto the land of Seir, the country of Edom.

4 And he commanded them, saying, Thus shall ye speak unto my lord Esau; Thy servant Jacob saith thus, I have sojourned with Laban, and stayed there until now:

5 And I have oxen, and asses, flocks, and menservants, and womenservants: and I have sent to tell my lord, that I may find grace in thy sight.

6 ¶ And the messengers returned to Jacob, saying, We came to thy brother Esau, and also he cometh to meet thee, and four hundred men with him.

7 Then Jacob was greatly afraid and distressed: and he divided the people that *was* with him, and the flocks, and herds, and the camels, into two bands;

8 And said, If Esau come to the one company, and smite it, then the other company which is left shall escape.

Jacob Seeks Peace With Esau

Jacob here recognizes that the man who serves God must be a peaceful man in his heart. First Peter 3:8-11 says:

"Finally, be ye all of one mind, having compassion one of another, love as brethren, be pitiful, be courteous: Not rendering evil for evil, or railing for railing: but contrariwise blessing; knowing that ye are thereunto called, that ye should inherit a blessing. For he that will love life, and see good days, let him refrain his tongue from evil, and his lips that they speak no guile: Let him eschew evil, and do good; let him seek peace, and ensue it."

Jesus said we are to love them that hate us, and pray for them that despitefully use us and persecute us (Matt. 5:44). Jesus commanded, "Agree with thine adversary quickly, whiles thou art in the way with him. . ." (Matt. 5:25). The man of God is to be "patient, not a brawler" (I Tim. 3:3).

Jacob had offended, had wronged his brother. Now it is right for him to try to make peace. But the messenger who is sent to seek peace comes back with an alarming report. "We came to thy brother Esau, and also he cometh to meet thee, and four hundred men with him."

That did not look like peace, and Jacob was greatly afraid and distressed. So he divided the flocks and herds and all into two bands so that if Esau should come to one company and smite it, then the other company might escape.

VERSES 9-12:

9 ¶ And Jacob said, O God of my father Abraham, and God of my father Isaac, the LORD which saidst unto me, Return unto thy country, and to thy kindred, and I will deal well with thee:

10 I am not worthy of the least of all the mercies, and of all the truth, which thou hast shewed unto thy servant; for with my staff I passed over this Jordan; and now I am become two bands.

11 Deliver me, I pray thee, from the hand of my brother, from the hand of Esau: for I fear him, lest he will come and smite me, *and the*

mother with the children.

12 And thou saidst, I will surely do thee good, and make thy seed as the sand of the sea, which cannot be numbered for multitude.

Jacob's Prayer for Deliverance

This is a wonderful prayer of Jacob's. First, he calls on the God of his father Abraham, the God of Isaac. That is the God of covenant. He has a claim there. He claims that those promises must be fulfilled.

Again, he claims the promise of God. God had plainly told him, "I will bring thee again into this land; for I will not leave thee until I have done that which I have spoken to thee of." Again twenty years later God had repeated the promise he gave at Bethel. We are told, "Return unto the land of thy fathers, and to thy kindred; and I will be with thee" (Gen. 31:3).

What a good example that is to us! We should claim the promises of God. We should repeat them to Him and expect Him to meet the obligation He has taken upon Himself in these promises. And He will.

Then there follows an honest confession of his unworthiness. A lonely, runaway boy, fleeing from his brother with a staff in hand more than twenty years before has now turned out to be a rich man with families, flocks, herds and servants. How good God has been! And Jacob acknowledges that all this came by the hand of God and not of his merit, and he must praise God for that.

Then he pleads, "Deliver me, I pray thee, from the hand of my brother, from the hand of Esau." He understands that that hate smoldered for many years, and now it could not simply be a peaceable visit when Esau comes with four hundred men.

He reminds God, How can Jacob's seed be "as the sand of the sea, which cannot be numbered for multitude" if Esau cuts off Jacob and his family? He was right to claim the promises of God. God will answer that prayer.

VERSES 13-21:

13 ¶ And he lodged there that same night; and took of that which came to his hand a present for Esau his brother;

14 Two hundred she goats, and twenty he goats, two hundred ewes, and twenty rams,

15 Thirty milch camels with their colts, forty kine, and ten bulls, twenty she asses, and ten foals.

16 And he delivered *them* into the hand of his servants, every drove by themselves; and said unto his servants, Pass over before me, and put a space betwixt drove and drove.

17 And he commanded the foremost, saying, When Esau my brother meeteth thee, and asketh thee, saying, Whose *art* thou? and whither goest thou? and whose *are* these be-

fore thee?

18 Then thou shalt say, *They be* thy servant Jacob's; it *is* a present sent unto my lord Esau: and, behold, also he *is* behind us.

19 And so commanded he the second, and the third, and all that followed the droves, saying, On this manner shall ye speak unto Esau, when ye find him.

20 And say ye moreover, Behold, thy servant Jacob *is* behind us. For he said, I will appease him with the present that goeth before me, and afterward I will see his face; peradventure he will accept of me.

21 So went the present over before him: and himself lodged that night in the company.

Jacob Makes Restitution for Wrong

It was not wrong that Jacob got the blessing which Esau wanted but it was wrong that he got it by deceit and by lying. Esau had a right to be offended there. And, perhaps Jacob did take advantage of Esau in demanding that he get the birthright for that bowl of red pottage. So now, Jacob honestly tries to make restitution. Note what a herd of animals, goats, sheep, camels, donkeys, cows, a good deal more than five hundred head of livestock. You can imagine he had great flocks and herds when, after the gift, he could still say, "I have enough" (Gen. 33:11). This is the kind of restitution that must impress any kindly heart. We are not surprised that Esau was won over as Jacob hoped he would be.

Notice that all the servants were to speak of Jacob as "thy servant Jacob"? They were to speak to Esau as "my lord Esau." And Jacob said, "I will appease him with the present that goeth before me, and afterward I will see his face; peradventure he will accept of me."

VERSES 22-32:

22 And he rose up that night, and took his two wives, and his two womenservants, and his eleven sons, and passed over the ford Jabbok.

23 And he took them, and sent them over the brook, and sent over that he had.

24 ¶ And Jacob was left alone; and there wrestled a man with him until the breaking of the day.

25 And when he saw that he prevailed not against him, he touched the hollow of his thigh; and the hollow of Jacob's thigh was out of joint, as he wrestled with him.

26 And he said, Let me go, for the day breaketh. And he said, I will not let thee go, except thou bless me.

27 And he said unto him, What is thy name? And he said, Jacob.

28 And he said, Thy name shall be called no more Jacob, but Israel: for as a prince hast thou power with God and with men, and hast prevailed.

29 And Jacob asked him, and said, Tell me, I pray thee, thy name. And he said, Wherefore is it that thou dost ask after my name? And he blessed him there.

30 And Jacob called the name of the place Pĕn-ĭ-ĕl: for I have seen God face to face, and my life is preserved.

31 And as he passed over Pĕn-ū-ĕl the sun rose upon him, and he halted upon his thigh.

32 Therefore the children of Israel eat not of the sinew which shrank, which is upon the hollow of the thigh, unto this day: because he touched the hollow of Jacob's thigh in the sinew that shrank.

Wrestling With God's Angel

Coming from the north, Jacob would cross the stream and has sent to Mamre, we suppose to Esau; now Esau comes to meet him with four hundred men. So that night Jacob sent over his wives, his children, his servants, his eleven sons, and all that he had. He is evidently showing himself and God that he honestly means to trust the Lord and go further into the land. He will trust God to take care of Esau. He himself must go back and wrestle all night with God until he has assurance. The best praying is often done alone. So, alone, Jacob wrestled. "And there wrestled a man with him until the breaking of the day." "A man." We remember that when God and two angels came to meet Abraham, they are called "three men" (Gen. 18:2). The two angels then are called "men" in Genesis 18:22. In the 19th chapter they are called angels, then they are called "men" again. They were angels in the form of men. So, no doubt this is a heavenly man.

An angel? Perhaps instead it is a pre-incarnation of

Christ Himself, for Jacob said in verse 30, "I have seen God face to face."

Why must men beg before God for great blessings? In the first place, we need the purification, the sense of our own unworthiness and the total abandonment of hope in human righteousness and human help that may come from long waiting on God. Often the waiting may include confession. It may include tears; and waiting itself is a matter of proof of faith. So Isaiah 40:31 says, "They that wait upon the Lord shall renew their strength; they shall mount up with wings as eagles; they shall run, and not be weary; they shall walk, and not faint."

Jesus gave the parable of the unjust judge: "And he spake a parable unto them to this end, that men ought always to pray, and not to faint." Even as that unjust judge would hear the widow's plea because her continual coming fretted and disturbed him and wearied him, just so would not God, who loves us and is not wearied, be so pleased to help His own who cry day and night unto Him? Luke 18.

We are commanded to pray always with all prayer and supplication and all perseverance and supplication (Eph. 6:18). The man who wanted bread at midnight for a friend who had come to him—that friend representing the Christian, we think, pleading for the Bread of Life for sinners—would not be heard because he was a friend, but "because of his importunity he will rise and give him as many as he needeth" (Luke 11:8).

Oh, remember the case of the Syrophenician woman who pleaded for her devil-possessed daughter (Matt. 15:21,22), and the pleading of the apostles and others before Pentecost as told in Acts 1:14: "These all continued with one accord in prayer and supplication, with the women, and Mary the mother of Jesus, and with his brethren."

These show us that oftentimes the greatest blessings are to come from those who continue to pray earnestly and steadfastly. In II Chronicles 7:14, the healing of the land and the reviving of God's work depend on those who "humble themselves, and pray, and seek MY FACE, and turn from their wicked ways." Oh, to plead with God, to wait on God, to seek God's face, is often the key to great victories.

Jacob would not be denied. When the angel of God touched his thigh and it went painfully out of joint, he would not give up. When the long night was gone and day was breaking, he still would not give up. "I will not let thee go, except thou bless me." And we have a right to pray that prayer when we come to God, provided our hearts are sincere in seeking His will and power.

What is your name? It is Jacob, the supplanter, the schemer, the trickster, the man who cheated his brother. Oh, but God will change that. It will now be "Israel: for as a prince hast thou power with God and with men, and hast prevailed." Notice the order of the statement here. Jacob got power with God; now he can prevail with Esau.

Some minister preaches and feels, "Oh, I cannot prevail on men to hear, to repent, to serve God." But your failure was not in the pulpit but in the secret closet before you entered the pulpit. If you had first prevailed with God, you could prevail with men.

Now the new name Israel will be for the nation established through the sons of Jacob.

Jacob has a way of giving names to the places that mark great experiences. He called Luz *Bethel*, where he saw the ladder to Heaven and where God gave him the covenant. He called the place where he saw the host of God *Mahanaim* (vs. 2). He called the place, the stone of witness between him and Laban, *Galeed* and *Mizpah*. Now he calls this Peniel, "the face of God." In this angel or in the face the Lord Jesus may have temporarily put on to appear to men before his birth, Jacob had seen "the face of God."

"He halted upon his thigh." I suppose that he will limp the rest of his life on that leg which was put out of joint by the touch of the angel as he wrestled. And the Israelites will remember and will not eat "of the sinew which shrank," which reminded them of Jacob's crippled limb, but also of his victory with God.

GENESIS 33

AND Jacob lifted up his eyes, and looked, and, behold, Esau came, and with him four hundred men. And he divided the children unto Leah, and unto Rachel, and unto the two handmaids.

2 And he put the handmaids and their children foremost, and Leah and her children after, and Rachel and Joseph hindermost.

3 And he passed over before them, and bowed himself to the ground seven times, until he came near to his brother.

4 And Esau ran to meet him, and embraced him, and fell on his neck, and kissed him: and they wept.

5 And he lifted up his eyes, and saw the women and the children; and said, Who *are* those with thee? And he said, The children which God hath graciously given thy servant.

6 Then the handmaidens came near, they and their children, and they bowed themselves.

7 And Leah also with her children came near, and bowed themselves: and after came Joseph near and Rachel, and they bowed themselves.

8 And he said, What *meanest* thou by all this drove which I met? And he said, *These are* to find grace in the sight of my lord.

9 And Esau said, I have enough, my brother; keep that thou hast unto thyself.

10 And Jacob said, Nay, I pray thee, if now I have found grace in thy sight, then receive my present at my hand: for therefore I have seen thy face, as though I had seen the face of God, and thou wast pleased with me.

11 Take, I pray thee, my blessing that is brought to thee; because God hath dealt graciously with me, and because I have enough. And he urged him, and he took *it*.

Jacob Meets Esau

It is a triumphal journey Jacob has now. He has moved before on the promise of God but with some fear. Now he has victory in his soul and is assured of God's blessing. His life is preserved and spared.

He divided his family, with the handmaids and their children in lead, then Leah and her children and, last of all, Rachel and her son, Joseph. It may be that in case of some vengeance yet in the heart of Esau, Jacob would want to preserve the best loved, Rachel and Joseph, most of all—so he sent them last. More likely it seems that this was a dramatic presentation of the blessing of God. The handmaids, then Leah and her children, then Rachel and

Joseph. His heart was proud and his greatest treasure was to climax the appearance.

Now he went over before this procession and bowed himself to the ground several times. That is not only a friendly appearance of humility but genuine, we are convinced, and Esau was convinced; it was genuine humility and genuinely seeking the favor of his brother. Oh, "Esau ran to meet him, and embraced him, and fell on his neck, and kissed him: and they wept."

They are weeping over more than twenty long years without any fellowship. They are weeping over the bitter thoughts, hatred, fears and misunderstandings of these long years. Oh, Esau's heart is changed! What need now of the four hundred men? Esau saw the family, all of them, and Jacob said, "The children which God hath graciously given thy servant." How graciously he bowed before Esau, and his heart was touched.

Now what about all these flocks and herds? Oh, they are a present. Jacob said, "I wanted to find grace in your heart, in your sight."

Oh, the hunger of Jacob's heart, the long years of loneliness, never seeing his twin brother and thinking only that to see him would mean judgment, strife, perhaps death: now he weeps for joy and thinks that the face of Esau is like the face of God!

Yes, Jacob had found that "a brother offended is harder to be won than a strong city: and their contentions like the bars of a castle" (Prov. 18:19). It was a brother, Cain, who killed his brother, Abel. It was Joseph's brothers who would have killed him and did sell him as a slave. Oh, how we ought to cherish those ties of blood and make sure that brotherly love is not changed to hate and spite.

Esau would have returned the gifts but Jacob would not have it. Oh, this brother must have some token of his earnest love and of his fellowship restored. And Esau consented.

VERSES 12-16:

12 And he said, Let us take our journey, and let us go, and I will go before thee.

13 And he said unto him, My lord knoweth that the children *are* tender, and the flocks and herds with young *are* with me: and if men should overdrive them one day, all the flock will die.

14 Let my lord, I pray thee, pass over before his servant: and I will lead on softly, according as the cattle that goeth before me and the children be able to endure, until I come unto my lord unto Seir.

15 And Esau said, Let me now leave with thee *some* of the folk that are with me. And he said, What needeth it? let me find grace in the sight of my lord.

16 ¶ So Esau returned that day on his way unto Seir.

A Happy Parting

Jacob would not accept the protective care of Esau and his four hundred men. In the first place, unencumbered men can march a good deal faster than the sheep with their lambs, the goats with their kids, the cattle with their calves. They must have time to graze and eat as they go. And they do not need the protection of Esau now for there is no other enemy that threatens them.

Jacob did not go down to the country of Esau. In the first place, both of these men will have great flocks and herds and each need plenty of room. Besides, Jacob may well have felt that the birthright and the blessing which had come to him might be a matter of unhappiness and quarreling and that the old enmities might be restored if they were thrust too much together.

VERSES 17-20:

17 And Jacob journeyed to Succoth, and built him an house, and made booths for his cattle: therefore the name of the place is called Succoth.

18 ¶ And Jacob came to Shalem, a city of Shḗ-chĕm, which *is* in the land of Cā́-nă-ăn, when he came from Pā́-dăn–aram; and pitched his tent before the city.

19 And he bought a parcel of a field, where he had spread his tent at the hand of the children of Hamor Shḗ-chĕm's father, for an hundred pieces of money.

20 And he erected there an altar and called it Ĕl-ĕl-ō-hĕ–Israel.

Jacob at Shechem

"And Jacob journeyed to Succoth, and built him an house, and made booths for his cattle." "Booths" may mean some kind of an arbor covered with brush for shade. So the place was called Succoth, meaning booths. If this is the same Succoth of Joshua 13:27, then it is still on the east side of Jordan, but in the land of Canaan and in the area of the kingdom later of Sihon, king of Heshbon, and it is near the little Sea of Galilee, called in Joshua 13:27 the Sea of Chinnereth.

Then he came to Shalem, a city of Shechem. How long he stayed in Succoth we do not know, probably not long. Then Jacob came over the Jordan River to Shechem in the land of Canaan and pitched his tent there. Here he bought a parcel of field, and that little field with the field that contained the Cave of Machpelah where Abraham and Sarah are buried, and where Isaac, with Rebekah, is to be buried, and where later Jacob and Leah will be buried—those two are the only pieces of land owned by Abraham, Isaac or Jacob. They were strangers and sojourners. Even when Jacob had been twenty years with Laban, he reported to Esau, "I have sojourned with Laban." But now he is in the land.

The Scofield Bible labels these last three verses as "Jacob's worship in self-will." Why Dr. Scofield thought so, we do not know. Now Jacob rears an altar. It is in the land of Canaan.

We must remember that though all the land of Canaan is promised to Jacob and his seed, he owns none of it permanently, even as Abraham had "not so much as to set his foot on." It is not surprising that as Abraham moved from Mamre to Hebron to Beer-sheba and elsewhere, so Jacob would dwell first in one part and then in another. The altar he calls "El-elohe-Israel"—God, the God of Israel. He has accepted and claimed the promises. God henceforth has been called the God of Abraham and "the God of my father Isaac." Now, Jacob said, "He is the God of Israel, my own personal God."

This little parcel of ground will later come to the children of Joseph and here Joseph's bones will be buried when the children of Israel come out of Egypt (Josh. 24:32).

GENESIS 34

VERSES 1-12:

AND Dinah the daughter of Leah, which she bare unto Jacob, went out to see the daughters of the land.

2 And when Shē-́chĕm the son of Hamor the Hivite, prince of the country, saw her, he took her, and lay with her, and defiled her.

3 And his soul clave unto Dinah the daughter of Jacob, and he loved the damsel, and spake kindly unto the damsel.

4 And Shē-́chĕm spake unto his father Hamor, saying, Get me this damsel to wife.

5 And Jacob heard that he had defiled Dinah his daughter: now his sons were with his cattle in the field: and Jacob held his peace until they were come.

6 ¶ And Hamor the father of Shē-́chĕm went out unto Jacob to commune with him.

7 And the sons of Jacob came out of the field when they heard it: and the men were grieved, and they were very wroth, because he had wrought folly in Israel in lying with Jacob's daughter; which thing ought not to be done.

8 And Hamor communed with them, saying, The soul of my son Shē-́chĕm longeth for your daughter: I pray you give her him to wife.

9 And make ye marriages with us, and give your daughters unto us, and take our daughters unto you.

10 And ye shall dwell with us: and the land shall be before you; dwell and trade ye therein, and get you possessions therein.

11 And Shē-́chĕm said unto her father and unto her brethren, Let me find grace in your eyes, and what ye shall say unto me I will give.

12 Ask me never so much dowry and gift, and I will give according as ye shall say unto me: but give me the damsel to wife.

Leah's Daughter Dinah Seduced by Prince Shechem

Dr. Scofield titled this chapter "Jacob reaps the harvest of his evil years." There is a sense in which all of us have evil years and have some harvest of our sinfulness. I doubt if there is enough direct connection to make that special charge against Jacob here. Dinah, daughter of Leah, went out to see the daughters of the land unchaperoned. The young prince Shechem saw her and found her very attractive, took her aside and seduced her and she was thus led into sin and defiled. That is a tragedy for any girl.

How much supervision Dinah had and how much more she ought to have had, we do not know. But in Israel, according to God's law, parents were accountable for the virtue of their daughters. The bloodstained bed clothes of the wedding night were kept to prove the daughter just married was a virgin (Deut. 22:13-19). The modern idea of young people dating without chaperones, sometimes riding in cars alone, sometimes left in a home or at the park or on the beaches without chaperones, is not only contrary to the Scriptures but is disgraceful and leads to sin and heartbreak for many. And of course it is a cheapening of the whole matter of marriage and a woman's virtue.

In the old times fathers and mothers made arrangements for their daughters' and sons' marriage. They determined that the family connections were right, that the character of the young man to marry their daughter was acceptable. They might know each other and come to love each other as did Jacob and Rachel, but there was no petting, no "going steady," no freedom about fondling and embracing.

A happy courtship, with the blessing of God upon it and helping to guarantee sober, godly choice among young people and safeguarding the virtue of young men and women, is not only possible but imperative, safe, and very rewarding.

Our six daughters had no unchaperoned dates in cars, were not left alone in the house or on the beach without a chaperone all the way through college, not even when engaged. All were very happy and very popular. The girls in high school and college were cheerleaders, intercollegiate debaters, sang in college choirs, had many dates, but always either two or more couples were together, or were in the home, or in the three blocks' walk to the church. All were brilliant students, fine musicians, very popular. All married very happily. A father and mother are responsible for the purity of their daughters.

Now that Dinah had been seduced, the Mosaic law had a simple, honest rule about it. Exodus 22:16 and 17 say, "And if a man entice a maid that is not betrothed, and lie with her, he shall surely endow her to be his wife. If her father utterly refuse to give her unto him, he shall pay money according to the dowry of virgins."

The young Shechem was a prince. He was very honorable. The father is mentioned as "Shechem's father." Shechem loved the girl, Dinah, and wanted her for his wife. That would have been the simplest and happiest solution. He insisted that arrangements be made that he should marry the girl. He would give any amount of dowry that was required. It would be understood that the people of Israel would live among them as they liked. Since Jacob had bought a bit of ground here, they had reason to suppose he meant to stay.

VERSES 13-29:

13 And the sons of Jacob answered Shē-chĕm and Hamor his father deceitfully, and said, because he had defiled Dinah their sister:

14 And they said unto them, We cannot do this thing, to give our sister to one that is uncircumcised; for that *were* a reproach unto us:

15 But in this will we consent unto you: If ye will be as we *be*, that every male of you be circumcised;

16 Then will we give our daughters unto you, and we will take your daughters to us, and we will dwell with you, and we will become one people.

17 But if ye will not hearken unto us, to be circumcised; then will we take our daughter, and we will be gone.

18 And their words pleased Hamor, and Shē-chĕm Hamor's son.

19 And the young man deferred not to do the thing, because he had delight in Jacob's daughter: and he *was* more honourable than all the house of his father.

20 ¶ And Hamor and Shē-chĕm his son came unto the gate of their city, and communed with the men of their city, saying,

21 These men *are* peaceable with us; therefore let them dwell in the land, and trade therein; for the land, behold, *it is* large enough for them; let us take their daughters to us for wives, and let us give them our daughters.

22 Only herein will the men consent unto us for to dwell with us, to be one people, if every male among us be circumcised, as they *are* circumcised.

23 *Shall* not their cattle and their substance and every beast of their's *be* our's? only let us consent unto them, and they will dwell with us.

24 And unto Hamor and unto Shē-chĕm his son hearkened all that went out of the gate of his city; and every male was circumcised, all that went out of the gate of his city.

25 ¶ And it came to pass on the third day, when they were sore, that two of the sons of Jacob, Simeon and Levi, Dinah's brethren, took each man his sword, and came upon the city boldly, and slew all the males.

26 And they slew Hamor and Shē-chĕm his son with the edge of the sword, and took Dinah out of Shē-chĕm's house, and went out.

27 The sons of Jacob came upon the slain, and spoiled the city, because they had defiled their sister.

28 They took their sheep, and their

oxen, and their asses, and that which *was* in the city, and that which *was* in the field.

29 And all their wealth, and all their little ones, and their wives took they captive, and spoiled even all that *was* in the house.

"The Sons of Jacob Answered Shechem and Hamor. . . ."

We suppose all of them were angry. Verse 7 says also, "The sons of Jacob came out of the field when they heard it: and the men were grieved. . . ." So all the sons of Jacob were greatly distressed that Dinah had been seduced and led into sin.

Now these brothers of Dinah insisted that she ought not be given in marriage to one who was uncircumcised. If they were honest in that, that meant that circumcision was a special mark of people separated for God. If they were deceitful, as seems likely, they simply meant to take advantage of these men.

At any rate, they pressed the point. All the men of the town of Shechem must be circumcised if they are to marry and intermarry with this family of Jacob. And since Jacob has great riches and flocks and herds, and since they are active, intelligent people, that seemed very attractive. And the young prince was popular and pressed the matter strongly. He wanted Dinah for his wife. Thus the men of the city consented.

No doubt there was some cupidity, some avarice in it, too. They said, "Shall not their cattle and their substance and every beast of their's be our's?" Circumcision would be a momentary inconvenience, a soreness for a few days; so they consented "and every male was circumcised, all that went out of the gate of his city."

But two of Jacob's sons, Simeon and Levi, sons of Leah, Dinah's brethren, took their swords and went into the city and literally killed every male. They sacked the city and took Dinah home with them. And besides, they took all the sheep, oxen, asses and the wealth of the city, the women and wives and spoiled everything in the houses! That is a sad story of wicked men. God regarded it so and Jacob never forgot that wickedness. In blessing the sons before dying in Genesis 49:5-7, Jacob was inspired to say:

"Simeon and Levi are brethren; instruments of cruelty are in their habitations. O my soul, come not thou into their secret; unto their assembly, mine honour, be not thou united: for in their anger they slew a man, and in their selfwill they digged down a wall. Cursed be their anger, for it was fierce; and their wrath, for it was cruel: I will divide them in Jacob, and scatter them in Israel."

God's punishment no doubt came on these men and Jacob said, speaking for God, "I will divide them in Jacob, and scatter them in Israel."

VERSES 30,31:

30 And Jacob said to Simeon and Levi, Ye have troubled me to make me to stink among the inhabitants of the land, among the Că-nă-ăn-ites and the Pĕ-rĭz-zites: and I *being* few in number, they shall gather themselves together against me, and slay me; and I shall be destroyed, I and my house.

31 And they said, Should he deal with our sister as with an harlot?

Jacob Fearful, Troubled

Inevitably now, Jacob and his sons would be hated as well as feared by the inhabitants of the country. They had proven themselves lawless and murderous. They were made to "stink among the inhabitants of the land." And Jacob's fear might have been fulfilled and he and his family might have been destroyed but for the command of God which came soon, that they were to leave this place and go to Bethel. In the next chapter, verse 5 tells us that "the terror of God was upon the cities that were round about them," and so Jacob and his family were not slaughtered.

GENESIS 35

VERSES 1-5:

AND God said unto Jacob, Arise, go up to Beth–el, and dwell there: and make there an altar unto God, that appeared unto thee when thou fleddest from the face of Esau thy brother.

2 Then Jacob said unto his household, and to all that *were* with him, Put away the strange gods that *are* among you, and be clean, and change your garments:

3 And let us arise, and go up to Beth–el; and I will make there an altar unto God, who answered me in the day of my distress, and was with me in the way which I went.

4 And they gave unto Jacob all the strange gods which *were* in their hand, and *all their* earrings which *were* in their ears; and Jacob hid them under the oak which *was* by Shĕ´-chĕm.

5 And they journeyed: and the terror of God was upon the cities that *were* round about them, and they did not pursue after the sons of Jacob.

Jacob Invited Back to Bethel Again

Bethel doubtless was the dearest spot in all of his memory to Jacob. There, as a young man, knowing that he was called of God and to have had certain blessings promised as the seed of Abraham and Isaac, yet he was heartsick at leaving home, going lonely and without means into a strange country. There God met him. There the great covenant of God with Abraham was renewed with Jacob. There were sweet promises, and Jacob made holy vows.

Now God says to him, "Arise, go up to Beth-el, and dwell there." Not only was he to go to Bethel, but he was "to dwell there," he was to make an altar there.

They must get ready. They must put away the strange gods that are among them. I do not know if any beside Rachel had images, but others should have a heart-searching and they need to be prepared in heart to come honestly before God in worship. They were to "be clean, and change your garments."

It is well that people dress up in nice clothes to attend the house of God. To be personally clean in body and in habits is good for Christians. Even the sin offering, the bullock whose blood and fat and kidneys were burned on the altar in Leviticus, chapter 4, had the body taken outside the camp "unto a clean place, where the ashes are poured out. . . ." Oh, that those who serve God be clean in mind, in heart, in habit.

One who comes to make an altar to God must count that a holy thing, and so one should "lay aside every weight, and the sin which doth so easily beset" you (Heb. 12:1). We should avoid even the very "appearance of evil." So they took off their earrings as well. Is there something wrong with earrings? Not necessarily, but a certain modesty and restraint is proper to those who serve God. Earrings might not be sinful if they are not "costly array" but one seeking to be personally beautiful, seeking to attract the praise and admiration of men, is not in a good state to worship.

Jacob had them lay their earrings aside and he hid them under an oak. We are not told that they are destroyed nor forsaken. Perhaps they were taken up again later.

But, just as it is sometimes proper and right for people to fast, that is to go without necessary food for a season while they pray and serve God, and sometimes proper for them to "watch and pray," that is, to stay awake in the night watches to pray, or as Luke 18:7 says, "day and night" pray, just so sometimes it is right to lay aside other pleasures and other interests. Never mind the rich clothing, the jewelry.

When God would speak to the people from Mount Sinai and the Ten Commandments were to be given, Moses commanded the people to sanctify themselves and wash their clothes. In Exodus 19:14,15, He commanded, "And Moses went down from the mount unto the people, and sanctified the people; and they washed their clothes. And he said unto the people, Be ready against the third day: come not at your wives."

We dress up for the company we greatly admire; why not for the Lord? We leave aside other business interests and pleasures to be with those we love; why not do that for the

Lord? So Jacob had them lay aside these images and even their earrings and wash themselves and be ready to come before God.

Oh, what a good day when they go back to Bethel where more than thirty years ago God had spoken and made His blessed promises to Jacob!

Note verse 5. They are protected as they journey because the terror of the Lord keeps the heathen people of the cities around them from attacking them—because of the murderous assault on Shechem by Levi and Simeon.

VERSES 6-15:

6 ¶ So Jacob came to Luz, which *is* in the land of Că-nă-ăn, that *is*, Beth–el, he and all the people that *were* with him.

7 And he built there an altar, and called the place Ĕl–bĕth-́ĕl: because there God appeared unto him, when he fled from the face of his brother.

8 But Deborah Rebekah's nurse died, and she was buried beneath Beth–el under an oak: and the name of it was called Al-́lŏn–bā–chûth.

9 ¶ And God appeared unto Jacob again, when he came out of Pā-́dăn-aram, and blessed him.

10 And God said unto him, Thy name *is* Jacob: thy name shall not be called any more Jacob, but Israel shall be thy name: and he called his name Israel.

11 And God said unto him, I *am* God Almighty: be fruitful and multiply; a nation and a company of nations shall be of thee, and kings shall come out of thy loins;

12 And the land which I gave Abraham and Isaac, to thee I will give it, and to thy seed after thee will I give the land.

13 And God went up from him in the place where he talked with him.

14 And Jacob set up a pillar in the place where he talked with him, *even* a pillar of stone: and he poured a drink offering thereon, and he poured oil thereon.

15 And Jacob called the name of the place where God spake with him, Beth–el.

Bethel Now Called "El-beth-el"

Now Jacob is at Luz, in the land of Canaan, Bethel, as Jacob had named it more than twenty years before. With him now are all the people God has given him. He built an altar there. That is what God had commanded in verse 1. Jacob had offered a sacrifice at Gilead where Laban met him (Gen. 31:51-54). Now he built an altar at Bethel where he had set up a stone for a monument more than twenty years before. He had built an altar at Shechem (Gen. 33:20).

Note the new name "El-beth-el," that is, "the God of the house of God." The Hebrew word *beth* is house, *el* is God.

It is good not only to go to the house of God but to be sure that we meet the God of the house of God. And wherever we meet God, that is a house of God.

Deborah, Rebekah's nurse, died and was buried "beneath Beth-el." We are not told what had happened to Jacob's mother, Rebekah. She may have died before and now the nurse may have come to live with and be cared for by Jacob. At any rate, she was buried here at Bethel, where Jacob was. And the oak was called Allon-bachuth (vs. 8), which means the oak of weeping.

The New Name, Israel

When Jacob wrestled with the angel in Genesis 32, we remember that a new name was given him, Israel, a prince, because he had prevailed with God and with man. Now, God reminds him of the new name. Here, too, must be a prophecy that Jews would scatter over the whole world and become a mighty people.

Here again is the promise of the whole land of Palestine. Jacob is still a sojourner but in the future the whole land of Palestine is to be given to him and "to thy seed after thee." That is a promise of the nation Israel, but a promise of the Messiah, too, no doubt. Again, Jacob set up a pillar. He must remember this place! He must remember these holy promises! And on the pillar of stone he poured a drink-offering and poured oil upon it.

This is the first mention of the drink-offering. It had not been given as a command, but a loving heart and dependent heart may give to God anything that has a special meaning to him. Dr. Scofield says the drink-offering "was always 'poured out,' never drunk, and may be considered a type of Christ in the sense of Psalm 22.14; Isaiah 53.12."

---

16 ¶ And they journeyed from Beth–el; and there was but a little way to come to Ē´-phrăth: and Rachel travailed, and she had hard labour.

17 And it came to pass, when she was in hard labour, that the midwife said unto her, Fear not; thou shalt have this son also.

18 And it came to pass, as her soul was in departing, (for she died) that she called his name ¹Bĕn–ō´-nī: but his father called him Benjamin.

19 And Rachel died, and was buried in the way to Ē´-phrăth, which is Beth–lehem.

20 And Jacob set a pillar upon her grave: that is the pillar of Rachel's grave unto this day.

21 ¶ And Israel journeyed, and spread his tent beyond the tower of Edar.

22 And it came to pass, when Israel dwelt in that land, that Reuben went and lay with Bilhah his father's concubine: and Israel heard it. Now the sons of Jacob were twelve:

23 The sons of Leah; Reuben, Jacob's firstborn, and Simeon, and Levi, and Judah, and Ĭs´-să-<u>ch</u>är, and Zĕ-bū´-lŭn:

24 The sons of Rachel; Joseph, and Benjamin:

25 And the sons of Bilhah, Rachel's handmaid; Dan, and Năph´-tă-lī:

26 And the sons of Zilpah, Leah's handmaid; Gad, and Asher: these are the sons of Jacob, which were born to him in Pā´-dăn–aram.

Birth of Benjamin and Death of Rachel

How Jacob loved Rachel! How dear to his heart was Joseph, Rachel's son! She had, by faith, prophesied in Genesis 30:24, "The Lord shall add to me another son." And He did. However, Rachel died following childbirth, and just before she died she called his name "Ben-oni" or "son of sorrow." But his father called him Benjamin, "son of my right hand."

They buried Rachel a little way out from Bethlehem, on the road to Jerusalem and there today is a tomb which traditionally is called "the tomb of Rachel." Leah will be buried in the Cave Machpelah, but Rachel was buried on the way to Bethlehem.

Jacob and his family are drifting down toward the plain of Mamre, near Hebron, the old home country of Abraham.

Here comes the sad story of the sin of Reuben who was guilty of adultery with Bilhah, his father's concubine. And Jacob remembered that sin and it was remembered prophetically when the old man was blessing the children, the sons, before he died.

Genesis 49:3,4 says, "Reuben, thou art my firstborn, my might, and the beginning of my strength, the excellency of dignity, and the excellency of power: Unstable as water, thou shalt not excel; because thou wentest up to thy father's bed; then defiledst thou it: he went up to my couch."

Reuben, the firstborn, who should have had the birthright, missed it and it was given to Joseph (I Chron. 5:1). The long years go by but the sin is remembered and brings a curse upon the generation to follow. So it often is that the sins of the father cause the sins of the children and their trouble.

Benjamin is born; now there are twelve sons. Remember Leah had six sons, Rachel two and each of the concubines, Bilhah and Zilpah, had two.

VERSES 27-29:

27 ¶ And Jacob came unto Isaac his father unto Mamre, unto the city of Arbah, which *is* Hebron, where Abraham and Isaac sojourned.

28 And the days of Isaac were an hundred and fourscore years.

29 And Isaac gave up the ghost, and died, and was gathered unto his people, *being* old and full of days: and his sons Esau and Jacob buried him.

Death of Isaac

Many years ago when Jacob was with Isaac they had lived adjacent to the Philistines; now he lives at Mamre and there Esau comes to be with his old father. Long years ago we are told that "Isaac was old, and his eyes were dim," when Jacob got the stolen blessing in Genesis 27:1. Now, more than twenty years have gone by and Isaac, 180 years old, died. He was "old and full of days." He was "gathered unto his people." I would suppose that means that this godly man went with all the saints of God in the past, including his ancestors Abraham and Sarah, of course.

GENESIS 36

NOW these *are* the generations of Esau, who *is* Edom.

2 Esau took his wives of the daughters of Că-́nă-ăn; Adah the daughter of Elon the Hittite, and Ă-hŏl-ĭ-bä-́măh the daughter of Anah the daughter of Zibeon the Hivite;

3 And Băsh-́ĕ-măth Ishmael's daughter, sister of Nĕ-bä-́jŏth.

4 And Adah bare to Esau Ĕ-lĭ-́phăz; and Băsh-́ĕ-măth bare Rĕu-́ĕl;

5 And Ă-hŏl-ĭ-bä-́măh bare Jĕ-́ŭsh, and Jä-́ă-lăm, and Korah: these *are* the sons of Esau, which were born unto him in the land of Că-́nă-ăn.

6 And Esau took his wives, and his sons, and his daughters, and all the persons of his house, and his cattle, and all his beasts, and all his substance, which he had got in the land of Că-́nă-ăn; and went into the country from the face of his brother Jacob.

7 For their riches were more than that they might dwell together; and the land wherein they were strangers could not bear them because of their cattle.

8 Thus dwelt Esau in mount Seir: Esau *is* Edom.

Esau Moves to Mount Seir

Dr. Scofield says:

> Edom (called also "Seir," Gen. 32.3; 36.8) is the name of the country lying south of the ancient kingdom of Judah, and extending from the Dead Sea to the Gulf of Akaba. It includes the ruins of Petra, and is bounded on the north by Moab. Peopled by descendants of Esau (Gen. 36. 1-19), Edom has a remarkable prominence in the prophetic word as (together with Moab) the scene of the final destruction of Gentile world-power in the day of the Lord.

This country called Edom and Seir is also called Idumea in Isaiah 34:5,6, and the name was given to Esau because he asked for that red pottage that Jacob had prepared. Genesis 25:30 says, "Feed me, I pray thee, with that same red pottage; for I am faint: therefore was his name called Edom." Here the sons of Esau's three wives are named. The following verses will give their grandsons.

VERSES 9-19:

9 ¶ And these *are* the generations of Esau the father of the Edomites in mount Seir:

10 These *are* the names of Esau's sons; Ĕ-lĭ-́phăz the son of Adah the wife of Esau, Rĕŭ-́ĕl the son of Băsh-́ĕ-măth the wife of Esau.

11 And the sons of Ĕ-lĭ-́phăz were Teman, Omar, Zĕ-́phō, and Gā-́tăm, and Kenaz.

12 And Timna was concubine to Ĕ-lĭ-́phăz Esau's son; and she bare to Ĕ-lĭ-́phăz Ăm-́ă-lĕk: these *were* the sons of Adah Esau's wife.

13 And these *are* the sons of Rĕŭ-́ĕl; Nā-́hăth, and Zerah, Shammah, and Mizzah: these were the sons of Băsh-́ĕ-măth Esau's wife.

14 ¶ And these were the sons of Ă-hŏl-ĭ-bä-́măh, the daughter of Anah the daughter of Zibeon, Esau's wife: and she bare to Esau Jĕ-́ŭsh, and Jā-́ă-lăm, and Korah.

15 ¶ These *were* dukes of the sons of Esau: the sons of Ĕ-lĭ-́phăz the firstborn *son* of Esau; duke Teman, duke Omar, duke Zĕ-́phō, duke Kenaz,

16 Duke Korah, duke Gā-́tăm, *and* duke Ăm-́ă-lĕk: these *are* the dukes *that came* of Ĕ-lĭ-́phăz in the land of Edom; these *were* the sons of Adah.

17 ¶ And these *are* the sons of Rĕŭ-́ĕl Esau's son; duke Nā-́hăth, duke Zerah, duke Shammah, duke Mizzah: these *are* the dukes *that came* of Rĕŭ-́ĕl in the land of Edom; these *are* the sons of Băsh-́ĕ-măth Esau's wife.

18 ¶ And these *are* the sons of Ă-hŏl-ĭ-bä-́măh Esau's wife; duke Jĕ-́ŭsh, duke Jā-́ă-lăm, duke Korah: these *were* the dukes *that came* of Ă-hŏl-ĭ-bä-́măh the daughter of Anah, Esau's wife.

19 These *are* the sons of Esau, who *is* Edom, and these *are* their dukes.

Descendants of Esau

"Dukes" here mean "chief of thousands." In these descendants the promises are fulfilled. The promise to Hagar is fulfilled in Genesis 16:10, "I will multiply thy seed exceedingly, that it shall not be numbered for multitude." He also fulfilled the promise to Abraham in Genesis 17:19, "And God said, Sarah thy wife shall bear thee a son indeed; and thou shalt call his name Isaac: and I will establish my covenant with him for an everlasting covenant, and with his seed after him."

Amalek (vs. 12), a grandson of Esau, grew into a great nation of people. When the children of Israel came out of Egypt four hundred years later, Exodus 17:8 says, "Then came Amalek, and fought with Israel in Rephidim." The children of Israel under Joshua, with Moses' hands upheld as a symbol, defeated the people of Amalek. "And the Lord said unto Moses, Write this for a memorial in a book, and rehearse it in the ears of Joshua: for I will utterly put out the remembrance of Amalek from under heaven. And Moses built an altar, and called the name of it Jehovah-nissi: For he said, Because the Lord hath sworn that the Lord will have war with Amalek from generation to generation" (Exod. 17:14-16).

Velikovsky and Courville both agree that the Hyksos, shepherd kings who invaded and ruled Egypt, were Amalekites.

This curse of God on the people of Amalek is repeated in Deuteronomy 25:17-19:

"Remember what Amalek did unto thee by the way, when ye were come forth out of Egypt; How he met thee by the way, and smote the hindmost of thee, even all that were feeble behind thee, when thou wast faint and weary; and he feared not God. Therefore it shall be, when the Lord thy God hath given thee rest from all thine enemies round about, in the land which the Lord thy God giveth thee for an inheritance to possess it, that thou shalt blot out the remembrance of Amalek from under heaven; thou shalt not forget it."

So the Amalekites were defeated by Gideon in Judges 7:25, and by Saul in I Samuel 14:48. Then God commanded King Saul, "Now go and smite Amalek, and utterly destroy all that they have, and spare them not; but slay both man and woman, infant and suckling, ox and sheep, camel and ass" (I Sam. 15:3). That means that the nation of the Amalekites should have been destroyed utterly, but they were not. Saul spared the best of the sheep and oxen, brought King Agag with him as a prisoner, and must have left many of the Amalekites alive because David fought against them again in I Samuel 27:8,9 and 30:17.

VERSES 20-30:

20 ¶ These *are* the sons of Seir the Horite, who inhabited the land; Lotan, and Shobal, and Zibeon, and Anah,

21 And Dishon, and Ezer, and Dishan: these *are* the dukes of the Horites, the children of Seir in the land of Edom.

22 And the children of Lotan were Hôr-í and Hemam; and Lotan's sister *was* Timna.

23 And the children of Shobal *were* these; Alvan, and Măn-́ă-hăth, and Ebal, Shepho, and Onam.

24 And these *are* the children of Zibeon; both Ajah, and Anah: this *was that* Anah that found the mules in the wilderness, as he fed the asses of Zibeon his father.

25 And the children of Anah *were* these; Dishon, and Ă-hŏl-ĭ-bä-́mäh the daughter of Anah.

26 And these *are* the children of Dishon; Hemdan, and Eshban, and Ithran, and Chē-́răn.

27 The children of Ezer *are* these; Bilhan, and Zā-́ă-văn, and Akan.

28 The children of Dishan *are* these; Uz, and Aran.

29 These *are* the dukes *that came* of the Horites; duke Lotan, duke Shobal, duke Zibeon, duke Anah,

30 Duke Dishon, duke Ezer, duke Dishan: these *are* the dukes *that came* of Hôr-́í, among their dukes in the land of Seir.

Descendants of Seir the Horite

We suppose that Mount Seir and the country of Edom was first called Seir after the name of this man who lived there, Seir the Horite. The word Horite means rock-dweller, and may have some reference to the city of Petra, carved out in rock and to the people who lived among those great stones even before the buildings were carved out of stone. These children of Seir, the Horites, evidently intermarried with the descendants of Esau. Lotan was a son of Seir (vs. 20). His sister and thus it is implied, daughter of Seir, was Timna, the concubine to Eliphaz, Esau's son; and from this union came Amalek (vs. 12). Zibeon (vs. 24) was the father of Anah and the grandfather of Aholibamah, Esau's wife, the daughter of Ishmael (vs. 2).

Since the people of Seir were in the land first, their leaders are mentioned along with those of Esau, with whom they intermarried.

Verse 24 is the first mention of mules in the Bible, crosses between the ass and the horse.

Uz (vs. 28) was son of Dishan (vs. 21) and grandson of Seir the Horite (vs. 20). From him may be named the land of Uz. Since in those days areas were generally named after the men who dwelt there and settled the country, we wonder if this area where Uz lived is the same land of Uz in which Job lived (Job 1:1), which is called by Dr. Scofield a "region at the south of Edom, and west of the Arabian desert, extending to Chaldea."

VERSES 31-39:

31 ¶ And these *are* the kings that reigned in the land of Edom, before there reigned any king over the children of Israel.

32 And Bela the son of Beor reigned in Edom: and the name of his city *was* Dĭn-́hă-bäh.

33 And Bela died, and Jobab the son of Zerah of Bozrah reigned in his stead.

34 And Jobab died, and Hū-́shăm of the land of Tē-́măn-ī reigned in his stead.

35 And Hū-́shăm died, and Hadad the son of Bē-́dăd, who smote Midian in the field of Moab, reigned in

his stead: and the name of his city *was* Avith.

36 And Hadad died, and Samlah of Măs-rē-́kăh reigned in his stead.

37 And Samlah died, and Saul of Rē-́hŏ-bōth *by* the river reigned in his stead.

38 And Saul died, and Bā-́ăl–hā-́năr the son of Ăch-́bôr reigned in his stead.

39 And Bā-́ăl–hā-́năn the son of Ăch-́bôr died, and Hadar reigned in his stead: and the name of his city *was* Pā-́ū; and his wife's name *was* Mĕ-hĕt-́ă-bĕl, the daughter of Matred, the daughter of Mē-́ză-hăb.

Kings of Edom

These are the kings that reigned in the area of Edom. Since that area is adjacent to the land of Israel and since Edom will be often mentioned in the Scriptures, here the kings are named.

We find it very interesting that the peoples adjacent to Israel were generally kin to Israel. Moab and Ammon were descendants from Lot and after the cities Sodom and Gomorrah, Admah and Zeboiim were destroyed by God's vengeance in Genesis 19, evidently the two illegitimate sons of Lot grew up and moved eastward and north to form the two nations of Moab and Ammon, east of the Dead Sea and east of Jordan.

Now Edom is peopled by Esau's people but there are also here descendants of Ishmael through his daughter Aholibamah who married Esau. Then the Midianites were descended from Midian, the son of Abraham by Keturah, wife of his old age (Gen. 25:2). When Moses had killed a man in Egypt and fled from Pharaoh at the age of forty, he dwelt in the land of Midian and married a daughter of a priest of Midian (Exod. 2:15-21). The Midianites sometimes plagued the Israelites in the days of the Judges.

We do not know that the Hittites on the north and the Philistines on the west were related to Israelites, but the Ammonites, Moabites, Edomites and Midianites were. And these largely make up now the great millions of Arab people.

VERSES 40-43:

40 And these *are* the names of the dukes *that came* of Esau, according to their families, after their places, by their names; duke Timnah, duke Alvah, duke Jetheth,

41 Duke Ă-hŏl-ĭ-bä′-mặh, duke Elah, duke Pī′-nŏn,

42 Duke Kenaz, duke Teman, duke Mibzar,

43 Duke Măg′-dĭ-ĕl, duke Iram: these *be* the dukes of Edom, according to their habitations in the land of their possession: he *is* Esau the father of the Edomites.

Dukes That Came of Esau

Here are eleven "chiefs of thousands" descended from Esau. It is interesting that Duke Aholibamah took the name of, we suppose, his grandmother (vs. 41).

Esau was the father of the Edomites.

GENESIS 37

VERSE 1:

AND Jacob dwelt in the land where- | the land of Cā́-nă-ăn.
in his father was a stranger, in |

Jacob a "Stranger," a Sojourner

Would you not have thought that men of great wealth like Abraham and Isaac and now Jacob, would have built them cities or at least great houses for themselves and their workers? No. It was the destiny of these men to be sojourners, temporary dwellers in a land that afterward God would give them. God had promised Abraham that after long years with the Israelites enslaved in Egypt, they would be brought forth and have the land, but not yet, "for the iniquity of the Amorites is not yet full" (Gen. 15:16). So Abraham "went down into Egypt to *sojourn* there; for the famine was grievous in the land" (Gen. 12:10). Genesis 21:34 says, "And Abraham *sojourned* in the Philistines' land many days." Again, Genesis 23:4, "I am a stranger and a *sojourner* with you. . . ."

And in Genesis 26:3 God said to Isaac, "*Sojourn* in this land, and I will be with thee, and will bless thee; for unto thee, and unto thy seed, I will give all these countries, and I will perform the oath which I sware unto Abraham thy father."

Now Jacob sent word to Esau, ". . . I have *sojourned* with Laban, and stayed there until now" (Gen. 32:4). May I remind you again of Hebrews 11:8-10 which says:

"By faith Abraham, when he was called to go out into a place which he should after receive for an inheritance, obeyed; and he went out, not knowing whither he went. By faith he sojourned in the land of promise, as in a strange country, dwelling in tabernacles with Isaac and Jacob, the heirs with him of the same promise: For he looked for a city

which hath foundations, whose builder and maker is God."

This matter of counting himself a temporary dweller, looking for eternal blessings later, was spiritually so important that Spirit-filled Stephen spoke of it in Acts 7:5, "And he gave him none inheritance in it, no, not so much as to set his foot on: yet he promised that he would give it to him for a possession, and to his seed after him, when as yet he had no child." So Jacob, still living in tents despite all his riches, is a stranger, a sojourner in the land of promise.

VERSES 2-4:

2 These *are* the generations of Jacob. Joseph, *being* seventeen years old, was feeding the flock with his brethren; and the lad *was* with the sons of Bilhah, and with the sons of Zilpah, his father's wives: and Joseph brought unto his father their evil report.

3 Now Israel loved Joseph more than all his children, because he *was* the son of his old age: and he made him a coat of *many* colours.

4 And when his brethren saw that their father loved him more than all his brethren, they hated him, and could not speak peaceably unto him.

The Beloved Son, Joseph

Now begins the wonderful story of Joseph who dominates 10 of the next 11 chapters of Genesis, through chapter 47.

The story begins when he was seventeen years old. He was reliable and trustworthy then and, as he worked with his older half brothers, he "brought unto his father their evil report." Perhaps he told of careless and wasteful ways and thus of losses to the flock. Israel loved Joseph more than all the children. He was a son of his old age and a mark of his affection was this coat of many colors. Oh, but the others were jealous of Joseph and hated him, partly because he was his father's favorite; and perhaps because the Spirit of God was on him.

So it often is. In I Samuel 18:12 we are told, "And Saul was afraid of David, because the Lord was with him, and was departed from Saul." In I Samuel 18:28,29 we are told, "Saul saw and knew that the Lord was with David . . . and Saul was yet the more afraid of David. . . ." We are told that Cain killed his brother Abel because "his own works were evil, and his brother's righteous" (I John 3:12). So the brothers of Joseph hated him.

VERSES 5-11:

5 ¶ And Joseph dreamed a dream, and he told it his brethren: and they hated him yet the more.

6 And he said unto them, Hear, I pray you, this dream which I have dreamed:

7 For, behold, we *were* binding sheaves in the field, and, lo, my sheaf arose, and also stood upright; and, behold, your sheaves stood round about, and made obeisance to my sheaf.

8 And his brethren said to him, Shalt thou indeed reign over us? or shalt thou indeed have dominion over us? And they hated him yet the more for his dreams, and for his words.

9 ¶ And he dreamed yet another dream, and told it his brethren, and said, Behold, I have dreamed a dream more; and, behold, the sun and the moon and the eleven stars made obeisance to me.

10 And he told it to his father, and to his brethren: and his father rebuked him, and said unto him, What *is* this dream that thou hast dreamed? Shall I and thy mother and thy brethren indeed come to bow down ourselves to thee to the earth?

11 And his brethren envied him; but his father observed the saying.

Dreams of Joseph

The Prophet Joel said, and Peter was inspired to quote it in Acts 2:17, ". . . I will pour out of my Spirit upon all flesh: and your sons and your daughters shall prophesy, and your young men shall see visions, and your old men shall dream dreams." So the Spirit of God is on this young Joseph. With prophetic dreams and visions he feels that God has some great future for him.

The first dream was obviously including the brothers binding the sheaves in the field and all the other sheaves of these brothers bowed down to Joseph's sheaf! They hated him for that, and said, "Shalt thou indeed reign over us?" Again he dreamed that the sun and the moon and the eleven stars made obeisance to him. The father understood the dream and said, "Shall I and thy mother and thy brethren indeed come to bow down ourselves to thee to the earth?" So his brothers envied and hated him, but old Jacob solemnly took it to heart.

No doubt the dream primarily referred to the time when he would be prime minister in Egypt. His mother had died before that time. But who knows but that Rachel, when God hearkened to her and gave her the boy Joseph, did not, after much prayer, know that Joseph would have the preeminence, and in her heart she bowed to him.

VERSES 12-27:

12 ¶ And his brethren went to feed their father's flock in Shē'-chĕm.

13 And Israel said unto Joseph, Do not thy brethren feed *the flock* in Shē'-chĕm? come, and I will send thee unto them. And he said to him, Here *am I*.

14 And he said to him, Go, I pray thee, see whether it be well with thy brethren, and well with the flocks; and bring me word again. So he sent him out of the vale of Hebron, and he came to Shē'-chĕm.

15 ¶ And a certain man found him, and, behold, *he was* wandering in the field: and the man asked him, saying, What seekest thou?

16 And he said, I seek my brethren: tell me, I pray thee, where they feed *their flocks*.

17 And the man said, They are departed hence; for I heard them say, Let us go to Dothan. And Joseph went after his brethren, and found them in Dothan.

18 And when they saw him afar off, even before he came near unto them, they conspired against him to slay him.

19 And they said one to another, Behold, this dreamer cometh.

20 Come now therefore, and let us slay him, and cast him into some pit, and we will say, Some evil beast hath devoured him: and we shall see what will become of his dreams.

21 And Reuben heard *it*, and he delivered him out of their hands; and said, Let us not kill him.

22 And Reuben said unto them, Shed no blood, *but* cast him into this pit that *is* in the wilderness, and lay no hand upon him; that he might rid him out of their hands, to deliver him to his father again.

23 ¶ And it came to pass when Joseph was come unto his brethren, that they stript Joseph out of his coat, *his* coat of *many* colours that *was* on him;

24 And they took him, and cast him into a pit: and the pit *was* empty, *there was* no water in it.

25 And they sat down to eat bread: and they lifted up their eyes and looked, and, behold, a company of Ĭsh'-mĕê-lītes came from Gĭl'-ĕ-ăd with their camels bearing spicery and balm and myrrh, going to carry *it* down to Egypt.

26 And Judah said unto his brethren, What profit *is it* if we slay our

brother, and conceal his blood?

27 Come, and let us sell him to the Ísh⸗mée⸗lítes, and let not our hand

be upon him; for he *is* our brother *and* our flesh. And his brethren were content.

Brothers Plot to Kill, Then Sell Joseph As a Slave

Jacob's flocks and herds are many. They must wander far to find sufficient grass. The older sons are with the flocks and Joseph goes to check up and bring word again.

At Shechem he found the brothers had gone on with the flocks to Dothan and went to find them. But the brothers, seeing him, called him "this dreamer" and planned to kill him.

Reuben heard it and delivered him and said, "Let us not kill him." He suggested that he be put in a pit temporarily, then he hoped to deliver him to his father whole.

They took off that beautiful coat of many colors which they hated because it was a sign of Jacob's love and put him into a pit with no water and no way could he climb out. But before Reuben can get him out and away to the father, as the brothers are gathered around the campfire and eating, they saw a caravan of Ishmeelites from Gilead that had crossed the Jordan and were going down to Egypt with this commerce. Judah, wanting to make sure that the brother was not killed, offered the suggestion that they sell him as a slave to the Ishmeelites, then they would never know of him any more.

To that the brethren agreed.

VERSES 28-36:

28 Then there passed by Midianites merchantmen; and they drew and lifted up Joseph out of the pit, and sold Joseph to the Ísh⸗mée⸗lítes for twenty *pieces* of silver: and they brought Joseph into Egypt.

29 ¶ And Reuben returned unto the pit; and, behold, Joseph *was* not in the pit; and he rent his clothes.

30 And he returned unto his brethren, and said, The child *is* not; and I, whither shall I go?

31 And they took Joseph's coat, and killed a kid of the goats, and dipped the coat in the blood;

32 And they sent the coat of *many* colours, and they brought *it* to their father; and said, This have we found:

know now whether it *be* thy son's coat or no.

33 And he knew it, and said, *It is* my son's coat; an evil beast hath devoured him; Joseph is without doubt rent in pieces.

34 And Jacob rent his clothes, and put sackcloth upon his loins, and mourned for his son many days.

35 And all his sons and all his daughters rose up to comfort him; but he refused to be comforted; and he said, For I will go down into the grave unto my son mourning. Thus his father wept for him.

36 And the Midianites sold him into Egypt unto Pŏt'-ĭ-phär, an officer of Phâr'-āōh's, *and* captain of the guard.

Sold Into Slavery, Joseph Goes to Egypt

Perhaps some of the men ate while others watched the flocks. At any rate, Reuben was not there when the Ishmeelite caravan came by and they sold Joseph, to go down to Egypt. Now Reuben was in great distress.

The Scriptures aren't quite clear here when it mentions the Ishmeelites in verses 25, 27, 28. But it was Midianite merchantmen who passed by. Did the brothers sell Joseph to these merchantmen, and they in turn, sell him to the Ishmeelites en route to Egypt? That is very possible. Or it may be that this was a mixed caravan. Ishmeelites and Midianites did intermarry. They often mingled. And you might call it a group of Ishmeelites or a group of Midianites—we do not know. If we had all the facts at hand, it would be perfectly clear and perfectly correct as the Word of God always is if properly translated and properly understood.

But they must answer to Jacob. Where is his beloved son? So they killed a kid, dipped the coat in the blood and sent the coat to Jacob, pretending some wild beast had killed the boy. For long years Jacob will grieve over the supposed death of Joseph; and how happy he will be to learn long years later that Joseph is yet alive.

Now Joseph has gone down to Egypt and the prophecy to Abraham in Genesis 15:13, 14 continues in progress. Joseph is in Egypt. There Jacob and the family will all come. Eventually they will become slaves to the Egyptians and be oppressed until Moses leads them out.

GENESIS 38

VERSES 1-10:

AND it came to pass at that time, that Judah went down from his brethren, and turned in to a certain Ă-dŭl'-lăm-īte, whose name *was* Hirah.

2 And Judah saw there a daughter of a certain Cā'-nă-ăn-īte, whose name *was* Shuah; and he took her, and went in unto her.

3 And she conceived, and bare a son; and he called his name Er.

4 And she conceived again, and bare a son; and she called his name Onan.

5 And she yet again conceived, and bare a son; and called his name Shē'-läh: and he was at Chē'-zĭb, when she bare him.

6 And Judah took a wife for Er his firstborn, whose name *was* Tamar.

7 And Er, Judah's firstborn, was wicked in the sight of the LORD; and the LORD slew him.

8 And Judah said unto Onan, Go in unto thy brother's wife, and marry her, and raise up seed to thy brother.

9 And Onan knew that the seed should not be his; and it came to pass, when he went in unto his brother's wife, that he spilled *it* on the ground, lest that he should give seed to his brother.

10 And the thing which he did displeased the LORD: wherefore he slew him also.

Judah's Ungodly Sons

Judah had three sons, Er, Onan and Shelah, by his wife, the daughter of Shuah a Canaanite.

But Er was "wicked in the sight of the Lord; and the Lord slew him" (vs. 7). How often in the Bible do we learn that God kills certain people. Sometimes it was with a great plague. When the people complained against God and Moses, He sent fiery serpents and much people of Israel died (Num. 21:5-9). When a certain prophet disobeyed the Lord's plain command, he had a lion kill him (I Kings 13:24). God announced that Saul and his sons would die and had them killed in battle with the Philistines. At one time God had the ground open up and men went down alive into the pit because of their rebellion. In Luke 13:1-5 the Lord Jesus indicates that those Galileans, whose blood Pilate mingled with the sacrifices, were slain in the will of God. And those men of Jerusalem were killed when the tower of Siloam fell, slain of God. God does kill people because of their sins.

We wonder how many of the approximately 55,000 who die yearly in automoble accidents in America are killed because of their sins. Sometimes it is obvious. They drive under the influence of liquor or dope; sometimes the chain of events is not clear. But no one dies against the will of God, and often people must die prematurely because of their sins. We should remember that the breath of every man and the heartbeat of every being is in the hands of God. Sin is certain to be punished and often it is with death. Ananias and Sapphira died for lying to God (Acts 5).

But it was the custom, later put into the Mosaic law, that a brother should take the wife of a brother who died and left childless and raise up seed to his brother. So Judah instructed another son, Onan, to take as his wife Tamar who had been wife to Er. But Onan evidently had rebellion in his heart. He did not want to have children who would be named after his brother and not counted his own children; so he avoided conception by withdrawal, and God killed him.

We have no doubt that God put this down in Scripture with the intent that we should see the sin of preventing conception in a normal course of events. Marriage is intended to produce children. Certainly in this case Onan sinned and was worthy of death in God's sight. Good men and women, intending and wanting to have children but seeking to space them perhaps, with some reasonable plan, might temporarily avoid having children. But to set out deliberately to never have children or to have few when God would give many, is counted as sin in the Bible. Children are a blessing, a heritage of God. What God gives, He can provide for. People should not trifle with marriage. The command given to Adam and to Noah to "multiply and replenish the earth" surely applies to married couples today.

VERSES 11-23:

11 Then said Judah to Tamar his daughter in law, Remain a widow at thy father's house, till Shē´-läh my son be grown: for he said, Lest peradventure he die also, as his brethren did. And Tamar went and dwelt in her father's house.

12 ¶ And in process of time the daughter of Shuah Judah's wife died; and Judah was comforted, and went up unto his sheepshearers to Timnath, he and his friend Hirah the Ā-dŭl´-lăm-īte.

13 And it was told Tamar, saying, Behold thy father in law goeth up to Timnath to shear his sheep.

14 And she put her widow's garments off from her, and covered her with a vail, and wrapped herself, and sat in an open place, which is by the way to Timnath; for she saw that Shē´-läh was grown, and she was not given unto him to wife.

15 When Judah saw her, he thought her to be an harlot; because she had covered her face.

16 And he turned unto her by the way, and said, Go to, I pray thee, let me come in unto thee; (for he knew not that she was his daughter in law.) And she said, What wilt thou give me, that thou mayest come in unto me?

17 And he said, I will send thee a kid from the flock. And she said, Wilt thou give me a pledge, till thou send it?

18 And he said, What pledge shall I give thee? And she said, Thy signet, and thy bracelets, and thy staff that is in thine hand. And he gave it her, and came in unto her, and she conceived by him.

19 And she arose, and went away, and laid by her vail from her, and put on the garments of her widowhood.

20 And Judah sent the kid by the hand of his friend the Ā-dŭl´-lăm-īte, to receive his pledge from the woman's hand: but he found her not.

21 Then he asked the men of that place, saying, Where is the harlot, that was openly by the way side? And they said, There was no harlot in this place.

22 And he returned to Judah, and said, I cannot find her; and also the men of the place said, that there was no harlot in this place.

23 And Judah said, Let her take it to her, lest we be shamed: behold, I sent this kid, and thou hast not found her.

Judah and Tamar

No doubt Judah intended that his third son Shelah, when he was old enough to marry, should take the wife, Tamar, of his older brother Er and of Onan. Judah seemed to fear that God would kill Shelah unless he took the proper responsibility for the wife of his brother. Meantime, Tamar went back to live in her father's house, now a widow, without children.

Then Judah's wife, the daughter of Shuah, died and Tamar planned that she would not die childless but would have a child by Judah if he would not have her married to the other son Shelah. So preparing herself to look like a harlot, with her face covered, she sat in an open place on the way to Timnath where her father-in-law was going to shear his sheep. Thinking she was a harlot, Judah the lonely, wifeless man, went in to this woman whom he supposed was a harlot.

But Tamar must have some evidence as to who is the father of the child-to-be, so she schemes to get his signet, bracelets and staff. Then she will keep these and the paternity of the child cannot be denied. Guileless Judah sent the kid he had promised by the hand of a friend. They could not find any harlot there! So Tamar has kept the signet ring, the bracelets and the walking stick of Judah!

VERSES 24-30:

24 ¶ And it came to pass about three months after, that it was told Judah, saying, Tamar thy daughter in law hath played the harlot; and also, behold, she *is* with child by whoredom. And Judah said, Bring her forth, and let her be burnt.

25 When she *was* brought forth, she sent to her father in law, saying, By the man, whose these *are, am* I with child: and she said, Discern, I pray thee, whose *are* these, the signet, and bracelets, and staff.

26 And Judah acknowledged *them*, and said, She hath been more righteous than I; because that I gave her not to Shē-läh my son. And he knew her again no more.

27 ¶ And it came to pass in the time of her travail, that, behold, twins *were* in her womb.

28 And it came to pass, when she travailed, that *the one* put out *his* hand: and the midwife took and bound upon his hand a scarlet thread, saying, This came out first.

29 And it came to pass, as he drew back his hand, that, behold, his brother came out: and she said, How hast thou broken forth? *this* breach *be* upon thee: therefore his name was called Phâr-ĕz.

30 And afterward came out his brother, that had the scarlet thread upon his hand: and his name was called Zarah.

A Child Born in Ancestral Line of Christ

Does it seem strange that an entire chapter of thirty verses should be given to this incident, told as somewhat of a parenthesis in the story of Joseph? But here is a relevant matter: the child to be born is to be in the ancestral line of Jesus!

Judah was shocked when he heard that Tamar, his daughter-in-law, had played the harlot and is pregnant. Judah said, perhaps rashly and Pharisaically, "Bring her forth, and let her be burnt." But she brought with her the signet ring, the bracelets, the staff of Judah and faced him with them. He acknowledged that she had been more righteous than he. He had not given Shelah the son as a husband as he had promised.

At the time of delivery, behold twins are born. The firstborn is Phares. The Lord tells us in Luke 3:33 that this Phares, son of Judah, is in the ancestral line from Abraham down to Christ. Christ is to be born of the tribe of Judah and through Judah's son Phares, by Tamar. That makes the birth of Phares so important that the chapter is included here.

It will give you great joy to go through the genealogical tables in Luke 3 and Matthew 1:1-17. Jesus came from Abraham, from Isaac, from Jacob, from Judah and Tamar. And we find that He came through Tamar who committed adultery with her father-in-law, and through Rahab the harlot who received the spies in peace and married Salmon. Here Christ came through Ruth the Moabitess who came to rest under the feathers of Jehovah, returning with Naomi to the Holy Land.

Ah, then, through peasants and paupers, through good men and bad, the Lord Jesus came because He is the Son of man, the Son of mankind, the Saviour of the whole world. He belongs to everybody.

GENESIS 39

VERSES 1-6:

AND Joseph was brought down to Egypt; and Pŏt-ĭ-phär, an officer of Phâr-'aōh, captain of the guard, an Egyptian, bought him of the hands of the Ish-'mē̂e-lĭtes, which had brought him down thither.

2 And the LORD was with Joseph, and he was a prosperous man; and he was in the house of his master the Egyptian.

3 And his master saw that the LORD *was* with him, and that the LORD made all that he did to prosper in his hand.

4 And Joseph found grace in his sight, and he served him: and he made him overseer over his house, and all *that* he had he put into his hand.

5 And it came to pass from the time *that* he had made him overseer in his house, and over all that he had, that the LORD blessed the Egyptian's house for Joseph's sake; and the blessing of the LORD was upon all that he had in the house, and in the field.

6 And he left all that he had in Joseph's hand; and he knew not ought he had, save the bread which he did eat. And Joseph was a goodly *person,* and well favoured.

Teenager, Joseph, Comes to Egypt

How old was Joseph when he arrived in Egypt and was sold to Potiphar, an officer of Pharaoh, captain of his guard? He had been seventeen when the story started in Genesis 37:2. Some months, or a year or so, have gone by, we suppose, since the period of his dreams and the growing hatred of his brothers.

He was not counted a grown man when he was sold as a slave and when Reuben wanted "to deliver him to his father again." Down in Egypt years later when the brothers, with guilty conscience, remembered, Reuben spoke up: "Spake I not unto you, saying, Do not sin against the child. . . ?" (Gen. 42:22).

So the young man yet in his teens comes to work as a slave in Potiphar's house. Here he, faithful and loyal as he was to his father, now proves himself faithful and loyal to this man who has become his owner, his master. He is not only faithful but wise, sensible and diligent. "And the Lord was with Joseph, and he was a prosperous man." So the captain of the guard soon "left all that he had in Joseph's hand" (vs. 6).

Some people whine that they "never had a chance." The circumstances were always against them. But prosperity is not really in the events and circumstances but in the character of the one who earns prosperity. I speak now not only of making money but more of making good wherever one is. Joseph would have been prosperous in any situation. So would David. God was with him and made whatever he did to prosper. So it was with Joshua. God had promised that wherever he set the sole of his foot, that God had given him.

Joseph prospers here in the house of Potiphar. He will prosper when he is in jail and will soon be running things there. He will prosper when he is prime minister of Egypt and the lives of millions are in his hands. God was with Joseph.

He was probably overseer over a number of servants, and over all the property the captain of the guard had.

But Joseph must get ready for great work ahead. There must be testing. He must learn to bear responsibility, must handle things, people and money. He must suffer and still trust God. He must prove himself loyal to Potiphar now, although he is a slave, and later he can be trusted to be loyal to Pharaoh. And since he is loyal to those God has put over him, we will find him also loyal to God and faithful.

We must remember how long God took to ripen Abraham, to answer his prayers about a son, and to teach him spiritual truths. Isaac and Rebekah needed to wait twenty years before God gave children. Now God must prepare Joseph. The green wood from the finest tree needs seasoning. Fruit needs to ripen. Seed must grow. He must be tempted now for only God knows the temptations that come with the unlimited power of the prime minister later.

We can see it now. Happily Joseph seemed to see it then. He was faithful and cheerful in the midst of great trials.

_____

VERSES 7-20:

7 ¶ And it came to pass after these things, that his master's wife cast her eyes upon Joseph; and she said, Lie with me.

8 But he refused, and said unto his master's wife, Behold, my master wotteth not what *is* with me in the house, and he hath committed all that he hath to my hand;

9 *There is* none greater in this house than I; neither hath he kept back any thing from me but thee, because thou *art* his wife: how then can I do this great wickedness, and sin against God?

10 And it came to pass, as she spake to Joseph day by day, that he hearkened not unto her, to lie by her, *or* to be with her.

11 And it came to pass about this time, that *Joseph* went into the house to do his business; and *there was* none of the men of the house there within.

12 And she caught him by his garment, saying, Lie with me: and he left his garment in her hand, and fled, and got him out.

13 And it came to pass, when she saw that he had left his garment in her hand, and was fled forth,

14 That she called unto the men of her house, and spake unto them, saying, See, he hath brought in an Hebrew unto us to mock us; he came in unto me to lie with me, and I cried with a loud voice:

15 And it came to pass, when he heard that I lifted up my voice and cried, that he left his garment with me, and fled, and got him out.

16 And she laid up his garment by her, until his lord came home.

17 And she spake unto him according to these words, saying, The Hebrew servant, which thou hast brought unto us, came in unto me to mock me:

18 And it came to pass, as I lifted up my voice and cried, that he left his garment with me, and fled out.

19 And it came to pass, when his master heard the words of his wife, which she spake unto him, saying, After this manner did thy servant to me; that his wrath was kindled.

20 And Joseph's master took him, and put him into the prison, a place where the king's prisoners *were* bound: and he was there in the prison.

A Sensuous, Lying Woman and Undeserved Imprisonment

Joseph's conscience held him true. Although he was a slave, he had been well treated. He felt a responsibility of a servant to his master. He could not betray that trust. One could understand if there had been some bitterness in his heart over being sold unjustly as a slave in a foreign country. And in this world it is God's will that some should be servants and some should be masters; that some should be rulers and others should be ruled; that some should be parents and others should be children; that some should be teachers and other students. Where God has allowed one to be a slave, then God has commands: "Servants, be subject to your masters with all fear; not only to the good and gentle, but also to the froward" (I Pet. 2:18).

Again Colossians 3:22 says, "Servants, obey in all things your masters according to the flesh; not with eyeservice, as menpleasers; but in singleness of heart, fearing God."

But a servant who serves well his master serves Christ. In this case, to be loyal and true to Potiphar meant to be loyal to God. So Joseph said, "How then can I do this great wickedness, and sin against God?"

Whether one is a general or a private in the army, he has an obligation to honesty, integrity, purity. To sin against those whom God has put over us would be to sin against God.

Some people foolishly say we should have no laws against the decisions of consenting adults whether for adultery or sodomy. Ah, but to sin with Potiphar's wife is to sin against Potiphar To sin against a single girl is to sin against the man who would one day marry her.

A poet has said, "Hell hath no fury like a woman scorned." So the woman who wanted Joseph now hated him. And what if he should tell her husband she had tried to seduce him? So with hate and perhaps for self-protection she schemed against him and accused him. Once when she tried to hold him, he slipped from his outer garment and ran away. That was wise. But she used that garment to pretend that he had sought to violate her. She enlisted the other servants over whom Joseph had been made overseer and who may have been jealous, and accused Joseph to her husband. Angrily, Potiphar commanded Joseph to be put in jail.

But note. It is not the ordinary prison but "a place where the king's prisoners were bound." Here he will meet the king's butler and baker when they are put in jail and have prophetic dreams. Here eventually Pharaoh will know that God is with this man to interpret dreams from God.

At first the case of Joseph seems hopeless. He is only a slave. He is in prison. There is no one to take his part and see to his release. He may have had some bitter thoughts and wonderings.

---

21 ¶ But the LORD was with Joseph, and shewed him mercy, and gave him favour in the sight of the keeper of the prison.

22 And the keeper of the prison committed to Joseph's hand all the prisoners that *were* in the prison; and whatsoever they did there, he was the doer *of it*.

23 The keeper of the prison looked not to any thing *that was* under his hand; because the LORD was with him, and *that* which he did, the LORD made *it* to prosper.

God With Joseph in Prison

Among the prisoners, criminals, violaters of the law, irresponsible people who had perhaps rebelled against the king or sinned against him, Joseph stands out before the warden as a bright light! Ah, the Lord was with Joseph, so he had peace of mind. He was courteous and industrious. He was sensible. It is said that responsibility gravitates to the shoulders of him who can bear responsibility. We remember that Joseph was "a prosperous man" (vs. 2). In any circumstances, real character, including peace of mind, a seizing of opportunities, a willingness to work, a willingness to obey orders, a willingness to earnestly do whatever is at hand, counting it as unto the Lord—that kind of character will shine, and the Lord being with Joseph "shewed him mercy, and gave him favour in the sight of the keeper of the prison." Are you surprised? It wasn't long till Joseph was in charge of all the prisoners in the prison, "And whatsoever they did there, he was the doer of it."

Fortunate was that warden of the prison! Fortunate is any executive, any pastor, any father over children, who has those who take upon them the responsibility offered and do what they are trusted to do and happily do their part.

God has great things for this man Joseph. There is testing and there will be more. He is young; he must mature; he must learn more. But God is preparing Joseph.

GENESIS 40

VERSES 1-4:

AND it came to pass after these things, *that* the butler of the king of Egypt and *his* baker had offended their lord the king of Egypt.

2 And Phâr-'aōh was wroth against two *of* his officers, against the chief of the butlers, and against the chief of the bakers.

3 And he put them in ward in the house of the captain of the guard, into the prison, the place where Joseph *was* bound.

4 And the captain of the guard charged Joseph with them, and he served them: and they continued a season in ward.

Joseph in Charge of Pharaoh's Chief Butler and Chief Baker

Two of Pharaoh's officers, the chief butler and the chief baker, had angered Pharaoh some way. Now despite the importance of their position they are put in jail and put in the charge of Joseph! So Joseph, evidently with the freedom of the jail, we suppose, brought their food and saw to their comfort, yet saw that they could not escape. Joseph is trusted. He will not release any prisoners, will not scheme against those in authority. Now two sad men, fearful of the future, are put in his charge.

VERSES 5-8:

5 ¶ And they dreamed a dream both of them, each man his dream in one night, each man according to the interpretation of his dream, the butler and the baker of the king of Egypt, which *were* bound in the prison.

6 And Joseph came in unto them in the morning, and looked upon them, and, behold, they *were* sad.

7 And he asked Phâr-'aōh's officers that *were* with him in the ward of his lord's house, saying, Wherefore look ye *so* sadly to day?

8 And they said unto him, We have dreamed a dream, and *there is* no interpreter of it. And Joseph said unto them, *Do* not interpretations *belong* to God? tell me *them*, I pray you.

Dreams? Joseph Has Had Dreams From God, Too!

As he served these two important officers of Pharaoh's, one morning he came to their cells and found them very sad. Why did they look so sad? They have dreamed each one a dream. It must have some meaning, but "there is no interpreter of it." Joseph answered, "Do not interpretations belong to God? tell me them [the dreams], I pray you."

Already Joseph knew that God had spoken to him in dreams. The dreams had not been fulfilled. He had trouble and heartache, a slave in a far-off land, yet he had confidence that the sheaves of his brothers would bow to his sheaf. The sun, moon and eleven stars would bow to his star!

That means that Joseph must have daily been in touch with God. He must have prayed about his trouble and found the answer. God was with him. He was willing to wait. God would reveal to this man the answer to the dreams. If God gives a dream with a message, He wants somebody to tell what the message is. He will give a dream to Nebuchadnezzar, and He wants Daniel to know the dream and interpret it. He will give a dream to Pharaoh, on which the lives of millions depend, and He will want Joseph to learn from God the answer. Now Joseph will undertake to find from God the meaning of the dream of the chief butler and the chief baker.

VERSES 9-19:

9 And the chief butler told his dream to Joseph, and said to him, In my dream, behold, a vine *was* before me;

10 And in the vine *were* three branches: and it *was* as though it budded, *and* her blossoms shot forth; and the clusters thereof brought forth ripe grapes:

11 And Phâr-ʻāōh's cup *was* in my hand: and I took the grapes, and pressed them into Phâr-ʻāōh's cup, and I gave the cup into Phâr-ʻāōh's hand.

12 And Joseph said unto him, This *is* the interpretation of it: The three branches *are* three days:

13 Yet within three days shall

Phâr-'aōh lift up thine head, and restore thee unto thy place: and thou shalt deliver Phâr-'aōh's cup into his hand, after the former manner when thou wast his butler.

14 But think on me when it shall be well with thee, and shew kindness, I pray thee, unto me, and make mention of me unto Phâr-'aōh, and bring me out of this house:

15 For indeed I was stolen away out of the land of the Hebrews: and here also have I done nothing that they should put me into the dungeon.

16 When the chief baker saw that the interpretation was good, he said unto Joseph, I also *was* in my dream, and, behold, *I had* three white baskets on my head:

17 And in the uppermost basket *there was* of all manner of bakemeats for Phâr-'aōh; and the birds did eat them out of the basket upon my head.

18 And Joseph answered and said, This *is* the interpretation thereof: The three baskets *are* three days:

19 Yet within three days shall Phâr-'aōh lift up thy head from off thee, and shall hang thee on a tree; and the birds shall eat thy flesh from off thee.

Meaning of the Dreams

In a dream the chief butler saw a vine with three branches and it brought forth grapes; he took the grapes, pressed them into Pharaoh's cup and brought the cup to Pharaoh. What did it mean? Joseph told him, "The three branches are three days: Yet within three days shall Pharaoh lift up thine head, and restore thee unto thy place: and thou shalt deliver Pharaoh's cup into his hand, after the former manner when thou wast his butler."

The chief baker took courage from the good interpretation given the butler's dream; so he told his dream. On his head were three white baskets with all manner of bakemeats. The birds did eat them out of the basket. Joseph gave the sad interpretation: the three baskets represented three days and within three days Pharaoh would take off his head, hang him on a tree and the birds would eat his flesh!

Oh, the chief baker could not help him. But the butler restored to daily service for Pharaoh could, so Joseph besought him, "But think on me when it shall be well with thee and shew kindness, I pray thee, unto me, and make mention of me unto Pharaoh, and bring me out of this house: For indeed I was stolen away out of the land of the Hebrews: and here also have I done nothing that they should put me into the dungeon." I am sure the butler intended and probably promised that he would remember Joseph.

VERSES 20-23:

20 ¶ And it came to pass the third day, *which was* Phâr-'aōh's birthday, that he made a feast unto all his servants: and he lifted up the head of the chief butler and of the chief baker among his servants.

21 And he restored the chief butler unto his butlership again; and he gave the cup into Phâr-'aōh's hand:

22 But he hanged the chief baker: as Joseph had interpreted to them.

23 Yet did not the chief butler remember Joseph, but forgat him.

Butler Forgets Kindness Done Him

But Joseph was left in prison. The butler went his happy way in three days, back in the great place of honor as cupbearer and chief butler to the mighty Pharaoh. Two years went by and he did not remember and did nothing to release Joseph.

Does that seem hard? But let us remember that when butlers forget, God always remembers. He remembered His covenant with Abraham. He remembered Rebekah and Rachel when they cried so long for children. He remembered Sarah. He remembered Hannah pleading for a son. He remembered Noah, tossed on the mighty deep with the world covered with water. So do not fear; some men mean Joseph harm, but God means it for good. Some people neglect their duty to Joseph and mistreat him, but God sees that it comes out right.

One of the blessings God promises and for which David thanked the Lord is, "The Lord executeth righteousness and judgment for all that are oppressed" (Ps. 103:6).

GENESIS 41

AND it came to pass at the end of two full years, that Phâr-́aōh dreamed: and, behold, he stood by the river.

2 And, behold, there came up out of the river seven well favoured kine and fatfleshed; and they fed in a meadow.

3 And, behold, seven other kine came up after them out of the river, ill favoured and leanfleshed; and stood by the *other* kine upon the brink of the river.

4 And the ill favoured and leanfleshed kine did eat up the seven well favoured and fat kine. So Phâr-̄aōh awoke.

5 And he slept and dreamed the second time: and, behold, seven ears of corn came up upon one stalk, rank and good.

6 And, behold, seven thin ears and blasted with the east wind sprung up after them.

7 And the seven thin ears devoured the seven rank and full ears. And Phâr-́aōh awoke, and, behold, *it was* a dream.

8 And it came to pass in the morning that his spirit was troubled; and he sent and called for all the magicians of Egypt, and all the wise men thereof: and Phâr-́aōh told them his dream; but *there was* none that could interpret them unto Phâr-́aōh.

Pharaoh's Strange Dreams

Two years went by while Joseph languished unremembered in prison. We are sure he did his duty daily, that he was still greatly trusted by the keeper of the prison and that God still prospered him. Now in the night the mighty Pharaoh dreamed troubled dreams. The first dream was of seven beautiful fat cattle that came out of the River Nile and fed in the meadow. But seven others came out of the river, lean and scrawny, and strangely they ate up the fat cattle. What could it mean?

Pharaoh went to sleep again and this time in his dream there were seven ears of corn upon one stalk, rank and good. But then seven thin ears, blasted by the east wind, sprang up after the others, and the seven thin ears devoured the seven full, rank ears. Pharaoh awoke and was troubled by the dream. What could it mean? He had a serious impression from God that some great and important matter was about to occur. So he called for all the magicians, those who knew about signs and wonders or pretended to know, those whom he would hope had some spiritual insight. What did the dreams mean? None of them could tell.

---

9 ¶ Then spake the chief butler unto Phâr-'āōh, saying, I do remember my faults this day:

10 Phâr-'āōh was wroth with his servants, and put me in ward in the captain of the guard's house, *both* me and the chief baker:

11 And we dreamed a dream in one night, I and he; we dreamed each man according to the interpretation of his dream.

12 And *there was* there with us a young man, an Hebrew, servant to the captain of the guard; and we told him, and he interpreted to us our dreams; to each man according to his dream he did interpret.

13 And it came to pass, as he interpreted to us, so it was; me he restored unto mine office, and him he hanged.

Butler Now Tells of Joseph

Pharaoh's butler now was deeply convicted. He had forgotten the blessings he had, the man who helped him, by revelations from God. How poorly he had repaid that young man in prison for no fault of his own! Now he told Pharaoh about it.

He and the chief baker had dreams. Joseph had interpreted the dreams. They came out just as Joseph had interpreted them from God. The butler was restored to his important place and the baker was executed. The answer was given by "a young man, an Hebrew, servant to the captain of the guard."

I am sure God arranged it that the butler can tell the thing now fresh, when it has real meaning and when Pharaoh's hungry heart seizes upon it, much better than if he had been telling it everywhere before or even if he had gotten Joseph out of jail and Joseph had gone. Now is God's time. God's train never comes in late.

VERSES 14-16:

14 ¶ Then Phâr-́aōh sent and called Joseph, and they brought him hastily out of the dungeon: and he shaved *himself*, and changed his raiment, and came in unto Phâr-́aōh.

15 And Phâr-́aōh said unto Joseph, I have dreamed a dream, and *there is* none that can interpret it: and I have heard say of thee, *that* thou canst understand a dream to interpret it.

16 And Joseph answered Phâr-́aōh, saying, *It is* not in me: God shall give Phâr-́aōh an answer of peace.

Joseph Brought Before Pharaoh

Joseph shaved himself and changed his garment, then he came to Pharaoh, who said, "I have heard say of thee, that thou canst understand a dream to interpret it." Joseph very wisely answered, "It is not in me: God shall give Pharaoh an answer of peace."

We are reminded of David's facing Goliath: ". . .Thou comest to me with a sword, and with a spear, and with a shield: but I come to thee in the name of the Lord of hosts, the God of the armies of Israel, whom thou hast defied. This day will the Lord deliver thee into mine hand. . . ." (I Sam. 17:45,46).

We are reminded of Daniel who said, when faced with the dream of Nebuchadnezzar, "The secret which the king hath demanded cannot the wise men, the astrologers, the magicians, the soothsayers, shew unto the king; But there is a God in heaven that revealeth secrets, and maketh known to the king Nebuchadnezzar what shall be in the latter days" (Dan. 2:27,28). Again he said in verse 30, "But as for me, this secret is not revealed to me for any wisdom that I have more than any living, but for their sakes that shall make known the interpretation to the king, and that thou mightest know the thoughts of thy heart."

So Gideon taught his men to cry, "The sword of the Lord, and of Gideon" (Judges 7:18,20).

VERSES 17-32:

17 And Phâr-́aōh said unto Joseph, In my dream, behold, I stood upon the bank of the river:

18 And, behold, there came up out of the river seven kine, fatfleshed and well favoured; and they fed in a meadow:

19 And, behold, seven other kine came up after them, poor and very ill favoured and leanfleshed, such as I never saw in all the land of Egypt for badness:

20 And the lean and the ill favoured kine did eat up the first seven fat kine:

21 And when they had eaten them up, it could not be known that they had eaten them; but they *were* still ill favoured, as at the beginning. So I awoke.

22 And I saw in my dream, and, behold, seven ears came up in one stalk, full and good:

23 And, behold, seven ears, withered, thin, *and* blasted with the east wind, sprung up after them:

24 And the thin ears devoured the seven good ears: and I told *this* unto the magicians; but *there was* none that could declare *it* to me.

25 ¶ And Joseph said unto Phâr-́aōh, The dream of Phâr-́aōh *is* one:

26 The seven good kine *are* seven years; and the seven good ears *are* seven years: the dream *is* one.

27 And the seven thin and ill favoured kine that came up after them *are* seven years; and the seven empty ears blasted with the east wind shall be seven years of famine.

28 This *is* the thing which I have spoken unto Phâr-́aōh: What God *is* about to do he sheweth unto Phâr-́aōh.

29 Behold, there come seven years of great plenty throughout all the land of Egypt:

30 And there shall arise after them seven years of famine; and all the plenty shall be forgotten in the land of Egypt; and the famine shall consume the land;

31 And the plenty shall not be known in the land by reason of that famine following; for it *shall be* very grievous.

32 And for that the dream was doubled unto Phâr-́aōh twice; *it is* because the thing *is* established by God, and God will shortly bring it to pass.

Pharaoh's Dreams Interpreted

In the dream, Pharaoh stood by the bank of the River Nile. We must remember that in those days the Nile overflowed its banks every year and enriched the whole valley, making possible the crops in that arid country. So out of the river seven fat cows came. That meant that for seven years the Nile would overflow at the right time and the ground would be wet and soaked and the seed could sprout and the ground, enriched with new silt from the river, would bring forth abundantly.

The second dream was like it. The seven ears represented

seven good years with great plenty. The seven thin, blasted ears represented great famine that would come. Doubtless the river would fail to water all the land and there would come famine.

The dream was doubled. The meaning was not only sure but very, very important!

VERSES 33-37:

33 Now therefore let Phâr-'aōh look out a man discreet and wise, and set him over the land of Egypt.

34 Let Phâr-'aōh do *this*, and let him appoint officers over the land, and take up the fifth part of the land of Egypt in the seven plenteous years.

35 And let them gather all the food of those good years that come, and lay up corn under the hand of Phâr-'aōh, and let them keep food in the cities.

36 And that food shall be for store to the land against the seven years of famine, which shall be in the land of Egypt; that the land perish not through the famine.

37 ¶ And the thing was good in the eyes of Phâr-'aōh, and in the eyes of all his servants.

Some Trustworthy Man Must Save and Administer in the Crisis

Joseph had God-given wisdom, and so he not only interpreted the dreams, but he gave necessary and wise advice. They must find some discreet and wise man and set him over the whole land of Egypt. He must have the power to demand that for seven years much of the rich crops be put away in storehouses. Granaries must be built, the crops collected, laid by and properly administered. Otherwise the land would perish in the famine.

The young man with the shining face and assured voice stood before Pharaoh and his officers. There could be no doubt that the hand of God was upon him. Where could they find some man wise and honest enough and enough in the favor of God to supervise this business?

VERSES 38-44:

38 And Phâr-́aōh said unto his servants, Can we find *such a one* as this *is*, a man in whom the Spirit of God *is?*

39 And Phâr-́aōh said unto Joseph, Forasmuch as God hath shewed thee all this, *there is* none so discreet and wise as thou *art:*

40 Thou shalt be over my house, and according unto thy word shall all my people be ruled: only in the throne will I be greater than thou.

41 And Phâr-́aōh said unto Joseph, See, I have set thee over all the land of Egypt.

42 And Phâr-́aōh took off his ring from his hand, and put it upon Joseph's hand, and arrayed him in vestures of fine linen, and put a gold chain about his neck;

43 And he made him to ride in the second chariot which he had; and they cried before him, Bow the knee: and he made him *ruler* over all the land of Egypt.

44 And Phâr-́aōh said unto Joseph, I *am* Phâr-́aōh, and without thee shall no man lift up his hand or foot in all the land of Egypt.

Joseph Made Prime Minister

Joseph is given powers almost of a dictator. Only in the throne itself was Pharaoh greater than Joseph. Pharaoh's signet ring with which he would sign orders and decrees was given to Joseph. I am sure he had the power to put to death or save alive whoever was necessary. He was given one of Pharaoh's chariots and before him ran men to cry, "Bow the knee." He was ruler over all the land of Egypt. Ah, in due time God has brought about what He intended—to save much people alive.

VERSES 45,46:

45 And Phâr-́aōh called Joseph's name Zăph-́năth–pā-ă-ne-́ăh; and he gave him to wife Ăs-́ĕ-năth the daughter of Pŏ-tĭ´–phĕr-ăh priest of On. And Joseph went out over *all* the land of Egypt.

46 ¶ And Joseph was thirty years old when he stood before Phâr-́aōh king of Egypt. And Joseph went out from the presence of Phâr-́aōh, and went throughout all the land of Egypt.

Joseph Now Prime Minister

Joseph was now thirty years old. That means he must

have spent some years in Potiphar's household proving himself and finally becoming master of all that was in Potiphar's house. Perhaps he had spent some years in prison before earning such respect and authority to run all the prison affairs. Then after the chief butler and chief baker came with their dreams and they were interpreted, two years had gone by. Now Joseph is a mature man, thirty years old, prime minister in Egypt. He was given to wife Asenath, the daughter of Poti-pherah, priest of On. Dr. Scofield thinks Joseph is a good type of Christ.

When Did Joseph Arrive in Egypt?

Egyptian chronology has been greatly misunderstood. Historians have largely misinterpreted the king lists of Manetho. He was an Egyptian priest in the third century before Christ and intended to give all the list of kings from the beginning. Inevitably he had to copy old records and go by traditions which were handed down through the long centuries. The dynasties of the Northern Kingdom and of the Southern Kingdom were recorded as if one line but they were not. But historians took for granted that the list of kings was consecutive, one after another.

Now there is much evidence that that is a mistake. Sometimes two kings reigned over different areas at the same time. Sometimes one of the kings named was a king over all Egypt; another king simply reigned under him over a "nome" or province but was called a prince or a king.

Two tremendous scholars have gone into this matter with very great care. One was Dr. Immanuel Velikovsky. His books, *Worlds in Collision, Ages in Chaos* and *Earth in Upheaval,* have aroused tremendous controversy. Dr. Velikovsky is a Jew, not a Christian, but he found that the largely accepted historical chronology of Egypt was wrong and that "600 ghost years" had crept into the history of Egypt.

Dr. Donovan A. Courville has two tremendously scholarly volumes, *The Exodus Problem and Its Ramifications.* He shows in much detail the same mistake of the unbelieving historians, and he contends that the Bible is accurate in every detail of history.

Velikovsky and Courville agree that the Hyksos, the Shepherd Kings who invaded Egypt and took over the rule for generations, were not the Jews, but were Amalekites. Rather, the Hyksos came in after the exodus. The armies of Pharaoh were destroyed and Pharaoh himself died. When the land was left desolate by the plagues, they took over. Courville shows that the exodus was about 1445 B.C., fitting in with the Scripture chronology and was in the 13th dynasty of Egyptian kings, not in the 18th or later dynasties, as many think. Then the exodus was about 1445, and Israel's conquest of Canaan forty years later.

The misinterpreting of Manetho's list of kings would put the history of Israel later than what the Scripture gives of it. Actually we understand that Mizraim (also spelled Mestraim or Menes), son of Ham, was the first king of Egypt and that would have been not much earlier than 2400 or 2500 B.C.

By placing the exodus in a later dynasty would put the conquest of Canaan about 1200 or later, and that would mess up not only the history of Egypt but of Israel, of Syria and Babylon and details of the Hittites. On that false assumption, Miss Kathleen Kenyon judged that the artifacts, buildings, pottery and instruments found in the land of Canaan after 1400 represented Canaanite civilization, before Israel's conquest, so they had no evidence of any higher civilization or moral standards of Israel than the heathen nations they replaced. She was wrong.

Also by this false chronology based on a misunderstanding of Egyptian chronology, people have given the Phoenicians credit for the alphabet when in fact the Canaanites and the Phoenicians must have learned that alphabet from Israel. Then the Pharaoh of the oppression and of the exodus was probably Koncharis. But if the exodus was in about 1445 B.C., then the coming of Jacob and his family to Egypt was about 215 years earlier, approximately 1660 B.C., and the coming of Joseph as a slave a few years before that.

Probably Joseph Came to Egypt in Reign of Sesostris I

Dr. Courville shows that in Egypt there were many inscriptions telling of extended famine some 215 years before the exodus and that Sesostris I was Pharaoh when Joseph had his dreams and the famine came and Joseph was put in charge as vizier or prime minister.

Courville says:

> The vizier of Sesostris I, who occupied this position second only to the king, is perhaps the most familiar figure in the Egyptian records of the many who held this office through the era of the Pharaohs. This fact makes possible a rather critical scrutiny of this identification which is demanded by the proposed reconstruction. The vizier of Sesostris I was known to the Egyptians as Mentuhotep. The extraordinary powers which were granted to Mentuhotep are clearly those also granted to Joseph. The vizier to the king of Egypt had powers which were great, irrespective of which one is under consideration, but the powers granted specifically to our Mentuhotep were so strikingly great that Breasted was prompted to comment on this point in the following words:

> > . . .When he [the vizier] also held the office of chief treasurer, as did the powerful vizier Mentuhotep under Sesostris I, the account which he could give of himself. . .read like the declaration of the king's powers.

> This is quite the same picture of Joseph's authority as stated in Scripture.

> > . . .See, I have set thee over all the land of Egypt. And Pharaoh took off his ring from his hand, and put it upon Joseph's hand and arrayed him in vestures of fine linen, and put a gold chain about his neck; And he made him to ride in the second chariot which he had; and they cried before him; Bow the knee; and he made him ruler over all the land of Egypt. And Pharaoh said to Joseph, I am Pharaoh, and without thee shall no man lift up his hand or foot in all the land of Egypt.

Speaking of Mentuhotep, Brugsch commented:

> In a word, our Mentuhotep, who was also invested with several priestly dignities, and was Pharaoh's treasurer, appears as the *alter ego* of the king. "When he arrived, *the*

> *great personages bowed down before him at the outer door
> of the royal palace.*" [Emphasis ours]

An examination of the inscriptions relative to Mentuhotep, which gave rise to the remarkable statements of Breasted, shows us that Mentuhotep carried, among others, the following titles: "Vizier, Chief Judge, Overseer of the Double Granary, Chief Treasurer, Governor of the Royal Castle, Wearer of the Royal Seal, Chief of all the works of the King, Hereditary Prince, Pilot of the People, Giver of Good—Sustaining Alive the People, Count, Sole Companion, Favorite of the King." Not before nor after the time of Sesostris I was there ever a man occupying this position who could claim such a list of titles. We compare these with the titles ascribed to Joseph in Scripture where he is "Lord of the Land," "Father of Pharaoh," "Lord of all his House," and "Ruler throughout the Land of Egypt." Since the recognition of Mentuhotep as Joseph was farthest from the mind of Breasted in making these comments on the powers of Mentuhotep, there is no call to underestimate the significance of these words which so clearly show that Joseph of the Bible meets in a most remarkable manner the power of the vizier of Sesostris I of the famine record.

The Egyptian papyrus records show that this Mentuhotep, or Joseph, had a tremendous canal built to irrigate more land and raise more food.

> An artificial canal was dug which ran parallel to the Nile northward to permit the flood waters of the Nile to flow into a natural basin. When the flood state was past, the impounded waters could be returned to the Nile by means of a second shorter canal. Examination of the remnants of this system indicates that it could well have doubled the tillable soil of the Nile Valley through which it passed. This canal which served to turn the waters of the Nile into this natural basin is still known to this day among the natives as the *Canal of Joseph*, and is so named on modern maps.

Dr. Courville says that with Velikovsky "he agrees that the Hyksos have been correctly identified as the Amalekites of Scripture, and that the absence of the expected repercussions of the expelled Hyksos on Palestine is explained by the near annihilation of this people by Saul."

VERSES 47-57:

47 And in the seven plenteous years the earth brought forth by handfuls.

48 And he gathered up all the food of the seven years, which were in the land of Egypt, and laid up the food in the cities: the food of the field, which *was* round about every city, laid he up in the same.

49 And Joseph gathered corn as the sand of the sea, very much, until he left numbering; for *it was* without number.

50 And unto Joseph were born two sons before the years of famine came, which Ăs-́ĕ-năth the daughter of Pŏ-tī́–phĕr-ăh priest of On bare unto him.

51 And Joseph called the name of the firstborn Mă-năs-́sēh: For God, *said he*, hath made me forget all my toil, and all my father's house.

52 And the name of the second called he Ē-́phră-ĭm: For God hath caused me to be fruitful in the land of my affliction.

53 ¶ And the seven years of plenteousness, that was in the land of Egypt, were ended.

54 And the seven years of dearth began to come, according as Joseph had said: and the dearth was in all lands; but in all the land of Egypt there was bread.

55 And when all the land of Egypt was famished, the people cried to Phâr-́aōh for bread: and Phâr-́aōh said unto all the Egyptians, Go unto Joseph; what he saith to you, do.

56 And the famine was over all the face of the earth: and Joseph opened all the storehouses, and sold unto the Egyptians; and the famine waxed sore in the land of Egypt.

57 And all countries came into Egypt to Joseph for to buy *corn;* because that the famine was *so* sore in all lands.

Years of Plenty and the Famine

Joseph had gone through all the land of Egypt. He had learned all the resources, all the people, had learned, no doubt, what officers he could trust. And so during the seven plentiful years when "the earth brought forth by handfuls," he had it gathered up for seven years. He must have built special granaries and cities of storage.

Then two sons were born to him, Manasseh and Ephraim. Manasseh means "forgetting." Oh, he forgot the days of slavery, the days in prison, the murderous hate of his brothers; forgot the lonely years. He had come to a place of usefulness and service. And when Ephraim was born, Joseph called him "fruitful," for he said, "God hath caused me to be fruitful in the land of my affliction."

The seven years of plenty have gone by, then the drought

came; Joseph and the people were ready, "and the dearth was in all lands." We will find the people of Palestine coming to Egypt for food.

GENESIS 42

VERSES 1-8:

NOW when Jacob saw that there was corn in Egypt, Jacob said unto his sons, Why do ye look one upon another?

2 And he said, Behold, I have heard that there is corn in Egypt: get you down thither, and buy for us from thence; that we may live, and not die.

3 ¶ And Joseph's ten brethren went down to buy corn in Egypt.

4 But Benjamin, Joseph's brother, Jacob sent not with his brethren; for he said, Lest peradventure mischief befall him.

5 And the sons of Israel came to buy *corn* among those that came: for the famine was in the land of Că-nă-ăn.

6 And Joseph *was* the governor over the land, *and* he *it was* that sold to all the people of the land: and Joseph's brethren came, and bowed down themselves before him *with* their faces to the earth.

7 And Joseph saw his brethren, and he knew them, but made himself strange unto them, and spake roughly unto them; and he said unto them, Whence come ye? And they said, From the land of Că-nă-ăn to buy food.

8 And Joseph knew his brethren, but they knew not him.

Joseph's Brothers Come for Grain

Caravans coming to and from Egypt brought the word. Everywhere but in Egypt the famine was great. Somebody had saved up grain for long years and now there was plenty.

Jacob and his ten older sons had anxious times. Would their family starve? But if there is grain in Egypt, surely they can buy some.

"Corn" here simply meant grain of any kind, mainly wheat and barley. (American Indian corn, so familiar to us, was not known then.) So Jacob sends his ten older sons down to buy corn in Egypt. Benjamin will stay at home "lest peradventure mischief befall him." Benjamin was already a mature man, and married, and when they went to Egypt a little later he had ten sons (see Gen. 46:21). But he is still the greatly beloved youngest son and Jacob must keep him at home.

The ten older brothers came bowing down, with their faces to the earth, before Joseph. He knew them, but they did not know him. He made himself strange and stern to them. They may have had some searchings of conscience about the young brother Joseph because of the long continued grief of Jacob, and verses 21 and 22 show that they had often considered their sin. They talked about it there in his presence thinking that Joseph could not understand their language for he spoke to them only through an interpreter.

More than twenty years have gone by since they sold him into Egypt. He is now more than thirty-seven years old. He was thirty when he stood before Pharaoh. Seven years of plenty have gone by; now it is in the time of famine.

They were foreigners and ten of them, so no underling could sell to them, we suppose. And an interpreter would ordinarily be needed with foreigners. Or perhaps Joseph saw them and took the case himself. At any rate, now the brothers face the stern prime minister. They bow with faces to the earth. If the mighty foreign ruler does not sell them grain, their families may well starve.

Ah, Joseph, your dreams have come true! Their empty, barren sheaves are falling down before his sheaves of filled granaries in all the land of Egypt. Their stars are bowing to the mighty ruler who can kill or keep alive. And while he means well to them, Joseph intends to see to it that there is genuine repentance.

VERSES 9-24:

9 And Joseph remembered the dreams which he dreamed of them, and said unto them, Ye *are* spies; to see the nakedness of the land ye are come.

10 And they said unto him, Nay, my lord, but to buy food are thy servants come.

11 We *are* all one man's sons; we *are* true *men*, thy servants are no spies.

12 And he said unto them, Nay, but to see the nakedness of the lan[d] ye are come.

13 And they said, Thy servants *ar[e]* twelve brethren, the sons of one ma[n] in the land of Că-́nă-ăn; and, behol[d] the youngest *is* this day with ou[r] father, and one *is* not.

14 And Joseph said unto them[,] That *is it* that I spake unto you, say[-] ing, Ye *are* spies:

15 Hereby ye shall be proved: B[y]

the life of Phâr-'āōh ye shall not go forth hence, except your youngest brother come hither.

16 Send one of you, and let him fetch your brother, and ye shall be kept in prison, that your words may be proved, whether *there be any* truth in you: or else by the life of Phâr-'āōh surely ye *are* spies.

17 And he put them all together into ward three days.

18 And Joseph said unto them the third day, This do, and live; *for* I *fear God:

19 If ye *be* true *men*, let one of your brethren be bound in the house of your prison: go ye, carry corn for the famine of your houses:

20 But bring your youngest brother unto me; so shall your words be verified, and ye shall not die. And they

did so.

21 ¶ And they said one to another, We *are* verily guilty concerning our brother, in that we saw the anguish of his soul, when he besought us, and we would not hear; therefore is this distress come upon us.

22 And Reuben answered them, saying, Spake I not unto you, saying, Do not sin against the child; and ye would not hear? therefore, behold, also his blood is required.

23 And they knew not that Joseph understood *them*; for he spake unto them by an interpreter.

24 And he turned himself about from them, and wept; and returned to them again, and communed with them, and took from them Simeon, and bound him before their eyes.

Joseph's Stern Treatment of His Brothers

A mighty famine was on. It sounded very plausible when Joseph accused them, "Ye are spies; to see the nakedness of the land ye are come." No, they came to buy food; they are all one man's sons.

They go into the story more carefully. There had been twelve sons in the land of Canaan. Benjamin was left at home with the father; "one is not." They did not elaborate. They intended to leave the impression he was dead. Joseph pretends not to believe them about the younger brother. He speaks as they would expect this strange Egyptian ruler to speak: "By the life of Pharaoh ye shall not go forth hence, except your youngest brother come hither." He repeats that saying again in verse 16. One of them must go fetch the brother! Dumbfounded, they wait. He put them all in jail for three days!

Then on the third day, he calls them together and says, "This do, and live." Well, he is not going to kill them all just now. He says, ". . .for I fear God." One of the brothers is to stay bound in prison while the others go home and carry food for their families and bring back the younger son Benjamin.

These brothers are heartsick. They know retribution is come upon them for their sin. They remember how he had anguish of soul when young Joseph had begged them to release him and they say that "therefore is this distress come upon us." And Reuben earnestly spake up, trying to free himself from guilt. He had not had a part in it. He had wanted to return the child to his father; now Joseph's blood is required! All this Joseph heard. They did not know this Egyptian prime minister spoke the Hebrew tongue.

Joseph was greatly moved. He went into an inner room and wept. Can you imagine the surprise, the joy, the trouble, the sense of fulfilled destiny when he faced his brothers? Great emotion shook him. Then he dried his tears and came back to his brothers.

Simeon is bound before their eyes. He will stay in prison until they return with Benjamin.

Why did Joseph keep Simeon in prison while the others were sent home? Probably because he was next to the oldest. He did not keep Reuben, the oldest, because Reuben was the one who had tried so hard to send him back to his father unharmed. And he had heard the protestation of Reuben: "Spake I not unto you, saying, Do not sin against the child; and ye would not hear?" So Joseph did not keep Reuben, but the next older one, Simeon, as a prisoner until they returned.

VERSES 25-38:

25 ¶ Then Joseph commanded to fill their sacks with corn, and to restore every man's money into his sack, and to give them provision for the way: and thus did he unto them.

26 And they laded their asses with the corn, and departed thence.

27 And as one of them opened his sack to give his ass provender in the inn, he espied his money; for, behold, it *was* in his sack's mouth.

28 And he said unto his brethren, My money is restored; and, lo, *it is* even in my sack: and their heart failed *them*, and they were afraid, saying one to another, What *is* this *that* God hath done unto us?

29 ¶ And they came unto Jacob their father unto the land of Cā́-nă-ăn, and told him all that befell unto them; saying,

30 The man, *who is* the lord of the land, spake roughly to us, and took us for spies of the country.

31 And we said unto him, We *are* true *men;* we are no spies:

32 We *be* twelve brethren, sons of our father; one *is* not, and the youngest *is* this day with our father in the land of Cā́-nă-ăn.

33 And the man, the lord of the country, said unto us, Hereby shall I know that ye *are* true *men;* leave one of your brethren *here* with me, and take *food for* the famine of your households, and be gone:

34 And bring your youngest brother unto me: then shall I know that ye *are* no spies, but *that* ye *are* true *men:* so will I deliver you your brother, and ye shall traffick in the land.

35 ¶ And it came to pass as they emptied their sacks, that, behold, every man's bundle of money *was* in his sack: and when *both* they and their father saw the bundles of money, they were afraid.

36 And Jacob their father said unto them, Me have ye bereaved *of my children:* Joseph *is* not, and Simeon *is* not, and ye will take Benjamin *away:* all these things are against me.

37 And Reuben spake unto his father, saying, Slay my two sons, if I bring him not to thee: deliver him into my hand, and I will bring him to thee again.

38 And he said, My son shall not go down with you; for his brother is dead, and he is left alone: if mischief befall him by the way in the which ye go, then shall ye bring down my gray hairs with sorrow to the grave.

Nine Troubled Men Carried Grain Back to Jacob and Their Families

How wise, how kindly was Joseph's treatment. Simeon was left in prison. He must not lose contact with these people. And they must know the seriousness of their sin. But he had their sacks filled with grain, restored every man's money in the sack, then gave them provisions for the way! They loaded their donkeys and started out.

They did not find the money until they stopped at an inn. Someone wanted to give his donkey a little grain, and then was when they found the money. They were startled and fearful. They think the thing is of God and so they go on home to Jacob and tell him, "The man, who is the lord of the land, spake roughly to us, and took us for spies of the country." They repeated the demand of Joseph that they must bring the younger son Benjamin and in no other way could they prove themselves honest men and no other way could they buy grain in Egypt.

They all emptied their sacks and, behold, a bundle of money was in every man's sack. They and their father saw the money and they were afraid. What scheme was this? Were they to be counted thieves? Was this a way of bringing them to trial and death? Jacob spoke sternly. They have bereaved him of children. Joseph is gone. He somewhat blames them. He does not know all the truth, but surely they were not blameless if the young man was killed by a wild beast when he was supposed to be with them. Now Simeon is bound down in Egypt and they want to take Benjamin away.

Reuben, tenderhearted but not always wise or reliable, was "unstable as water." He committed adultery with his father's wife. He makes a wild suggestion: Jacob might slay his two sons if he did not bring Benjamin back alive! But Jacob would not hear. Oh, Benjamin is the only child left of his beloved Rachel. His sorrowing will take him to the grave if he loses Benjamin, thinks Jacob.

GENESIS 43

AND the famine *was* sore in the land.

2 And it came to pass, when they had eaten up the corn which they had brought out of Egypt, their father said unto them, Go again, buy us a little food.

3 And Judah spake unto him, saying, The man did solemnly protest unto us, saying, Ye shall not see my face, except your brother *be* with you.

4 If thou wilt send our brother with us, we will go down and buy thee food:

5 But if thou wilt not send *him*, we will not go down: for the man said unto us, Ye shall not see my face, except your brother *be* with you.

6 And Israel said, Wherefore dealt ye *so* ill with me, *as* to tell the man whether ye had yet a brother?

7 And they said, The man asked us straitly of our state, and of our kindred, saying, *Is* your father yet alive? have ye *another* brother? and we told him according to the tenor of these words: could we certainly know that he would say, Bring your brother down?

8 And Judah said unto Israel his father, Send the lad with me, and we will arise and go; that we may live, and not die, both we, and thou, *and* also our little ones.

9 I will be surety for him; of my hand shalt thou require him: if I bring him not unto thee, and set him before thee, then let me bear the blame for ever:

10 For except we had lingered, surely now we had returned this second time.

Judah Stands Surety for Benjamin; They Return to Egypt

The famine is sore in the land. The grain bought by the ten brothers is gone after awhile. Again hunger stares them in the face. Jacob urged them to go again and buy them a little food.

Now Judah spoke up. They need not go back unless they have Benjamin with them. Joseph, stern, wise and with the power of God upon him, certainly had made believers of these men. They dare not face that stern man unless Benjamin comes with them.

Now Judah makes a sensible, honest plea. Jacob would not listen to Reuben. What joy would it give to Jacob to slay the two sons of Reuben just because Benjamin did not come back? But Judah is a different kind of man. He is serious, trustworthy and greatly respected. Judah is "he whom thy brethren shall praise." He is "a lion's whelp." Through him the Messianic covenant is to be fulfilled, and Christ the Lawgiver would come (Gen. 49:8-12). How much of all this Jacob knew before he spoke it prophetically on his deathbed, we cannot know. But he did know Judah could be trusted. Jacob sadly conceded to the request lest they all starve. They must take again the money they had gotten in their sacks; they must take Benjamin.

Judah says plainly about Benjamin, "I will be surety for him; of my hand shalt thou require him: if I bring him not unto thee, and set him before thee, then let me bear the blame for ever." They are in dire emergency and lest the children starve, the eleven now will go back down to Egypt for bread.

VERSES 11-14:

11 And their father Israel said unto them, If it must be so now, do this; take of the best fruits in the land in your vessels, and carry down the man a present, a little balm, and a little honey, spices, and myrrh, nuts, and almonds:

12 And take double money in your hand; and the money that was brought again in the mouth of your sacks, carry it again in your hand; peradventure it was an oversight:

13 Take also your brother, and arise, go again unto the man:

14 And God Almighty give you mercy before the man, that he may send away your other brother, and Benjamin. If I be bereaved of my children, I am bereaved.

With Double Money They Take Benjamin to Egypt

They must take some of the best fruits of the land and a present, "a little balm, and a little honey, spices, and myrrh, nuts, and almonds." They must take double money in their hands, and the money that was brought back, they must take it again. Everything possible must be done to please the stern man in Egypt and to get food for their families.

VERSES 15-26:

15 ¶ And the men took that present, and they took double money in their hand, and Benjamin; and rose up, and went down to Egypt, and stood before Joseph.

16 And when Joseph saw Benjamin with them, he said to the ruler of his house, Bring *these* men home, and slay, and make ready; for *these* men shall dine with me at noon.

17 And the man did as Joseph bade; and the man brought the men into Joseph's house.

18 And the men were afraid, because they were brought into Joseph's house; and they said, Because of the money that was returned in our sacks at the first time are we brought in; that he may seek occasion against us, and fall upon us, and take us for bondmen, and our asses.

19 And they came near to the steward of Joseph's house, and they communed with him at the door of the house,

20 And said, O sir, we came indeed down at the first time to buy food:

21 And it came to pass, when we came to the inn, that we opened our sacks, and, behold, *every* man's money *was* in the mouth of his sack, our money in full weight: and we have brought it again in our hand.

22 And other money have we brought down in our hands to buy food: we cannot tell who put our money in our sacks.

23 And he said, Peace *be* to you, fear not: your God, and the God of your father, hath given you treasure in your sacks: I had your money. And he brought Simeon out unto them.

24 And the man brought the men into Joseph's house, and gave *them* water, and they washed their feet; and he gave their asses provender.

25 And they made ready the present against Joseph came at noon: for they heard that they should eat bread there.

26 ¶ And when Joseph came home, they brought him the present which *was* in their hand into the house, and bowed themselves to him to the earth.

Now Eleven Brothers Face Joseph

It was certainly a very humble group that came down to Egypt this second time and stood before Joseph. Joseph instructed the ruler of his house to bring these men to his home and make ready a feast. They would dine with Joseph at noon.

The brothers were more afraid. Were they to be taken to dungeons? Was it because of the money that was returned in their sacks the first time? Is this ruler seeking occasion to make them all slaves?

But they go with the steward to Joseph's house. They try to explain to Joseph's steward. They had brought money before and they were surprised to find the money in their sacks. They brought some more money now to buy food.

The man explained, "Peace be to you, fear not: your God, and the God of your father, hath given you treasure in your sacks: I had your money. And he brought Simeon out unto them." They are courteously treated, given water to wash their feet, and the donkeys are fed. They make ready the present they had brought when Joseph will come to the house at noon. I suppose they had it beautifully arranged to impress him as well as they could. Then they "bowed themselves to him to the earth."

VERSES 27-34:

27 And he asked them of *their* welfare, and said, *Is* your father well, the old man of whom ye spake? *Is* he yet alive?

28 And they answered, Thy servant our father *is* in good health, he *is* yet alive. And they bowed down their heads, and made obeisance.

29 And he lifted up his eyes, and saw his brother Benjamin, his mother's son, and said, *Is* this your younger brother, of whom ye spake unto me? And he said, God be gracious unto thee, my son.

30 And Joseph made haste; for his bowels did yearn upon his brother: and he sought *where* to weep; and he entered into *his* chamber, and wept there.

31 And he washed his face, and went out, and refrained himself, and said, Set on bread.

32 And they set on for him by himself, and for them by themselves, and for the Egyptians, which did eat with him, by themselves: because the Egyptians might not eat bread with the Hebrews; for that *is* an abomination unto the Egyptians.

33 And they sat before him, the firstborn according to his birthright, and the youngest according to his youth: and the men marvelled one at another.

34 And he took *and sent* messes unto them from before him: but Benjamin's mess was five times so much as any of their's. And they drank, and were merry with him.

Joseph Sees Brother Benjamin: His Father Is Yet Alive!

Can you imagine the deep emotion of Joseph as he looks upon his brother Benjamin? He had not seen this, his only full brother, for more than twenty years! And he did not altogether trust the other brothers. Jacob was getting old. Was he still alive? He pretends that he does not know the younger brother, and he speaks of his father as "the old man of whom ye spake." Oh, how glad he was to hear that Jacob was still alive!

He said to Benjamin, "God be gracious unto thee, my son," and then he hasted away to an inner room where he might weep. Oh, the memories of childhood and of lost years! Then he washed his face and came out again and they served the meal.

He ate by himself, as a mighty ruler. These Hebrews ate by themselves, and the Egyptians who were present must eat by themselves.

They were startled when Joseph seated them at the table in the order of their ages. Did he have some supernatural knowledge? He served the plates. When he sent the messes to Benjamin, his overflowing heart piled up more than the young man could eat, five times as much as any of the others. Now the men were somewhat relaxed and they drank and were merry.

GENESIS 44

AND he commanded the steward of his house, saying, Fill the men's sacks *with* food, as much as they can carry, and put every man's money in his sack's mouth.

2 And put my cup, the silver cup, in the sack's mouth of the youngest, and his corn money. And he did according to the word that Joseph had spoken.

3 As soon as the morning was light, the men were sent away, they and their asses.

4 *And* when they were gone out of the city, *and* not *yet* far off, Joseph said unto his steward, Up, follow after the men; and when thou dost overtake them, say unto them, Wherefore have ye rewarded evil for good?

5 *Is* not this *it* in which my lord drinketh, and whereby indeed he divineth? ye have done evil in so doing.

6 ¶ And he overtook them, and he spake unto them these same words.

7 And they said unto him, Wherefore saith my lord these words? God forbid that thy servants should do according to this thing:

8 Behold, the money, which we found in our sacks' mouths, we brought again unto thee out of the land of Cā-nă-ăn: how then should we steal out of thy lord's house silver or gold?

9 With whomsoever of thy servants it be found, both let him die, and we also will be my lord's bondmen.

10 And he said, Now also *let* it *be* according unto your words: he with whom it is found shall be my servant; and ye shall be blameless.

11 Then they speedily took down every man his sack to the ground, and opened every man his sack.

12 And he searched, *and* began at the eldest, and left at the youngest: and the cup was found in Benjamin's sack.

13 Then they rent their clothes, and laded every man his ass, and returned to the city.

Joseph's Ruse to Further Convict Brothers

Joseph's heart is full. He thinks about his old father Jacob and all the family. Do they have enough to eat? So Joseph commanded the stewards, "Fill the men's sacks with food, as much as they can carry, and put every man's money in his sack's mouth." Although he feels he must teach these wicked brothers a lesson, he has deep concern for the welfare of the families at home.

Joseph was concerned. Knowing the wickedness of these brothers, he must choose how to deal with them. Could he bring judgment and punishment on them for their wickedness, as they deserved? He might have put to death some of them, or put some into slavery, or he could have taken their animals. They deserved punishment. Or should he receive them as if they had done no harm? Should he trust them, give them full fellowship? Could he ignore the wickedness of their hearts and their hatred and, perhaps, allow them to go on with their scheming? No. He must love them and forgive them. They are his family. For the father's and Benjamin's sakes, he must keep the family ties. But they must be brought to humility, to repentance.

It is not wrong that they should fear Joseph, that they should see that his dreams have come true, the dreams he had from God. Joseph must make it so these guilty brothers will walk softly before him.

And where are they most vulnerable? How could he bring fear to their hearts? Mainly through Benjamin! There would be no way to guarantee the angry wrath of their father whom they feared, as to leave Benjamin here! Not a one of them will dare go back to face the old father if Benjamin does not return. And so Joseph selected Benjamin, had the silver cup put in his sack, then instructed the steward to chase them down and accuse them, find the silver cup and then bring them back.

It was a solemn, protesting crowd when they unloaded their donkeys and searched every man's sack, beginning with Reuben, Simeon, Levi, Judah, and down from the oldest to the youngest, until he came to Benjamin and there, behold, was the silver cup!

Joseph instructed his steward to tell them that the silver cup was the one "whereby. . .he divineth." And the same thing he said in verse 15, "Wot ye not that such a man as I can certainly divine?" They could tell that Joseph knew things about them that a heathen Egyptian would have no way of knowing unless they were especially revealed to him.

Did Joseph, then, this austere, stern prime minister, have some way of communicating with deity, to know things others did not know? Joseph let them think so. He is not speaking to them as if he were one trusting and believing in their father's God but as one who would worship the gods of

Egypt and through this silver cup, perhaps, could foretell things not revealed. So he pretended that through this silver cup he could divine and know things about them. Oh, then, this great man knew the wicked secrets of their heart!

Now it is a sad procession as they retrace their steps back to Joseph's house. Some way the cup got in Benjamin's possession. It is threatened now that Benjamin must stay and they must face an angry father alone even if they are allowed to go back to Palestine. What will they do!

VERSES 14-17:

14 ¶ And Judah and his brethren came to Joseph's house; for he *was* yet there: and they fell before him on the ground.

15 And Joseph said unto them, What deed *is* this that ye have done? wot ye not that such a man as I can certainly divine?

16 And Judah said, What shall we say unto my lord? what shall we speak? or how shall we clear ourselves? God hath found out the iniquity of thy servants: behold, we *are* my lord's servants, both we, and *he* also with whom the cup is found.

17 And he said, God forbid that I should do so: *but* the man in whose hand the cup is found, he shall be my servant; and as for you, get you up in peace unto your father.

Conscience-Stricken, Fearful Brothers Return

Joseph had not gone to his offices at the palace; he was still at home waiting for them. Now they came and in anguish and trouble fall down before him on the ground. What has happened to them! Joseph adds to their fear. Didn't they know that he could divine, could foretell the secrets of the heart? Judah, perhaps the most honest of the group and forthright, said, "How shall we clear ourselves? God hath found out the iniquity of thy servants."

No doubt they have in mind their sin in selling Joseph as a slave. They were hounded with conscience because all these years their father had grieved. It is very likely that these men had been wicked in more ways than that. When Joseph was just a boy he had reported about the brothers to his father. "And Joseph brought unto his father their evil report." And Judah had been the one to protest that they should not kill the lad, but suggested selling him as a slave (Gen. 37:26,27). Now he speaks for them all: "God hath found out the iniquity of thy servants." No doubt that was the purpose Joseph had in mind in his serious dealing with these men. And Judah offers, "We'll be servants, all of us, as well as Benjamin."

But Joseph said, "No, I'll only keep Benjamin and the rest can go in peace!"

In peace? How could they go and face their father, and how could Judah go, who had guaranteed to bring the lad safely or bear the blame forever!

VERSES 18-34:

18 ¶ Then Judah came near unto him, and said, Oh my lord, let thy servant, I pray thee, speak a word in my lord's ears, and let not thine anger burn against thy servant: for thou *art* even as Phâr-āoh.

19 My lord asked his servants, saying, Have ye a father, or a brother?

20 And we said unto my lord, We have a father, an old man, and a child of his old age, a little one; and his brother is dead, and he alone is left of his mother, and his father loveth him.

21 And thou saidst unto thy servants, Bring him down unto me, that I may set mine eyes upon him.

22 And we said unto my lord, The lad cannot leave his father: for *if* he should leave his father, *his father* would die.

23 And thou saidst unto thy servants, Except your youngest brother come down with you, ye shall see my face no more.

24 And it came to pass when we came up unto thy servant my father, we told him the words of my lord.

25 And our father said, Go again, *and* buy us a little food.

26 And we said, We cannot go down: if our youngest brother be with us, then will we go down: for we may not see the man's face, except our youngest brother *be* with us.

27 And thy servant my father said unto us, Ye know that my wife bare me two *sons:*

28 And the one went out from me, and I said, Surely he is torn in pieces; and I saw him not since:

29 And if ye take this also from me, and mischief befall him, ye shall bring down my gray hairs with sorrow to the grave.

30 Now therefore when I come to thy servant my father, and the lad *be* not with us; seeing that his life is bound up in the lad's life;

31 It shall come to pass, when he seeth that the lad *is* not *with us*, that he will die: and thy servants shall bring down the gray hairs of thy servant our father with sorrow to the grave.

32 For thy servant became surety for the lad unto my father, saying, If I

bring him not unto thee, then I shall bear the blame to my father for ever.

33 Now therefore, I pray thee, let thy servant abide instead of the lad a bondman to my lord; and let the lad go up with his brethren.

34 For how shall I go up to my father, and the lad *be* not with me? lest peradventure I see the evil that shall come on my father.

Judah's Eloquent Plea

Judah wants a private word with the prime minister. He reviews the matter very seriously and honestly. On the previous visit Joseph had asked them, "Have ye a father or a brother?" They had told of their aged father and their younger brother and Joseph had insisted that the young man Benjamin must be brought down to him. They had explained then that if Benjamin were to be brought away, their aged father, doting on the only child left from his beloved Rachel, would die with a broken heart. Joseph had insisted they must bring back their brother. Now they have done so. As honestly as he can, Judah tells a moving story of the old man's love for these two sons, Joseph and Benjamin. Now if Benjamin does not come, Jacob will die of grief.

Judah explained that he had made the promise and the guarantee. "For thy servant became surety for the lad unto my father, saying, If I bring him not unto thee, then I shall bear the blame to my father for ever."

What can they do then? Judah offers himself to be a slave that Benjamin may go back to the father. Judah has family and loved ones back at home, but, never mind; if need be he will stay as a slave and never see them again in order that he may keep his vow to the old father. He said, "Now therefore, I pray thee, let thy servant abide instead of the lad a bondman to my lord; and let the lad go up with his brethren."

Judah could not bear to see the old father grieving these years over Joseph and now to die of a broken heart, perhaps, if Benjamin did not return!

How, Then, Can We Face the Lord Jesus Without Loved Ones We Should Win to Him?

We remember that ten chapters in Genesis are taken up with the story of Joseph, chapters 37 down to 47, with the exception of chapter 38, which is about Judah. It is a beautiful and charming story, but did God not have some eternal truths, too, to put upon our hearts here? I think surely He did. Judah could not bear to think of facing his old father, knowing that he had not kept his vow, that he must bear the blame forever for Benjamin to be a slave, he thought, in Egypt. How could he face his father and the lad not be with him?

It was a wonderful, sacrificial offer Judah made to stay as a bondservant that the lad might go home. But the shame and heartbreak of Judah to go home to an old father and not bring back the lad he had vowed to bring on a safe return—that would not be as bad as for us to face Jesus Christ at our death or at the second coming and not have loved ones with us whose souls are entrusted for us to win.

> How can I meet Him without my loved ones,
> How can I smile and know they are lost,
> When I see Jesus up in the glory
> Without the souls He bought at such cost?
>
> Time now for warning, time now for pleading,
> Time now to weep, to cling to the cross.
> Too late in Heaven, to win our loved ones;
> Too late to pray, to weep o'er the lost.
>
> Solemn accounting, facing our Saviour.
> Rewards receiving, suffering loss!
> Judgment seat, facing Jesus in Heaven;
> Wood, hay and stubble, burning as dross.
>
> How poor investment, in land or bus'ness;
> What cheap returns we'll have for our pains!
> But how the wise will shine in their glory,
> When souls appear, what eternal gain!

How glad the greeting, praises and singing
When we meet Jesus, with all our own!
Then will our labor seem but a trifle,
And all our tears, and toiling be done!

Oh, bring your loved ones, Bring them to Jesus!
Bring ev'ry brother and sister to Him!
When come the reapers, home with the harvest,
May all our dear ones be safe gathered in!

Oh, that is the burden God lays upon us through the message of Ezekiel:

"Son of man, I have made thee a watchman unto the house of Israel: therefore hear the word at my mouth, and give them warning from me. When I say unto the wicked, Thou shalt surely die; and thou givest him not warning, nor speakest to warn the wicked from his wicked way, to save his life; the same wicked man shall die in his iniquity; but his blood will I require at thine hand."—Ezek. 3:17,18.

Jesus told a parable of one who goes at midnight begging for three loaves of bread (all the power of the Father, Son and Holy Spirit), the Bread of Life, for, "A friend of mine in his journey is come to me, and I have nothing to set before him" (Luke 11:6).

Oh, someone is come to me, someone is come to each reader; God has sent him your way for you to win, and do you have no bread? Then plead with God for the power of God to win that one. For one day we must face the Lord Jesus, even as Judah had to face his father knowing that he had failed of his promises and duty and had not brought Benjamin safely home to him again.

Let us then bring our loved ones to the Lord at any cost.

GENESIS 45

THEN Joseph could not refrain himself before all them that stood by him; and he cried, Cause every man to go out from me. And there stood no man with him, while Joseph made himself known unto his brethren.

2 And he wept aloud: and the Egyptians and the house of Phâr-ʹaōh heard.

3 And Joseph said unto his brethren, I *am* Joseph; doth my father yet live? And his brethren could not answer him; for they were troubled at his presence.

4 And Joseph said unto his brethren, Come near to me, I pray you. And they came near. And he said, I *am* Joseph your brother, whom ye sold into Egypt.

Joseph Reveals Himself to His Brethren

Can you imagine the surging emotions in this crowd? Benjamin, who feels he is falsely accused, is about to be slave over a silver cup he did not steal. And the guilty brothers keep remembering the brother they sold into slavery and their deceit of their father. But most of all, here is Joseph who, after more than twenty long years, is about to make himself known to his brothers. He cried out for all the Egyptians to leave the room, then wept aloud. The Egyptians in the house of Pharaoh heard the sobbing of the prime minister in the room with these strange Hebrews from Palestine! Then Joseph said to his brothers, "I am Joseph; doth my father yet live?" They might have lied to him before—they were not too good to do it. And pressed by his great love for his father, he must know. Yes, his father was alive. They stand away from him, troubled, uncertain, but he begs them, "Come near to me, I pray you. And they came near." Yes, he told them again, "I am Joseph your brother, whom ye sold into Egypt."

VERSES 5-8:

5 Now therefore be not grieved, nor angry with yourselves, that ye sold me hither: for God did send me before you to preserve life.

6 For these two years *hath* the famine *been* in the land: and yet *there are* five years, in the which *there shall* neither *be* earing nor harvest.

7 And God sent me before you to preserve you a posterity in the earth, and to save your lives by a great deliverance.

8 So now *it was* not you *that* sent me hither, but God: and he hath made me a father to Phâr-́aōh, and lord of all his house, and a ruler throughout all the land of Egypt.

God Sent Joseph to Egypt

I wonder how long he had known that all this was the hand of God? Surely he could see it now. I think he knew, ever since he had been put in power, that his dreams to rule were being fulfilled. But now his brethren had come to bow down before him, and that fulfilled his dream also. But he realizes that this is the hand of God. God made all these plans to keep millions of people alive in the famine and to keep his own loved ones alive back in Palestine!

God sent Joseph into Egypt to preserve life. He even sent him to Egypt to save the lives of these brothers and their families. So, then, there is no bitterness in his heart against these brothers. He has taken care to see that they should repent, but he is not berating them. The hand of God was only for good.

He will say the same thing again after his father dies and is buried, and they will again be fearful. Will Joseph punish them now? In Genesis 50:20 he said to them, "But as for you, ye thought evil against me, but God meant it unto good. . . ." Joseph says it modestly enough. He has really been like a father to Pharaoh and he is the lord of all the palace and ruler for all the land of Egypt. God put Joseph there as the one man to know the will of God and save the food and administer it.

VERSES 9-15:

9 Haste ye, and go up to my father, and say unto him, Thus saith thy son Joseph, God hath made me lord of all Egypt: come down unto me, tarry not:

10 And thou shalt dwell in the land of Goshen, and thou shalt be near unto me, thou, and thy children, and thy children's children, and thy flocks, and thy herds, and all that thou hast:

11 And there will I nourish thee; for yet *there are* five years of famine; lest thou, and thy household, and all that thou hast, come to poverty.

12 And, behold, your eyes see, and the eyes of my brother Benjamin, that *it is* my mouth that speaketh unto you.

13 And ye shall tell my father of all my glory in Egypt, and of all that ye have seen; and ye shall haste and bring down my father hither.

14 And he fell upon his brother Benjamin's neck, and wept; and Benjamin wept upon his neck.

15 Moreover he kissed all his brethren, and wept upon them: and after that his brethren talked with him.

They Are Instructed to Bring Jacob and Their Families to Egypt

There are yet five years of famine. Jacob and all his family should come down to Egypt so Joseph can care for them. They will dwell in the land of Goshen and be near Joseph and his children. These older brothers can see them, but Benjamin, dearly beloved and full brother, would be the one to tell the father the truth.

There was tender embracing with Benjamin, then, graciously, he kissed his brothers, each one on the cheek, as is still the Oriental custom, and wept upon them. Afterwards they talked with him. I can imagine they told Joseph about each family and how they had grown in these more than twenty years since he had gone away.

VERSES 16-20:

16 ¶ And the fame thereof was heard in Phâr-'aoh's house, saying, Joseph's brethren are come: and it pleased Phâr-'aoh well, and his servants.

17 And Phâr-'aoh said unto Joseph, Say unto thy brethren, This do ye;

lade your beasts, and go, get you unto the land of Cā-'nă-ăn;

18 And take your father and your households, and come unto me: and I will give you the good of the land of Egypt, and ye shall eat the fat of the land.

19 Now thou art commanded, this do ye; take you wagons out of the land of Egypt for your little ones, and for your wives, and bring your father, and come.

20 Also regard not your stuff; for the good of all the land of Egypt *is* your's.

Pharaoh Pleased to Have Israel's Family Come to Egypt

You can be sure that whatever Joseph did pleased Pharaoh. Now, they are to come back and bring their father and families. They are to take wagons out of the land of Egypt to bring back the little ones and their wives. And if they cannot bring all their possessions, they must leave them; there will be plenty for them in Egypt.

VERSES 21-28:

21 And the children of Israel did so: and Joseph gave them wagons, according to the commandment of Phâr-́āōh, and gave them provision for the way.

22 To all of them he gave each man changes of raiment; but to Benjamin he gave three hundred *pieces* of silver, and five changes of raiment.

23 And to his father he sent after this *manner;* ten asses laden with the good things of Egypt, and ten she asses laden with corn and bread and meat for his father by the way.

24 So he sent his brethren away, and they departed: and he said unto them, See that ye fall not out by the way.

25 ¶ And they went up out of Egypt, and came into the land of Cā-nă-ăn unto Jacob their father,

26 And told him, saying, Joseph *is* yet alive, and he *is* governor over all the land of Egypt. And Jacob's heart fainted, for he believed them not.

27 And they told him all the words of Joseph, which he had said unto them: and when he saw the wagons which Joseph had sent to carry him, the spirit of Jacob their father revived:

28 And Israel said, *It is* enough; Joseph my son *is* yet alive: I will go and see him before I die.

Brothers Sent Happily Away

Joseph gave them provisions for the way. Each man got a change of garments, and Benjamin was given three hundred pieces of silver and five changes of raiment! He sent along ten donkeys laden with the good things of Egypt, ten she asses laden with corn and bread and meat for his father by the way.

They are distinctly warned, "See that ye fall not out by the way." They are not to quarrel nor divide but are to rush on to complete the mission and bring their father.

How animated are their faces as they meet the old man Jacob and tell him the wonderful news that "Joseph is alive in Egypt. He is the prime minister and he has sent for them." Jacob could not believe all this. But when he saw the wagons that were sent to carry him back to Egypt, his spirit revived and he said, "It is enough; Joseph my son is yet alive: I will go and see him before I die."

GENESIS 46

AND Israel took his journey with all that he had, and came to Beer–sheba, and offered sacrifices unto the God of his father Isaac.

2 And God spake unto Israel in the visions of the night, and said, Jacob, Jacob. And he said, Here *am* I.

3 And he said, I *am* God, the God of thy father: fear not to go down into Egypt; for I will there make of thee a great nation:

4 I will go down with thee into Egypt; and I will also surely bring thee up *again*: and Joseph shall put his hand upon thine eyes.

God Reassures Jacob

Now the caravan heads for Egypt. From Mamre they came down to Beer-sheba, which is still in the land of Canaan and there Jacob (Israel) offered sacrifices to the God of his father Isaac.

God gave Israel visions in the night. The God of his father Isaac is assuring him he may safely go down to Egypt. He will be there with them and make a great nation of them in Egypt, then will bring them again into the land of Canaan.

That is a restatement of the promise God gave to Abraham in Genesis 15:13-16:

"And he said unto Abram, Know of a surety that thy seed shall be a stranger in a land that is not their's, and shall serve them; and they shall afflict them four hundred years; And also that nation, whom they shall serve, will I judge: and afterward shall they come out with great substance. And thou shalt go to thy fathers in peace; thou shalt be buried in a good old age. But in the fourth generation they shall come hither again: for the iniquity of the Amorites is not yet full."

All the plan of God is working. He will fill out the things that are promised. There is to be persecution and trouble, but God will give to Abraham's seed and descendants the land of Canaan.

VERSES 5-28:

5 And Jacob rose up from Beer-sheba: and the sons of Israel carried Jacob their father, and their little ones, and their wives, in the wagons which Phâr-́aōh had sent to carry him.

6 And they took their cattle, and their goods, which they had gotten in the land of Cā-́nă-ăn, and came into Egypt, Jacob, and all his seed with him:

7 His sons, and his sons' sons with him, his daughters, and his sons' daughters, and all his seed brought he with him into Egypt.

8 ¶ And these are the names of the children of Israel, which came into Egypt, Jacob and his sons: Reuben, Jacob's firstborn.

9 And the sons of Reuben; Hā-́nŏ<u>ch</u>, and Phallu, and Hezron, and Cär-́mī.

10 ¶ And the sons of Simeon; Jĕ-mū-́ĕl, and Jamin, and Ohad, and Jā-́<u>ch</u>ĭn, and Zohar, and Shā-́ŭl the son of a Cā-nă-ăn-ĭ-́tĭsh woman.

11 ¶ And the sons of Levi; Gershon, Kohath, and Mĕ-rär-́ī.

12 ¶ And the sons of Judah; Er, and Onan, and Shē-́läh, and Phâr-́ĕz, and Zarah: but Er and Onan died in the land of Cā-́nă-ăn. And the sons of Phâr-́ĕz were Hezron and Hamul.

13 ¶ And the sons of Ĭs-́să-<u>ch</u>är; Tō-́lă, and Phū-́väh, and Job, and Shimron.

14 ¶ And the sons of Zĕ-bū-́lŭn; Sē-́rĕd, and Elon, and Jäh-́lêĕl.

15 These be the sons of Leah, which she bare unto Jacob in Pā-́dăn–aram, with his daughter Dinah: all the souls of his sons and his daughters were thirty and three.

16 ¶ And the sons of Gad; Ziphion, and Haggi, Shû-́nī, and Ezbon, Ē-́rī, and Ă-rō-́dī, and Ă-rē-́lī.

17 ¶ And the sons of Asher; Jimnah, and Ĭsh-́ū-ăh, and Ĭs-́ū-ī, and Bĕ-rī-́ăh, and Sē-́răh their sister: and the sons of Bĕ-rī-́ăh; Heber, and Măl-́chĭ-ĕl.

18 These are the sons of Zilpah, whom Laban gave to Leah his daughter, and these she bare unto Jacob, even sixteen souls.

19 The sons of Rachel Jacob's wife; Joseph, and Benjamin.

20 ¶ And unto Joseph in the land of Egypt were born Mă-năs-́sēh and Ē-́phră-im, which Ăs-́ĕ-năth the daughter of Pŏ-tī-́–phĕr-ăh priest of On bare unto him.

21 ¶ And the sons of Benjamin were Belah, and Bĕ-́chĕr, and Ashbel, Gera, and Nā-́ă-măn, Ē-́hī, and Rosh, Muppim, and Huppim, and Ard.

22 These are the sons of Rachel, which were born to Jacob: all the souls were fourteen.

23 ¶ And the sons of Dan; Hū-́shĭm.

24 ¶ And the sons of Năph-́tă-lī; Jäh-́zêĕl, and Gū-́nī, and Jĕ-́zĕr, and Shillem.

25 These are the sons of Bilhah, which Laban gave unto Rachel his daughter, and she bare these unto Jacob: all the souls were seven.

26 All the souls that came with Jacob into Egypt, which came out of his loins, besides Jacob's sons' wives, all the souls were threescore and six;

27 And the sons of Joseph, which were born him in Egypt, were two souls: all the souls of the house of Jacob, which came into Egypt, were threescore and ten.

28 ¶ And he sent Judah before him unto Joseph, to direct his face unto Goshen; and they came into the land of Goshen.

Genealogy of Those Who Went to Egypt

Dr. Scofield thought that Israel made a mistake to go down to Egypt, that God permitted it but that he should have remained in Canaan. But he seems to be mistaken since God had plainly put Joseph there to save the people alive and since He had promised to Abraham they would be in Egypt.

In the caravan going to Egypt, with wagons and camels, with herds of sheep, goats, cattle, camels and donkeys, were sixty-six people (vs. 26) besides Jacob. Then Joseph and his two sons in Egypt make seventy. Dr. Scofield says:

> A discrepancy has been imagined. The "souls that came with Jacob" were 66. The "souls of the house of Jacob" (vs. 27, i.e. the entire Jacobean family) were 70, viz. the 66 which came with Jacob, Joseph and his two sons, already in Egypt=69; Jacob himself=70.

Then Acts 7:14 speaks of this: "Then sent Joseph, and called his father Jacob to him, and all his kindred, threescore and fifteen souls." Dr. Scofield adds there:

> There is no real contradiction. The "house of Jacob" numbered seventy, but the "kindred" would include the wives of Jacob's sons.

There are a few matters of interest in the names of these of the family of Jacob going down to Egypt.

Carmi (vs. 9), son of Reuben, will have a descendant, Achan, who will steal the wedge of gold, the shekels of silver and a Babylonish garment in the taking of Jericho, and will be stoned (Josh. chap. 7).

The three sons of Levi (vs. 11) will be mentioned frequently in Exodus and Leviticus—in Exodus particularly, since the three groups of Levites will be divided with separate services.

Pharez, son of Judah (vs. 12), is in the ancestral line of Christ as will be Hezron, his son (Luke 3:33).

It is amazing that out of all the sixty-six people—Jacob's descendants—only two daughters are mentioned, Dinah, the daughter of Leah (vs. 15) and Serah, daughter of Asher. Does that mean that other daughters were born but not counted, but only these men; or does it mean that, making special plans for the nation Israel, God chose to give men to head families?

Now Israel sends Judah, most responsible of his older sons, before him to see Joseph and so direct where they will need to go to settle in Goshen.

VERSES 29-34:

29 And Joseph made ready his chariot, and went up to meet Israel his father, to Goshen, and presented himself unto him; and he fell on his neck, and wept on his neck a good while.

30 And Israel said unto Joseph, Now let me die, since I have seen thy face, because thou *art* yet alive.

31 And Joseph said unto his brethren, and unto his father's house, I will go up, and shew Phâr'-āōh, and say unto him, My brethren, and my father's house, which *were* in the land of Cā'-nă-ăn, are come unto me;

32 And the men *are* shepherds, for their trade hath been to feed cattle; and they have brought their flocks, and their herds, and all that they have.

33 And it shall come to pass, when Phâr'-āōh shall call you, and shall say, What *is* your occupation?

34 That ye shall say, Thy servants' trade hath been about cattle from our youth even until now, both we, *and* also our fathers: that ye may dwell in the land of Goshen; for every shepherd *is* an abomination unto the Egyptians.

Jacob Meets His Son Joseph!

What a joyful meeting it was! Joseph, in his chariot, went up to meet his father when the caravan stopped in the land of Goshen nearby. What a greeting, with tears of joy! Now Israel is ready to die. The lonely years slip away from his memory, seeing Joseph alive.

Here Joseph instructs his brothers. They should say to Pharaoh that they are shepherds and accustomed to cattle and flocks so that they may dwell in the land of Goshen, separated somewhat from the Egyptians, to whom they would be an abomination.

So now Jacob and his families settle in Egypt and there they will grow to be a great nation and then will be enslaved and then led out under Moses with great signs and wonders.

GENESIS 47

VERSES 1-12:

THEN Joseph came and told Phâr-́aōh, and said, My father and my brethren, and their flocks, and their herds, and all that they have, are come out of the land of Cā-́nă-ăn; and, behold, they *are* in the land of Goshen.

2 And he took some of his brethren, *even* five men, and presented them unto Phâr-́aōh.

3 And Phâr-́aōh said unto his brethren, What *is* your occupation? And they said unto Phâr-́aōh, Thy servants *are* shepherds, both we, *and* also our fathers.

4 They said moreover unto Phâr-́aōh, For to sojourn in the land are we come; for thy servants have no pasture for their flocks; for the famine *is* sore in the land of Cā-́nă-ăn: now therefore, we pray thee, let thy servants dwell in the land of Goshen.

5 And Phâr-́aōh spake unto Joseph, saying, Thy father and thy brethren are come unto thee:

6 The land of Egypt *is* before thee; in the best of the land make thy father and brethren to dwell; in the land of Goshen let them dwell: and if thou knowest *any* men of activity among them, then make them rulers over my cattle.

7 And Joseph brought in Jacob his father, and set him before Phâr-́aōh: and Jacob blessed Phâr-́aōh.

8 And Phâr-́aōh said unto Jacob, How old *art* thou?

9 And Jacob said unto Phâr-́aōh, The days of the years of my pilgrimage *are* an hundred and thirty years: few and evil have the days of the years of my life been, and have not attained unto the days of the years of the life of my fathers in the days of their pilgrimage.

10 And Jacob blessed Phâr-́aōh, and went out from before Phâr-́aōh.

11 ¶ And Joseph placed his father and his brethren, and gave them a possession in the land of Egypt, in the best of the land, in the land of Răm-́ĕ-sĕs̄, as Phâr-́aōh had commanded.

12 And Joseph nourished his father, and his brethren, and all his father's household, with bread, according to *their* families.

Jacob and Family in Egypt

Joseph wanted to keep his brothers separate and not have them mingle and intermarry with these Egyptian heathens. So he instructed them to say they are shepherds, for shepherds are an abomination to the Egyptians. They are to ask for the land of Goshen which no doubt has some grazing and room for the flocks and herds. Pharaoh agrees with Joseph, and they are to have the area of Goshen, the northeastern part of Egypt proper.

Note these Israelites say they only want to "sojourn" in

the land until the famine be over (vs. 4).

Joseph presented his father to Pharaoh. The question is, "How old are you?"

Jacob says rather sadly, "The days of the years of my pilgrimage are an hundred and thirty years: few and evil have the days of the years of my life been." You see, Abraham lived to be 175 (Gen. 25:7). Isaac had lived to be 180 (Gen. 35:28). Jacob is thus far much short of these, but already he feels an old and beaten man.

"Few and evil," he says, are the years of his life. Evil? He had been a sad man for many years. When they brought him word that Joseph was missing and brought the bloody garment which he thought meant Joseph had been killed by wild beasts, then "all his sons and all his daughters rose up to comfort him; but he refused to be comforted; and he said, For I will go down into the grave unto my son mourning. Thus his father wept for him."

When the older brothers first came back from Egypt and left Simeon a prisoner there, "Jacob their father said unto them, Me have ye bereaved of my children: Joseph is not, and Simeon is not, and ye will take Benjamin away: all these things are against me" (Gen. 42:36). His beloved Rachel had died at the birth of Benjamin. Now for more than twenty years he had grieved over Joseph. So his days seemed evil to old man Jacob.

From verse 11 it appears that the country of Rameses is another name for the land of Goshen where the children of Israel settled. This has caused trouble in history because a later Pharaoh Rameses is better known than the one for whom the area was evidently named.

Joseph, in charge of all the granaries of Egypt, now provided for his father and brethren and their households.

———

VERSES 13-26:

13 ¶ And *there was* no bread in all the land; for the famine *was* very sore, so that the land of Egypt and *all* the land of Cā́-nă-ăn fainted by

reason of the famine.

14 And Joseph gathered up all the money that was found in the land of Egypt, and in the land of Cā-́nă-ăn, for the corn which they bought: and Joseph brought the money into Phâr-́āōh's house.

15 And when money failed in the land of Egypt, and in the land of Cā-́nă-ăn, all the Egyptians came unto Joseph, and said, Give us bread: for why should we die in thy presence? for the money faileth.

16 And Joseph said, Give your cattle; and I will give you for your cattle, if money fail.

17 And they brought their cattle unto Joseph: and Joseph gave them bread *in exchange* for horses, and for the flocks, and for the cattle of the herds, and for the asses: and he fed them with bread for all their cattle for that year.

18 When that year was ended, they came unto him the second year, and said unto him, We will not hide *it* from my lord, how that our money is spent; my lord also hath our herds of cattle; there is not ought left in the sight of my lord, but our bodies, and our lands:

19 Wherefore shall we die before thine eyes, both we and our land? buy us and our land for bread, and we and our land will be servants unto Phâr-́āōh: and give *us* seed, that we may live, and not die, that the land

be not desolate.

20 And Joseph bought all the land of Egypt for Phâr-́āōh; for the Egyptians sold every man his field, because the famine prevailed over them: so the land became Phâr-́āōh's.

21 And as for the people, he removed them to cities from *one* end of the borders of Egypt even to the *other* end thereof.

22 Only the land of the priests bought he not; for the priests had a portion *assigned them* of Phâr-́āōh, and did eat their portion which Phâr-́āōh gave them: wherefore they sold not their lands.

23 Then Joseph said unto the people, Behold, I have bought you this day and your land for Phâr-́āōh: lo, *here is* seed for you, and ye shall sow the land.

24 And it shall come to pass in the increase, that ye shall give the fifth *part* unto Phâr-́āōh, and four parts shall be your own, for seed of the field, and for your food, and for them of your households, and for food for your little ones.

25 And they said, Thou hast saved our lives: let us find grace in the sight of my lord, and we will be Phâr-́āōh's servants.

26 And Joseph made it a law over the land of Egypt unto this day, *that* Phâr-́āōh should have the fifth *part*; except the land of the priests only, *which* became not Phâr-́āōh's.

Egyptians Give Their Money, Cattle, Land to Pharaoh for Food

We're distressed to see that farmers all over Egypt had to give up to Pharaoh their money for food, then their cattle, then the land itself in order to have food. But it is only fair to say that without some dictator and strong central government, the country could not have lasted through the seven years' famine. Someone must see that the food is saved and stored in those seven plenteous years. Someone must see that it is carefully and honestly given out through this seven years of famine. Government as a plan is from God, and frail, sinful men must have a human government, but the result of the seven years' famine is that now the land is in the hands of Pharaoh, and those who till the soil must pay rent on it. But the land of the priests is not taken, since these priests of the idol gods of Egypt were supported by the public fund. The truth is, to pay one fifth of the crop to the government then, is not as bad as paying fifty percent of one's total income to the government, as many people in America must do.

VERSES 27-31:

27 ¶ And Israel dwelt in the land of Egypt, in the country of Goshen; and they had possessions therein, and grew, and multiplied exceedingly.

28 And Jacob lived in the land of Egypt seventeen years: so the whole age of Jacob was an hundred forty and seven years.

29 And the time drew nigh that Israel must die: and he called his son Joseph, and said unto him, If now I have found grace in thy sight, put, I pray thee, thy hand under my thigh, and deal kindly and truly with me; bury me not, I pray thee, in Egypt:

30 But I will lie with my fathers, and thou shalt carry me out of Egypt, and bury me in their buryingplace. And he said, I will do as thou hast said.

31 And he said, Swear unto me. And he sware unto him. And Israel bowed himself upon the bed's head.

Jacob Spends Last Seventeen Years in Egypt

These descendants of Jacob are thrifty people. Their possessions grew and multiplied exceedingly. Jacob lived 17 years, making his age 147 years before he died.

But Jacob remembers he has a covenant with God. His seed are to inherit the land of Canaan. So his sons must take his body back to Israel and bury him in the Cave of Machpelah near Hebron where Abraham and Sarah, Isaac and Rebekah and Jacob's wife Leah were buried. Joseph swore to his father he would see that his last wishes were carried out. Israel is only "sojourning" in Egypt.

GENESIS 48

VERSES 1-7:

AND it came to pass after these things, that *one* told Joseph, Behold, thy father *is* sick: and he took with him his two sons, Mă-năs´-sĕh and E´-phră-ĭm.

2 And *one* told Jacob, and said, Behold, thy son Joseph cometh unto thee: and Israel strengthened himself, and sat upon the bed.

3 And Jacob said unto Joseph, God Almighty appeared unto me at Luz in the land of Că´-nă-ăn, and blessed me,

4 And said unto me, Behold, I will make thee fruitful, and multiply thee, and I will make of thee a multitude of people; and will give this land to thy seed after thee *for* an everlasting possession.

5 ¶ And now thy two sons, E´-phră-ĭm and Mă-năs´-sĕh, which were born unto thee in the land of Egypt before I came unto thee into Egypt, *are* mine; as Reuben and Simeon, they shall be mine.

6 And thy issue, which thou begettest after them, shall be thine, *and* shall be called after the name of their brethren in their inheritance.

7 And as for me, when I came from Padan, Rachel died by me in the land of Că´-nă-ăn in the way, when yet *there was* but a little way to come unto E´-phrăth: and I buried her there in the way of E´-phrăth; the same *is* Beth-lehem.

Jacob Meets Joseph's Two Sons

Jacob was now sick and will soon die. Joseph took with him his two sons, Manasseh, the firstborn, and Ephraim. Evidently Jacob has seen little of them. No doubt Joseph wants them to have a dying blessing from their grandfather. We have seen that Isaac had a gift of prophecy in blessing his sons, Jacob and Esau. That prophecy was given by divine revelation and must be fulfilled. But Jacob has the same gift to bless the brothers, as you will see in the next chapter.

Abraham was "a prophet" as God told Abimelech (Gen. 20:7). We must remember that in Old Testament times as in New Testament times people must come to put their trust in God's Saviour, although they did not know a great deal about Him. Even so, Abraham "believed in the Lord; and he counted it to him for righteousness" (Gen. 15:6; Rom. 4:3). And men had the leading of the Spirit of God in the Old Testament times and the fullness of the Spirit, too. They did not have the indwelling Spirit in their bodies, which Jesus promised in John 14:17, "He dwelleth with you" (before Christ's resurrection) "and shall be in you" (after Christ's resurrection). But the Spirit of God dealt with God's people in old time too.

Jacob reminded Joseph of that glorious time at Luz (later called Bethel) in the land of Canaan when as a boy fleeing from his brother Esau, God had confirmed to Jacob the covenant He had made with Abraham and Isaac. God had promised to make him fruitful with many descendants, a multitude, and his descendants were to have the land of Canaan for an everlasting possession.

Thinking of those descendants, he mentions Ephraim and Manasseh. They are to be counted Jacob's children because there are to be twelve tribes.

There were twelve sons already come, but one will found the tribe of Levi, the priestly tribe. There must be twelve other tribes. So Joseph's two sons now make up the eleventh and twelfth. The land of Canaan will be divided to them later under Joshua as tribes.

Thinking of Joseph's descendants, he is reminded of Rachel, Joseph's mother who died near Bethlehem and was buried there. And there, it may be, Jacob buried part of his heart also. Remember that Jacob keeps mentioning the land of Canaan (vss. 3,7). Oh, Joseph, your mother died leaving only two children, but you will have a multitude of descendants.

VERSES 8-20:

8 And Israel beheld Joseph's sons, and said, Who *are* these?

9 And Joseph said unto his father, They *are* my sons, whom God hath given me in this *place*. And he said, Bring them, I pray thee, unto me, and I will bless them.

10 Now the eyes of Israel were dim for age, *so that* he could not see. And he brought them near unto him; and he kissed them, and embraced them.

11 And Israel said unto Joseph, I had not thought to see thy face: and, lo, God hath shewed me also thy

seed.

12 And Joseph brought them out from between his knees, and he bowed himself with his face to the earth.

13 And Joseph took them both, E-phră-ĭm in his right hand toward Israel's left hand, and Mă-năs-sēh in his left hand toward Israel's right hand, and brought *them* near unto him.

14 And Israel stretched out his right hand, and laid *it* upon E-phră-ĭm's head, who *was* the younger, and his left hand upon Mă-năs-sēh's head, guiding his hands wittingly; for Mă-năs-sēh *was* the firstborn.

15 ¶ And he blessed Joseph, and said, God, before whom my fathers Abraham and Isaac did walk, the God which fed me all my life long unto this day,

16 The Angel which redeemed me from all evil, bless the lads; and let my name be named on them, and the name of my fathers Abraham and Isaac; and let them grow into a multitude in the midst of the earth.

17 And when Joseph saw that his father laid his right hand upon the head of E-phră-ĭm, it displeased him: and he held up his father's hand, to remove it from E-phră-ĭm's head unto Mă-năs-sēh's head.

18 And Joseph said unto his father, Not so, my father: for this *is* the firstborn; put thy right hand upon his head.

19 And his father refused, and said, I know *it*, my son, I know *it*: he also shall become a people, and he also shall be great: but truly his younger brother shall be greater than he, and his seed shall become a multitude of nations.

20 And he blessed them that day, saying, In thee shall Israel bless, saying, God make thee as E-phră-ĭm and as Mă-năs-sēh: and he set E-phră-ĭm before Mă-năs-sēh.

Prophesied Blessing on Ephraim and Manasseh

Jacob is sick and will soon die. So after he had made plans about his burial and Joseph had sworn to carry his body back to Mamre to the Cave Machpelah for burial, Joseph came to see Jacob and brought the two sons. One might think that they are children, but they were born before the years of plenty (Gen. 41:50), and the seven years of famine went by and then seventeen years that Jacob had lived in Egypt; so they must be twenty-four or twenty-five years old at least. So they are young men. However, when men lived so old, young men didn't marry young. Isaac was forty before he thought of marriage.

Jacob's eyes were dimmed for age. He could not recognize the young men until Joseph said, "These are my sons, whom God hath given me in this place." So he kissed and embraced each of them, in the eastern way, kissing first one cheek, then the other. How glad he is to see not only Joseph but Joseph's children!

Manasseh was the firstborn, but Joseph thought to put him under Jacob's right hand for the blessing of the firstborn. But Jacob, by prophetic knowledge, changed the plan and took Ephraim to his right hand and gave him the first blessing. The younger son would be the greater (vs. 19) "and his seed shall become a multitude of nations." We need not be surprised that when the northern tribes separated from Judah and Levi, the northern nation was sometimes called Samaria, but often it was called Ephraim.

The prayer of Jacob is wonderfully suggestive. He prays, "The Angel which redeemed me from all evil; bless the lads." Oh, he knew, "The angel of the Lord encampeth round about them that fear him, and delivereth them" (Ps. 34:7). He had seen angels ascending and descending on the ladder at Bethel; he had wrestled with the angel of God (Gen. 32) and he said, "I have seen God face to face." How would one know to talk about this pre-incarnation appearance of Christ, as it probably was? So I think "the Angel which redeemed me from all evil" is a reference to the Lord Jesus who dimly was seen by Jacob.

VERSES 21,22:

21 And Israel said unto Joseph, Behold, I die: but God shall be with you, and bring you again unto the land of your fathers.
22 Moreover I have given to thee one portion above thy brethren, which I took out of the hand of the Amorite with my sword and with my bow.

Another Promise of Palestine, and Joseph Gets Reuben's Birthright

The thing is clear in Jacob's mind. God would bring Israel back into Palestine, the promised land. He was certain of that. Now he said to Joseph, "Moreover I have given to thee one portion above thy brethren, which I took out of the hand of the Amorite with my sword and with my bow." Above his brethren? Evidently he is giving Joseph the birthright that would normally have gone to Reuben, the firstborn. But I Chronicles 5:1,2 tells us:

"Now the sons of Reuben the firstborn of Israel, (for he was the firstborn; but, forasmuch as he defiled his father's bed, his birthright was given unto the sons of Joseph the son of Israel: and the genealogy is not to be reckoned after the birthright. For Judah prevailed above his brethren, and of him came the chief ruler; but the birthright was Joseph's:)"

Judah was the most reputable and steady, and most honored among the other brethren, but the birthright is given to Joseph because Reuben defiled his father's bed.

GENESIS 49

AND Jacob called unto his sons, and said, Gather yourselves together, that I may tell you *that* which shall befall you in the last days.

2 Gather yourselves together, and hear; ye sons of Jacob; and hearken unto Israel your father.

Prophetic Blessing on Twelve Tribes

The Spirit of God was on Jacob. He was ready to die and all the sons are gathered to hear his prophetic blessing.

---

3 ¶ Reuben, thou *art* my firstborn, my might, and the beginning of my strength, the excellency of dignity, and the excellency of power:

4 Unstable as water, thou shalt not excel; because thou wentest up to thy father's bed; then defiledst thou *it:* he went up to my couch.

Reuben, Firstborn

It was an enlightenment and a dignified event when God gave a child. Reuben was the firstborn, and the beginning of Jacob's family. But, alas, he was "unstable as water." He was likable but not strong. He went up to his father's bed and committed adultery with Jacob's concubine Bilhah (Gen. 35:22).

So he does not keep the birthright; it is given to Joseph and Joseph's sons.

---

5 ¶ Simeon and Levi *are* brethren; instruments of cruelty *are in* their habitations.

6 O my soul, come not thou into their secret; unto their assembly, mine honour, be not thou united:

for in their anger they slew a man, and in their selfwill they digged down a wall.

7 Cursed *be* their anger, for *it* was fierce; and their wrath, for it was cruel: I will divide them in Jacob, and scatter them in Israel.

Simeon and Levi

The two are named together; the one great event in their life was their murderous attack on the city of Shechem after the prince had led Dinah into sin and defiled her. By trickery and deceit they had all the men of the city circumcised and when they were sore, these two men went in with the sword and killed every male in the place and took the women and children and spoil of the city. It is strange that the curse on these sons would go to the others. "I will divide them in Jacob, and scatter them in Israel," said Jacob.

VERSES 8-12:

8 ¶ Judah, thou *art he* whom thy brethren shall praise: thy hand *shall be* in the neck of thine enemies; thy father's children shall bow down before thee.

9 Judah *is* a lion's whelp: from the prey, my son, thou art gone up: he stooped down, he couched as a lion, and as an old lion; who shall rouse him up?

10 The sceptre shall not depart from Judah, nor a lawgiver from between his feet, until Shiloh come; and unto him *shall* the gathering of the people *be.*

11 Binding his foal unto the vine, and his ass's colt unto the choice vine; he washed his garments in wine, and his clothes in the blood of grapes:

12 His eyes *shall be* red with wine, and his teeth white with milk.

Judah

Judah is wonderfully praised, "a lion's whelp." Here is a promise of the coming Messiah: "The sceptre shall not depart from Judah, nor a lawgiver from between his feet, until Shiloh come; and unto him shall the gathering of the people be." That is a reference to Christ, and not only that Christ will come to redeem people but that He will come again to reign on Jacob's throne and will reign in the land of Palestine.

Isaiah 9:6,7 says:

"For unto us a child is born, unto us a son is given: and the government shall be upon his shoulder: and his name shall be called Wonderful, Counsellor, The mighty God, The everlasting Father, The Prince of Peace. Of the increase of his government and peace there shall be no end, upon the throne of David, and upon his kingdom, to order it, and to establish it with judgment and with justice from henceforth even for ever. The zeal of the Lord of hosts will perform this."

VERSE 13:

13 ¶ Zĕ-bū-ʹlŭn shall dwell at the haven of the sea; and he *shall be* for an haven of ships; and his border *shall be* unto Zidon.

Zebulun

Zebulun is to be given land in Palestine in the country of Zidon and Tyre, in the Mount Carmel range.

VERSES 14,15:

14 ¶ Ĭs-ʹsă-<u>ch</u>är *is* a strong ass couching down between two burdens: 15 And he saw that rest *was* good, and the land that *it was* pleasant; and bowed his shoulder to bear, and became a servant unto tribute.

Issachar

A kindly, good word about solid, unprepossessing people of no great leadership in the nation.

VERSES 16-18:

16 ¶ Dan shall judge his people, as one of the tribes of Israel.

17 Dan shall be a serpent by the way, an adder in the path, that biteth the horse heels, so that his rider shall fall backward.

18 I have waited for thy salvation, O LORD.

Dan

Dan shall be in the northern boundary of the land of Palestine. Those boundaries shall often be described as "from Dan to Beer-sheba." Not nationwide leadership but one of the twelve tribes.

Dan as a "serpent by the way, an adder." His role is not leadership in the nation but a solid part of it here. He will be a respectable tribe.

VERSE 19:

19 ¶ Gad, a troop shall overcome him: but he shall overcome at the last.

Gad

Reuben and Gad will have part east of the Jordan River, taking over the country after they help conquer Canaan.

VERSE 20:

20 ¶ Out of Asher his bread *shall be* fat, and he shall yield royal dainties.

Asher

Here will be a breadbasket, an especially blessed part of the land as far as fruit and food is concerned.

VERSE 21:

21 ¶ Năph-́tă-lī *is* a hind let loose: | he giveth goodly words.

Naphtali

A rather ordinary blessing.

VERSES 22-26:

22 ¶ Joseph *is* a fruitful bough, *even* a fruitful bough by a well; *whose* branches run over the wall:

23 The archers have sorely grieved him, and shot *at him*, and hated him:

24 But his bow abode in strength, and the arms of his hands were made strong by the hands of the mighty God of Jacob; (from thence *is* the shepherd, the stone of Israel:)

25 *Even* by the God of thy father, who shall help thee; and by the Almighty, who shall bless thee with blessings of heaven above, blessings of the deep that lieth under, blessings of the breasts, and of the womb:

26 The blessings of thy father have prevailed above the blessings of my progenitors unto the utmost bound of the everlasting hills: they shall be on the head of Joseph, and on the crown of the head of him that was separate from his brethren.

Joseph

The most comforting blessing is given to Joseph, "a fruitful bough," because he saved the lives of so many as an agent in Egypt in the great famine. "The archers have sorely grieved him, and shot at him, and hated him." Oh, the hatred of his brothers, the period in jail, accused by a wicked woman. But these are forgotten; he has been victorious now. He had been especially blessed of God and led by God and the blessings of the father had been given to him. God promises great prosperity to Joseph's kindred.

VERSES 27,28:

27 ¶ Benjamin shall ravin *as* a wolf: in the morning he shall devour the prey, and at night he shall divide the spoil.

28 ¶ All these *are* the twelve tribes of Israel: and this *is it* that their father spake unto them, and blessed them; every one according to his blessing he blessed them.

Benjamin

Benjamin is the youngest of the men. However, he is the father of a tribe and good words are said about him.

Here are the twelve tribes foretold in the future in the deathbed blessing of Jacob.

VERSES 29-33:

29 And he charged them, and said unto them, I am to be gathered unto my people: bury me with my fathers in the cave that *is* in the field of Ephron the Hittite,

30 In the cave that *is* in the field of Măch-pē-́läh, which *is* before Mamre, in the land of Cā-́nă-ăn, which Abraham bought with the field of Ephron the Hittite for a possession of a buryingplace.

31 There they buried Abraham and Sarah his wife; there they buried Isaac and Rebekah his wife; and there I buried Leah.

32 The purchase of the field and of the cave that *is* therein *was* from the children of Heth.

33 And when Jacob had made an end of commanding his sons, he gathered up his feet into the bed, and yielded up the ghost, and was gathered unto his people.

Jacob's Last Exhortation

He reminds the people again, as Joseph had sworn to him already, that he must be buried in the Cave Machpelah, "which is before Mamre, in the land of Canaan," where Abraham, Sarah, Isaac and Rebekah and Leah were buried.

His message from God is done. This old man, 147 years old, sitting boldly to make his prophecy, now gathered his feet up into the bed and "was gathered unto his people."

GENESIS 50

AND Joseph fell upon his father's face, and wept upon him, and kissed him.

2 And Joseph commanded his servants the physicians to embalm his father: and the physicians embalmed Israel.

3 And forty days were fulfilled for him; for so are fulfilled the days of those which are embalmed: and the Egyptians mourned for him threescore and ten days.

4 And when the days of his mourning were past, Joseph spake unto the house of Phâr-́āōh, saying, If now I have found grace in your eyes, speak, I pray you, in the ears of Phâr-́āōh, saying,

5 My father made me swear, saying, Lo, I die: in my grave which I have digged for me in the land of Cā-́nă-ăn, there shalt thou bury me. Now therefore let me go up, I pray thee, and bury my father, and I will come again.

6 And Phâr-́āōh said, Go up, and bury thy father, according as he made thee swear.

7 ¶ And Joseph went up to bury his father: and with him went up all the servants of Phâr-́āōh, the elders of his house, and all the elders of the land of Egypt,

8 And all the house of Joseph, and his brethren, and his father's house: only their little ones, and their flocks, and their herds, they left in the land of Goshen.

9 And there went up with him both chariots and horsemen: and it was a very great company.

10 And they came to the threshing-floor of Atad, which *is* beyond Jordan, and there they mourned with a great and very sore lamentation: and he made a mourning for his father seven days.

11 And when the inhabitants of the land, the Cā-́nă-ăn-ītes, saw the mourning in the floor of Atad, they said, This *is* a grievous mourning to the Egyptians: wherefore the name of it was called Ā-́běl-mĭz-́rā-ĭm, which *is* beyond Jordan.

12 And his sons did unto him according as he commanded them:

13 For his sons carried him into the land of Cā-́nă-ăn, and buried him in the cave of the field of Măch-pē-́läh, which Abraham bought with the field for a possession of a burying-place of Ephron the Hittite, before Mamre.

14 ¶ And Joseph returned into Egypt, he, and his brethren, and all that went up with him to bury his father, after he had buried his father.

Burial of Jacob

It does not take many words to tell of the burial of Jacob. Jacob was embalmed according to the Egyptian custom, a process of forty days that often left it so the dried mummy might last for centuries in that dry climate of Egypt. Then there were seventy days of mourning. Then Joseph asked permission of Pharaoh to carry out the oath he had sworn and take his father back to Mamre in Canaan for burial in the Cave of Machpelah.

So a fine procession is formed. All the men, we suppose, of the house of Jacob went back with the funeral cortege. Wives, little ones, the flocks and herds stayed in Egypt. The other went forth. Many chariots and horsemen of Egyptians went along with them. "And they came to the threshing-floor of Atad which is beyond Jordan, and there they mourned. . .seven days" after they were in the land of Canaan and all the Canaanites saw the mourning and they called the place Abel-mizraim.

This place of Abel-mizraim is said to be "beyond Jordan" and again "beyond Jordan." Did they go around the Dead Sea and east of Jordan crossing the river to come to Mamre at Hebron? It so appears. Abel-mizraim is east of Jordan.

The International Standard Bible Encyclopedia says:

> It is remarkable that the funeral should have taken this circuitous route, instead of going directly from Egypt to Hebron. Possibly a reason may be found as we obtain additional details in Egypt history.

Now the great procession goes back to Egypt. Israel is gone. The nation will multiply greatly.

Heretofore God has been dealing principally with individuals—Abraham, then Isaac, then Jacob. Now we know that Judah is to be in the ancestral line, his son and grandson. But now, principally, God will be dealing with the whole nation Israel, until the time for the Messiah.

VERSES 15-21:

15 ¶ And when Joseph's brethren saw that their father was dead, they said, Joseph will peradventure hate us, and will certainly requite us all the evil which we did unto him.

16 And they sent a messenger unto Joseph, saying, Thy father did command before he died, saying,

17 So shall ye say unto Joseph, Forgive, I pray thee now, the trespass of thy brethren, and their sin; for they did unto thee evil: and now,

we pray thee, forgive the trespass of the servants of the God of thy father. And Joseph wept when they spake unto him.

18 And his brethren also went and fell down before his face; and they said, Behold, we *be* thy servants.

19 And Joseph said unto them, Fear not: for *am* I in the place of God?

20 But as for you, ye thought evil against me: *but* God meant it unto good, to bring to pass, as *it is* this day, to save much people alive.

21 Now therefore fear ye not: I will nourish you, and your little ones. And he comforted them, and spake kindly unto them.

Fearful Brothers

The brothers have been thoroughly cowed by the strong hand of Joseph. Seventeen years have gone by since they moved down into Egypt, yet they fear he will take vengeance upon them. They pretend that the father commanded them to say to Joseph that he must forgive their sins. I do not believe that Jacob took up the matter. He no doubt trusted Joseph and understood him much more thoroughly than did these older brothers. Now they fell down before him.

And Joseph modestly said, "Fear not: for am I in the place of God? But as for you, ye thought evil against me; but God meant it unto good, to bring to pass, as it is this day, to save much people alive." And so he will nourish them and their children. "He comforted them and spake kindly unto them." And the repentance and forgiveness of sin is all now made good, as far as it can be.

VERSES 22-26:

22 ¶ And Joseph dwelt in Egypt, he, and his father's house: and Joseph lived an hundred and ten years.

23 And Joseph saw E̓-phră-ĭm's children of the third *generation*: the children also of Mā-̓chir the son of Mă-năs-̓sēh were brought up upon Joseph's knees.

24 And Joseph said unto his brethren, I die: and God will surely visit you, and bring you out of this land unto the land which he sware to Abraham, to Isaac, and to Jacob.

25 And Joseph took an oath of the children of Israel, saying, God will surely visit you, and ye shall carry up my bones from hence.

26 So Joseph died, *being* an hundred and ten years old: and they embalmed him, and he was put in a coffin in Egypt.

Last Days of Joseph

Joseph lived to be 110. He had first appeared before Pharaoh when he was 30. My, 80 long years he had lived and we suppose he kept the power of government in his hands most of that time.

Oh, but he has a great inheritance from Abraham, Isaac, and Jacob. He must be buried back in the land of Canaan. So, just as Israel did of his sons, Joseph took an oath of the children of Israel. God would visit them. They will be taken back to the land of Canaan. "Ye shall carry up my bones from hence." So Joseph was embalmed and his body carefully kept for many, many years in Egypt until the time of the departure.

Joshua 24:32 tells us, "And the bones of Joseph, which the children of Israel brought up out of Egypt, buried they in Shechem, in a parcel of ground which Jacob bought of the sons of Hamor the father of Shechem for an hundred pieces of silver: and it became the inheritance of the children of Joseph."

List of References

Buttrick, George A. *The Christian Fact and Modern Doubt.* New York: Charles Scribner's Sons, 1934. Pages 48, 94.

Courville, Donovan A. *The Exodus Problem and Its Ramifications.* Loma Linda, Ca.: Challenge Books, 1971. Pages 474, 505-508.

Ellicott, Charles J. *Ellicott's Commentary on the Whole Bible.* Grand Rapids: Zondervan, 1954. Page 95.

Erdman, Charles R. *The Book of Genesis.* Old Tappan, N.J.: Revell, 1950. Page 336.

Fausset, A. R. *Bible Encyclopaedia and Dictionary.* Grand Rapids: Zondervan, no date. Pages 258 and 259.

Free, Joseph P. *Archaeology and Bible History.* Wheaton, Illinois: Scripture Press, 1959. Pages 254 and 255, 289, 317 and 318.

Halley, Henry H. *Halley's Bible Handbook.* Grand Rapids: Zondervan, 1965. Pages 168, 275.

Henkel, M. Footnote on page 49 in *Modern Science and Christian Faith.* Wheaton: Van Kampen Press, 1950. Page 40.

Henry, Matthew. *Matthew Henry's Commentary on the Whole Bible,* Vol. I. Old Tappan, N.J.: Revell. Pages 186 and 187, 259, 285, 322, 330, 342, 349 and 350, 382, 383, 389, 390.

Josephus. *Josephus' Complete Works.* Grand Rapids: Kregel, 1960. Page 284.

Kyle, Melvin Grove. *Explorations at Sodom.* Old Tappan, N.J.: Revell, 1928. Pages 268, 328-330.

Lange, John P. *Lange's Commentary on the Holy Scriptures—Genesis.* Grand Rapids: Zondervan, no date. Pages 282,286.

Leupold, H. C. *Exposition of Genesis.* Grand Rapids: Baker, 1950. Page 187.

Luther, Martin. *Luther's Commentary on Genesis.* Grand Rapids: Zondervan, 1958. Pages 187, 283, 285.

Maclaren, Alexander. *Expositions of Holy Scripture,* Vol I. Grand Rapids: Eerdmans, 1944. Page 95.

Meldau, Fred John. *Why We Believe in Creation, Not in Evolution.* Denver: Christian Victory Publishing Co., 1959. Pages 57, 61 and 62.

Morris, Henry M. *The Genesis Flood*. Nutley, N.J.: Presbyterian and Reformed Publishing Co., 1967. Pages 47, 222.

Morris, Henry M. *The Troubled Waters of Evolution*. San Diego: Creation-Life Publishers, 1975. Page 89 and 90.

Nelson, Byron C. *The Deluge Story in Stone*. Minneapolis: Bethany Fellowship, 1968. Pages 47, 63.

Patten, Donald W. *The Biblical Flood and the Ice Epoch*. Seattle: Pacific Meridian Publishing Co., 1966. Pages 246 and 247.

Pember, G. H. *Earth's Earliest Ages*. Old Tappan, N.J.: Revell, no date. Pages 39, 50, 169 and 179.

Rehwinkel, Alfred M. *The Flood*. St. Louis, Concordia, 1951. Page 47.

Rice, Bill. *Cowboy Boots in Darkest Africa*. Murfreesboro: Sword of the Lord. 1968. Page 26.

Rice, John R. *"And God Remembered. . ."* Murfreesboro: Sword of the Lord, 1941. Page 206.

Rice, John R. *The Ruin of a Christian*. Murfreesboro: Sword of the Lord, 1944. Pages 332 and 333.

Rice, John R. *Seeking a City*. Murfreesboro: Sword of the Lord, 1957. Pages 270, 275, 305.

Rimmer, Harry. *Dead Men Tell Tales*. Berne, Indiana: Berne Witness, 1941. Pages 69-71.

Sampey, John R. *The System Bible Study*. Chicago: System Bible Co., 1922. Page 76.

Scofield, C. I. *The Scofield Reference Bible*. Fairlawn, N.J.: Oxford, 1945. Pages 37, 38, 40, 42, 87, 93, 119, 154, 162, 186, 241, 264, 292, 361, 449, 459, 461, 469, 472, 476, 536.

Thomas, W. H. Griffith. *Through the Pentateuch Chapter by Chapter*. Grand Rapids: Eerdmans, 1957. Page 275.

Velikovsky, Immanuel. *Worlds in Collision*. Garden City, N.J.: Doubleday, 1950. Pages 215, 474, 505-508.

Whitcomb, John C., Jr. *The Early Earth*. Nutley, N.J.: Presbyterian and Reformed Publishing Co., 1973. Pages 225 and 226.

Whitcomb, John C., Jr. *The Genesis Flood*. Nutley, N.J.: Presbyterian and Reformed Publishing Co., 1967. Pages 47, 222.

Wright, George Frederick. *The International Standard Bible Encyclopaedia*. Grand Rapids: Eerdmans, 1946. Pages 210-212, 554.

Young, Robert. *Analytical Concordance to the Bible*. Grand Rapids: Eerdmans, no date. Pages 367, 374.

Encyclopaedia Britannica Chicago: Encyclopaedia Britannica Inc., 1950. Pages 219 and 220, 249 and 250, 272.

The Interpreter's Bible, Vol. I. Nashville: Abingdon, 1952. Page 94.

Oxford Bible Atlas. Fairlawn, N.J.: Oxford, 1962. Page 353.

Webster's Dictionary. Webster's New Twentieth Century Dictionary of the English Language. Cleveland: World, 1971. Page 67.

Baker, Bruce F. *Bible-Science Newsletter*, July of 1975. Pages 173-176.

Libby, W. F. *American Scientist*, January of 1956. Pages 257 and 258.

National Geographic. Page 58.

For a complete list of books available from the Sword of the Lord, write to Sword of the Lord Publishers, P. O. Box 1099, Murfreesboro, Tennessee 37133.

This book may be kept

FOURTEEN DAYS

A fine will be charged for each day the book is kept overtime.

GAYLORD 142			PRINTED IN U.S.A